国际公法
英文教程

COURSES FOR PUBLIC INTERNATIONAL LAW IN ENGLISH

主　编　王云鹏　陈亚芸
副主编　李　亮　贺　赞　冯静茹

图书在版编目(CIP)数据

国际公法英文教程/王云鹏,陈亚芸主编. —北京:北京大学出版社,2023.1
ISBN 978-7-301-33636-6

Ⅰ.①国…　Ⅱ.①王…②陈…　Ⅲ.①国际公法—教材—英文　Ⅳ.①D99

中国版本图书馆 CIP 数据核字(2022)第 230195 号

书　　名	国际公法英文教程 GUOJI GONGFA YINGWEN JIAOCHENG
著作责任者	王云鹏　陈亚芸　主编
责 任 编 辑	孙维玲
标 准 书 号	ISBN 978-7-301-33636-6
出 版 发 行	北京大学出版社
地　　址	北京市海淀区成府路 205 号　100871
网　　址	http://www.pup.cn　新浪微博:@北京大学出版社
电 子 信 箱	sdyy_2005@126.com
电　　话	邮购部 010-62752015　发行部 010-62750672　编辑部 021-62071998
印 刷 者	天津中印联印务有限公司
经 销 者	新华书店
	730 毫米×980 毫米　16 开本　32.5 印张　669 千字 2023 年 1 月第 1 版　2023 年 1 月第 1 次印刷
定　　价	118.00 元

未经许可,不得以任何方式复制或抄袭本书之部分或全部内容。
版权所有,侵权必究
举报电话:010-62752024　电子信箱:fd@pup.pku.edu.cn
图书如有印装质量问题,请与出版部联系,电话:010-62756370

编 写 说 明

习近平总书记强调,"要坚持统筹推进国内法治和涉外法治"。随着中国日益走近世界舞台中央,中国经济发展的外部环境发生了重大的改变。在新一轮对外开放的格局下,为更好地维护国家主权、安全和发展利益,需要加强涉外法治人才的培养。通晓国际法律规则、善于处理涉外法律事务是涉外法治人才应当具备的基本能力,而这种能力的培养依赖于专业人才培养体系的完善。然而,当前涉外法治人才的培养体系存在明显短板,其中就包括课程和教材建设上的严重滞后,特别是本科阶段的国际法学专业课程体系和教材建设。教育部2018年召开的新时代全国高等学校本科教育工作会议强调要坚持"以本为本",明确"人才培养是大学的本质职能,本科教育是大学的根和本"。追根溯源,提高本科阶段的人才培养质量是涉外法治人才队伍建设的源头,而教材建设就是保证本科教学质量的关键之一。

我们的初衷是编写一本适应本科教学实际的英文教材。编者都是承担"国际公法学"全英文或双语教学的青年教师。内容的选择和体例编排充分考虑了当前国际法学课程本科教学的现状:第一,强调对条约文本、案例原文和经典原著的阅读,节选重要公约、经典案例和经典著作作为学习材料。第二,强调中国问题,凸显中国贡献和中国立场,选编了很多与中国有关的条约、文件和案例。第三,注重知识体系的完整性,基本涵盖了经典的《国际公法学》中文教材(以马工程教材为例)所覆盖的章节内容和关键概念。第四,凸显学生的教学主体地位,内容编排符合中国学生的认知特征;通过文本阅读确立问题导向和规则框架,通过概念阐释建构知识体系,通过案例研读理解规则与知识的具体应用。第五,契合实际教学环节,充分适应当前以双语(全英文)教学、案例教学和翻转课堂为特征的教学模式,凸显本科教学应以学生为教学主体的基本理念,每一章节均布置学生文献检索和案例报告的学习任务。本教材既可以单独使用,作为"国际公法学"英文课程的教学用书,也可以作为"国际公法学"课程中文教学的辅助教材。

英文教材的编写难度超出了我们的预期。因此,从确定编写计划、教材立项到正式编写,都超出了我们原先预定的计划。特别感谢北京大学出版社孙维玲老师及时的督促和对我们教材编写进程延宕的耐心与容忍。当然,编写进度缓慢也说明了我们能力的不足。本教材的疏漏之处在所难免,欢迎随时批评指正。

缩略语简表

（按缩略语首字母排序）

缩略语	英文全称	中文全称
ARSIWA	Draft Articles on Responsibility of State for Internationally Wrongful Act	《国家对国际不法行为的责任条款草案》
ECHR	European Court of Human Rights	欧洲人权法院
EEZ	Exclusive Economic Zone	专属经济区
EU	European Union	欧洲联盟
GA	the General Assembly of UN	联合国大会
ICAO	International Civil Aviation Organization	国际民航组织
ICC	International Criminal Court	国际刑事法院
ICJ	International Court of Justice	国际法院
ICRC	International Committee of the Red Cross	国际红十字会
ILC	International Law Commission	国际法委员会
PCIJ	Permanent Court of International Justice	常设国际法院
SC	The Security Council of UN	联合国安理会
UNCLOS	The United Nations Convention on the Law of the Sea	《联合国海洋法公约》
UN	United Nations	联合国
VCLT	Vienna Convention on the Law of Treaties	《维也纳条约法公约》
USSR	(the former) Union of Soviet Socialist Republics	(前)苏联，苏维埃社会主义共和国联盟
WTO	World Trade Organization	世界贸易组织
WHO	World Health Organization	世界卫生组织

拉丁语简表

de jure 法律上

de facto 事实上

erga omnes 对世义务

inter alia 除了其他事物之外

ipso facto 根据事实本身

jus cogens 国际强行法

jus in bello 战争法规

lex specialis 特别法

lex generalis 一般法

opinio juris 法律确信

pacta sunt servanda 有约必守

res iudicata 既判力

res nullius 无主物

res communis 共有物

terra nullius 无主土地

usus 通常实践

Contents

Chapter I **International Law: General Introduction** .... (1)
    1. Introduction .... (1)
    2. Preliminary Reading and Assignment .... (1)
    3. Terminologies and Discussions .... (11)
    4. Further Reading Materials: China and International Law .... (18)
    5. References and Recommended Reading Materials ...... (43)

Chapter II **Sources of International Law** .... (44)
    1. Introduction .... (44)
    2. Preliminary Reading and Assignment .... (45)
    3. Terminologies and Discussions .... (50)
    4. Cases and Materials .... (63)
    5. References and Recommended Reading Materials ...... (87)

Chapter III **International Law and Municipal Law** .... (88)
    1. Introduction .... (88)
    2. Preliminary Reading and Assignment .... (89)
    3. Terminologies and Discussions .... (103)
    4. Cases and Materials .... (107)
    5. References and Recommended Reading Materials ...... (117)

Chapter IV	**General Principle of International Law** (118)
	1. Introduction (118)
	2. Preliminary Reading and Assignment (119)
	3. Terminologies and Explanations (127)
	4. Cases and Materials (130)
	5. References and Recommended Reading Materials (134)
Chapter V	**The State** (135)
	1. Introduction (135)
	2. Preliminary Reading and Assignment (136)
	3. Terminologies and Explanations (143)
	4. Cases and Materials (148)
	5. References and Recommended Reading Materials (159)
Chapter VI	**International Organization** (160)
	1. Introduction (160)
	2. Preliminary Reading and Assignment (160)
	3. Terminologies and Explanations (164)
	4. Cases and Materials (167)
	5. References and Recommended Reading Materials (184)
Chapter VII	**Individual** (185)
	1. Introduction (185)
	2. Preliminary Reading and Assignment (185)
	3. Terminologies and Explanations (199)
	4. Cases and Materials (202)
	5. References and Recommended Reading Materials (214)
Chapter VIII	**Territory** (215)
	1. Introduction (215)
	2. Preliminary Reading and Assignment (216)

3. Terminologies and Explanations ……………………… (229)
4. Cases and Materials ………………………………… (236)
5. References and Recommended Reading Materials ………………………………………………… (248)

Chapter IX Law of the Sea ……………………………………… (249)
1. Introduction ……………………………………… (249)
2. Preliminary Reading and Assignment ……………… (250)
3. Terminologies and Discussions ……………………… (262)
4. Cases and Materials ………………………………… (273)
5. References and Recommended Reading Materials …… (294)

Chapter X International Space Law …………………………… (295)
1. Introduction ……………………………………… (295)
2. Preliminary Reading and Assignment ……………… (296)
3. Terminologies and Explanations …………………… (304)
4. Further Reading Materials ………………………… (308)
5. References and Recommended Reading Materials …… (322)

Chapter XI Treaty Law ………………………………………… (323)
1. Introduction ……………………………………… (323)
2. Preliminary Reading and Assignment ……………… (324)
3. Key Concepts and Discussions ……………………… (330)
4. Cases and Materials ………………………………… (343)
5. References and Recommended Reading Materials …… (355)

Chapter XII Diplomacy and Immunity ……………………… (356)
1. Introduction ……………………………………… (356)
2. Preliminary Reading and Assignment ……………… (357)
3. Terminologies and Explanations …………………… (365)
4. Cases and Materials ………………………………… (373)

　　　　　　5. References and Recommended Reading Materials ⋯⋯ (392)

Chapter XIII　**The Law of Responsibility** ⋯⋯⋯⋯⋯⋯⋯⋯⋯⋯ (393)
　　　　　　1. Introduction ⋯⋯⋯⋯⋯⋯⋯⋯⋯⋯⋯⋯⋯⋯⋯⋯⋯⋯ (393)
　　　　　　2. Preliminary Reading and Assignment ⋯⋯⋯⋯⋯⋯ (394)
　　　　　　3. Terminologies and Explanations ⋯⋯⋯⋯⋯⋯⋯⋯ (404)
　　　　　　4. Cases and Materials ⋯⋯⋯⋯⋯⋯⋯⋯⋯⋯⋯⋯⋯⋯ (417)
　　　　　　5. References and Recommended Reading
　　　　　　　　Materials ⋯⋯⋯⋯⋯⋯⋯⋯⋯⋯⋯⋯⋯⋯⋯⋯⋯⋯ (439)

Chapter XIV　**Peaceful Settlement of Disputes** ⋯⋯⋯⋯⋯⋯⋯⋯ (440)
　　　　　　1. Introduction ⋯⋯⋯⋯⋯⋯⋯⋯⋯⋯⋯⋯⋯⋯⋯⋯⋯⋯ (440)
　　　　　　2. Preliminary Reading and Assignment ⋯⋯⋯⋯⋯⋯ (441)
　　　　　　3. Terminologies and Explanations ⋯⋯⋯⋯⋯⋯⋯⋯ (454)
　　　　　　4. Cases and Materials ⋯⋯⋯⋯⋯⋯⋯⋯⋯⋯⋯⋯⋯⋯ (459)
　　　　　　5. References and Recommended Reading
　　　　　　　　Materials ⋯⋯⋯⋯⋯⋯⋯⋯⋯⋯⋯⋯⋯⋯⋯⋯⋯⋯ (475)

Chapter XV　**International Human Rights and Humanitarian Law** ⋯⋯ (476)
　　　　　　1. Introduction ⋯⋯⋯⋯⋯⋯⋯⋯⋯⋯⋯⋯⋯⋯⋯⋯⋯⋯ (476)
　　　　　　2. Preliminary Reading and Assignment ⋯⋯⋯⋯⋯⋯ (478)
　　　　　　3. Terminologies and Discussions ⋯⋯⋯⋯⋯⋯⋯⋯⋯ (491)
　　　　　　4. Further Reading Materials ⋯⋯⋯⋯⋯⋯⋯⋯⋯⋯⋯ (498)
　　　　　　5. References and Recommended Reading Materials ⋯ (509)

Chapter Ⅰ International Law: General Introduction

1. Introduction

This chapter explores the concepts and historical development of international law by introducing some edited classic material and historical documents. By reading these materials, some fundamental issues concerning international law are to be briefly explained, e. g. , the definition of international law, the basis of its obligation, and why the global society needs it. Also, we present some essays reflecting China's changing role and contribution to the evolution of international law.

2. Preliminary Reading and Assignment

Read the materials excepted from classic textbooks and think about the following questions:

(1) What is international law?

(2) Why does the world need it?

(3) Is international law the LAW you learned in classes about municipal law? Why?

2.1 Emer de Vattel: On the Concept and Function of International Law[①]

Nations or States are bodies politic, societies of men united together for

---

① See Emer de Vattel, *The Law of Nations*, Liberty Fund, 2008, pp. 67-79.

the purpose of promoting their mutual safety and advantage by the joint efforts of their combined strength. Such a society has her affairs and her interests; she deliberates and takes resolutions in common; thus becoming a moral person, who possesses an understanding and a will peculiar to herself, and is susceptible of obligations and rights. **The Law of nations is the science which teaches the rights subsisting between nations or States, and the obligations correspondent to those rights.** as such, In this treatise it will appear, in what manner States, ought to regulate all their actions. We shall examine the obligations of a people, as well towards themselves as towards other nations; and by that means we shall discover the rights which result from those obligations.

Nations being composed of men naturally free and independent, and who, before the establishment of civil societies, lived together in the State of nature—nations or sovereign States are to be considered as so many free persons living together in the State of nature. It is a settled point with writers on the natural law, that all men inherit from nature a perfect liberty and independence, of which they cannot be deprived without their own consent. In a State, the individual citizens do not enjoy them fully and absolutely, because they have made a partial surrender of them to the sovereign. But the body of the nation, the State, remains absolutely free and independent with respect to all other men, all other nations, as long as it has not voluntarily submitted to them. As men are subject to the laws of nature, the entire nation, whose common will is but the result of the united wills of the citizens, remains subject to the laws of nature, and is bound to respect them in all her proceedings. And since right arises from obligation, the nation possesses also the same rights which nature has conferred upon men in order to enable them to perform their duties.

We must therefore apply to nations the rules of the Law of nature, in order to discover what their obligations are, and what their rights are: consequently the Law of nations is originally no other than the Law of nature applied to nations. But as the application of a rule cannot be just and reasonable unless it be made in a manner suitable to the subject, we are not to imagine that the Law of nations is precisely and in every case the same as the Law of nature, with the difference only of the subjects to which it is applied, so as to allow of our substituting nations for individuals. A State or civil society is a subject very different from an individual of the human race: from which circumstance, pursuant to the Law of nature itself, there result, in many cases, very different obligations and rights; since the same general rule, applied to two subjects, cannot produce exactly the same decisions, when the subjects are different; and a particular rule which is perfectly just with respect to one subject, is not applicable to another subject of a quite different nature. There are many cases, therefore, in which the Law of nature does not decide between State and State in the same manner as it would between man and man. We must therefore know how to accommodate the application of it to different subjects; and it is the art of thus applying it with a precision founded on right reason, that renders the Law of nations a distinct science.

We call that the necessary Law of nations which consists in the application of the Law of nature to nations. It is necessary, because nations are absolutely bound to observe it. This Law contains the precepts prescribed by the Law of nature to States, on whom that Law is not less obligatory than on individuals, since States are composed of men, their resolutions are taken by men, and the Law of nature is binding on all men, under whatever relation they act. This is the Law which Grotius, and those who follow him, call the internal Law of nations, on account of its being obligatory on nations in point of conscience. Several writers term it the natural Law of nations. Whence, as this Law is immutable, and the obligations that arise from it necessary and indispensable, nations can neither make any changes in it by their conventions, dispense with it in their own conduct, nor reciprocally release each other from the observance of it. This is the principle by which we may distinguish lawful conventions or treaties from those that are not lawful, and innocent and rational customs from those that are unjust or censurable.

There are things, just in themselves, and allowed by the necessary Law of nations, on which States may mutually agree with each other, and which they may consecrate and enforce by their manners and customs. There are others, of an indifferent nature, respecting which, it rests at the option of nations to make in their treaties whatever agreements they please, or to introduce whatever custom or practice they think proper. But every treaty or custom, which contravenes the injunctions or prohibitions of the necessary Law of nations, is unlawful. It will appear, however, that it is only by the internal Law, by the Law of conscience, such conventions or treaties are always condemned as unlawful. Nations being free and independent, the others are bound to acquiesce in it, when it does not infringe upon their perfect rights. The liberty of that nations would not remain entire, if the others were to arrogate to themselves the right of inspecting and regulating their actions; an assumption on their part, that would be contrary to the Law of nature, which declares every nation free and independent of all the others.

Hence is deduced the establishment of natural society among men. The general Law of that society is, that each individual should do everything which their necessities require for the others, and which he can perform without neglecting the duty that he owes to himself. Within this nature society, all men must observe in order to live in a manner consonant to their nature, and conformable to the views of their common creator. Our own safety, our happiness, our dearest interests, ought to render sacred to every one of us. Such is the general obligation that binds us to the observance of our duties: let us fulfill them with care, if we would wisely endeavor to promote our own advantage. If only all men willing to observe the rule that we have just laid down, the world would enjoy exalted felicity. On the contrary, if each man wholly and immediately directs all his thoughts to his own interest, if he does nothing for the sake of other men, the whole human race together will be immersed in the deepest wretchedness. Let us therefore endeavor to promote the general happiness of mankind; all mankind, in return, will endeavor to promote ours; and thus we shall establish our felicity on the most solid foundations.

The universal society of the human race is an institution of nature herself. All men, in whatever stations they are placed, cannot liberate themselves from the obligation by any convention, by any private association. Therefore, when they unite in civil society for the purpose of forming a separate State or nation, they may indeed enter into particular engagements towards those with whom they associate themselves; but they remain still bound to the performance of their duties towards the rest of mankind. Since the men have resigned their rights and submitted their will to the body of the society, everything concerns their common welfare henceforward belongs to that body, that State, and its rulers. This body of the society shall fulfill the duties of humanity towards strangers. Consequently, it is the State more particularly to perform those duties aforesaid towards other States. The men united in society remain subject to the obligations imposed upon them by human nature.

Since the object of the natural society established between all mankind is that they should lend each other mutual assistance in order to attain perfection themselves and to render their condition as perfect as possible, and, since nations, considered as so many free persons living together in a State of nature, are bound to cultivate human society with each other, the object of the great society established by nature between all nations is also the interchange of mutual assistance for their own improvement and that of their condition. The first general Law that we discover in the very object of the society of nations, is that each individual nation is bound to contribute everything in her power to the happiness and perfection of all the others.

Nations being free and independent of each other, in the same manner as men are naturally free and independent. The second general Law of their society is, that each nation should be left in the peaceable enjoyment of that liberty which she inherits from nature. The natural society of nations cannot subsist, unless the natural rights of each be duly respected. No nation is willing to renounce her liberty: she would rather break off all commerce with those States that should attempt to infringe upon it. As a consequence of that liberty and independence, it exclusively belongs to each nation to form her own judgment of what her conscience prescribes to her (of what she can or cannot do, and of what it is proper or improper for her to do), and of course it rests solely with her to examine and determine whether she can perform any office for another nation without neglecting the duty which she owes to herself.

Since men are naturally equal, and a perfect equality prevails in their rights and obligations, as equally proceeding from nature, and considering that nations composed of men, and considered as so many free persons living together in the State of nature, these nations are naturally equal, and inherit from nature the same obligations and rights. Power or weakness does not in this respect produce any difference. A dwarf is as much a man as a giant, a small republic is no less a sovereign State than the most powerful kingdom. By a necessary consequence of that equality, whatever is lawful for one nation, is equally lawful for any other; whatever is unjustifiable in the one, is equally so in the other.

Nations are free, independent and equal. Since each State possesses the right of judging, according to the dictates of her conscience, what conduct she is to pursue in order to fulfil her duties, thus, the nations own a perfect equality of rights between them, in the administration of their affairs and the pursuit of their pretensions, without regard to the intrinsic justice of their conduct. Actually, each nation can in fact maintain that she has justice on her side in every dispute that happens to arise. The party who is in the wrong is guilty of a crime against her own conscience. But as there exists a possibility that she may perhaps have justice on her side, we cannot accuse her of violating the laws of society. It is therefore necessary, on many occasions, that nations should suffer certain things to be done, though in their own nature unjust and condemn able. Because they cannot oppose them by open force, without violating the liberty of some particular State, and destroying the foundations of their natural society.

And since all nations are bound to cultivate that society, it is of course presumed that they have consented to the principle we have just established. The rules that are deduced from it, constitute what Monsieur Wolf calls "the voluntary law of nations". The laws of natural society are of such importance to the safety of all States. All nations have therefore a right to resort to forcible means for the purpose of repressing any one particular nation who openly violates the laws of the society which nature has established between them, or who directly attacks the welfare and safety of that society.

2.2　John Austin: Positive Moral Rule and International Law

The science of jurisprudence (or, simply and briefly, jurisprudence) is concerned with positive laws, or with laws strictly so called, as considered without regard to their goodness or badness. Positive morality, as considered without regard to its goodness or badness, might be the subject of a science closely analogous to jurisprudence. We say "might be", since it is only in one of its branches (namely, the law of nations or international Law), that positive morality, as considered without regard to its goodness or badness, has been treated by writers in a scientific or systematic manner. [1]

The positive moral rules which are laws improperly so called, are laws set or imposed by general opinion: that is to say, by the general opinion of any class or any society of persons. For example, some are set or imposed by the general opinion of persons who are members of a profession or calling;

---

[1]　See John Austin, *The Province of Jurisprudence Determined*, Wilfrid E. Rumble (ed.), Cambridge University Press, 1995, p. 112.

others, by that of persons who inhabit a town or province; others, by that of a nation or independent political society; others, by that of a larger society formed of various nations.

A few species of the laws which are set by general opinion have gotten appropriate names. For example, there are laws or rules imposed upon gentlemen by opinions current among gentlemen. And these are usually styled the rules of honor, or the laws or law of honor. There are laws or rules imposed upon people of fashion by opinions current in the fashionable world. And these are usually styled the Law set by fashion. There are laws which regard the conduct of independent political societies in their various relations to one another. Or, rather, there are laws which regard the conduct of sovereigns or supreme governments in their various relations to one another. And laws or rules of this species, which are imposed upon nations or sovereigns by opinions current among nations, are usually styled the Law of nations or international Law. [1]

Grotius, Puffendorf, and other writers on the so-called Law of nations, have fallen into a similar confusion of ideas: they have confounded positive international morality, or the rules which actually obtain among civilized nations in their mutual intercourse, with their own vague conceptions of international morality as it ought to be, with that indeterminate something which they conceived it would be, if it conformed to that indeterminate something which they call the Law of nature. [2]

2.3　Kelsen's View on International Law[3]

According to the traditional definition, international law is a complex of norms regulating the mutual behavior of States, the specific subjects of

---

[1] See John Austin, *The Province of Jurisprudence Determined*, Wilfrid E. Rumble (ed.), Cambridge University Press, 1995, p. 123.
[2] Ibid., p. 170.
[3] See Hans Kelsen, *Pure Theory of Law*, Harvard University Press, 1949, pp. 320-325.

international Law. International Law is "law" in the same sense as national law, and therefore a possible object of a science of law. In accordance with the concept of law here accepted, so-called international law is "law," if it is a coercive order, that is to say, a set of norms regulating human behavior by attaching certain coercive acts (sanctions) as consequences to certain facts, as delicts, determined by this order as conditions, and if, therefore, it can be described in sentences which may be called "rules of law".

At the moment we want to answer the question whether international law regulates the behavior of States in such a way that it reacts against a certain behavior as a delict by providing for a sanction as the consequence of the delict. The decisive question, then, is that **does international law establish coercive acts as sanctions?**

The specific sanctions of international law are reprisals and war. It is easy to demonstrate that this assumption is correct with respect to reprisals. For it is a principle of general international law that a State which considers some of its interests violated by another State is authorized to reprisals against the State responsible for the violation. A "reprisal" is an interference, under normal circum stances forbidden by international law, in the sphere of interest of a State. It is an interference that takes place without and against the will of the State concerned and is in this sense a coercive act, even if it is executed without physical force (e. g., without force of arms) when the affected State does not resist. Reprisal may be executed by force of arms if necessary, but this coercive act has the character of a reprisal only as long as the action of the armed force has not assumed—because of its intensity and magnitude—the character of war.

The difference between armed reprisal and war is only one of degree. A reprisal is limited to the violation of certain interests; war is unlimited interference in the sphere of interest of another State. Since reprisals are admissible only as reactions against the violation of certain interests of one State by another, they have the character of sanctions; and the violation of interests conditioning the reprisals have the character of a violation of international law, that is, the character of an international delict. In this way international law protects some (not all possible) interests of the States subject to it. The interests of a State protected by general international law are precisely those against whose violation the State is authorized by international law to reprisals. The limited interference in the sphere of interest of another State is itself an international delict if it is not a reaction against a violation of the law. Then, the interference is either sanction or delict.

Does this also apply to the unlimited interference in the sphere of interests of another State, called "war"? In this respect two opposing views are maintained. The first holds that according to general international law, war is neither delict nor sanction. Every State may go to war for whatever reason, without violating international law. The second holds that war, even according to general international law, is permissible only as a reaction against a violation of international law. War, like reprisal, is itself a delict, unless it is a sanction. This is the so-called principle of *bellum iustum*.

These sanctions, like the sanctions of national law, consist in the forcible deprivation of life, liberty and other goods, notably economic values. In a war, human beings are killed, maimed, imprisoned, national or private property is destroyed; by way of reprisals national or private property is confiscated and other legal rights are infringed. These sanctions of international Law are not different in content from those of national law. But they are directed against the State.

2.4 Assignment and Questions

(1) Search information about Emer de Vattel, John Austin and Hans Kelsen.

(2) Give a five-minute speech in English about your understanding of why human society needs **the Law of Nations**.

3. Terminologies and Discussions

3.1 International Law

(1) What is international law

International law (IL) sometimes could be seen as a concept including the public international law, private international law and international economic law. In English textbooks, authors always give a brief description. E. g., James Crawford defines it as "a specialized body of legal thinking about the relations between rulers, reflective of custom and practice in such matters as treaty-making, the status of ambassadors, the use of the oceans, and the modalities of warfare"①. Malcolm Shaw uses the term of "public international law" and gives a short explanation. He points out that IL governs relations between States in all their myriad forms, from war to satellites and from trade to human rights, and regulates the operations of the many international and regional institutions. ② Besides, he clarifies that IL is different from what is called "international comity" or practices such as saluting the flags of foreign warships at sea. They are implemented solely through courtesy and are not regarded as legally binding. Moreover, IL shall be distinguished from international morality.

IL is the rules and principles governing the relationships between the States, international organizations, and other recognized subjects in the global society. Within the interdependent and solidary world, the State, including its nationals, corporations, and other forms of organizations within its jurisdiction or under its jurisdiction, has to make contacts with the other

---

① James Crawford (ed.), *Brownlie's Principles of Public International Law*, 8th Ed., Oxford University Press, 2012, p. 6.
② See Malcolm N. Shaw, *International Law*, 8th Ed., Cambridge University Press, 2017, p. 238.

States and those counterparts in politics, economy, culture, and other social spheres. Modern technologies have expanded the domains and depth of the global communications, making intrenational law developed in theories and practices. IL applies in traditional issues such as war and peace, State and territory, diplomatic and treaty, and embraces rules and principles regarding individuals and international organization, sea, air and outer space, or other domains influenced by human activity in cyberspace. It is still in a continuous evolution contributed by the dynamics of globalization and emerging transboundary crises, such as climate change and global health crises.

(2) *IL and international relation(IR)*

The end of the Cold War heralded the end of a bipolar world in which Law was subjugated to the imperatives of superpower spheres of influence. With the perceived transformation of State sovereignty as the basis for power politics, the structure of international relations has changed: issues that transcend or disrupt traditional State interests, such as arms flows, human rights, terrorism, migration and displacement of populations, international finance, and the increasingly legalized nature of relations at the multilateral level, have risen to prominence. Under this situation, some scholars believe that the divide between IR and IL is both tenuous and tendentious. They advocated that, "without IL, IR's theory and practice would amount to little more than a constant reaffirmation that might is right. Without IR, we would not be able to expose instances when IL is an instrument of might or to advocate what needs to be done to reaffirm the principle of right not might. And, our ability to succeed strategically in developing new IL, founded on the principle of right not might, would be considerably limited."[1]

From different IR theorists' views, IL plays various functions in global politics. The realist school, represented by Morgenthau, Waltz and

---

[1] Thomas J. Biersteker, et al. (eds.), *International Law and International Relations: Bridging Theory and Practice*, Routledge, 2007, pp. 278-279.

Mearsheimer, has insisted that IR theory is about States, their interests, and their power, and IL is inconsequential in a world in which "rational self-interest and geopolitical capacities, not law, explained the global dynamic". It inherits Austinian notions of law and power to consider IL to be not law at all. In the contemporary world after the end of the Cold War, though the State actions remain centric, the non-State actors, e. g. , the individual and governmental and non-governmental international organizations, have become increasingly important in shaping transnational relationships. In considering these new phenomena, the school of liberalism provides a different description. It assumes that all States will benefit from the flourishing of free markets and the open exchange of ideas. And, wars can be avoided if countries work together cooperatively. Scholars believe liberalism make critics against realists because they focus on power and conflict. They claim that the growth of transnational forces, economic interdependence, regional integration, and cooperation in areas where war appeared unlikely are beyond the explanatory ability of the theoretical paradigm of realist analysis. It seems that the liberal model is more appropriate than realist theory in describing and explaining international relations in a globalized, post-Cold War world. However, making such a conclusion after the 2008 crisis is too arbitrary.

(3) *IL, private international law and international economic law*

In a classic textbook, IL is divided into private international law and public international law.① The former deals with those cases in which foreign elements obtrude, raising questions about the application of foreign law or the role of foreign courts. E. g. , acceptance and enforcement of a judgment made by a U. S. court in China, or, if two Chinese make a contract to sell the property situated in England, the court with jurisdiction will apply the law of England to decide the validity of that contract. Public international law is not

---

① See Malcolm N. Shaw, *International Law*, 8th Ed. , Cambridge University Press, 2017, p. 238.

merely an adjunct of a legal order but a separate system altogether. As implied before, public international law covers relations between States in all their myriad forms, from war to satellites and from trade to human rights, and regulates the operations of the many international and regional institutions. Discussion about the connection and distinction between IL and international economic law is a theoretical issue well developed by scholars in many Chinese international economic law textbooks. The international economic law needs to prove its distinction from IL. The main argument is that international economic law applies to particular international economic relations established between States and relations among non-State actors. It does not mean the two are unrelated. On the contrary, they share many overlapped norms concerning the economic relationships between States and international organizations. But, a broad interpretation of international economic law extends all cross-border economic intercourse, especially those vertical legal relations between States and individuals or entities conducting transboundary economic activity, such as trade, investment, or transfer of intellectual property. [1]

3.2 Basis of Obligation

The basis of obligation in IL is a fundamental theoretical issue, encompassing discussions about the nature of international society, the concept of modern sovereign State, the legal character of IL and its defects, and the application of IL in domestic court. [2] In a famous Chinese IL textbook, the basis of obligation is mainly about the ground of IL's validity as the Law to bind States. That is, why the State complies with the IL or why the State should be bound to observe the rules of IL in this anarchic world;

---

[1] See An Chen, *The Voice from China: An Chen on International Economic Law*, Springer, 2013, pp. 3-6.

[2] See Andrew Clapham (ed.), *Brierly's Law of Nations: An Introduction to the Role of International Law in International Relations*, 7th Ed., Oxford University Press, 2012, pp. 42-100.

or, what is the ultimate foundation of IL's legal obligation. ① These questions go to the root of the legal phenomenon. In *Oppenheim's Inte Law*, the basis of (obligation) of IL is the "common consent" of the State member of the international community. It provides that: "It is not possible to say why IL as a whole is binding upon the international community without entering the realm of non-legal considerations. It is, however, in accord with practical realities to see the basis of IL in the existence of an international community the common consent of whose members is that there shall be a body of rules of law—IL—to govern their conduct as members of that community."② In this sense "common consent" could be the basis of IL as a legal system. As indicated by Oppenheim, it is impossible to require that all States must at all times expressly consent to every part of the body of rules constituting IL, for such common consent could never in practice be established. The common consent is thus not consented to particular rules but the express or tacit consent of States to the body of rules comprising IL as a whole at any particular time. And, dissent from a particular rule is not to be taken as withdrawal of consent to the system as a whole.

  The view that the basis of IL is grounded on common consent is a typical theory held by positivists. It is one of the two traditional competing doctrines that try to answer why States should be bound to observe the rules of IL. According to the doctrine of positivism, IL is the rules by which the States have consented to abide.

  The other is the doctrine of the natural or fundamental rights of States. As Brierly pointed out that, "the doctrine of 'natural rights' is a corollary of the doctrine of the 'State of nature', in which individuals are supposed to have lived before they formed themselves into political communities or States;

---

  ① See Robert Kolb, *Theory of International Law*, Hart Publishing, 2016, p. 121.
  ② Robert Jennings and Arthur Watts (eds.), *Oppenheim's International Law*, 9th Ed., Longman, 1996, pp. 14-15.

for States, not having formed themselves into a super-State, are still supposed by the adherents of this doctrine to be living in such a condition."① Under this doctrine, States are endowed with certain inherent natural rights, such as self-preservation, independence, equality, respect and intercourse. Brierly makes a critical commentary that this doctrine is only a transfer of the old theory of "natural right of man" from an individual to a State.②

It may be helpful to iterate Grotius' notion about the law of nations. At the times of Grotius, the law was considered to limit State's liberty on two planes: through heteronomous natural law constraints; and through autonomous positive law constraints, based on conventional and thus voluntary bonds. It seems that Brierly's critic against natural Law on the issue overlooks the complexity of the natural right theory. This complexity comes mostly from the ambiguous of the term "natural". Sometimes it indicates an ethical cosmos; sometimes it is reduced to the observation of causal forces dominating reality. The interaction between these two wings makes the natural law doctrines more complicated. Generally, it assumes two orientations. One is spiritualistic, ideal and ethical natural law theory, which is founded on values such as justice, reason or natural sociability of the human being. The other is existentialist or empirical natural law theory, which founds the Law on nature understood as a reality. The core of this doctrine is notions such as cries for self-conservation and self-aggrandizement, the law that the stronger prevails over the weaker, the struggle for survival and the like.③

The common aspects of this natural law theory include at least the following: First, it concerns elements that are exterior to any voluntary act of man. The doctrine seeks the foundation of the law in the given of a

---

① Andrew Clapham (ed.), *Brierly's Law of Nations: An Introduction to the Role of International Law in International Relations*, 7th Ed., Oxford University Press, 2012, p. 47.
② Ibid., p. 47.
③ See Robert Kolb, *Theory of International Law*, Hart Publishing, 2016, pp. 112-113.

transcendental idea representing a supreme value: God, justice, the common good or some conception of Man in his moral and physical needs. It rejects the idea that Law could ultimately be founded on the arbitrary will of some persons invested with power, which makes it different from positivism and sociologism. The concept of natural Law offers something eternal: it corresponds to a fundamental need of the human spirit and soul. Those general principles of IL, provided in the Charter of the United Nations, could be seen as a modern expression of this notion of natural right law.[1] The theories of "Building of a Human Community with a Shared Future", proposed by China as fundamental for global governance, also have some origins from it. It seems that natural Law provides dynamics for theory evolution during grand transition of international society, e. g., during the World War II.

After refuting natural law's view based on obligations, *Brierly* also present his explanation. It States as follow: "The ultimate explanation of the binding force of all law is that individuals, whether as single human beings, or whether associated with others in a State, are constrained, in so far as they are reasonable beings, to believe that order and not chaos is the governing principle of the world in which they have to live."[2] This explanation seems to resemble the subjective sociological theories on law, which is a third explanation of the foundation of law or basis of obligation for IL. As commented by Robert Kolb, "the foundation of the law can be a value (natural law), or may be created and sanctioned by a power (positivism), or may be taken as the fact of the observation of the rule in practice (sociologism)."[3]

The theory about the basis of obligation for IL is more complicated than

---

[1] See Robert Kolb, *Theory of International Law*, Hart Publishing, 2016, pp. 114-115.
[2] Andrew Clapham (ed.), *Brierly's Law of Nations: An Introduction to the Role of International Law in International Relations*, 7th Ed., Oxford University Press, 2012, p. 53.
[3] Robert Kolb, *Theory of International Law*, Hart Publishing, 2016, p. 105.

aforesaid. It relates closely with another basic question of IL, the compliance theory. It tries to make a sketch of why the States choose to comply with IL in an anarchic world. Also, to better understand the foundation of IL, the relation between municipal Law and IL is worthy of being explored by an illustration of China and IL.

4. Further Reading Materials: China and International Law

Read the following materials reflecting China and international law and think about the following questions:

(1) Why did China accept the modern international law that originated from Europe?

(2) What effect has, or had, international law brought on China?

(3) Will China reconstruct the international law in the future, and How?

4.1 Materials before World War I: Treaty of Nanjing (1842)[①]

Article I There shall henceforward be Peace and Friendship between Her Majesty the Queen of the United Kingdom of Great Britain and Ireland, and His Majesty the Emperor of China, and between their respective Subjects, who shall enjoy full security and protection for their persons and property within the Dominions of the other.

Article II His Majesty the Emperor of China agrees that British Subjects, with their families and establishments, shall be allowed to reside, for the purpose of carrying on their Mercantile pursuits, without molestation or restraint at the Cities and Towns of Canton, Amoy, Foochow-fu, Ningpo, and Shanghai, and Her Majesty the Queen of Great Britain, etc., will

---

① Treaty of Nanjing (August 29, 1842), the treaty that ended the first Opium War, is the first of the unequal treaties between China and foreign imperialist powers. China paid the British an indemnity, ceded the territory of Hong Kong, and agreed to establish a "fair and reasonable" tariff.

appoint Superintendents or Consular Officers, to reside at each of the above-named Cities or Towns, to be the medium of communication between the Chinese Authorities and the said Merchants, and to see that the just Duties and other Dues of the Chinese Government is hereafter provided for, are duly discharged by Her Britannic Majesty's Subjects.

4.2 Materials around the Two World Wars

(1) Treaty of Versailles (1919)[①]

Article 128 Germany renounces in favour of China all benefits and privileges resulting from the provisions of the final Protocol signed at Peking on September 7, 1901 and from all annexes, notes and documents supplementary thereto. She likewise renounces in favour of China any claim to indemnities accruing thereunder subsequent to March 14, 1917.

Article 129 From the coming into force of the present Treaty the High Contracting Parties shall apply, in so far as concerns them respectively: (1) The Arrangement of August 29, 1902 regarding the new Chinese customs tariff; (2) The Arrangement of September 27, 1905, regarding Whang-Poo, and the provisional supplementary Arrangement of April 4, 1912; China, however, will no longer be bound to grant to Germany the advantages or privileges which she allowed Germany under these Arrangements. ···

Article 156 Germany renounces, in favor of Japan, all her rights, title

---

① A peace document signed at the end of World War I by the Allied and associated powers and by Germany in the Hall of Mirrors in the Palace of Versailles, France, on June 28, 1919; it took force on January 10, 1920. The treaty was drafted during the Paris Peace Conference in the spring of 1919, which was dominated by the national leaders known as the "Big Four"—David Lloyd George of Britain, Georges Clemenceau of France, Woodrow Wilson of the United States, and Vittorio Orlando of Italy. The population and territory of Germany was reduced by about 10 percent by the treaty. All Germany's overseas colonies in China, in the Pacific, and in Africa were taken over by Britain, France, Japan, and other Allied nations. The representative of Chinese government, Wellington Koo, refused to sign the treaty and the Chinese delegation at the Paris Peace Conference was the only nation that did not sign the Treaty of Versailles at the signing ceremony. The sense of betrayal led to great demonstrations in China such as the May 4th Movement.

and privileges particularly those concerning the territory of Kiaochow, railways, mines and submarine cables—which she acquired in virtue of the Treaty concluded by her with China on March 6, 1898, and of all other arrangements relative to the Province of Shantung. All German rights in the Tsingtao—Tsinanfu Railway, including its branch lines, together with its subsidiary property of all kinds, stations, shops, fixed and rolling stock, mines, plant and material for the exploitation of the mines, are and remain acquired by Japan, together with all rights and privileges attaching thereto. The German State submarine cables from Tsingtao to Shanghai and from Tsingtao to Chefoo, with all the rights, privileges and properties attaching thereto, are similarly acquired by Japan, free and clear of all charges and encumbrances.

Article 157 The movable and immovable property owned by the German State in the territory of Kiaochow, as well as all the rights which Germany might claim in consequence of the works or improvements made or of the expenses incurred by her, directly or indirectly, in connection with this territory, are and remain acquired by Japan, free and clear of all charges and encumbrances. …

(2) *Cairo Communiqué* (*1943*)[①]

"The several military missions have agreed upon future military operations against Japan. The Three Great Allies expressed their resolve to bring unrelenting pressure against their brutal enemies by sea, land, and air. This pressure is already rising.

"The Three Great Allies are fighting this war to restrain and punish the aggression of Japan. They covet no gain for themselves and have no thought

---

① It was the outcome of the Cairo Conference in Cairo, Egypt, on November 27, 1943. The declaration developed ideas from the 1941 Atlantic Charter, which was issued by the Allies of World War Ⅱ to set goals for the post-war order.

of territorial expansion. It is their purpose that Japan shall be stripped of all the islands in the Pacific which she has seized or occupied since the beginning of the first World War in 1914, and that all the territories Japan has stolen from the Chinese, such as Northeast China, Taiwan Region, and the Penghu Islands, shall be restored to China. Japan will also be expelled from all other territories which she has taken by violence and greed. The aforesaid three great powers, mindful of the enslavement of the people of Korea, are determined that in due course Korea shall become free and independent. ···"

(3) *The Japanese Instrument of Surrender* (*1945*)[①]

We hereby proclaim the unconditional surrender to the Allied Powers of the Japanese Imperial General Headquarters and of all Japanese Armed Forces and all Armed Forces under Japanese control wherever situated. ···

We hereby undertake for the Emperor, the Japanese Government, and their successors to carry out the provisions of the Potsdam Declaration in good faith, and to issue whatever orders and take whatever action may be required by the Supreme Commander for the Allied Powers or by any other designated representative of the Allied Powers for the purpose of giving effect to that declaration. ···

4.3 Materials before 1978

(1) *Text of the Korean War Armistice Agreement* (*1953*)[②]

Preamble

The undersigned, the Commander-in-Chief, United Nations Command,

---

[①] It was the written agreement that formalized the surrender of the Empire of Japan, marking the end of World War II. It was signed by representatives from the Empire of Japan, the United States of America, China, the United Kingdom of Great Britain and Northern Ireland, the Union of Soviet Socialist Republics, the Commonwealth of Australia, the Dominion of Canada, the Provisional Government of the French Republic, the Kingdom of the Netherlands, and the Dominion of New Zealand.

[②] Agreement between the Commander-in-Chief, United Nations Command, on the one hand, and the Supreme Commander of the Korean People's Army and the Commander of the Chinese People's Volunteers, on the other hand, concerning a military armistice in Korea.

on the one hand, and the Supreme Commander of the Korean People's Army and the Commander of the Chinese People's Volunteers, on the other hand, in the interest of stopping the Korean conflict, with its great toil of suffering and bloodshed on both sides, and with the objective of establishing an armistice which will insure a complete cessation of hostilities and of all acts of armed force in Korea until a final peaceful settlement is achieved, do individually, collectively, and mutually agree to accept and to be bound and governed by the conditions and terms of armistice set forth in the following articles and paragraphs, which said conditions and terms are intended to be purely military in character and to pertain solely to the belligerents in Korea. ⋯

Article Ⅱ: Concrete Arrangements for Cease-Fire and Armistice

……

12. The Commanders of the opposing sides shall order and enforce a complete cessation of all hostilities in Korea by all armed forces under their control, including all units and personnel of the ground, naval, and air forces, effective twelve hours after this armistice agreement is signed. (See paragraph 63 hereof for effective date and hour of the remaining provisions of this armistice agreement.)

13. In order to insure the stability of the military armistice so as to facilitate the attainment of a peaceful settlement through the holding by both sides of a political conference of a higher level, the Commanders of the opposing sides shall:

(a) Within seventy-two hours after this armistice agreement becomes effective, withdraw all of their military forces, supplies, and equipment from the demilitarized zone except as otherwise provided herein. All demolitions, minefields, wire entanglements, and other hazards to the safe movement of personnel of the Military Armistice Commission or its Joint Observer Teams, known to exist within the demilitarized zone after the withdrawal of military forces therefrom, together with lanes known to be free of all such hazards,

Chapter I   International Law: General Introduction   23

shall be reported to the MAC by the Commander of the side whose forces emplaced such hazards. Subsequently, additional safe lanes shall be cleared; and eventually, within forty-five days after the termination of the seventy-two hour period, all such hazards shall be removed from the demilitarized zone as directed by the under the supervision of the MAC. At the termination of the seventy-two hour period, except for unarmed troops authorized forty-five day period to complete salvage operations under MAC and agreed to by the MAC and agreed to by the Commanders of the opposing sides, and personnel authorized under paragraphs 10 and 11 hereof, no personnel of either side shall be permitted to enter the demilitarized zone.

(b) Within ten days after this armistice agreement becomes effective, withdraw all of their military forces, supplies, and equipment from the rear and the coastal islands and waters of Korea of the other side. If such military forces are not withdrawn within the stated time limit, and there is no mutually agreed and valid reason for the delay, the other side shall have the right to take any action which it deems necessary for the maintenance of security and order. …

(c) Cease the introduction into Korea of Reinforcing military personnel; provided, however, that the rotation of units and personnel, the arrival in Korea of personnel on a temporary duty basis, and the return to Korea of personnel after short periods of leave or temporary duty outside of Korea shall be permitted within the scope prescribed below…

(d) Cease the introduction into Korea of reinforcing combat aircraft, armored vehicles, weapons, and ammunition; provided however, that combat aircraft, armored vehicles, weapons, and ammunition which are destroyed, damaged, worn out, or used up during the period of the armistice may be replaced on the basis piece-for-piece of the same effectiveness and the same type. Such combat aircraft, armored vehicles, weapons, and ammunition shall be introduced into Korea only through the ports of entry enumerated in paragraph 43 hereof. In order to justify the requirements for combat aircraft, armored vehicles, weapons, and ammunition to be introduced into Korea for replacement purposes, reports concerning every incoming shipment of these items shall be made to the MAC and the NNSC; such reports shall include Statements regarding the disposition of the items being replaced. Items to be replace which are removed from Korea shall be removed only through the ports of entry enumerated in paragraph 43 hereof. The NNSC, through its Neutral Nations Inspection Teams, shall conduct supervision and inspection of the replacement of combat aircraft, armored vehicles, weapons, and ammunition authorized above, at the ports of entry enumerated in paragraph 43 hereof.

(e) Insure that personnel of their respective commands who violate any of the provisions of this armistice agreement are adequately punished.

(f) In those cases where places of burial are a matter of record and graves are actually found to exist, permit graves registration personnel of the other side to enter, within a definite time limit after this armistice agreement becomes effective, the territory of Korea under their military control, for the purpose of proceeding to such graves to recover and evacuate the bodies of the deceased military personnel of that side, including deceased prisoners of war. The specific procedures and the time limit for the performance of the above task shall be determined by the Military Armistice Commission. The Commanders of the opposing sides shall furnish to the other side all available information pertaining to the places of burial of the deceased military personnel of the other side.

······

(2) *The Asian-African Conference* (1955)[①]

······

[①] The Asian-African Conference, also known as the Bandung Conference, was held in Bandung, Indonesia from April 18 to 24, 1955. Representatives from 29 Asian and African countries and regions, most of which were newly independent, gathered to discuss independence, peace and economic prosperity. The conference was jointly proposed by Indonesia, Burma (now Myanmar), Ceylon (now Sri Lanka), India and Pakistan. China played a prominent part in the conference and strengthened friendly relations with other nations.

The Asian-African Conference considered problems of common interest and concern to countries of Asia and Africa and discussed ways and means by which their people could achieve fuller economic, cultural and political co-operation.

A. Economic co-operation

a. The Asian-African Conference recognized the urgency of promoting economic development in the Asian-African region. There was general desire for economic co-operation among the participating countries on the basis of mutual interest and respect for national sovereignty. The proposals with regard to economic cooperation within the participating countries do not preclude either the desirability or the need for cooperation with countries outside the region, including the investment of foreign capital. ⋯

b. The participating countries agreed to provide technical assistance to one another, to the maximum extent practicable, in the form of: experts, trainees, pilot projects and equipment for demonstration purposes; exchange of know-how and establishment of national, and where possible, regional training and research institutes for imparting technical knowledge and skills in co-operation with the existing international agencies. ⋯

B. Human rights and self-determination

a. The Asian-African Conference declared its full support of the fundamental principles of Human Rights as set forth in the Charter of the United Nations and took note of the Universal Declaration of Human Rights as a common standard of achievement for all peoples and all nations. The Conference declared its full support of the principle of self-determination of peoples and nations as set forth in the Charter of the United Nations and took note of the United Nations resolutions on the rights of peoples and nations to self-determination, which is a pre-requisite of the full enjoyment of all fundamental Human Rights.

b. The Asian-African Conference deplored the policies and practices of racial segregation and discrimination which form the basis of government and human relations in large regions of Africa and in other parts of the world. ···

C. Promotion of world peace and co-operation

a. The Asian-African Conference, taking note of the fact that several States have still not been admitted to the United Nations (UN), considered that for effective co-operation for world peace membership in the United Nations should be universal, called on the Security Council to support the admission of all those States which are qualified for membership in terms of the Charter. In the opinion of the Asian-African Conference, the following among participating countries, viz. Cambodia, Ceylon, Japan, Jordan, Libya, Nepal, a unified Vietnam were so qualified. ···

b. The Asian-African Conference having considered the dangerous situation of international tension existing and the risks confronting the whole human race from the outbreak of global war in which the destructive power of all types of armaments, including nuclear and thermo-nuclear weapons, would be employed, invited the attention of all nations to the terrible consequences that would follow if such a war were to break out. The Conference considered that disarmament and the prohibition of the production, experimentation and use of nuclear and thermo-nuclear weapons of war are imperative to save mankind and civilization from the fear and prospect of wholesale destruction. ······

The Conference declared that universal disarmament is an absolute necessity for the preservation of peace and requested the United Nations to continue its efforts and appealed to all concerned speedily to bring about the regulation, limitation, control and reduction of all armed forces and armaments, including the prohibition of the production, experimentation and use of all weapons of mass destruction, and to establish effective international control to this end.

D. Declaration on the promotion of world peace and co-operation

The Asian-African Conference gave anxious thought to the question of world peace and co-operation. It viewed with deep concern the present State of international tension with its danger of an atomic world war. ···Free from mistrust and fear, and with confidence and goodwill towards each other, nations should practice tolerance and live together in peace with one another as good neighbours and develop friendly co-operation on the basis of the following principles:

a. Respect for fundamental human rights and for the purposes and principles of the Charter of the United Nations.

b. Respect for the sovereignty and territorial integrity of all nations.

c. Recognition of the equality of all races and of the equality of all nations large and small.

d. Abstention from intervention or interference in the internal affairs of another country.

e. Respect for the right of each nation to defend itself singly or collectively, in conformity with the Charter of the United Nations.

f. (a) Abstention from the use of arrangements of collective defence to serve the particular interests of any of the big powers. (b) Abstention by any country from exerting pressures on other countries.

g. Refraining from acts or threats of aggression or the use of force against the territorial integrity or political independence of any country.

h. Settlement of all international disputes by peaceful means, such as negotiation, conciliation, arbitration or judicial settlement as well as other peaceful means of the parties' own choice, in conformity with the Charter of the United Nations.

i. Promotion of mutual interests and co-operation.

j. Respect for justice and international obligations.

······

(3) *Restoration of the Lawful Rights of the People's Republic of China in the United Nations UN DOC. A/RES/2758(XXVI) (1971)*
The General Assembly:

······

Recognizing that the representatives of the Government of **the People's Republic of China are the only lawful representatives of China to the United Nations** and that the People's Republic of China is one of the five permanent members of the Security Council,

Decides to restore all its rights to the People's Republic of China and to recognize the representative of its Government as the only legitimate representatives of China to the United Nations…

4.4 Materials during 1978-2008

(1) *Joint Communique on the Establishment of Diplomatic Relations Between the United States of American and the People's Republic of China* (1979)

The United States of America and the People's Republic of China have agreed to recognize each other and to establish diplomatic relations as of January 1, 1979.

The United States of America recognizes the Government of the People's Republic of China as **the sole legal Government of China**. Within this context, the people of the United States will maintain cultural, commercial, and **other unofficial relations** with the people of Taiwan.

……

Neither should **seek hegemony in the Asia-Pacific region** or in any other region of the world and each is opposed to efforts by any other country or group of countries to establish such hegemony.

Neither is prepared to negotiate on behalf of any third party or to enter into agreements or understandings with the other directed at other States.

……

The Government of the United States of America acknowledges the Chinese **position that there is but one China and Taiwan is part of China.**

(2) *Accession of the People's Republic of China (Decision of 10 November 2001)*

The Ministerial Conference,

Decides as follows:

The People's Republic of China may accede to the Marrakesh Agreement Establishing the World Trade Organization on the terms and conditions set out in the Protocol annexed to this decision.

······

4.5 Materials after 2008

(1) *Follow the Trend of the Times and Promote Peace and Development in the World*[①]

······

Dear faculty members and students,

The Institute of International Relations, as an institution of higher learning specialized in the study of international issues, surely pays a close attention to international landscape and can appreciate even more keenly the enormous changes the world has gone through over the past decades. Indeed, We live in a time of kaleidoscopic changes that make the world constantly different.

It is a world where peace, development, cooperation and mutual benefit have become the trend of the times. The old colonial system has since disintegrated, confrontation between blocs as during the Cold War has long gone. No country or group of countries can dominate world affairs single-handedly.

---

① See Follow the Trend of the Times and Promote Peace and Development in the World, Speech by Xi Jinping, President of the People's Republic of China at Moscow State Institute of International Relations, 23 March 2013, http://www.fmcoprc.gov.hk/eng/jbwzlm/xwdt/zt/xzxcf/201304/t20130419_10095330.htm, last visited on Jan. 8, 2022.

......

It is a world where countries are linked with and dependent on one another at a level never seen before. Mankind, by living in the same global village within the same time and space where history and reality meet, have increasingly emerged as a community of common destiny in which everyone has in himself a little bit of others.

And it is a world where mankind are beset with numerous difficulties and challenges. They range from continued underlying impact of the international financial crisis, an apparent upsurge of all kinds of protectionism, incessant regional hotspots, rising hegemonism, power politics, and neo-interventionism, to interlaced traditional and non-conventional security threats, such as arms race, terrorism and cyber-security. Upholding world peace and promoting common development remain a long and uphill battle.

......

In the face of the profoundly changed international landscape and the objective need for the world to rally closely together like passengers in the same boat, **all countries should join hands in building a new type of international relations featuring cooperation and mutual benefit,** and all peoples should work together to safeguard world peace and promote common development.

We stand for the sharing of dignity by all countries and peoples in the world. All countries, irrespective of size, strength and wealth, are equal. The right of the people to independently choose their development paths should be respected, interference in the internal affairs of other countries opposed and international fairness and justice maintained. Only the wearer of the shoes knows if they fit or not. Only the people can best tell if the development path they have chosen for their country suits or not.

We stand for the sharing of the fruits of development by all countries and peoples in the world. Every country, while pursuing its own development, should actively facilitate the common development of all countries. ...

We stand for the sharing of security by all countries and peoples in the world. Countries should make concerted efforts to properly address the issues and challenges in their face. …

As the trends of world multipolarity and economic globalization deepen and those of upholding cultural diversity and applying information technology in social life continue to make progress, mankind have never been better blessed for taking strides towards peace and development. And win-win cooperation provides the only practical way to achieve such a goal.

The destiny of the world must be left in the hands of the people of all countries. Matters that fall within the sovereign rights of a country should be managed only by the government and people of that country. And affairs of the world should be addressed by the governments and peoples of all countries through consultation. Herein lies the democratic principle in the handling of international affairs which should be universally observed by the international community.

……

(2) *Work Together to Build a Community of Shared Future for Mankind* [1]

……

I just attended the World Economic Forum Annual Meeting. In Davos, many speakers pointed out in their speeches that today's world is full of uncertainties and that people long for a bright future but are bewildered about what will come. What has happened to the world and how should we respond? The whole world is reflecting on this question, and it is also very much on my mind.

I believe that to answer this question, we need to get clear about a

---

[1] See Work Together to Build a Community of Shared Future for Mankind, Speech by Xi Jinping, at the United Nations Office at Geneva, 18 January 2017, http://www.xinhuanet.com/english/2017-01/19/c_135994707.htm, last visited on Jan. 8, 2022.

fundamental issue: Where did we come from? Where are we now? And where are we going?

Over the past century and more, mankind has gone through bloody hot wars and the chilling Cold War, but also achieved remarkable development and huge progress. In the first half of 20th century, mankind suffered the scourges of two world wars, and the people yearned for the end of war and the advent of peace. In the 1950s and 1960s, people in colonies awakened and fought to shake off shackles and achieve independence. Since the end of the Cold War, people have pursued a shared aspiration, namely, to expand cooperation and promote common development.

......

Pass on the torch of peace from generation to generation, sustain development and make civilization flourish: this is what people of all countries long for; it is also the responsibility Statesmen of our generation ought to shoulder. **And China's proposition is: build a community of shared future for mankind and achieve shared and win-win development.**

Vision guides action and direction determines the future. As modern history shows, to establish a fair and equitable international order is the goal mankind has always striven for. From the principles of equality and sovereignty established in the Peace of Westphalia over 360 years ago to international humanitarianism affirmed in the Geneva Convention 150-plus years ago; from the four purposes and seven principles enshrined in the UN Charter more than 70 years ago to the Five Principles of Peaceful Coexistence championed by the Bandung Conference over 60 years ago, many principles have emerged in the evolution of international relations and become widely accepted. These principles should guide us in building a community of shared future for mankind.

Sovereign equality is the most important norm governing state-to-state relations over the past centuries and the cardinal principle observed by UN and all other international organizations. The essence of sovereign equality is that the sovereignty and dignity of all countries, whether big or small, strong or weak, rich or poor, must be respected, their internal affairs allow no interference and they have the right to independently choose their social system and development path. In organizations such as United Nations, World Trade Organization, World Health Organization, World Intellectual Property Organization, World Meteorological Organization, International Telecommunication Union, Universal Postal Union, International Organization for Migration and International Labor Organization, countries have an equal voice in decision-making, constituting an important force for improving global governance. In a new era, we should uphold sovereign equality and work for equality in right, opportunity and rules for all countries.

……

Great visions can be realized only through actions. Actions hold the key to building a community of shared future for mankind. To achieve this goal, the international community should promote partnership, security, growth, inter-civilization exchanges and the building of a sound ecosystem.

We should stay committed to building a world of lasting peace through dialogue and consultation. … Major powers should respect each other's core interests and major concerns, keep their differences under control and build a new model of relations featuring non-conflict, non-confrontation, mutual respect and win-win cooperation. As long as we maintain communication and treat each other with sincerity, the "Thucydides trap" can be avoided. Big countries should treat smaller ones as equals instead of acting as a hegemon imposing their will on others. No country should open the Pandora's box by willfully waging wars or undermining the international rule of law. …

We should build a world of common security for all through joint efforts. No country in the world can enjoy absolute security. A country cannot have security while others are in turmoil, as threats facing other countries may haunt itself also. When neighbors are in trouble, instead of tightening his own fences, one should extend a helping hand to them. As a saying goes, "United we stand, divided we fall." All countries should pursue common, comprehensive, cooperative and sustainable security.

Fighting terrorism is the shared responsibility of all countries. In fighting terror, we should not just treat the symptoms, but remove its root causes. We should enhance coordination and build a global united front against terrorism so as to create an umbrella of security for people around the world. The number of refugees has hit a record high since the end of the Second World War. While tackling the crisis, we should also get to its roots. Why would anyone want to be displaced if they have a home to return to? UNHCR and the International Organization for Migration should act as the coordinator to mobilize the whole world to respond effectively to the refugee crisis. China has decided to provide an additional 200 million yuan of humanitarian assistance for refugees and the displaced of Syria. As terrorism and refugee crises are closely linked to geopolitical conflicts, resolving conflicts provides the fundamental solution to such problems. Parties directly involved should return to the negotiating table, and other parties should work to facilitate talks for peace, and we should all respect the role the UN plays as the main channel for mediation. Pandemic diseases such as bird flu, Ebola and Zika have sounded the alarm for international health security. The WHO should play a leadership role in strengthening epidemic monitoring and sharing of information, practices and technologies. The international community should step up support and assistance for public health in African countries and other developing countries.

We should build a world of common prosperity through win-win cooperation. Development is the top priority for all countries. Instead of beggaring thy neighbor, countries should stick together like passengers in the same boat. All countries, the main economies in particular, should strengthen macro policy coordination, pursue both current and long-term interests and focus on resolving deep-seated problems. We should seize the historic opportunity presented by the new round of scientific and technological revolution and industrial transformation, shift growth models, drive growth through innovation and further unleash social productivity and social creativity. We should uphold WTO rules, support an open, transparent, inclusive and nondiscriminatory multilateral trading regime and build an open world economy. Trade protectionism and self-isolation will benefit no one.

Economic globalization, a surging historical trend, has greatly facilitated trade, investment, flow of people and technological advances. Since the turn of the century, under the auspices of the UN and riding on the waves of economic globalization, the international community has set the Millennium Development Goals and the 2030 Agenda for Sustainable Development. Thanks to these initiatives, 1.1 billion people have been lifted out of poverty, 1.9 billion people now have access to safe drinking water, 3.5 billion people have gained access to the Internet, and the goal has been set to eradicate extreme poverty by 2030. All this demonstrates that economic globalization is moving in the right direction. Of course, challenges such as development disparity, governance dilemma, digital divide and equity deficit still exist. But they are growing pains. We should face these problems and tackle them, instead of taking no action, as we Chinese like to say, one should not stop eating for fear of getting choked.

......

We should build an open and inclusive world through exchanges and mutual learning. Delicious soup is made by combining different ingredients. Diversity of human civilizations not only defines our world, but also drives progress of mankind. There are more than 200 countries and regions, over 2500 ethnic groups and multiple religions in our world. Different histories, national conditions, ethnic groups and customs give birth to different civilizations and make the world a colorful one. There is no such thing as a superior or inferior civilization, and civilizations are different only in identity and location. Diversity of civilizations should not be a source of global conflict; rather, it should be an engine driving the advance of human civilizations.

Every civilization, with its own appeal and root, is a human treasure. Diverse civilizations should draw on each other to achieve common progress. We should make exchanges among civilizations a source of inspiration for advancing human society and a bond that keeps the world in peace.

We should make our world clean and beautiful by pursuing green and low-carbon development. Man coexists with nature, which means that any harm to nature will eventually come back to haunt man. We hardly notice natural resources such as air, water, soil and blue sky when we have them. But we won't be able to survive without them. Industrialization has created material wealth never seen before, but it has also inflicted irreparable damage to the environment. We must not exhaust all the resources passed on to us by previous generations and leave nothing to our children or pursue development in a destructive way. Clear waters and green mountains are as good as mountains of gold and silver. We must maintain harmony between man and nature and pursue sustainable development.

We should pursue green, low-carbon, circular and sustainable way of life and production, advance the 2030 Agenda for Sustainable Development in a balanced manner and explore a model of sound development that ensures growth, better lives and a good environment. The Paris Agreement is a milestone in the history of climate governance. We must ensure this endeavor is not derailed. All parties should work together to implement the Paris Agreement. China will continue to take steps to tackle climate change and fully honor its obligations.

……

First, China remains unchanged in its commitment to uphold world peace. Amity with neighbors, harmony without uniformity and peace are values cherished in the Chinese culture. The Art of War, a Chinese classic, begins with this observation, "The art of war is of vital importance to the State. It is a matter of life and death, a road to either survival or ruin. Hence it demands

Chapter I International Law: General Introduction 37

careful study. " What it means is that every effort should be made to prevent a war and great caution must be exercised when it comes to fighting a war. For several millennia, peace has been in the blood of us Chinese and a part of our DNA.

......

China has grown from a poor and weak country to the world's second largest economy not by committing military expansion or colonial plunder, but through the hard work of its people and our efforts to uphold peace. China will never waver in its pursuit of peaceful development. No matter how strong its economy grows, China will never seek hegemony, expansion or sphere of influence. History has borne this out and will continue to do so.

Second, China remains unchanged in its commitment to pursue common development. An old Chinese saying goes, when you reap fruits, you should remember the tree; when you drink water, you should remember its source. China's development has been possible because of the world, and China has contributed to the world's development. We will continue to pursue a win-win strategy of opening-up, share our development opportunities with other countries and welcome them aboard the fast train of China's development.

Between 1950 and 2016, China provided foreign countries with over 400 billion yuan of aid, and we will continue to increase assistance to others as its ability permits. Since the outbreak of the international financial crisis, China has contributed to over 30% of global growth each year on average. In the coming five years, China will import eight trillion US dollars of goods, attract 600 billion US dollars of foreign investment, make 750 billion US dollars of outbound investment, and Chinese tourists will make 700 million outbound visits. All this will bring more development opportunities to other countries.

China pursues a path of development in keeping with its national conditions. We always put people's rights and interests above everything else and have worked hard to advance and uphold human rights. China has met the basic living needs of its 1.3 billion-plus people and lifted over 700 million people out of poverty, which is a significant contribution to the global cause of human rights. The Belt and Road initiative I put forward aims to achieve win-win and shared development. Over 100 countries and international organizations have supported the initiative, and a large number of early harvest projects have been launched. China supports the successful operation of the Asian Infrastructure Investment Bank and other new multilateral financial institutions in order to provide more public goods to the international community.

Third, China remains unchanged in its commitment to foster partnerships. China pursues an independent foreign policy of peace, and is ready to enhance friendship and cooperation with all other countries on the basis of the Five Principles of Peaceful Coexistence. China is the first country to make partnership-building a principle guiding state-to-state relations. It has formed partnerships of various forms with over 90 countries and regional organizations, and will build a circle of friends across the world.

China will endeavor to put in place a framework of relations with major powers featuring general stability and balanced growth. We will strive to build a new model of major country relations with the United States, a comprehensive strategic partnership of coordination with Russia, partnership for peace, growth, reform and among different civilizations with Europe, and a partnership of unity and cooperation with BRICS countries. China will continue to uphold justice and friendship and pursue shared interests, and boost pragmatic cooperation with other developing countries to achieve common development. We will further enhance mutually beneficial cooperation with our neighbors under the principle of amity, sincerity, mutual benefit and inclusiveness. We will pursue common development with African countries in a spirit of sincerity, being result oriented, affinity and good faith. And we will elevate our comprehensive cooperative partnership with Latin America to a higher level.

Fourth, China remains unchanged in its commitment to multilateralism.

Multilateralism is an effective way to preserve peace and promote development. For decades, UN and other international institutions have made a universally recognized contribution to maintaining global peace and sustaining development.

China is a founding member of UN and the first country to put its signature on the UN Charter. China will firmly uphold the international system with the UN as its core, the basic norms governing international relations embodied in the purposes and principles of the UN Charter, the authority and stature of the UN, and its core role in international affairs.

The China-UN Peace and Development Fund has been officially inaugurated. We will make funds available to peace and development oriented programs proposed by the UN and its agencies in Geneva on a priority basis. China's support for multilateralism will increase as the country continues to develop itself.

……

(3) *China and the World in the New Era*[1]

……

Ⅳ. China Contributes to a Better World

China cannot develop in isolation from the rest of the world, nor can the world as a whole maintain peace, development, prosperity and stability without China. China will do well only when the world does well, and vice versa. China continues to place its own development in the coordinate system of human development, seeing that its future is closely connected with that of the rest of the world and the interests of the Chinese people are integrated with the common interests of the peoples of other countries. China is always a builder of world peace, a contributor to global development, and a guardian of

---

[1] See The State Council Information Office of the People's Republic of China, China and the World in the New Era, September 2019, http://english.scio.gov.cn/2019-09/28/content_75252746_5.htm, last visited on Jan. 8, 2022.

global order, contributing Chinese wisdom and strength to building a global community of shared future and developing a better world.

......

Guided by Xi Jinping Thought on Socialism with Chinese Characteristics for a New Era, China will continue to forge ahead on its socialist path. We have committed to a people-centered approach and given top priority to development. We have implemented the five-sphere integrated plan to advance economic, political, cultural, social and ecological development, and the four-pronged comprehensive strategy to complete a moderately prosperous society in all respects, further reform, advance the rule of law and strengthen Party discipline. We should strive to build China into a strong, modern socialist country and march towards national rejuvenation.

China places economic development at the center of its national rejuvenation, promotes high-quality development and pursues with firmness of purpose the new vision of innovative, coordinated, green, open and inclusive development. ⋯

......

Promoting high-quality development along the Belt and Road. ⋯ China will join forces with all parties concerned to follow the principles of extensive consultation, joint contribution and shared benefits, and uphold open and green development and clean government. ⋯

China is an active participant in and a firm supporter of economic globalization. We are ready to join the international community in taking proactive measures and strengthening guidance to make the process of economic globalization more dynamic, more inclusive and more sustainable. ⋯

Opposing unilateralism and protectionism. China is fully committed to a multilateral trading system with the WTO at its core. It is keen to extend cooperation with other countries on the basis of equality and mutual respect, and to jointly maintain the stability and development of the global economy and trade. China advocates compliance with the WTO rules to address issues in international trade through dialogue and consultation based on mutual respect, equality, mutual benefit, cooperation and good faith. …

Opening wider to the outside world. … We have launched and will continue to implement a host of major opening-up measures, giving equal emphasis to "bringing in" and "going global", and making new ground in opening China further through links running eastward and westward, across land and over sea. With lower overall tariffs, a shorter negative list, easier market access, more transparent market rules, and a more attractive business environment, China will build an open economy of higher quality, bringing more opportunities for growth, transformation and innovation to the world. …

Moving faster to promote regional economic integration. China will speed up the implementation of its free trade zone strategy, and build a high-standard network of free trade zones that focuses on neighboring countries and regions, radiates out through the Belt and Road, and opens to the world. We will continue to help secure agreement on the Regional Comprehensive Economic Partnership, and speed up negotiations on the China-Japan-ROK Free Trade Agreement and the China-EU investment treaty. …

Continuing internationalization of the Renminbi. The internationalization of the Renminbi has broadened monetary settlement options for global trade and promoted diversity in the international monetary system. …

Developing global partnerships.

China gives priority to expanding partnerships. Those who cherish the same ideals and follow the same path can be partners, and so can those who seek common ground while reserving differences. China will carry forward this spirit, remain committed to a new approach to state-to-state relations, one that features dialogue rather than confrontation, and seeks partnerships rather than alliances. …

Taking a lead in reforming and developing the global governance system.

As a major and responsible country, China will continue to enjoy its rights in balance with fulfilling its obligations, taking account of both its requirements of the world and the international community's expectations for China. We will take an active part in reforming and developing the global governance system. As a participant in, builder of, and contributor to that system, China hopes to help the system move with the times through innovation and improvement, rather than reinvent the wheel.

······

China gives active support to reforming the UN, helping it better meet the new requirements of global governance in its underlying guidelines, organization and operations, better fulfill the responsibilities prescribed in the UN Charter, and better play an expanding role in safeguarding world peace and promoting common development. We support necessary reform of the WTO on the basis of equity and justice. China advocates that reform of the WTO should safeguard its core values and basic principles, especially the interests and policy space of developing countries. ···

China makes active efforts to advance the quota and governance reform of the IMF and the World Bank, better reflecting changes to the international architecture. We will promote the role of the G20 as the premier forum for international economic cooperation, and help it transform from a crisis-management body to a long-term and effective governance mechanism, making a bigger contribution to world economic growth and global economic governance. In leading and promoting an open world economy, China will push for new breakthroughs in the Asia-Pacific Economic Cooperation (APEC), and ensure that more people embrace the spirit of an Asia-Pacific family and the idea of a community of shared future. We will ensure sustained and steady progress of the BRICS cooperation mechanism, so that it can play a greater role among international platforms.

······

5. References and Recommended Reading Materials

(1) Philippe Sands, *Lawless World: Making and Breaking Global Rules*, Penguin, 2006. 〔英〕菲利普·桑斯:《无法无天的世界:当代国际法的产生与破灭》,单文华、赵宏、吴双全译,人民出版社 2011 年版。

(2) Immanuel C. Y. Hsü, *China's Entrance into the Family of Nations: The Diplomatic Phase, 1858-1880*, Harvard University Press, 1960. 〔美〕徐中约:《中国进入国际大家庭:1958—1980 年间的外交》,屈文生译,商务印书馆 2018 年版。

(3) Hans J. Morgenthau, *Politics Among Nations: The Struggle for Power and Peace*, 4th Ed., Alfred A. Knopf, Inc., 1967. 〔美〕汉斯·摩根索:《国家间政治:权力斗争与和平(第七版)》,徐昕等译,北京大学出版社 2006 年版。

Chapter Ⅱ　Sources of International Law

1. Introduction

　　The concept of sources of law is important because it enables the rules of international law to be ascertained and distinguished from others. And it also concerns how the new rules of conduct are established and how the existing rules are changed. [1] In practice, the sources of international law constitute one of the most central patterns around which international legal discourses and legal claims are built. It is not contested that speaking like an international lawyer entails, first and foremost, the ability to deploy the categories put in place by the sources of international law. [2]

　　This chapter will provide a basic outline of the theory and practice of the **sources** of international law. Part 2 excerpts several articles in the Statute of ICJ, ICC and other international tribunals. Part 3 briefly discusses some terminologies, such as the concept of sources of international law, treaty, custom, general principle, and other subsidiary sources. Part 4 provides famous cases decided by ICJ or other international tribunals.

---

　　[1]　See Robert Jennings and Arthur Watts (eds.), *Oppenheim's International Law*, 9th Ed., Longman, 1996, p. 23.

　　[2]　See Samantha Besson and Jean d'Aspremont (eds.), *The Oxford Handbook on the Sources of International Law*, Oxford University Press, 2017, p. 1.

2. Preliminary Reading and Assignment

2.1 Some Problems Regarding the Formal Sources of International Law[①]

The sources of law are commonly classified as "formal" and "material". Side by side with these there are the "evidences" or records of law. Thus, if State practice, for instance, is a source of law, it would be incorrect to regard such things as documents embodying diplomatic representations, notes of protest, etc., as constituting sources of law. They are evidences of it because they demonstrate certain attitudes on the part of States, but it is the State practice so evidenced which is the source of law.

Accepting this classification, it is of course possible to use other terms to describe the formal and material sources. Thus they may be described as, respectively, the legal sources and the historical sources, as direct and indirect, as proximate or immediate, and remote or ultimate, and so on. Or, as has been suggested, the material sources might better be described as the "origins" of law. But whatever the terminology used, the essence of the distinction remains the same. Material, historical, indirect sources represent, so to speak, the stuff out of which the law is made. It is they which go to form the content of the law. These are the sources to which the lawgiver goes, so to speak, in order to obtain ideas, or to decide what the law is to consist of, and this is broadly true whether the lawgiver be conceived of as a national legislature, or as the international community evolving customary rules through State practice. The formal, legal, and direct sources consist of the acts or facts whereby this content, whatever it may be and from whatever material source it may be drawn, is clothed with legal validity and obligatory

---

[①] See G. Fitzmaurice, Some Problems Regarding the Formal Sources of International Law, in F. M. van Asbeck, *et al.* (eds), Martinus Nijhoff, 1958, pp. 153-76.

force. The essence of the distinction therefore is between the thing which inspires the content of the law, and the thing which gives that content its obligatory character as law.

Considered in themselves, and particularly in their inception, treaties are, formally, a source of obligation rather than a source of law. In their contractual aspect they are no more a source of law than an ordinary private law contract; which simply creates rights and obligations. Such instruments (as also, on the international plane, a commercial treaty, for example) create obligations and rights, not law. In this connexion, the attempts which have been made to ascribe a law-making character to all treaties irrespective of the character of their content or the number of the parties to them, by postulating that some treaties create "particular" international law and others "general", is of extremely dubious validity. There is really no such thing as "particular" international treaty law, though there are particular international treaty rights and obligations. The only "law" that enters into these is derived, not from the treaty creating them—or from any treaty—but from the principle *pacta sunt servanda*—an antecedent general principle of law. The law is that the obligation must be carried out, but the obligation is not, in itself, law. A genuine law may of course be applicable only to certain particular subjects of the legal system, but if so it is usually as members of a class, not as individuals. For instance, a law relating to married women obviously applies only to women who are married. But it applies automatically and *ipso facto* to all such women, not merely to those individual women who have set their hands to some particular instrument.

2.2 Statute of International Tribunals

(1) *Statute of the ICJ*[①]

Article 38

1. The Court, whose function is to decide in accordance with

[①] See ICJ, Statute of the International Court of Justice, https://www.icj-cij.org/en/statute, last visited on Jan. 8, 2022.

international law such disputes as are submitted to it, shall apply:

a) international conventions, whether general or particular, establishing rules expressly recognized by the contesting States;

b) international custom, as evidence of a general practice accepted as law;

c) the general principles of law recognized by civilized nations;

d) subject to the provisions of Article 59, judicial decisions and the teachings of the most highly qualified publicists of the various nations, as subsidiary means for the determination of rules of law.

2. This provision shall not prejudice the power of the Court to decide a case *ex aequo et bono*, if the parties agree thereto.

Article 59

The decision of the Court has no binding force except between the parties and in respect of that particular case.

(2) *Rome Statute of the International Criminal Court*[1]

Article 21: Applicable law

1. The Court shall apply:

a) In the first place, this Statute, Elements of Crimes and its Rules of Procedure and Evidence;

b) In the second place, where appropriate, applicable treaties and the principles and rules of international law, including the established principles of the international law of armed conflict;

c) Failing that, general principles of law derived by the Court from national laws of legal systems of the world including, as appropriate, the national laws of States that would normally exercise jurisdiction over the crime, provided that those principles are not inconsistent with this Statute

---

[1] See ICC, Rome Statute of the International Criminal Court, chrome-extension://efaidnbmnnnibpcajpcglclefindmkaj/viewer. html？pdfurl＝https％3A％2F％2Fwww. icc-cpi. int％2Fresource-library％2Fdocuments％2Frs-eng. pdf&clen＝381805&chunk＝true, last visited on Jan. 8, 2022. Hereinafter called "Rome Statute".

and with international law and internationally recognized norms and standards.

2. The Court may apply principles and rules of law as interpreted in its previous decisions.

3. The application and interpretation of law pursuant to this article must be consistent with internationally recognized human rights, and be without any adverse distinction founded on grounds such as gender as defined in article 7, paragraph 3, age, race, color, language, religion or belief, political or other opinion, national, ethnic or social origin, wealth, birth or other status.

(3) *Understanding on Rules and Procedures Governing the Settlement of Disputes*[①]

Article 1 Coverage and Application

1. The rules and procedures of this Understanding shall apply to disputes brought pursuant to the consultation and dispute settlement provisions of the agreements listed in Appendix 1 to this Understanding (referred to in this Understanding as the "covered agreements"). The rules and procedures of this Understanding shall also apply to consultations and the settlement of disputes between Members concerning their rights and obligations under the provisions of the Agreement Establishing the World Trade Organization (referred to in this Understanding as the "WTO Agreement") and of this Understanding taken in isolation or in combination with any other covered agreement.

2. The rules and procedures of this Understanding shall apply subject to such special or additional rules and procedures on dispute settlement contained in the covered agreements as are identified in Appendix 2 to this Understanding. To the extent that there is a difference between the rules and procedures of this Understanding and the special or additional rules and

---

[①] See WTO, Understanding on Rules and Procedures Governing the Settlement of Disputes, https://www.wto.org/english/tratop_e/dispu_e/dsu_e.htm, last visited on Jan. 8, 2022.

procedures set forth in Appendix 2, the special or additional rules and procedures in Appendix 2 shall prevail. In disputes involving rules and procedures under more than one covered agreement, if there is a conflict between special or additional rules and procedures of such agreements under review, and where the parties to the dispute cannot agree on rules and procedures within 20 days of the establishment of the panel, the Chairman of the Dispute Settlement Body provided for in paragraph 1 of Article 2 (referred to in this Understanding as the "DSB"), in consultation with the parties to the dispute, shall determine the rules and procedures to be followed within 10 days after a request by either Member. The Chairman shall be guided by the principle that special or additional rules and procedures should be used where possible, and the rules and procedures set out in this Understanding should be used to the extent necessary to avoid conflict.

Article 7　Terms of Reference of Panels

1. Panels shall have the following terms of reference unless the parties to the dispute agree otherwise within 20 days from the establishment of the panel: "To examine, in the light of the relevant provisions in (name of the covered agreement(s) cited by the parties to the dispute), the matter referred to the DSB by (name of party) in document... and to make such findings as will assist the DSB in making the recommendations or in giving the rulings provided for in that/those agreement(s)."

2. Panels shall address the relevant provisions in any covered agreement or agreements cited by the parties to the dispute.

3. In establishing a panel, the DSB may authorize its Chairman to draw up the terms of reference of the panel in consultation with the parties to the dispute, subject to the provisions of paragraph 1. The terms of reference thus drawn up shall be circulated to all Members. If other than standard terms of reference are agreed upon, any Member may raise any point relating thereto in the DSB.

(4) *United Nations Convention on the Law of the Sea*[①]
Article 293　Applicable law

1. A court or tribunal having jurisdiction under this section shall apply this Convention and other rules of international law not incompatible with this Convention.

2. Paragraph Ⅰ does not prejudice the power of the court or tribunal having jurisdiction under this section to decide a case *ex aequo et bono*, if the parties so agree.

2.3 Assignment and Questions

(1) Retreat one theoretical paper on the sources of international law and brief the key points.

(2) Retreat information about ICJ, ICC, DSB and International Tribunal for the Law of the Sea and find at least one case each decided by them.

(3) How many sources of international law mentioned and what are they?

(4) Brief your understanding of the difference between sources of municipal law and sources of international law in a 5-10 minutes speech in English.

3. Terminologies and Discussions

3.1 Concept of Sources of International Law

Oppenheim points out that the sources of law is used with an unavoidable degree of flexibility and overlapped with the terms such as "cause", "basis" and "evidence". The concept of a "source" is important since it enables rules

---

[①] See UN, United Nations Convention on the Law of the Sea, https://www.un.org/depts/los/convention_agreements/texts/unclos/part15.htm, last visited on Jan. 8, 2022.

of law to be identified and distinguished from other rules.[①] It is about the process by which it first becomes identifiable as a rule of conduct with legal force and from which it derives its legal validity. The sources of law, also, are distinct from the basis of law. They concern the particular rules which constitute the system and the processes by which the rules become identifiable as rules of law. When an international scholar uses the term "sources of international law", what he intends to express is a survey of the process whereby rules of international law emerge. Scholars always debate on two related concepts, formal sources and material sources. The former is the source from which the legal rules derive their validity, while the latter denotes the provenance of the substantive content of that rule. A more specific explanation on the two confusing terms provides that "formal sources are those methods for the creation of rules of general application which are legally binding on their addressees, the material sources provide evidence of the existence of rules which, when established, are binding and of general application."[②] The distinction between formal sources and material sources is difficult to maintain, since they show the variety of material sources. These are the all-important evidence of a normative consensus among States and other relevant actors concerning particular rules or practices. Decisions of the ICJ, resolutions of the UN General Assembly (GA), and law-making multilateral treaties are evidence of the attitude of these actors toward particular rules and of the presence or absence of consensus.[③] This may be the reason why scholars in China generally support the idea that the sources of international law indicated those specific forms of expression of the rules of international law.

[①] See Robert Jennings and Arthur Watts (eds.), *Oppenheim's International Law*, 9th Ed., Longman, 1996, pp. 23-24.

[②] James Crawford (ed.), *Brownlie's Principles of Public International Law*, 8th Ed., Oxford University Press, 2012, p. 20.

[③] Ibid., p. 21.

However, ascertainment of the international law on any given point is more complex than in the domestic legal order. There is a definite method of discovering what the law is. In the common law system, lawyers and other practitioners could see whether the matter at issue is covered by an act of parliament or congress, or examine the case decided by the court to find a precedent to follow. In the civil law system, the process is more simplified to check the statutes codified by the legislative authority. These sources of law in domestic legal order also demonstrate how the law is created, namely, by parliamentary legislation or judicial case law. It reflects the hierarchical character of a national legal order with its gradations of authority imparting to the law a large measure of stability and predictability.[1] In the situation of international law, there exists no centralized body to create laws internationally binding upon everyone, nor a proper system of courts with comprehensive and compulsory jurisdiction to interpret and extend the law. The anarchic nature of world affairs and the clash of competing sovereignties reinforce the difficulty of finding the proper rule of law and ascertain whether a particular proposition amounts to a binding legal rule. The difficulty and uncertainties persisting in the construction and understanding of the sources of international law are weakening by Article 38 of the Statute of the ICJ, which has been treated as authoritative. Note that this formalization is only partial. The system remains open-ended. They reflect the previous practice of arbitral tribunals. Some emerging problems are beyond this Article, though Article 38 is often put forward as a complete statement of the sources of international law, e. g., the hierarchy between the sources specified in the Article, the soft law, decisions made by the UN, and the most controversial "source" of international law, the *Jus Cogens* or peremptory rules.

---

[1] See Malcolm N. Shaw, *International Law*, Cambridge University Press, 2017, pp. 339-340.

3.2 Treaties or Conventions

Treaties and conventions are the paramount importance sources of law in the contemporary world, for they are the most evident ways in which rules binding on two or more States may come into existence, and thus an evident formal source of law. The obligatory nature of treaties is founded upon the customary international law principle that agreements are binding (*pacta sunt servanda*). Treaties may be divided into law-making treaties, which have universal or general relevance, and treaty contracts, which apply only as between two or a small number of States. [1] This distinction reflect the general or local applicability of a particular treaty and the range of obligations imposed.

Treaties are written agreements binding States legally to act in a particular way or to establish specific relations between or among themselves. ILC defined Treaty as follow: "Any international agreement in written form, whether embodied in a single instrument or in two or more related instruments and whatever its particular designation (treaty, convention, protocol, covenant, charter, statute, act, declaration, concordat, exchange of notes, agreed minute, memorandum of agreement, modus vivendi or any other appellation), concluded between two or more States or other subjects of international law and governed by international law."

3.3 Custom

Article 38 of Statute of the ICJ defines custom as "a general practice accepted as law". It seems that all the custom could be seen as a form of tacit agreement: States behave towards each other in given circumstances in specific ways, which are found acceptable, and thus tacitly assented to, first as a guide to future conduct and then, little by little, as legally determining

---

[1] See Malcolm N. Shaw, *International Law*, Cambridge University Press, 2017, p. 365.

future conduct.① The existence of a custom is the conclusion drawn by someone (a legal adviser, a court, a government, a commentator) as to two related questions: (a) is there a general practice; (b) is it accepted as international law?②

Unlike the treaty as a source of international law, identifying a custom is more difficult. How can one tell when a particular line of action adopted by a State reflects a legal rule or is merely prompted by, for example, courtesy. Indeed, how can one discover what precisely a State is doing, since there is no living "State" but rather thousands of officials in scores of departments exercising governmental functions. Because of its dynamic evolution with the transforming State practice, writers have disagreements with the value of a customary system in international law. However, the custom remains important. While States in dispute enter no agreement between them, they can claim that a custom exit to apply without showing that the other party has expressly accepted it or participated in the practice from which the rule derives. It indicates that an essential difference between customary law and law that is derived from the treaty. In principle, customary law is applicable to all States without exception, while treaty law is applicable as such only to the parties of particular treaty.

Customary law's universal applicability has two exceptions. First, it is in principle possible for a State which does not accept a rule that is in the process of becoming standard international practice to make clear its opposition to it, in which case it will be exempted from the rule when it does become the rule of law, having the status of what is generally called a persistent objector. Second, alongside general customary law, there exist rules of special or local customary law, which are applicable only within a defined group of States.

---

① See Hugh Thirlway, *The Sources of International Law*, 2nd Ed., Oxford University Press, 2019, pp. 60-61.
② See James Crawford (ed.), *Brownlie's Principles of Public International Law*, 8th Ed., Oxford University Press, 2012, p 23.

And, when a claim is based upon an asserted custom of this kind, it is necessary to show that the respondent State had accepted the custom as one binding upon it by appropriate acts of practice indicating their intention to take it as law.

There is persisting debate on how to identify a custom from dynamic State practices. ILC made an "Identification of Customary International Law" report to provide a helpful directive.[①] Its conclusions could be seen as a detailed interpretation of the two constituent elements of a custom: general practice (*or usus*) and *opinio juris* (or *opinio juris sive necessitates*). Conclusion 2 of this draft provides that, "to determine the existence and content of a rule of customary international law, it is necessary to ascertain whether there is a general practice among the States concerned that is accepted as law." The commentary for this Conclusion read as follow: "A general practice and acceptance of that practice as law (*opinio juris*) are the two constituent elements of customary international law: together they are the essential conditions for the existence of a rule of customary international law. The identification of such a rule thus involves a careful examination of available evidence to establish their presence in any given case. This has been confirmed, *inter alia*, in the case law of the ICJ, which refers to 'two conditions (that) must be fulfilled' and has repeatedly laid down that 'the existence of a rule of customary international law requires that there be a settled practice together with *opinio juris*'. To establish that a claim concerning the existence or the content of a rule of customary international law is well-founded thus entails a search for a practice that has gained such acceptance among States that it may be considered to be the expression of a legal right or obligation (namely, that it is required, permitted or prohibited

---

[①] See ILC, Draft Conclusions on Identification of Customary International Law, with Commentaries, 2018, https://legal.un.org/ilc/texts/instruments/english/commentaries/1_13_2018.pdf, last visited on Nov. 17, 2021.

as a matter of law). The test must always be: is there a general practice that is accepted as law?"

Clearly, this draft clarifies some key problems that have confused international law new learners. E. g. , what practice could evolve into customary law? Is there two or one constituent element for customary law? On what conditions and to what extent could those practices be treated as general? What role can the international organization play in the forming of customary law? Are there objective indicators to help us comprehend the subjective standard of *opinio juris*? What is the co-relation between treaty and custom? Is there an exception to the university of customary law and to what extent that this exception could not be applied?

3.4 General Principles

Article 38(1)(c) of the Statute of the ICJ refers to "the general principles of law recognized by civilized nations". The general principle remains as a formal source of international law besides treaty and custom mainly for two reasons. First, it enables rules of law that can fill gaps or weaknesses in the law which might otherwise be left by the operation of custom or treaty. Second, it provides a background of legal principles in the light of which custom and treaties have to be applied and as such it may act to modify their application. When considering the drafting history of the statute, the function of general principles is to avoid that the Court make decisions solely on subjective concepts associated with principles of justice. The wording used, inevitably, grant the Court a certain power to develop and refine such principles. Does this bring a persisting debating on which principle could amount to the "general principle" referred to in the statute? This question turns complicated since the customary law also contains established principles or norms derived by extrapolation or analysis from the general principles.

There is broad agreement but no unanimity among scholars as to the nature of the principles that may be invoked under Article 38(1)(c). Two possible interpretations were provided by the members of the Advisory Committee of Jurists who prepared the ICJ Statute. One interpretation provides that, the principles in question can be derived from a comparison of the various systems of municipal law and the extraction of such principles as appear to be shared by all, or a majority, of them. This interpretation gives force to the reference in Article 38 to the principles being those "recognized by civilized nations". The other interpretation of the intention underlying Article 38(1)(c) is that, while *the Committee of Jurists* may have had primarily in view the legal principles shared by municipal legal orders, the recognized principles also include general principles that apply directly to international legal relations, and general principles applicable to legal relations generally. E. g., the *pacta sunt servanda*, the principle that the special prevails over the general and that the later prevails over the earlier.[①] Examples of this type of general principle of international law also include the principles of consent, reciprocity, equality of States, the finality of awards and settlements, the legal validity of agreements, good faith, domestic jurisdiction, and the freedom of the seas. Certain fundamental principles of international law enjoy heightened normativity as peremptory norms.

  Tribunals, including arbitral tribunals and ICJ, based their judgment sparingly solely on the principles. However, they have shown that the principle is important to the legal reasoning in their practice. In *Factory at Chorzów Case* the PCIJ observed that: "one Party cannot avail himself of the fact that the other has not fulfilled some obligation or has not had recourse to some means of redress, if the former Party has, by some illegal act, prevented the latter from fulfilling the obligation in question, or from having recourse to the tribunal which would have been open, to him."[②] The PCIJ

---

  ① See Hugh Thirlway, *The Sources of International Law*, 2nd Ed., Oxford University Press, 2019, pp. 108-109.
  ② *Factory at Chorzów (Germ. v. Pol.)*, PCIJ, Ser. A, No. 9 (1927), p. 31.

went on to observe that: "it is a principle of international law, and even a general conception of law, that any breach of an engagement involves an obligation to make reparation."① This general notion of responsibility underlies the law about State responsibility. The principle of estoppel or acquiescence also has been relied upon by the court. The most frequent and successful use of domestic law analogies has been in the field of evidence, procedure, and jurisdiction. Thus, there have been references to the rule that no one can be a judge in his own suit, to *res iudicata*, to various principles governing the judicial process, to the burden and the standard of proof.② In *Corfu Channel Case* the ICJ considered circumstantial evidence and remarked that "this indirect evidence is admitted in all systems of law, and its use is recognized by international decisions"③.

3.5 Judicial Decisions and Other Subsidiary Sources

Judicial decisions and teachings are not formal sources of international law but material sources having a particular degree of authority.④ Paragraph 1 (d) of Article 38 of the ICJ Statute makes a clear distinction between them. The reason for this is quite apparent. If a rule of international law is stated in a judicial decision or in a textbook, it will be stated as a rule deriving either from the treaty, custom, or the general principles of law. The decision, or the textbook, will not assert that the rule stated is law because the judge or the author has said it; it will be so stated because the judge or the author considers that it derives from one of the three principal sources indicated in paragraphs (a) to (c) of Article 38. After the enactment of the statute, some other materials have the like degree of authority as the judicial decisions, such

---

① *Factory at Chorzów* (Germ. v. Pol.), Merits, PCIJ, Ser. A, No. 17 (1928), p. 29.
② See James Crawford (ed.), *Brownlie's Principles of Public International Law*, 8th Ed., Oxford University Press, 2012, p. 36.
③ *Corfu Channel Case*, ICJ Reports 1949, pp. 4, 18.
④ See Hugh Thirlway, *The Sources of International Law*, 2nd Ed., Oxford University Press, 2019, p. 131.

as the conclusion of international conferences, resolution of the UN General Assembly and codification and the work of the ILC.

(1) Judicial Decisions

Judicial decisions are derivative. As Robert Jennings has observed, "even where a court creates law in the sense of developing, adapting, modifying, filling gaps, interpreting, or even branching out in a new direction, the decision must be seen to emanate reasonably and logically from existing and previously ascertainable law. A court has no purely legislative competence."① This intention is stated clearly in Article 59 of Statute of the ICJ. The Committee of Jurists clearly indicates that the Article 59 was not intended merely to express the principle of *res iudicata*, but rather to rule out a system of binding precedent.② The Court reaffirmed this position in *Polish Upper Silesia Case*, "the object of this Article (Article 59) is simply to prevent legal principles accepted by the Court in a particular case from being binding on other States or in other disputes."③

The PICJ and ICJ did not follow the doctrine of precedent. However, a coherent body of previous jurisprudence still has essential consequences in any given case. In practice, it strives to maintain judicial consistency. E. g., in *Exchange of Greek and Turkish Populations Case*, the Court referred to "the precedent afforded by" the *Wimbledon*, reflecting the principle that treaty obligations do not entail an abandonment of sovereignty.④ In *Reparation for Injuries Case*, the ICJ relied on a pronouncement in a previous advisory opinion for a statement of the principle of effectiveness in interpreting

---

① Robert Y. Jennings, The Role of the International Court of Justice, 68 *British Yearbook of International Law* 1(1997), p. 43.

② See James Crawford (ed.), *Brownlie's Principles of Public International Law*, 8th Ed., Oxford University Press, 2012, p. 38.

③ *German Interests in Polish Upper Silesin (Germ. v. Pol.)*, PCIJ, Ser. A, No. 7 (1926), p. 19.

④ See *Exchange of Greek and Turkish Populations*, PCIJ, Ser. B, No. 10 (1925), p. 21.

treaties.①

In short, judicial decisions are important evidence of the law. Besides the international court, such as PICJ, ICJ, ICC, and the WTO's Appellate Body, awards of international arbitral tribunals also have similar authority. There have been many international arbitral tribunals, such as the Permanent Court of Arbitration created by The Hague Conferences of 1899 and 1907 and the various mixed-claims tribunals, including Iran-US Claims Tribunal. The authority of their decisions depends on the status of the tribunals and their members and on the conditions under which it conducts its work. E. g., the judgment of the International Military Tribunal for the Trial of German Major War Criminals, the decisions of the Iran-United States Claims Tribunal, and the decisions of the International Criminal Tribunal for the Former Yugoslavia, among others, contain significant findings on issues of international law.

Besides, the decisions made by national courts also have value. Some decisions provide indirect evidence of the practice of the forum State on the question involved. Others may offer a careful exposition of the law on a particular point. Municipal judicial decisions have been an important source of material on the recognition of governments and States, State succession, sovereign immunity, diplomatic immunity, extradition, war crimes, belligerent occupation, the concept of a "State of war", and the law of prize.②

(2) Teachings of the Most Highly Qualified Publicists

Article 38 of Statute of the ICJ includes a subsidiary means for the determination of rules of law, e. g., "the teachings of the most highly qualified publicists of the various nations". In early history, some important

---

① See *Reparation for Injuries Suffered in the Service of the United Nations*, ICJ Reports 1949, pp. 174, 182-183.

② See James Crawford (ed.), *Brownlie's Principles of Public International Law*, 8th Ed., Oxford University Press, 2012, p. 41.

writers, Gentili, Grotius, Pufendorf, Bynkershoek and Vattel, played as the supreme authorities to determine the scope, form and content of international law. The increasing emphasis on State sovereignty makes the treaties and customs the dominant position in the exposition of international law, causing the decline of the importance of the writers. Some writers still have a formative impact upon the evolution of particular laws, e. g., Gidel on the law of the sea, Bin Cheng on the air law. These books' importance is primarily in arranging and putting into focus the structure and form of international law and elucidating the nature, history, and practice of the rules of law. [1]

In practice, the opinions of publicists are still widely used in arbitral tribunals and national courts. It is due to the generally unfamiliarity of the national courts towards State practice. Thus, they are ready to rely on secondary sources as a substitute. The international courts, for example, ICJ, ICC and the Appellate Body of WTO, seem to make little or no use of jurists' writings. This is because of the need to avoid an invidious selection of citations, reducing prejudice in the judgment.

(3) *Resolution of the UN General Assembly*

According to the UN Charter, GA resolutions are not binding on member States except certain UN organizational matters. However, the situation is different, while these resolutions are concerned with general norms of international law. The acceptance by all or most members constitutes evidence of the rules of international law which receive the widest consent. When resolutions are framed as general principles, they can provide a basis for the progressive development of the law and the speedy consolidation of customary rules. This kind of resolution is recognized as a "law-making"

---

[1] See Malcolm N. Shaw, *International Law*, Cambridge University Press, 2017, p. 384.

resolution.① Examples of these resolutions are listed in some popular textbooks, such as General Assembly's Affirmation of the Principles of International Law Recognized by the Charter of the Nürnberg Tribunal, the Declaration of Legal Principles Governing Activities of States in the Exploration and Use of Outer Space, the Rio Declaration on Environment and Development, and Resolution 1803 on Permanent Sovereignty over Natural Resources.

Besides, resolution may have effect as an authoritative interpretation and application of the principles of the UN Charter, e. g., the Friendly Relations Declaration of 1970, or restatement of established customary law. The practice of ICJ reinforced this view. For example, in *Nicaragua Case*, ICJ noted that, "the wording of certain General Assembly declarations adopted by States demonstrates their recognition of the principle of the prohibition of force as definitely a matter of customary international law"②. Another opinion often cited by academic writings is: "General Assembly resolutions, even if they are not binding, may sometimes have normative value. They can, in certain circumstances, provide evidence important for establishing the existence of a rule or the emergence of an *opinio juris*."③

(4) *Conclusion of International Conferences*

The final declaration or the other statement of conclusions of States might be a form of a bilateral or multilateral treaty, e. g., the three Joint Communiqués between China and the United States. Provided that it is an instrument recording decision not adopted unanimously, the result may still be evidence of the law on that subject. A convention embodied in a final act and expressed as a codification of existing principle is influential, even it

---

① See James Crawford (ed.), *Brownlie's Principles of Public International Law*, 8th Ed., Oxford University Press, 2012, p. 42.
② *Military and Paramilitary Activities in and against Nicaragua (Nicaragua v. United States of America)*. Merits, Judgment, ICJ Reports 1986, p. 14.
③ *Legality of the Threat or Use of Nuclear Weapons*, ICJ Reports 1996, p. 226.

receives ratifications less than the necessary number. E. g., Vienna Convention on the Law of Treaties (VCLT) at the time was open for signature.

(5) *Codification and the Work of the ILC*

The General Assembly established the ILC in 1947 to promote the progressive development of international law and its codification. Its codification and work, including its articles and commentaries, reports, and secretariat memoranda, are analogous to the writings of publicists.

4. Cases and Materials

Read the materials below and think about the following questions:

(1) Who shall prove that there is a customary law applied to a dispute?

(2) Are there any other material sources of international law? For example, what do you think about the function of the "soft law" and "unilateral State acts" forms the traditional sources of international law?

(3) How do the treaty and custom interplay with each other?

4.1 *North Sea Continental Shelf Case* [①]

(1) *Facts and Arguments made by Parties*

The North Sea has to some extent the general look of an enclosed sea

---

① *North Sea Continental Shelf Cases*, Judgment, ICJ Reports 1969, p. 3. Judges in this case provide an insight on two important sources of international law: treaty and custom. It is a landmark case for its articulation of important principles relating to the sources of international law and their interaction. The Court rejected the contention of Denmark and the Netherlands to the effect that the delimitations in question had to be carried out in accordance with the principle of equidistance as defined in Article 6 of the Convention on the Continental Shelf (1958), holding: (a) That the Federal Republic, which had not ratified the Convention, was not legally bound by the provisions of Article 6. (b) That the equidistance principle was not a necessary consequence of the general concept of continental shelf rights, and was not a rule of customary international law. (c) That the boundary lines in question were to be drawn by agreement between the Parties and in accordance with equitable principles, and it indicated certain factors to be taken into consideration for that purpose.

without actually being one. Round its shores are situated, on its eastern side and starting from the north, Norway, Denmark, the Federal Republic of Germany, the Netherlands, Belgium and France; while the whole western side is taken up by Great Britain, together with the island groups of the Orkneys and Shetlands.

Much the greater part of this continental shelf has already been the subject of delimitation by a series of agreements concluded between the United Kingdom (which, as stated, lies along the whole western side of it) and certain of the States on the eastern side, namely Norway, Denmark and the Netherlands. These three delimitations were carried out by the drawing of what are known as "median lines" which, for immediate present purposes, may be described as boundaries drawn between the continental shelf areas of "opposite" States, dividing the intervening spaces equally between them. Even if these median lines were drawn however, the question would arise whether the United Kingdom, Norway and the Netherlands could take advantage of them as against the parties to the existing delimitations, since these lines would, it seems, in each case lie beyond (i.e., respectively to the east, south and north of) the boundaries already effective under the existing agreements at present in force.

Under the agreements of December 1964 and June 1965, the partial boundaries represented by the map lines had been drawn mainly by application of the principle of equidistance, using that term as denoting the abstract concept of equidistance. A line so drawn, known as an "equidistance line", may be described as one which leaves to each of the parties concerned all those portions of the continental shelf that are nearer to a point on its own coast than they are to any point on the coast of the other party. An equidistance line may consist either of a "median" line between "opposite" States, or of a "lateral" line between "adjacent" States.

The further negotiations between the Parties for the prolongation of the partial boundaries broke down mainly because Denmark and the Netherlands

Chapter II Sources of International Law   65

respectively wished this prolongation also to be effected on the basis of the equidistance principle; whereas the Federal Republic of Germany considered that such an outcome would be inequitable because it would unduly curtail what the Republic believed should be its proper share of continental shelf area, on the basis of proportionality to the length of its North Sea coastline.

After the negotiations, separately held between the Federal Republic and the other two Parties respectively, had in each case, failed to result in any agreement about the delimitation of the boundary extending beyond the partial one already agreed…The Court has to determine what principles and rules of international law are applicable to the delimitation of the areas of continental shelf involved.

Submission from the Federal Republic of Germany

The delimitation of the continental shelf between the Parties in the North Sea is governed by the principle that each coastal State is entitled to a just and equitable share.

i. The delimitation of the continental shelf between the Parties in the North Sea is governed by the principle that each coastal State is entitled to a just and equitable share.

ii. (**a**) The method of determining boundaries of the continental shelf in such a way that every point of the boundary is equidistant from the nearest points of the baselines from which the breadth of the territorial sea of each State is measured (equidistance method) is not a rule of customary international law.

(**b**) The rule contained in the second sentence of paragraph 2 of Article 6 of the Continental Shelf Convention, prescribing that in the absence of agreement, and unless another boundary is justified by special circumstances, the boundary shall be determined by application of the principle of equidistance, has not become customary international law.

(**c**) Even if the rule under (b) would be applicable between the Parties, special circumstances within the meaning of that rule would exclude the application of the equidistance method in the present case.

iii. (a) The equidistance method cannot be used for the delimitation of the continental shelf unless it is established by agreement, arbitration, or otherwise, that it will achieve a just and equitable apportionment of the continental shelf among the States concerned.

(b) As to the delimitation of the continental shelf between the Parties in the North Sea, the Kingdom of Denmark and the Kingdom of the Netherlands cannot rely on the application of the equidistance method, since it would not lead to an equitable apportionment.

iv. Consequently, the delimitation of the continental shelf, on which the Parties must agree pursuant to paragraph 2 of Article I of the Special Agreement, is determined by the principle of the just and equitable share, based on criteria relevant to the particular geographical situation in the North Sea.

Memorial of Denmark and Netherland Jointly

According to Denmark and the Netherlands, the relevant rules and principles of international law declare:

a) that the boundary line as between Denmark and the Federal Republic (or as between the Netherlands and the Federal Republic, as the case may be) is to be determined by application of the principle of equidistance from the nearest points of the baselines from which the breadth of the territorial sea of each State is measured, unless another boundary is justified by special circumstances, and

b) that, as between Denmark and the Federal Republic (or as between the Netherlands and the Federal Republic, as the case may be), there are no special circumstances which would justify another boundary line.

(2) *Court Opinions*

Non-Applicability of Article 6 of the 1958 Continental Shelf Convention

21. The Court will now turn to the contentions advanced on behalf of Denmark and the Netherlands. Their general character, the most convenient

Chapter II Sources of International Law 67

way of dealing with them will be on the basis of the following question—namely, does the equidistance-special circumstances principle constitute a mandatory rule, either on a conventional or on a customary international law basis, in such a way as to govern any delimitation of the North Sea continental shelf areas between the Federal Republic and the Kingdoms of Denmark and the Netherlands respectively? Another and shorter way of formulating the question would be to ask whether, in any delimitation of these areas, the Federal Republic is under a legal obligation to accept the application of the equidistance-special circumstances principle.

22. Particular attention is directed to the use, in the foregoing formulations, of the terms "mandatory" and "obligation". It has never been doubted that the equidistance method of delimitation is a very convenient one, the use of which is indicated in a considerable number of cases. It constitutes a method capable of being employed in almost all circumstances, however singular the results might sometimes be, and has the virtue that if necessary,—if for instance, the Parties are unable to enter into negotiations,—any cartographer can *de facto* trace such a boundary on the appropriate maps and charts, and those traced by competent cartographers will for all practical purposes agree.

23. In short, it would probably be true to say that no other method of delimitation has the same combination of practical convenience and certainty of application. Yet these factors do not suffice of themselves to convert what is a method into a rule of law, making the acceptance of the results of using that method obligatory in all cases in which the parties do not agree otherwise, or in which "special circumstances" cannot be shown to exist. Juridically, if there is such a rule, it must draw its legal force from other factors than the existence of these advantages, important though they may be. …

24. The plea that, however this may be, the results can never be inequitable, because the equidistance principle is by definition an equitable

principle of delimitation, involves postulate that clearly begs the whole question at issue.

25. The Court now turns to the legal position regarding the equidistance method. The first question to be considered is whether the Convention on the Continental Shelf (1958) is binding for all the Parties in this case—that is to say, whether the use of this method is rendered obligatory for the present delimitations by virtue of the delimitations provision (Article 6) of that instrument, according to the conditions laid down in it. Clearly, if this is so, then the provisions of the Convention will prevail in the relations between the Parties, and would take precedence of any rules having a more general character, or derived from another source. That is to say constituted the Law of Parties—and is sole remaining task would be to interpret those provisions, in so far as their meaning was disputed or appeared to be uncertain, and to apply them to the particular circumstances involved.

26. The relevant provisions of Article 6 of the Geneva Convention, paragraph 2 read as follows: ⋯ The Convention received 46 signatures and, up-to-date, there have been 39 ratifications or accessions. It came into force on 10 June 1964, having received the 22 ratifications or accessions required for that purpose (Article 11), and was therefore in force at the time when the various delimitations of continental shelf boundaries described earlier (paragraphs 1 and 5) took place between the Parties. But, under the formal provisions of the Convention, it is in force for any individual State only in so far as, having signed it within the time-limit provided for that purpose, that Stale has also subsequently ratified it; or, not having signed within that time-limit, has subsequently acceded to the Convention. Denmark and the Netherlands have both signed and ratified the Convention, and are parties to it, the former since 10 June 1964, the latter since 20 March 1966. The Federal Republic was one of the signatories of the Convention, but has never ratified it, and is consequently not a party.

27. It is admitted on behalf of Denmark and the Netherlands that in these

circumstances the Convention cannot, as such, be binding on the Federal Republic. But it is contended that the Convention, or the regime of the Convention, and in particular of Article 6, has become binding on the Federal Republic in another way, —namely because, by conduct, by public statements and proclamations, and in other ways, the Republic has unilaterally assumed the obligations of the Convention; or has manifested its acceptance of the conventional regime; or has recognized it as being generally applicable to the delimitation of continental shelf areas. ···

28. As regards these contentions, It is clear that only a very definite, very consistent course of conduct on the part of a State in the situation of the Federal Republic could justify the Court in upholding them; and, if this had existed—that is to say if there had been a real intention to manifest acceptance or recognition of the applicability of the conventional regime—then it must be asked why it was that the Federal Republic did not take the obvious step of giving expression to this readiness by simply ratifying the Convention. ··· It is not lightly to be presumed that a State which has not carried out these formalities, though at all times fully able and entitled to do so, has nevertheless somehow become bound in another way. Indeed if it were a question not of obligation but of rights, —if, that is to say, a State which, though entitled to do so, had not ratified or acceded, attempted to claim rights under the convention, on the basis of a declared willingness to be bound by it, or of conduct evincing acceptance of the conventional regime, it would simply be told that, not having become a party to the convention it could not claim any rights under it until the professed willingness and acceptance had been manifested in the prescribed form.

29. A further point, not in itself conclusive, but to be noted, is that if the Federal Republic had ratified the Geneva Convention, it could have entered—and could, if it ratified now, enter—a reservation to Article 6, by reason of the faculty to do so conferred by Article 12 of the Convention. ···

30. Having regard to these considerations of principle, it appears to the

Court that only the existence of a situation of estoppel could suffice to lend substance to this contention. That is to say, if the Federal Republic were now precluded from denying the applicability of the conventional regime, by reason of past conduct, declarations, etc., which not only clearly and consistently evinced acceptance of that regime, but also had caused Denmark or the Netherlands, in reliance on such conduct, detrimentally to change position or suffer some prejudice. Of this there is no evidence whatever in the present case.

The Equidistance Principle not Inherent in the Basic Doctrine of the Continental Shelf

37. It is maintained by Denmark and the Netherlands that the Federal Republic, whatever its position may be in relation to the Geneva Convention, considered as such, is in any event bound to accept delimitation on an equidistance-special circumstances basis, because the use of this method is not in the nature of a merely conventional obligation, but is, or must now be regarded as involving, a rule that is part of the *corpus* of general international law; —and, like other rules of general or customary international law, is binding on the Federal Republic automatically and independently of any specific assent, direct or indirect, given by the latter. … In its fundamentalist aspect, the view put forward derives from what might be called the natural law of the continental shelf, in the sense that the equidistance principle is seen as a necessary expression in the field of delimitation of the accepted doctrine of the exclusive appurtenance of the continental shelf to the nearby coastal State, and therefore as having an *a priori* character of so to speak juristic inevitability.

39. The *a priori* argument starts from the position described in para. 19, according to which the right of the coastal State to its continental shelf areas is based on its sovereignty over the land domain, of which the shelf area is the natural prolongation into and under the sea. From this notion, the Court accepts, that the coastal State's rights exist *ipso facto* and *ab initio* without

there being any question of having to make good a claim to the areas concerned, or of any apportionment of the continental shelf between different States. ⋯ Denmark and the Netherlands, for their part, claim that the test of appurtenance must be "proximity", or more accurately "closer proximity": all those parts of the shelf being considered as appurtenant lo a particular coastal State which are (but only if they are) closer to it than they are to any point on the coast of another State. Hence delimitation must be effected by a method which will leave to each one of the States concerned all those areas that are nearest to its own coast. Only a line drawn on equidistance principles will do this. Therefore, it is contended, only such a line can be valid because only such a line can be thus consistent with basic continental shelf doctrine.

40. This view clearly has much force; for there can be no doubt that as a matter of normal topography, the greater part of a State's continental shelf areas will in fact, and without the necessity for any delimitation at all, be nearer to its coasts than to any other. But *post hoc* is not *propter hoc*, and this situation may only serve to obscure the real issue, which is whether it follows that every part of the area concerned must be placed in this way. The Court does not consider that it does follow, either from the notion of proximity itself, or from the more fundamental concept of the continental shelf as being the natural prolongation of the land domain.

41. As regards the notion of proximity, the idea of absolute proximity is certainly not implied by the rather vague and general terminology employed in the literature of the subject, and in most State proclamations and international conventions and other instruments. ⋯ This would be even truer of localities where, physically, the continental shelf begins to merge with the ocean depths. Equally, a point inshore situated near the meeting place of the coasts of two States can often properly be said to be adjacent to both coasts, even though it may be fractionally closer to the one than the other. Local geographical configuration may sometimes cause it to have a closer physical connection with the coast to which it is not in fact closest.

42. Even if proximity may afford one of the tests to be applied and an important one in the right conditions, it may not necessarily be the only, nor in all circumstances, the most appropriate one. Hence it would seem that the notion of adjacency, so constantly employed in continental shelf doctrine from the start, only implies proximity in a general sense, and does not imply any fundamental or inherent rule the ultimate effect of which would be to prohibit any State from exercising continental shelf rights in respect of areas closer to the coast of another State.

43. More fundamental than the notion of proximity appears to be the principle—constantly relied upon by all the Parties—of the natural prolongation or continuation of the land territory or domain, or land sovereignty of the coastal State, into and under the high seas, via the bed of its territorial sea which is under the full sovereignty of that State. … It is this idea of extension which is, in the Court's opinion, determinant. Submarine areas do not really appertain to the coastal State because—or not only because—they are near it. But this would not suffice to confer title. …

44. In the present case… As regards equidistance, it clearly cannot be identified with the notion of natural prolongation or extension, since the use of the equidistance method would frequently cause areas which are the natural prolongation or extension of the territory of one State to be attributed to another. …

46. The conclusion drawn by the Court from the foregoing analysis is that the notion of equidistance as being logically necessary, in the sense of being an inescapable *a priori* accompaniment of basic continental shelf doctrine, is incorrect. 1t is said not to be possible to maintain that there is a rule of law ascribing certain areas to a State as a matter of inherent and original right, without also admitting the existence of some rule by which those areas can be obligatorily delimited. The Court cannot accept the logic of this view. The problem arises only where there is a dispute and only in respect of the marginal areas involved. …

47. A review of the genesis and development of the equidistance method of delimitation can only serve to confirm the foregoing conclusion. Such a review may appropriately start with the instrument, generally known as the "Truman Proclamation". ··· It stated that boundaries "shall be determined by the United States and the State concerned in accordance with equitable principles". These two concepts, of delimitation by mutual agreement and delimitation in accordance with equitable principles, have underlain all the subsequent history of the subject. ···

49. In the records of the International Law Commission, which had the matter under consideration from 1950 to 1956, there is no indication at all that any of its members supposed that it was incumbent on the Commission to adopt a rule of equidistance because this gave expression to, and translated into linear terms, a principle of proximity inherent in the basic concept of the continental shelf, causing every part of the shelf to appertain to the nearest coastal State and to no other, and because such a rule must therefore be mandatory as a matter of customary international law. Such an idea does not seem ever to have been propounded. Had it been, and had it had the self-evident character contended for by Denmark and the Netherlands, the Commission would have had no alternative but to adopt it, and its long continued hesitations over this matter would be incomprehensible.

53. When the Commission was finalizing the whole complex of drafts comprised under the topic of the Law of the Sea, various doubts about the equidistance principle were still being voiced in the Commission, on such grounds for instance as that its strict application would be open, in certain cases, to the objection that the geographical configuration of the coast would render a boundary drawn on this basis inequitable.

54. A further point of some significance is that neither in the Committee of Experts, nor in the Commission itself, nor subsequently at the Geneva Conference, does there appear to have been any discussion of delimitation in the context, not merely of two adjacent States, but of three or more States on

the same coast, or in the same vicinity, —from which it can reasonably be inferred that the possible resulting situations, some of which have been described in paragraph 8 above, were never really envisaged or taken into account. …

55. In the light of this history, and of the record generally, it is clear that at no time was the notion of equidistance as an inherent necessity of continental shelf doctrine entertained. Quite a different outlook was indeed manifested from the start in current legal thinking. It was, and it really remained to the end, governed by two beliefs. First, no one single method of delimitation was likely to prove satisfactory in all circumstances, and that delimitation should, therefore, be carried out by agreement (or by reference to arbitration). Second, it should be effected on equitable principles. It was in pursuance of the first of these beliefs that in the draft that emerged as Article 6 of the Geneva Convention, the Commission gave priority to delimitation by agreement, and in pursuance of the second that it introduced the exception in favor of "special circumstances". Yet the record shows that, even with these mitigations, doubts persisted, particularly as to whether the equidistance principle would in all cases prove equitable.

The Equidistance Principle not a Rule of Customary International Law

60. The condusions so far reached leave open, and still to be considered, the question whether the equidistance principle has come to be regarded as a rule of customary international law, so that it would be obligatory for the Federal Republic. For this purpose it is necessary to examine the status of the principle as it stood when the Convention was drawn up, as it resulted from the effect of the Convention, and in the light of State practice subsequent to the Convention.

61. Denmark and the Netherlands' contention was, rather, that although prior to the Conference, continental shelf law was only in the formative stage, and State practice lacked uniformity, yet "the process of the definition and consolidation of the emerging customary law took place through the work of

the International Law Commission, the reaction of governments to that work and the proceedings of the Geneva Conference"; and this emerging customary law became "crystallized in the adoption of the Continental Shelf Convention by the Conference".

62. The Court cannot accept it as regards the delimitation provision (Article 6), the relevant parts of which were adopted almost unchanged from the draft of the International Law Commission that formed the basis of discussion at the Conference. The status of the rule in the Convention therefore depends mainly on the processes that led the Commission to propose it. These processes have already been reviewed in connection with the Danish-Netherlands contention of an *a priori* necessity for equidistance, and the Court considers this review sufficient for present purposes. It now figures, somewhat on an experimental basis, at most *de lege ferenda*, and not at all *de lege lata* or as an emerging rule of customary international law. This is clearly not the sort of foundation on which Article 6 of the Convention could be said to have reflected or crystallized such a rule.

63. The foregoing conclusion receives significant confirmation from the fact that Article 6 is one of those reservations may be made by any State on signing, ratifying or acceding. Speaking generally, it is a characteristic of purely conventional rules and obligations that some faculty of making unilateral reservations may, within certain limits, be admitted. This cannot be so in the case of general or customary law rules and obligations which, by their very nature, must have equal force for all members of the international community, and cannot therefore be the subject of any right of unilateral exclusion exercisable at will. ···

70. The Court must now proceed to the last stage in the argument put forward on behalf of Denmark and the Netherlands. This is to the effect that even if there was at the date of the Geneva Convention no rule of customary international law in favor of the equidistance principle, and no such rule was crystallized in Article 6 of the Convention, nevertheless such a rule has come

into being a rule of customary international law binding on all States, partly because of its own impact, partly on the basis of subsequent State practice. And this rule, being now, including therefore the Federal Republic, should be declared applicable to the delimitation of the boundaries between the Parties' respective continental shelf areas in the North Sea.

71. This contention (foregoing) clearly involves treating that Article as a norm-creating provision which has constituted the foundation of the general corpus of international law, and is now accepted as such by the *opinio juris*, so as to have become binding even for countries which have never, and do not, become parties to the Convention. There is no doubt that this process is a perfectly possible one and does from time to time occur: it constitutes indeed one of the recognized methods by which new rules of customary international law may be formed.

72. It would in the first place be necessary that the provision concerned should, at all events potentially, be of a fundamentally norm-creating character such as forming the basis of a general rule of law. Yet in the particular form in which it is embodied in Article 6 of the Geneva Convention, and having regard to the relationship of that Article to other provisions of the Convention, this must be open to some doubt. First, Article 6 is so framed as to put second the obligation to make use of the equidistance method, causing it to come after a primary obligation to effect delimitation by agreement. Such a primary obligation constitutes an unusual preface to what is claimed to be a potential general rule of law. Second, the part played by the notion of special circumstances relative to the principle of equidistance as embodied in Article 6, and the very considerable, still unresolved controversies as to the exact meaning and scope of this notion, must raise further doubts as to the potentially norm-creating character of the rule. Finally, the faculty of making reservations to Article 6 does add considerably to the difficulty of regarding this result as having been brought about on the basis of the Convention.

73. With respect to the other elements usually regarded as necessary

before a conventional rule can be considered to have become a general rule of international law, it might be that, even without the passage of any considerable period of time, a very widespread and representative participation in the convention might suffice of itself, provided it included that of States whose interests were specially affected. However, the Court notes that, the number of ratifications and accessions so far secured is, though respectable, hardly sufficient.

74. As regards the time element, the Court notes that it is over ten years since the Convention was signed, but that it is even now less than five since it came into force in June 1964, and that when the present proceedings were brought it was less than three years. Although the passage of only a short period of time is not necessarily, or of itself, a bar to the formation of a new rule of customary international law on the basis of what was originally a purely conventional rule, an indispensable requirement would be that State practice, including that of States whose interests are specially affected should have been both extensive and virtually uniform in the sense of the provision invoked, and should moreover have occurred in such a way as to show a general recognition that a rule of law or legal obligation is involved.

75. The Court must now consider whether State practice in the matter of continental shelf delimitation has, subsequent to the Geneva Convention, been of such a kind as to satisfy this requirement (foregoing discussed). There are some fifteen cases have been cited in the course of the present proceedings, occurring mostly since the signature of the 1958 Geneva Convention, in which continental shelf boundaries have been delimited according to the equidistance principle.

77. The essential point in this connection is (that), even if those instances of action by non-parties to the Convention were much more numerous than they in fact are, they would not, even in the aggregate, suffice in themselves to constitute the *opinio juris*, for in order to achieve this result, two conditions must be fulfilled. Not only must the acts concerned

amount to a settled practice, but they must also be such, or be carried out in such a way, as to be evidence of a belief that this practice is rendered obligatory by the existence of a rule of law requiring it. The States concerned must therefore feel that they are conforming to what amounts to a legal obligation. The frequency, or even habitual character of the acts is not in itself enough. There are many international acts, e. g., in the field of ceremonial and protocol, which are performed almost invariably, but which are motivated only by considerations of courtesy, convenience or tradition, and not by any sense of legal duty.

78. In this respect the Court follows the view adopted by the Permanent Court of International Justice in the *Lotus Case*, as stated in the following passage, the principle of which is, by analogy, applicable almost word for word, *mutatis mutandis*, to the present case (P. C. I. J, Series A, No. 10, 1927, at p. 28):

"Even if the rarity of the judicial decisions to be found... were sufficient to prove... the circumstance alleged..., it would merely show that States had often, in practice, abstained from instituting criminal proceedings, and not that they recognized themselves as being obliged to do so; for only if such abstention were based on their being conscious of having a duty to abstain would it be possible to speak of an international custom. The alleged fact does not allow one to infer that States have been conscious of having such a duty; on the other hand, ... there are other circumstances calculated to show that the contrary is true."

79. Finally, it appears that in almost all of the cases cited, the delimitations concerned were median-line delimitations between opposite States, not lateral delimitations between adjacent States. …… The Court simply considers that they are inconclusive, and insufficient to bear the weight sought to be put upon them as evidence of such a settled practice, manifested in such circumstances, as would justify the inference that

delimitation according to the principle of equidistance amounts to a mandatory rule of customary international law.

......

4.2 Asylum Case [1]

(1) Brief of the Fact

On October 3rd, 1948, a military rebellion broke out in Peru. It was suppressed the same day. On the following day, a decree was published charging against a political party, the American People's Revolutionary Party. The head of the Party, Victor Ratil Maya de la Torre ("Torre"), was denounced as being responsible. He was prosecuted on a charge of military rebellion. On January 3rd, 1949, he was granted asylum in the Colombian Embassy in Lima. On January 4th, 1949, the Colombian Ambassador in Lima informed the Peruvian Government of the asylum granted to Torre; at the same time he asked that a safe-conduct be issued to enable the refugee to leave the country. On January 14th, he further stated that the refugee had been qualified as a political refugee. The Peruvian Government disputed this qualification and refused to grant a safe-conduct. On August 31th, 1949, the two Governments agreed to submit the case to the International Court of Justice.

(2) Judgment of the Court

The Application concludes by requesting the Court ··· pass judgment on and answer the following questions:

a) Within the limits of the obligations resulting in particular from the

---

[1] *Colombian-Peruvian Asylum Case*, Judgment of November 20th, 1950, ICJ Reports 1950, p. 266. The question in dispute was whether Colombia, as the State granting the asylum, was entitled unilaterally to "qualify" the offence committed by the refugee in a manner binding on the territorial State—that is, to decide whether it was a political offence or a common crime. Furthermore, the Court was asked to decide whether the territorial State was bound to afford the necessary guarantees to enable the refugee to leave the country in safety. To answer the questions, the Court made an explanation on constituent elements of a customary law.

Bolivarian Agreement on Extradition of July 18th, 1911, and the Convention on Asylum of February 20th, 1928, both in force between Colombia and Peru, and in general from American international law, was Colombia competent, as the country granting asylum, to qualify the offence for the purposes of said asylum?

b) In the specific case under consideration, was Peru, as the territorial State, bound to give the guarantees necessary for the departure of the refugee from the country, with due regard to the inviolability of his person?

······

The Colombian Government has finally invoked "American international law in general". In addition to the rules arising from agreements which have already been considered, it has relied on an alleged regional or local custom peculiar to Latin-America States.

The Party which relies on a custom of this kind must prove that this custom is established in such a manner that it has become binding on the other Party. The Colombian Government must prove that the rule invoked by it is in accordance with a constant and uniform usage practised by the States in question, and that this usage is the expression of a right appertaining to the State granting asylum and a duty incumbent on the territorial State. This follows from Article 38 of the Statute of the Court, which refers to international custom "as evidence of a general practice accepted as law".

In support of its contention concerning the existence of such a custom, the Colombian Government has referred to a large number of extradition treaties which, can have no bearing on the question now under consideration. It has cited conventions and agreements which do not contain any provision concerning the alleged rule of unilateral and definitive qualification such as the Montevideo Convention of 1889 on international penal law, the Bolivarian Agreement of 1911 and the Havana Convention of 1928. ···

The Colombian Government has referred to a large number of particular cases in which diplomatic asylum was in fact granted and respected. But it has not shown that the alleged rule of unilateral and definitive qualification was invoked or—if in some cases it was in fact invoked—that it was, apart from conventional stipulations, exercised by the States granting asylum as a right appertaining to them and respected by the territorial States as a duty incumbent on them and not merely for reasons of political expediency.

The facts brought to the knowledge of the Court disclose so much uncertainty and contradiction, so much fluctuation and discrepancy in the exercise of diplomatic asylum and in the official views expressed on various occasions, there has been so much inconsistency in the rapid succession of conventions on asylum, ratified by some States and rejected by others, and the practice has been so much influenced by considerations of political expediency in the various cases, that it is not possible to discern in all this any constant and uniform usage, accepted as law, with regard to the alleged rule of unilateral and definitive qualification of the offence.

The Court cannot therefore find that the Colombian Government has proved the existence of such a custom. But even if it could be supposed that such a custom existed between certain Latin-American States only, it could not be invoked against Peru which, far from having by its attitude adhered to it, has, on the contrary, repudiated it by refraining from ratifying the Montevideo Conventions of 1933 and 1939, which were the first to include a rule concerning the qualification of the offence in matters of diplomatic asylum.

(3) *Dissenting Opinion by Alvarez*

The dispute between Colombia and Peru concerning asylum is of great importance for the countries of the New World who await the Court's answer with lively interest. This dispute also presents considerable importance for all the other countries, since asylum has been written into the Universal Declaration of Human Rights, it is necessary to consider unilateral acts in international law and their nature in their broad outlines:

A distinction must be made in international law between unilateral acts, or acts which are the result of the will of one State alone, and multilateral acts in which the will of two or more States participate. Unilateral acts occupy an important place and play an important role in international law. We shall not expatiate upon this point but shall confine ourselves to giving three examples of this kind of act:

(a) those which concern the freedom of the individual and the sovereignty of States, on the one hand, and the sovereignty of one or more States, on the other;

(b) some acts relating to conventional international law;

(c) certain acts which relate to politics.

Acts under the first head refer particularly to the admission of aliens to a State, immigration, refuge, asylum, extradition, internment and expulsion, etc. The acts of the second category arise in connexion with certain conventions: the latter may be adhered to, denounced, etc.; moreover, some conventions may contain certain special provisions as, for instance, those excluding from arbitration those questions which related to the vital interests of the parties. Finally, in the third category are included unilateral acts qualifying certain individuals as *persona grata* or *persona non grata*, desirable or undesirable, etc.

In all the examples mentioned above, the appreciation of the facts or circumstances depends on the will of one of the parties. In certain cases, this unilateral appreciation may not be disputed; it may at most be criticized. For example, in matters of immigration, it is the State in which the immigrants wish to settle which appreciates unilaterally whether they should be admitted and, if so, under what conditions. The result of such an appreciation may be prejudicial to the interests of thousands of persons who wish to emigrate to these countries, as well as to the interests of their national State; but nobody disputes the fact that the government of the receiving country has the right to act unilaterally and that its decisions cannot be disputed. In other cases, the unilateral appreciation may be challenged by the party concerned; this is precisely what happens in the *Asylum Case*.

4.3 *Factory at Chorzów Case* [1]

It is a principle of international law that the breach of an engagement involves an obligation to make reparation in an adequate form. Reparation therefore is the indispensable complement of a failure to apply a convention and there is no necessity for this to be stated in the convention itself. Differences relating to reparations, which may be due by reason of failure to apply a convention, are consequently differences relating to its applications.

It is, moreover, a principle generally accepted in the jurisprudence of international arbitration, as well as by municipal courts, that one Party cannot avail himself of the fact that the other has not fulfilled some obligation or has not had recourse to some means of redress, if the former Party has, by some illegal act, prevented the latter from fulfilling the obligation in question, or from having recourse to the tribunal which would have been open, to him.

Comment by Chester Brown: The case is most well-known for its authoritative statement on the law of reparation, which has been widely applied by other international courts and tribunals, forms the basis of the relevant provisions of the ILC's Articles on State Responsibility, and unquestionably reflects customary international law. It is thus deserving of its

---

[1] *Factory at Chorzów* (*Germ. v. Pol.*), Jurisdiction PCIJ, Ser. A, No. 9 (1927). The case concerned a claim by Germany against Poland which was brought in relation to Poland's alleged breach of its international obligations under Article 6 of the Geneva Convention of 15 May 1922, and the amount of reparation that Poland owed in respect of its conduct towards two German companies—namely, the "Oberschlesische Stickstoffwerke A.-G." and the "Bayerische Stickstoffwerke A.-G."—at the time it took possession of the "private factory situated at Chorzów". It is primarily significant for the contribution it makes to the rules of international law on issues of State responsibility, the law of reparation, and the assessment of damages, but it also deals with issues which are of contemporary concern, such as the effect of multiple or parallel proceedings, the inherent powers of international courts and tribunals concerning the consequences of an internationally wrongful act. The case edited here is to illustrate the general principle's function as a formal source.

place in this collection of "landmark cases" of international law. [1]

4.4　Legality of the Threat or Use of Nuclear Weapons: Advisory Opinion of 8 July 1996[2]

……

13. The question put to the Court by the General Assembly is indeed a legal one, since the Court is asked to rule on the compatibility of the threat or use of nuclear weapons with the relevant principles and rules of international law. To do this, the Court must identify the existing principles and rules, interpret them and apply them to the threat or use of nuclear weapons, thus offering a reply to the question posed based on law.

The fact that this question also has political aspects, as, in the nature of things, is the case with so many questions which arise in international life, does not suffice to deprive it of its character as a "legal question" and to "deprive the Court of a competence expressly conferred on it by its Statute" (*Application for Review of Judgement No. 158 of the United Nations Administrative Tribunal*, Advisory Opinion, I.C.J. Reports 1973, p. 172, para. 14). Whatever its political aspects, the Court cannot refuse to admit the legal character of a question which invites it to discharge an

---

[1]　See Eirik Bjorge and Cameron Miles (eds.), *Landmark Cases in Public International Law*, Hart Publishing, 2017, pp. 87-88.

[2]　*Legality of the Threat or Use of Nuclear Weapons*, ICJ Reports 1996, p. 226. In 19 December 1994, the Secretary-General officially submits to the Court for advisory opinion of the following question: "is the threat or use of nuclear weapons in any circumstance permitted under international law?" The Court considered the question of the legality or illegality of the use of nuclear weapons in the light of the provisions of the UN Charter relating to the threat or use of force. And, the Court then turned to the law applicable in situations of armed conflict from a consideration of customary and conventional law. The Court indicated that, although the applicability to nuclear weapons of the principles and rules of humanitarian law and of the principle of neutrality was not disputed, the conclusions to be drawn from it were, on the other hand, controversial. As to international law, the opinions also provided clarity on a number of important basic questions about international law: the relationship between international human rights law and international humanitarian law, the significance of General Assembly resolutions in the development of international law, the development of environmental law and its relationship to the law of armed conflict, and the constraints imposed by the law of armed conflict on the use of force in self-defense.

Chapter Ⅱ Sources of International Law   85

essentially judicial task, namely, an assessment of the legality of the possible conduct of States with regard to the obligations imposed upon them by international law. ···

20. The Court must next address certain matters arising in relation to the formulation of the question put to it by the General Assembly. The English text asks: "Is the threat or use of nuclear weapons in any circumstance permitted under international law?" ··· It was suggested that the Court was being asked by the General Assembly whether it was permitted to have recourse to nuclear weapons in every circumstance, and it was contended that such a question would inevitably invite a simple negative answer. ···

32. General Assembly resolution 47/37 of 25 November 1992 on the "Protection of the Environment in Times of Armed Conflict" is also of interest in this context. It affirms the general view according to which environmental considerations constitute one of the elements to be taken into account in the implementation of the principles of the law applicable in armed conflict: it States that "destruction of the environment, not justified by military necessity and carried out wantonly, is clearly contrary to existing international law". ···

68. According to certain States, the important series of General Assembly resolutions, beginning with resolution 1653 (ⅩⅥ) of 24 November 1961, that deal with nuclear weapons and that affirm, with consistent regularity, the illegality of nuclear weapons, signify the existence of a rule of international customary law which prohibits recourse to those weapons. According to other States, however, the resolutions in question have no binding character on their own account and are not declaratory of any customary rule of prohibition of nuclear weapons; some of these States have also pointed out that this series of resolutions not only did not meet with the approval of all of the nuclear-weapon States but of many other States as well.

69. States which consider that the use of nuclear weapons is illegal indicated that those resolutions did not claim to create any new rules, but were confined to a confirmation of customary law relating to the prohibition of

means or methods of warfare which, by their use, overstepped the bounds of what is permissible in the conduct of hostilities. In their view, the resolutions in question did no more than apply to nuclear weapons the existing rules of international law applicable in armed conflict; they were no more than the "envelope" or *instrumentum* containing certain pre-existing customary rules of international law. For those States it is accordingly of little importance that the *instrumentum* should have occasioned negative votes, which cannot have the effect of obliterating those customary rules which have been confirmed by treaty law.

70. The Court notes that General Assembly resolutions, even if they are not binding, may sometimes have normative value. They can, in certain circumstances, provide evidence important for establishing the existence of a rule or the emergence of an *opinio juris*. To establish whether this is true of a given General Assembly resolution, it is necessary to look at its content and the conditions of its adoption; it is also necessary to see whether an *opinio juris* exists as to its normative character. Or a series of resolutions may show the gradual evolution of the *opinio juris* required for the establishment of a new rule.

71. Examined in their totality, the General Assembly resolutions put before the Court declare that the use of nuclear weapons would be "a direct violation of the Charter of the United Nations"; and in certain formulations that such use "should be prohibited". The focus of these resolutions has sometimes shifted to diverse related matters; however, several of the resolutions under consideration in the present case have been adopted with substantial numbers of negative votes and abstentions; thus, although those resolutions are a clear sign of deep concern regarding the problem of nuclear weapons, they still fall short of establishing the existence of an *opinio juris* on the illegality of the use of such weapons.

72. The Court further notes that the first of the resolutions of the General Assembly expressly proclaiming the illegality of the use of nuclear

weapons, resolution 1653 (XVI) of 24 Novermber 1961 (mentioned in subsequent resolutions), after referring to certain international declarations and binding agreements, from the Declaration of St. Petersburg of 1868 to the Geneva Protocol of 1925, proceeded to qualify the legal nature of nuclear weapons, determine their effects, and apply general rules of customary international law to nuclear weapons in particular. That application by the General Assembly of general rules of customary law to the particular case of nuclear weapons indicates that, in its view, there was no specific rule of customary law which prohibited the use of nuclear weapons; if such a rule had existed, the General Assembly could simply have referred to it and would not have needed to undertake such an exercise of legal qualification.

74. The Court not having found a conventional rule of general scope, nor a customary rule specifically proscribing the threat or use of nuclear weapons *per se*, it will now deal with the question whether recourse to nuclear weapons must be considered as illegal in the light of the principles and rules of international humanitarian law applicable in armed conflict and of the law of neutrality.

……

5. References and Recommended Reading Materials

(1) Bin Cheng, *General Principles of Law as Applied by International Courts and Tribunals*, Cambridge University Press, 1987. 〔英〕郑斌:《国际法院与法庭适用的一般法律原则》,韩秀丽、蔡从燕译,法律出版社 2012 年版。

(2) Samantha Besson and Jean d'Aspremont (eds.), *The Oxford Handbook on the Sources of International Law*, Oxford University Press, 2017.

(3) Dinah Shelton, *Commitment and Compliance: The Role of Nonbinding Norms in the International Legal System*, Oxford University Press, 2003.

Chapter Ⅲ International Law and Municipal Law

1. Introduction

The relationship between international law and municipal law is another important issue in the preliminary topics constituting general principles of public international law in some popular textbooks. It contains mainly two questions. First, how does the national court or the sovereign State apply international law within its jurisdiction? Second, how do the international tribunals, i. e., ICJ, treat the municipal law? Most of the States have promulgated provisions in their constitutions or statutes to provide basic norms on the status of treaties and customary law. And, the municipal courts have developed some established patterns on the application of international law. So do the international tribunals. E. g., the Unites States have developed a mix of constitutional, statutory, judicial and executive branch materials defining the role of international law in its legal system.

Part 2 provides some provisions from constitutional, statutory and judicial decisions demonstrating main patterns concerned followed by States, e. g., the United States(US), the United Kingdom(UK), China and EU countries, to demonstrate how the practice developed in various States with different legal traditions. Part 3 briefly discusses the Monist and Dualist theory to make a snapshot about the theoretical debate over this issue. Part 4 proceeds with some papers written by politicians or scholars as further reading materials to show the current practice at issue.

2. Preliminary Reading and Assignment

2.1 Practice of United States

(1) *Constitutional and Statutory Provisions*
Articles in the US Constitution
Article I Section 10

Para. 1 No State shall enter into any Treaty, Alliance, or Confederation; grant Letters of Marque and Reprisal; coin Money; emit Bills of Credit; make any Thing but gold and silver Coin a Tender in Payment of Debts; pass any Bill of Attainder, ex post facto Law, or Law impairing the Obligation of Contracts, or grant any Title of Nobility.

Para. 3 No State shall, without the Consent of Congress, lay any Duty of Tonnage, keep Troops, or Ships of War in time of Peace, enter into any Agreement or Compact with another State, or with a foreign Power, or engage in War, unless actually invaded, or in such imminent Danger as will not admit of delay.

Article II Section 2

Para. 2 He (*the President*) shall have Power, by and with the Advice and Consent of the Senate, to make Treaties, provided two thirds of the Senators present concur; and he shall nominate, and by and with the Advice and Consent of the Senate, shall appoint Ambassadors, other public Ministers and Consuls, Judges of the supreme Court, and all other Officers of the United States, whose Appointments are not herein otherwise provided for, and which shall be established by Law: but the Congress may by Law vest the Appointment of such inferior Officers, as they think proper, in the President alone, in the Courts of Law, or in the Heads of Departments.

Article Ⅵ

Para. 2 This Constitution, and the Laws of the United States which shall be made in Pursuance thereof; and all Treaties made, or which shall be made, under the Authority of the United States, shall be the supreme Law of the Land; and the Judges in every State shall be bound thereby, any Thing in the Constitution or Laws of any State to the Contrary notwithstanding.

1 U.S.Code § 112b- United States International Agreements; Transmission to Congress

(a) The Secretary of State shall transmit to the Congress the text of any international agreement (including the text of any oral international agreement, which agreement shall be reduced to writing), other than a treaty, to which the United States is a party as soon as practicable after such agreement has entered into force with respect to the United States but in no event later than sixty days thereafter. However, any such agreement the immediate public disclosure of which would, in the opinion of the President, be prejudicial to the national security of the United States shall not be so transmitted to the Congress but shall be transmitted to the Committee on Foreign Relations of the Senate and the Committee on International Relations of the House of Representatives under an appropriate injunction of secrecy to be removed only upon due notice from the President. Any department or agency of the United States Government which enters into any international agreement on behalf of the United States shall transmit to the Department of State the text of such agreement not later than twenty days after such agreement has been signed.

(c) Notwithstanding any other provision of law, an international agreement may not be signed or otherwise concluded on behalf of the United States without prior consultation with the Secretary of State. Such consultation may encompass a class of agreements rather than a particular agreement.

(2) *Judicial Decisions*

A. The Paquete Habana[1]

MR. Justice Gray delivered the opinion of the court:

International law is part of our law, and must be ascertained and administered by the courts of justice of appropriate jurisdiction, as often as questions of right depending upon it are duly presented for their determination. For this purpose, where there is no treaty, and no controlling executive or legislative act or judicial decision, resort must be had to the customs and usages of civilized nations; and, as evidence of these, to the works of jurists and commentators, who by years of labor, research and experience, have made themselves peculiarly well acquainted with the subjects of which they treat. Such works are resorted to by judicial tribunals, not for the speculations of their authors concerning what the law ought to be, but for trustworthy evidence of what the law really is.

······

This review of the precedents and authorities on the subject appears to us abundantly to demonstrate that at the present day, by the general consent of the civilized nations of the world, and independently of any express treaty or other public act, it is an established rule of international law, founded on considerations of humanity to a poor and industrious order of men, and of the mutual convenience of belligerent States, that coast fishing vessels, with their implements and supplies, cargoes and crews, unarmed, and honestly pursuing their peaceful calling of catching and bringing in fresh fish, are exempt from capture as prize of war.

······

---

[1] *The Paquete Habana*, 175 U. S. 677 (1900), https://case-law.vlex.com/vid/175-u-s-677-606300378, last visited on Jan. 8, 2022.

B. Sei Fujii v. State of California[①]

Plaintiff, an alien Japanese who is ineligible to citizenship under our naturalization laws, appeals from a judgment declaring that certain land purchased by him in 1948 had escheated to the State. There is no treaty between this country and Japan which confers upon plaintiff the right to own land, and the sole question presented on this appeal is the validity of the California Alien Land Law.

It is first contended that the land law has been invalidated and superseded by the provisions of the United Nations Charter pledging the member nations to promote the observance of human rights and fundamental freedoms without distinction as to race. Plaintiff relies on Statements in the preamble and in articles 1, 55 and 56 of the charter.

It is not disputed that the charter is a treaty, and our federal Constitution provides that treaties made under the authority of the United States are part of the supreme law of the land and that the judges in every State are bound thereby. (U. S. Const., art. Ⅵ) **A treaty, however, does not automatically supersede local laws which are inconsistent with it unless the treaty provisions are self-executing.** In the words of Chief Justice Marshall: A treaty is "to be regarded in courts of justice as equivalent to an act of the Legislature, whenever it operates of itself, without the aid of any legislative provision. But when the terms of the stipulation import a contract—when either of the parties engages to perform a particular act, the treaty addresses itself to the political, not the judicial department; and the Legislature must execute the contract, before it can become a rule for the court."

In determining whether a treaty is self-executing courts look to the intent of the signatory parties as manifested by the language of the instrument, and, if the instrument is uncertain, recourse may be had to the circumstances

---

[①] *Sei Fujii v. State of California*, 38 Cal. 2d 718, 242 P. 2d 617 (1952), https://casetext.com/case/sei-fujii-v-state-of-california, last visited on Jan. 8, 2022.

surrounding its execution. In order for a treaty provision to be operative without the aid of implementing legislation and to have the force and effect of a statute, it must appear that the framers of the treaty intended to prescribe a rule that, standing alone, would be enforceable in the courts.

It is clear that the provisions of the preamble and of article 1 of the charter which are claimed to be in conflict with the alien land law are not self-executing. They State general purposes and objectives of the United Nations Organization and do not purport to impose legal obligations on the individual member nations or to create rights in private persons. It is equally clear that none of the other provisions relied on by plaintiff is self-executing. Article 55 declares that the United Nations "shall promote... universal respect for, and observance of, human rights and fundamental freedoms for all without distinction as to race, sex, language, or religion", and in article 56, the member nations "pledge themselves to take joint and separate action in cooperation with the Organization for the achievement of the purposes set forth in Article 55". Although the member nations have obligated themselves to cooperate with the international organization in promoting respect for, and observance of, human rights, it is plain that it was contemplated that future legislative action by the several nations would be required to accomplish the declared objectives, and there is nothing to indicate that these provisions were intended to become rules of law for the courts of this country upon the ratification of the charter.

The language used in Articles 55 and 56 is not the type customarily employed in treaties which have been held to be self-executing and to create rights and duties in individuals. For example, the treaty involved in *Clark v. Allen* (67 S. Ct. 1431, 1434, 91 L. Ed. 1633, 170 A. L. R. 953), relating to the rights of a national of one country to inherit real property located in another country, specifically provided that "such national shall be allowed a term of three years in which to sell the property... and withdraw the proceeds..." free from any discriminatory taxation. In *Nielsen v.*

Johnson (49 S. Ct. 223, 73 L. Ed. 607), the provision treated as being self-executing was equally definite. There each of the signatory parties agreed that "no higher or other duties, charges, or taxes of any kind, shall be levied" by one country on removal of property therefrom by citizens of the other country "than are or shall be payable in each State, upon the same, when removed by a citizen or subject of such State respectively". In other instances treaty provisions were enforced without implementing legislation where they prescribed in detail the rules governing rights and obligations of individuals or specifically provided that citizens of one nation shall have the same rights while in the other country as are enjoyed by that country's own citizens.

It is significant to note that when the framers of the charter (UN Charter) intended to make certain provisions effective without the aid of implementing legislation they employed language which is clear and definite and manifests that intention. For example, Article 104 provides: "The Organization shall enjoy in the territory of each of its Members such legal capacity as may be necessary for the exercise of its functions and the fulfillment of its purposes." Article 105 provides: "The Organization shall enjoy in the territory of each of its Members such privileges and immunities as are necessary for the fulfillment of its purposes. …"

The provisions in the charter pledging cooperation in promoting observance of fundamental freedoms lack the mandatory quality and definiteness which would indicate an intent to create justiciable rights in private persons immediately upon ratification. Instead, they are framed as a promise of future action by the member nations. Secretary of State Stettinius, chairman of the United States delegation at the San Francisco Conference where the charter was drafted, stated in his report to President Truman that Article 56 "pledges the various countries to cooperate with the organization by joint and separate action in the achievement of the economic and social objectives of the organization without infringing upon their right to order their national affairs according to their own best ability, in their own way, and in accordance with their own political and economic institutions and processes. " The same view was repeatedly expressed by delegates of other nations in the debates attending the drafting of Article 56.

The humane and enlightened objectives of the UN Charter are, of course, entitled to respectful consideration by the courts and legislatures of every member nation, since that document expresses the universal desire of thinking men for peace and for equality of rights and opportunities. The charter represents a moral commitment of foremost importance, and we must not permit the spirit of our pledge to be compromised or disparaged in either our domestic or foreign affairs. We are satisfied, however, that the charter provisions relied on by plaintiff were not intended to supersede existing domestic legislation, and we cannot hold that they operate to invalidate the Alien Land Law.

……

This case today is probably not of such immediately grave importance to the citizens of California, and to the United States as a nation, as it would have been prior to the events of the period between December 7, 1941, and August 14, 1945. The long-planned occupation and conquest of California by Japan has been at least for the foreseeable future averted. That nation, finally defeated at horrible cost to the United States and to other freedom-loving peoples of the world, as well as to itself, is now building a new government. It is to be hoped that this new government may in time prove its right to, and thereupon be welcomed in, the family of nations as a champion of peace and good will and a defender against aggressors, their stealth, their devices, their cunning and their violence. It is indeed to be fervently hoped that the people of this late enemy nation, though perhaps unwillingly rescued from totalitarianism, may espouse the principles of democracy, and of forthrightness, honesty, reason and gentleness for their own government and in their dealings with all. But the validity of a law should be decided on facts as they existed at the time of its enactment, not on social theories or expectation for the future, or speculation that the United States Supreme Court may eventually change its ruling on a constitutional issue. Justice is pictured as being blind but not in the posture of an ostrich, and judicial duty is not performed when a court refuses to follow a law because it conjectures that a higher court which has previously upheld the law may eventually reverse itself.

……

I agree that the United Nations Charter, as presently constituted and accepted was not intended to, and does not, supersede existing domestic legislation of the United States or of the several States and territories.

……

(3) *Executive Branch Materials*: *US Foreign Affair Manual*

11 FAM 723. Exercise of the International Agreement Power

11 FAM 723. 1 Determination of Type of Agreement The following considerations will be taken into account along with other relevant factors in determining whether an international agreement shall be dealt with by the United States as a treaty to be brought into force with the advice and consent of the Senate or as an agreement to be brought into force on some other constitutional basis.

11 FAM 723. 2 Constitutional Requirements There are two procedures under the Constitution through which the United States becomes a party to an international agreement. Those procedures and the constitutional parameters of each are found below.

(a) *Treaties* International agreements (regardless of their title, designation, or form) whose entry into force with respect to the United States takes place only after the Senate has given its advice and consent are "treaties". The President, with the advice and consent of two-thirds of the Senators present, may enter into an international agreement on any subject genuinely of concern in foreign relations, so long as the agreement does not contravene the United States Constitution.

(*b*) ***International Agreements Other Than Treaties*** International agreements brought into force with respect to the United States on a constitutional basis other than with the advice and consent of the Senate are "international agreements other than treaties". (The term "executive agreement" is appropriately reserved for agreements made solely on the basis of the constitutional authority of the President.) There are three constitutional bases for international agreements other than treaties as set forth below. An international agreement may be concluded pursuant to one or more of these constitutional bases:

i. Treaty. The President may conclude an international agreement pursuant to a treaty brought into force with the advice and consent of the Senate, the provisions of which constitute authorization for the agreement by the Executive without subsequent action by the Congress.

ii. Legislation. The President may conclude an international agreement on the basis of existing legislation, or subject to legislation to be adopted by the Congress, or upon the failure of Congress to adopt a disapproving joint or concurrent resolution within designated time periods.

iii. The Constitutional authority of the President. The President may conclude an international agreement on any subject within his constitutional authority so long as the agreement is not inconsistent with legislation enacted by the Congress in the exercise of its constitutional authority. The constitutional sources of authority for the President to conclude international agreements include:

a) The President's authority as Chief Executive to represent the nation in foreign affairs;

b) The President's authority to receive ambassadors and other public ministers, and to recognize foreign governments;

c) The President's authority as "Commander-in-Chief"; and

d) The President's authority to "take care that the laws be faithfully executed".

2.2 Practice of UK and Other European States

(1) UK: *Case and Statute*

A. Thomas and Haniff Hilaire v. Cipriani Baptiste[①]

Background The appellants T and H had both been convicted of murder and sentenced to death. They had exhausted all possible avenues of appeal. In October 1997, the Government of Trinidad and Tobago issued "Instructions relating to applications from persons under sentence of death" establishing a series of successive time limits for petitions to the Inter-American Commission of Human Rights (the "IACHR") and the UN Human Rights Committee by persons who had been condemned to death. These were intended to restrict the time following the passing of sentence of death which might be taken up by petitioning these bodies. The appellants both petitioned the IACHR. Subsequently, and before the IACHR had concluded its procedures, warrants were read for the execution of the appellants. Both appellants (in separate proceedings) issued constitutional motions. The appellant T's motion was heard by Jamadar J who allowed it, vacated the sentence of death and ordered that the appellant be held in custody at the President's pleasure. The motion of the appellant H was dismissed by Kangaloo J. The Prison Commissioner in the case of the appellant T and the appellant H appealed to the Court of Appeal, and their appeals were heard consecutively. The Court of Appeal allowed the appeal in the case of the appellant T (in effect reinstating the death sentence) and dismissed it in the case of the appellant H; the court gave leave to appeal to the Privy Council in both cases. In reaching its decision, the court ruled that the appalling conditions in which the appellants had been detained in prison, although in breach of the Prison Rules, did not constitute

---

[①] *Thomas and Haniff Hilaire v. Cipriani Baptiste*, (1999) UKPC 13, https://lawassociationtt.com/wp-content/uploads/2017/05/Thomas_and_Another_v_Baptiste_and_Others.pdf, last visited on Jan. 8, 2022.

a breach of their constitutional rights not to be subjected to cruel and unusual treatment or punishment (of Constitution of Trinidad an Tobago, section 5(2)(b)). On the appeal to the Privy Council, the appellants argued that they had a constitutional right to have their petitions to the IACHR determined before their sentences were carried out, and that the conditions under which they had been held in prison constituted a breach of section 5(2)(b) entitling them to a commutation of sentence. Further, the appellant T argued that, following its decision, the Court of Appeal had had no power to impose or to reinstate the death sentence.

Opinion delivered by Lord Millett:

......

26. Their Lordships recognize the constitutional importance of the principle that international conventions do not alter domestic law except to the extent that they are incorporated into domestic law by legislation. The making of a treaty, in Trinidad and Tobago as in England, is an act of the executive government, not of the legislature. It follows that the terms of a treaty cannot effect any alteration to domestic law or deprive the subject of existing legal rights unless and until enacted into domestic law by or under authority of the legislature. When so enacted, the Courts give effect to the domestic legislation, not to the terms of the treaty. The many authoritative Statements to this effect are too well known to need citation. It is sometimes argued that human rights treaties form an exception to this principle. It is also sometimes argued that a principle which is intended to afford the subject constitutional protection against the exercise of executive power cannot be invoked by the executive itself to escape from obligations which it has entered into for his protection. Their Lordships mention these arguments for completeness. They do not find it necessary to examine them further in the present case.

27. In their Lordships' view, however, the appellants, claim does not infringe the principle which the Government invoke. The right for which they

contend is not the particular right to petition the IACHR or even to complete the particular process which they initiated when they lodged their petitions. It is the general right accorded to all litigants not to have the outcome of any pending appellate or other legal process pre-empted by executive action. This general right is not created by the Convention; it is accorded by the common law and affirmed by section 4(a) of the Constitution. The appellants are not seeking to enforce the terms of an unincorporated treaty, but a provision of the domestic law of Trinidad and Tobago contained in the Constitution. By ratifying a treaty which provides for individual access to an international body, the Government made that process for the time being part of the domestic criminal justice system and thereby, temporarily at least, extended the scope of the "due process" clause in the Constitution.

……

B. Diplomatic Privileges Act 1964

Article 2 Application of Vienna Convention

(1) Subject to section 3 of this Act, the Articles set out in Schedule 1 to this Act (being Articles of the Vienna Convention on Diplomatic Relations signed in 1961) shall have the force of law in the United Kingdom and shall for that purpose be construed in accordance with the following provisions of this section.

(2) *Germany: Germany's Constitution of 1949 with Amendments through 2014*

Article 25 Primacy of International Law

The general rules of international law shall be an integral part of federal law. They shall take precedence over the laws and directly create rights and duties for the inhabitants of the federal territory.

Article 100 Concrete Judicial Review

1. If a court concludes that a law on whose validity its decision depends is unconstitutional, the proceedings shall be stayed, and a decision shall be obtained from the Land court with jurisdiction over constitutional disputes

Chapter III International Law and Municipal Law   101

where the constitution of a Land is held to be violated, or from the Federal Constitutional Court where this Basic Law is held to be violated. This provision shall also apply where the Basic Law is held to be violated by Land law and where a Land law is held to be incompatible with a federal law.

2. If, in the course of litigation, doubt exists whether a rule of international law is an integral part of federal law and whether it directly creates rights and duties for the individual (Article 25), the court shall obtain a decision from the Federal Constitutional Court.

3. If the constitutional court of a Land, in interpreting this Basic Law, proposes to deviate from a decision of the Federal Constitutional Court or of the constitutional court of another Land, it shall obtain a decision from the Federal Constitutional Court.

(3) *France*: *France's Constitution of 1958 with Amendments Through 2008*

Preamble The French Republic, faithful to its traditions, shall respect the rules of public international law. It shall undertake no war aimed at conquest, nor shall it ever employ force against the freedom of any people. Subject to reciprocity, France shall consent to the limitations upon its sovereignty necessary to the organisation and preservation of peace. ⋯

Article 53 Peace Treaties, Trade agreements, treaties or agreements relating to international organization, those committing the finances of the State, those modifying provisions which are the preserve of statute law, those relating to the status of persons, and those involving the ceding, exchanging or acquiring of territory, may be ratified or approved only by an Act of Parliament. They shall not take effect until such ratification or approval has been secured. No ceding, exchanging or acquiring of territory shall be valid without the consent of the population concerned.

Article 54 If the Constitutional Council, on a referral from the President of the Republic, from the Prime Minister, from the President of one or the other Houses, or from sixty Members of the National Assembly or sixty

Senators, has held that an international undertaking contains a clause contrary to the Constitution, authorization to ratify or approve the international undertaking involved may be given only after amending the Constitution.

Article 55 Treaties or agreements duly ratified or approved shall, upon publication, prevail over Acts of Parliament, subject, with respect to each agreement or treaty, to its application by the other party.

2.3 Kelsen's View on Municipal Law and International Law[①]

Thus, the international legal order is significant only as part of a universal legal order which comprises also all the national legal order. The analysis has further led to the conclusion that the international legal order determines the territorial, personal, and temporal spheres of validity of the national legal orders, thus making possible the coexistence of a multitude of States. We have finally seen that the international legal order restricts the material sphere of validity of the national legal orders by subjecting them to a certain regulation of their own matters that could otherwise have been arbitrarily regulated by the State.

But the pluralistic view is untenable also on logical grounds. International law and national law cannot be different and mutually independent systems of norms if the norms of both systems are considered to be valid for the same space, and at the same time. It is logically not possible to assume that simultaneously valid norms belong to different, mutually independent systems.

The unity of national and international law is an epistemological Postulate. A jurist who accepts both as sets of valid norms must try to comprehend them as parts of one harmonious system. This is a priori possible in either of two different ways. Two sets of norms can be part of one

---

① See Hans Kelsen, *Pure Theory of Law*, Harvard University Press, 1949, pp. 363-374.

normative system because one, being an inferior order, derives its validity from the other, a superior order. The superior order can either itself State the procedure in which the norms of the inferior order are to be created, or merely empower an authority to create norms for a certain sphere at its own discretion. The relationship of international and national law must correspond to one of these two types. International law can be superior to national law or vice versa; or international law can be coordinated to national law. Coordination presupposes a third order superior to both. Since there is no third order superior to both, they themselves must be in a relationship of superiority and inferiority. Entirely excluded is the possibility that they should exist side by side, one independent of the other, without being coordinated by a superior order.

2.4 Assignment and Questions

(1) Could a treaty be directly applied in a US court? Why?

(2) What are the patterns that the UK applies international law in its court?

(3) What is the executive agreement in US law system?

(4) Find out the pattern that China applies international law and make a 5-10 minutes speech in English.

3. Terminologies and Discussions

3.1 Municipal Law and International Law

Most popular textbooks define the relation between municipal law and international law as an important preliminary issue before the detailed discussion about subject, territory, sea and other material contents. The practice of the States does not resolve the theoretical debate. On the contrary, international development, such as the increasing role of individuals as subjects, the convergence of internal law by the uniform codification of treaties and deepening involvement of the international or supranational organization in internal affairs, have made the distinction between international law and municipal law unclear and more complex. The questions, e. g. , how do States, within the framework of their internal legal order, apply the rules of international law, and how is a conflict between a rule of international law and a national rule of law to be resolved, are increasingly answered by reference to various national laws, rather than the doctrine of monistic doctrine or dualistic doctrine.

Some basic views could be drawn based on the survey of the various practices of States. First, it is generally accepted that the rules of international law can operate as part of municipal law with expressed municipal adoption. The way of adoption might be different in various legal systems. E. g. , transformation by a specific stature or incorporation grounded on constitutional provisions or a precedent created by the court with authority. States show considerable flexibility in the procedures whereby they give effect within their territories to the rules of international law, although a great many States adopt the doctrine that international law is part of the law of the land. Also, the national court could apply various sources of international law in different ways. It is more complicated, for it always put the court to ascribe conflict between the two systems. E. g. , between State immunity and the prohibition of torture, treaty rules of human rights and binding Security Council resolutions.

Second, a State cannot plead provisions of its law or deficiencies in that law in answering to a claim against it for a breach of its obligations under international law. This principle is reflected in Article 3 of the ARSIWA 2001 which provides that: "The characterization of an act of a State as internationally wrongful is governed by international law. Such characterization is not affected by the characterization of the same act as lawful by internal law." There is a general duty to bring national law into conformity with obligations under international law, but what this entails depends on the obligation in question.

Third, there is an established principle that national laws are merely facts before international tribunals. A national court decision or a legislative measure may constitute evidence of a breach of a treaty or customary international law. However, international tribunals cannot declare the unconstitutionality or invalidity of rules of national law. In practice, to decide whether particular acts are in breach of obligations under treaties or customary law, ICJ has had to examine national law relating to a wide range of topics including expropriation, fishing limits, nationality, guardianship and welfare of infants, the rights of shareholders in respect of damage suffered by corporations, and the arbitrary arrest and expulsion of aliens. National law is very frequently implicated in cases concerning individuals, including those relating to the protection of human rights and the exhaustion of local remedies.

3.2 Monism and Dualism

Monism and Dualism are the two competing schools on the relationship between international law and national law. Dualists believe that international law and the internal law of States are separate legal systems. They emphasize the distinct and independent character of the international and national legal systems. International law is the law between States, whereas national law applies within a State, regulating the relations of its citizens with each other and with that State. Neither legal order has the power to create or alter the rules of the other. In case of a conflict between international law and national law, the dualists would assume that a national court would apply national law, or at least that it is for the national system to decide which rule is to prevail.

The monist approach postulates that municipal and international law constitute one legal order or interlocking order that should be coherent and consistent. International law can be applied directly within the national legal order. Those writers of monism tend to fall into two distinct categories. The difference could be represented by Hersch Lauterpacht① and Hans Kelsen. Lauterpacht emphasized that individuals are the ultimate subjects of international law, representing both the justification and moral limit of the legal order. International law is seen as the best available moderator of human affairs and also as a condition of the legal existence of States and, therefore, of the national legal systems. Kelsen's view is grounded on the formal methods of analysis depending on a theory of knowledge. According to him, monism is scientifically established if international law and national law are part of the same system of norms receiving their validity and content by an intellectual operation involving the assumption of a single basic norm (Grundnorm). Only that assumption makes sense of the shared normativity of law. Under his theory, the law is a hierarchical system whereby each legal norm derives its validity from a higher norm. This chain of validity can be traced to the Grundnorm, which is not a norm of positive law but rather a "hypothesis of juristic thinking". International and national law form a single system of norms because they receive their validity from the same source, the Grundnorm.

Besides, there is a third theory. It denies that any common field of operation exists between international law and municipal law by which one system is superior or inferior to the other. Instead, each order is supreme in its spheres, such as French and English laws in France and England. They are both the legal elements contained within the domestic and international systems, respectively, within different juridical orders.

---

① Sir Hersch Lauterpacht (16 August 1897—8 May 1960) was a prominent British international lawyer and judge at the International Court of Justice. Lauterpacht was a member of the UN' ILC from 1952 to 1954 and a Judge of the ICJ from 1955 to 1960. Hersch's writings and (concurring and dissenting) opinions continue, nearly 50 years after his death, to be cited frequently in briefs, judgments, and advisory opinions of the World Courts. He famously said "international law is at the vanishing point of law".

4. Cases and Materials

Read the materials below and think about the following questions:

(1) Which theory do you think is more compatible with Chinese practice on applying international law?

(2) Are there customary rules on the relationship between international law and municipal law? If yes, why do States adopt unilateral measures in contradiction with international law?

(3) What are the essence of the issue of international law and municipal law bring into the practice?

4.1 Two Cases about the International Law in Municipal Court

(1) Regina v. Jones (Margaret)[①]

There are 20 appellants before the House. All of them committed acts in February or March 2003 which were, or are alleged to have been, criminal offences, unless there was legal justification for what they did or are said to have done. The common feature of all the appeals, and the feature which makes the cases important, is that they all raise the question whether the crime of aggression, if established in customary international law, is a crime recognized by or forming part of the domestic criminal law of England and Wales. The appellants acted as they did because they wished to impede, obstruct or disrupt the commission of that crime, or what they believed would be the commission of that crime, by Her Majesty's Government or the

---

① *Regina v. Jones (Margaret)*, (2006) UKHL 16, https://publications.parliament.uk/pa/ld200506/ldjudgmt/jd060329/jones.pdf, last visited on Jan. 8, 2022. This case confirms that general Statements to the effect: "the common law incorporates the rule of customary international law do not mean that a crime that is recognized by customary international law is thereby automatically incorporated into United Kingdom Law so as to provide a basis for prosecution in its municipal courts or otherwise amount to a 'crime' in that law; constitutional considerations by which only Parliament may create a criminal offence come into play."

Government of the United States against Iraq in the weeks and days before (as we now know) hostilities began. They accordingly contend, or have contended, that they were legally justified in acting as they did. The House is not asked to rule whether, in preparing to make war against Iraq, the United Kingdom or the United States committed the international law crime of aggression, but it must rule whether, if they may have done, that would justify the appellants' otherwise criminal conduct.

Lord Bingham of Cornhill:

10(1) Customary international law is (without the need for any domestic statute or judicial decision) part of the domestic law of England and Wales.

11. The appellants contended that the law of nations in its full extent is part of the law of England and Wales. The Crown did not challenge the general truth of this proposition, for which there is indeed old and high authority. … I would for my part hesitate, at any rate without much fuller argument, to accept this proposition in quite the unqualified terms in which it has often been stated. … and I am content to accept the general truth of the proposition for present purposes since the only relevant qualification is the subject of consideration below. …

22. It is true that certain practices have, since mediaeval times, been regarded as contrary to the laws and usages of war. After the Second World War some countries provided for the trial of those accused of this crime by statute (as in Australia), or Order in Council under statutory authority (Canada), and the United States appointed military commissions, a practice which predated the Constitution and was recognised but not established by statute. … but in the event a Royal Warrant was issued under the royal prerogative on 18 June 1945 to provide for the trial in military courts of persons charged with "violations of the laws and usages of war", which were treated as synonymous with war crimes. Such courts were to take judicial notice of the laws and usages of war. Pursuant to this instrument some 500 trials were held during the years 1945-1949. … Since, by 1945, the creation

of new offences lay out with the royal prerogative, the underlying premise of the Royal Warrant must, I think, have been that war crimes, recognised as such in customary international law, had been assimilated into our domestic law. It was, however, contemplated that an Act of Indemnity should be passed to give retrospective validity to the proceedings, which may betray some uncertainty on the point. But hiseory has movedon. In 1950 the International Law Commission, summarising the Principles of International Law Recognized in the Charter of the Nürnberg Tribunal and in the Judgment of the Tribunal, listed war crimes ("Violations of the laws or customs of war") as crimes under international law. In section 1(1) of the War Crimes Act 1991, jurisdiction was conferred on British courts to try charges of murder, manslaughter or culpable homicide against a person in this country irrespective of his nationality at the time of the alleged offence if that offence was committed between 1 September 1939 and 5 June 1945 in a place which at the time was part of Germany or under German occupation and "constituted a violation of the laws and customs of war", an expression which it was not thought necessary to define. …

23. I would accordingly accept that a crime recognised in customary international law may be assimilated into the domestic criminal law of this country. …I respectfully agree with the observations of Sir Franklin Berman answering the question whether customary international law is capable of creating a crime directly triable in a national court:

"The first question is open to a myriad of answers, depending on the characteristic features of the particular national legal system in view. Looking at it simply from the point of view of English law, the answer would seem to be no; international law could not create a crime triable directly, without the intervention of Parliament, in an English court. …"

28. The lack of any statutory incorporation is not, however, a neutral factor, for two main reasons. The first is that there now exists no power in

the courts to create new criminal offences, as decided by a unanimous House in *Knuller (Publishing, Printing and Promotions) Ltd. v. Director of Public Prosecutions* (1973) AC 435. While old common law offences survive until abolished or superseded by statute, new ones are not created. Statute is now the sole source of new criminal offences. The second reason is that when it is sought to give domestic effect to crimes established in customary international law, the practice is to legislate. Examples may be found in the Geneva Conventions Act 1957 and the Geneva Conventions (Amendment) Act 1995, dealing with breaches of the Geneva Conventions of 1949 and the Additional Protocols of 1977; the Genocide Act 1969, giving effect to the Genocide Convention of 1948; the Criminal Justice Act 1988, s 134, giving effect to the Torture Convention of 1984; the War Crimes Act 1991, giving jurisdiction to try war crimes committed abroad by foreign nationals; the Merchant Shipping and Maritime Security Act 1997, s 26, giving effect to provisions of the United Nations Convention on the Law of the Sea 1982 relating to piracy; and sections 51 and 52 of the International Criminal Court Act 2001, giving effect to the Rome Statute by providing for the trial here of persons accused of genocide, crimes against humanity and war crimes, but not, significantly, the crime of aggression. …

30. In the present case, involving the crime of aggression, there are compelling reasons for not departing. A charge of aggression, if laid against an individual in a domestic court, would involve determination of his responsibility as a leader but would presuppose commission of the crime by his own State or a foreign State. Thus resolution of the charge would (unless the issue had been decided by the Security Council or some other third party) call for a decision on the culpability in going to war either of Her Majesty's Government or a foreign government, or perhaps both if the States had gone to war as allies. But there are well established rules that the courts will be very slow to review the exercise of prerogative powers in relation to the conduct of foreign affairs and the deployment of the armed services, and very

slow to adjudicate upon rights arising out of transactions entered into between sovereign States on the plane of international law. … Lord Wilberforce cited with approval the words of Fuller CJ in the United States Supreme Court in *Underhill v. Hernandez* 168 US 250 (1897), 252:

> "Every sovereign State is bound to respect the independence of every other sovereign State, and the courts of one country will not sit in judgment on the acts of the government of another done within its own territory. Redress of grievances by reason of such acts must be obtained through the means open to be availed of by sovereign powers as between themselves."

(2) *Trendtex Trading v. Bank of Nigeria*[①]

Fact:

In July 1975 the Central Bank of issued an irrevocable letter of credit to pay for quantities of cement ordered by the Nigerian Ministry of Defence. The credit was, properly, transferred to the plaintiffs who shipped the cement to Nigeria. Because of complications at port caused by substantial over-ordering of cement, the plaintiffs' vessels were delayed prior to discharge; the Bank refused to make payments under the letter of credit upon the plaintiffs applying for the same in respect of demurrage. Upon the plaintiffs issuing proceedings for breach and repudiation of the letter of credit, the Bank contended successfully before Donaldson J. that it was entitled to sovereign immunity.

Lord Denning:

A fundamental question arises for decision. What is the place of international law in our English law? One school of thought holds to the doctrine of incorporation. It says that the rules of international law are

---

[①] *Trendtex Trading v. Bank of Nigeria*, (1977) 1 QB 529, http://www.uniset.ca/other/css/1977QB529.html, last visited on Jan. 8, 2022.

incorporated into English law automatically and considered to be part of English law unless they are in conflict with an Act of Parliament. The other school of thought holds to the doctrine of transformation. It says that the rules of international law are not to be considered as part of English law except in so far as they have been already adopted and made part of our law by the decisions of the judges, or by Act of Parliament, or long established custom. The difference is vital when you are faced with a change in the rules of international law. Under the doctrine of incorporation, when the rules of international law change, our English law changes with them. But, under the doctrine of transformation, the English law does not change. It is bound by precedent. It is bound down to those rules of international law which have been accepted and adopted in the past. It cannot develop as international law develops.

……

Which is correct? As between these two schools of thought, I now believe that the doctrine of incorporation is correct. Otherwise I do not see that our courts could ever recognise a change in the rules of international law. It is certain that international law does change. I would use of international law the words which Galileo used of the earth: "But it does move." International law does change: and the courts have applied the changes without the aid of any Act of Parliament. Thus, when the rules of international law were changed (by the force of public opinion) so as to condemn slavery, the English courts were justified in applying the modern rules of international law. Again, the extent of territorial waters varies from time to time according to the rule of international law current at the time, and the courts will apply it accordingly. The bounds of sovereign immunity have changed greatly in the last 30 years. The changes have been recognised in many countries, and the courts—of our country and of theirs—have given effect to them, without any legislation for the purpose. …

4.2 Two Cases about Municipal Law in International Tribunal

(1) *Serbian Loans* [1]

Para. 38 Accordingly, in all cases with which the Court has so far had to deal and in which private interests have been involved, the State's claim has been based upon an alleged breach of an international agreement. The controversy submitted to the Court in the present case, on the contrary, solely relates to the existence and extent of certain obligations which the Serbian State is alleged to have assumed in respect, of the holders of certain loans. It therefore is exclusively concerned with relations between the borrowing State and private persons, that is to say, relations which are, in themselves, within the domain of municipal law.

Para. 40 From a general point of view, it must be admitted that the true function of the Court is to decide disputes between States or Members of the League of Nations on the basis of international law: Article 38 of the Statute contains a clear indication to this effect.

Para. 41 But it would be scarcely accurate to say that only questions of international law may form the subject of a decision of the Court. It should be recalled in this respect that paragraph 2 of Article 36 of the Statute provides that States may recognize as compulsory the jurisdiction of the Court in legal disputes concerning "the existence of any fact which, if established, would constitute a breach of an international obligation". And Article 13 of the Covenant includes disputes of the sort above mentioned "among those which are generally suitable for submission to arbitration or judicial settlement". Clearly, amongst others, disputes concerning pure matters of fact are contemplated, for the States concerned may agree that the fact to be established would constitute a breach of an international obligation; it is unnecessary to add that the facts the existence of which the Court has to

---

[1] *Serbian Loans*, PCIJ, Ser. A, No. 20 (1929).

establish may be of any kind.

Para. 42 Is the case altered if the point at issue between two States is a question which must be decided by application of the municipal law of a particular country? There are cases—as the Court has already had occasion to observe in Judgment No. 8—in which an action cannot be brought before an international tribunal when there are legal remedies still open to the individuals concerned. But, apart from cases of this kind, and when the two States have agreed to have recourse to the Court, the latter's duty to exercise its jurisdiction cannot be affected, in the absence of a clause in the Statute on the subject, by the circumstance that the dispute relates to a question of municipal law rather than to a pure matter of fact. ...

Para. 43 Article 38 of the Statute cannot be regarded as excluding the possibility of the Court's dealing with disputes which do not require the application of international law, seeing that the Statute itself expressly provides for this possibility. ...

Para. 86 Any contract which is not a contract between States in their capacity as subjects of international law is based on the municipal law of some country. The question as to which this law is forms the subject of that branch of law which is at the present day usually described as private international law or the doctrine of the conflict of laws. The rules thereof may be common to several States and may even be established by international conventions or customs, and in the latter case may possess the character of true international law governing the relations between States. But apart from this, it has to be considered that these rules form part of municipal law.

Para. 87 The Court, which has before it a dispute involving the question as to the law which governs the contractual obligations at issue, can determine what this law is only by reference to the actual nature of these obligations and to the circumstances attendant upon their creation, though it may also take into, account the expressed or presumed intention of the

Parties. Moreover, this would seem to be in accord with the practice of municipal courts in the absence of rules of municipal law concerning the settlement of conflicts of law.

Para. 88 Before proceeding to determine which this law is, it should however be observed that it may happen that the law which may be held by the Court to be applicable to the obligations in the case, may in a particular territory be rendered inoperative by a municipal law of this territory—that is to say, by legislation enacting a public policy the application of which is unavoidable even though the contract has been concluded under the auspices of some foreign law.

Para. 105 The Court, having in these circumstances to decide as to the meaning and scope of a municipal law, makes the following observations: For the Court itself to undertake its own construction of municipal law, leaving on one side existing judicial decisions, with the ensuing danger of contradicting the construction which has been placed on such law by the highest national tribunal and which, in its results, seems to the Court reasonable, would not be in conformity with the task for which the Court has been established and would not be compatible with the principles governing the selection of its members. It would be a most delicate matter to do so, especially in cases concerning public policy—a conception the definition of which in any particular country is largely dependent on the opinion prevailing at any given time in such country itself—and in cases where no relevant provisions directly relate to the question at issue. It is French legislation, as applied in France, which really constitutes French law, and if that law does not prevent the fulfillment of the obligations in France in accordance with the stipulations made in the contract, the fact that the terms of legislative provisions are capable of a different construction is irrelevant.

Para. 106 In these circumstances, the Court will confine itself to observing that, according to the information furnished by the Parties, the doctrine of French courts, after some oscillation, has now been established in the manner indicated by the French Government, and that consequently there is nothing to prevent the creditor from claiming in France, in the present case, the gold value stipulated for.

(2) *India-Patents* (US) [①]

In public international law, an international tribunal may treat municipal law in several ways.

Municipal law may serve as evidence of facts and may provide evidence of State practice. However, municipal law may also constitute evidence of compliance or non-compliance with international obligations.

In this case, the Panel was simply performing its task in determining whether India's "administrative instructions" for receiving mailbox applications were in conformity with India's obligations under Article 70.8 of the TRIPS Agreement. It is clear that an examination of the relevant aspects of Indian municipal law and, in particular, the relevant provisions of the Patents Act as they relate to the "administrative instructions", is essential to determining whether India has complied with its obligations under Article 70.8. There was simply no way for the Panel to make this determination without engaging in an examination of Indian law. But, as in the case cited above before the Permanent Court of International Justice, in this case, the Panel was not interpreting Indian law "as such"; rather, the Panel was examining Indian law solely for the purpose of determining whether India had met its obligations under the TRIPS Agreement. To say that the Panel should have done otherwise would be to say that only India can assess whether Indian law is consistent with India's obligations under the WTO Agreement. This, clearly, cannot be so.

---

① India -Patent Protection for Pharmaceutical and Agricultural Chemical Products, WT/DS50/R., 1997.

5. References and Recommended Reading Materials

(1) 万鄂湘主编:《国际法与国内法关系研究》,北京大学出版社 2011 年版。

(2) Daniel P. O'Connell, The Relationship Between International Law and Municipal Law, 48 *GEO. L. J.* 3 (1960).

(3) D. J. Devine, The Relationship Between International Law and Municipal Law in Light of the Constitution of the Republic of Namibia, 26 *Case W. Res. J. Int'l L.* 2 (1994).

(4) John H. Jackson, The Great 1994 Sovereignty Debate: United States Acceptance and Implementation of the Uruguay Round Results, 36 *Colum. J. Transnat'l L.* (1997).

(5) Curtis A. Bradley, Unratified Treaties, Domestic Politics, and the U.S. Constitution, 48 *HARV. INT'l L. J.* 2 (2007).

Chapter Ⅳ General Principle of International Law

1. Introduction

The rubric "general principles of international law" may be alternately referred to as rules of customary international law, general principles of law as in Article 38 (1) (c) of ICJ Stature, or certain logical propositions underlying judicial reasoning based on existing international law. This shows that a rigid categorization of sources is inappropriate. Examples of this type of general principle are the principles of consent, reciprocity, equality of States, the finality of awards and settlements, the legal validity of agreements, good faith, domestic jurisdiction, and the freedom of the seas. They are primarily abstractions and have been accepted for so long and so generally as no longer to be directly connected to State practice. Certain fundamental principles of international law enjoy heightened normativity as peremptory norms. ①

Under *the UN Charter*, *the UN General Assembly's Declaration on Principles of International Law* and other international law documents, the basic principles of international law mainly include the principle of sovereign equality of States, the principle of non-aggression and non-interference in each other's internal affairs, the principle of prohibiting the use of force or threat use of force, the principle of peaceful settlement of international disputes, and

---

① James Crawford (ed.), *Brownlie's Principles of Public International Law*, 8th Ed., Oxford University Press, 2012, pp. 36-37.

Chapter Ⅳ General Principle of International Law

the principle of fulfilling international obligations in good faith. The Five Principles of Peaceful Coexistence, which is a great contribution made by China to international law and international relations, share the same essences with these principles.

2. Preliminary Reading and Assignment

2.1 The Declaration on Principles of International Law①

(1) The principle that States shall refrain in their international relations from the threat or use of force against the territorial integrity or political independence of any State, or in any other manner inconsistent with the purposes of the United Nations

Every State has the duty to refrain in its international relations from the threat or use of force against the territorial integrity or political independence of any State, or in any other manner inconsistent with the purposes of the United Nations. Such a threat or use of force constitutes a violation of international law and the Charter of United Nations and shall never be employed as a means of settling international issues.

A war of aggression constitutes a crime against the peace, for which there is responsibility under international law.

… States have the duty to refrain from propaganda for wars of aggression.

Every State has the duty to refrain from the threat or use of force to violate the existing international boundaries of another State or as a means of solving international disputes, including territorial disputes and problems

---

① *The Declaration on Principles of International Law concerning Friendly Relations and Co-operation among States in accordance with the Charter of United Nations* was adopted by the General Assembly on 24 October 1970 (resolution 26/25 (XXV)), during a commemorative session to celebrate the twenty-fifth anniversary of the United Nations (A/PV. 1883).

concerning frontiers of State.

Every State likewise has the duty to refrain from the threat or use of force to violate international lines of demarcation, such as armistice lines, established by or pursuant to an international agreement to which it is a party or which it is otherwise bound to respect. Nothing in the foregoing shall be construed as prejudicing the positions of the parties concerned with regard to the status and effects of such lines under their special regimes or as affecting their temporary character.

States have a duty to refrain from acts of reprisal involving the use of force.

Every State has the duty to refrain from any forcible action which deprives peoples referred to in the elaboration of the principle of equal rights and self-determination of their right to self-determination and freedom and independence.

Every State has the duty to refrain from organizing or encouraging the organization of irregular forces or armed bands including mercenaries, for incursion into the territory of another State. Every State has the duty to refrain from organizing, instigating, assisting or participating in acts of civil strife or terrorist acts in another State or acquiescing in organized activities within its territory directed towards the commission of such acts, when the acts referred to in the present paragraph involve a threat or use of force.

The territory of a State shall not be the object of military occupation resulting from the use of force in contravention of the provisions of the Charter. The territory of a State shall not be the object of acquisition by another State resulting from the threat or use of force. No territorial acquisition resulting from the threat or use of force shall be recognized as legal. ⋯

……

All States shall comply in good faith with their obligations under the generally recognized principles and rules of international law with respect to the maintenance of international peace and security, and shall endeavor to make the United Nations security system based on the Charter more effective.

Nothing in the foregoing paragraphs shall be construed as enlarging or diminishing in any way the scope of the provisions of the Charter concerning cases in which the use of force is lawful.

(2) The principle that States shall settle their international disputes by peaceful means in such a manner that international peace and security and justice are not endangered

Every State shall settle its international disputes with other States by peaceful means in such a manner that international peace and security and justice are not endangered.

States shall accordingly seek early and just settlement of their international disputes by negotiation, inquiry, mediation, conciliation, arbitration, judicial settlement, resort to regional agencies or arrangements or other peaceful means of their choice. In seeking such a settlement the parties shall agree upon such peaceful means as may be appropriate to the circumstances and nature of the dispute.

The parties to a dispute have the duty, in the event of failure to reach a solution by any one of the above peaceful means, to continue to seek a settlement of the dispute by other peaceful means agreed upon by them.

States parties to an international dispute, as well as other States shall refrain from any action which may aggravate the Situation so as to endanger the maintenance of international peace and security, and shall act in accordance with the purposes and principles of the United Nations.

International disputes shall be settled on the basis of the Sovereign equality of States and in accordance with the Principle of free choice of means. Recourse to, or acceptance of, a settlement procedure freely agreed to by States with regard to existing or future disputes to which they are parties shall not be regarded as incompatible with sovereign equality.

Nothing in the foregoing paragraphs prejudices or derogates from the applicable provisions of the Charter, in particular those relating to the pacific settlement of international disputes.

(3) The principle concerning the duty not to intervene in matters within the domestic jurisdiction of any State, in accordance with the Charter

No State or group of States has the right to intervene, directly or indirectly, for any reason whatever, in the internal or external affairs of any other State.

Consequently, armed intervention and all other forms of interference or attempted threats against the personality of the State or against its political, economic and cultural elements, are in violation of international law.

No State may use or encourage the use of economic political or any other type of measures to coerce another State in order to obtain from it the subordination of the exercise of its sovereign rights and to secure from it advantages of any kind. Also, no State shall organize, assist, foment, finance, incite or tolerate subversive, terrorist or armed activities directed towards the violent overthrow of the regime of another State, or interfere in civil strife in another State.

(4) The duty of States to co-operate with one another in accordance with the Charter

States have the duty to co-operate with one another, irrespective of the differences in their political, economic and social systems, in the various spheres of international relations, in order to maintain international peace and security and to promote international economic stability and progress, the general welfare of nations and international co-operation free from discrimination based on such differences.

To this end: (a) States shall co-operate with other States in the maintenance of international peace and security; (b) States shall co-operate in the promotion of universal respect for, and observance of, human rights and fundamental freedoms for all, and in the elimination of all forms of racial discrimination and all forms of religious intolerance; (c) States shall conduct their international relations in the economic, social, cultural, technical and trade fields in accordance with the principles of sovereign equality and non-intervention; (d) States Members of the United Nations have the duty to take joint and separate action in co-operation with the United Nations in accordance with the relevant provisions of the Charter.

States should co-operate in the economic, social and cultural fields as well as in the field of science and technology and for the promotion of international cultural and educational progress. States should co-operate in the promotion of economic growth throughout the world, especially that of the developing countries.

(5) The principle of equal rights and self-determination of peoples

By virtue of the principle of equal rights and self-determination of peoples enshrined in the Charter of the United Nations, all peoples have the right freely to determine, without external interference, their political status and to pursue their economic, social and cultural development, and every State has the duty to respect this right in accordance with the provisions of the Charter.

Every State has the duty to promote, through joint and separate action, realization of the principle of equal rights and self-determination of peoples, in accordance with the provisions of the Charter, and to render assistance to the United Nations in carrying out the responsibilities entrusted to it by the Charter regarding the implementation of the principle, in order: (a) To promote friendly relations and co-operation among States; and (b) To bring a speedy end to colonialism, having due regard to the freely expressed will of the peoples concerned; and (c) bearing in mind that subjection of peoples to alien subjugation, domination and exploitation constitutes a violation of the principle, as well as a denial of fundamental human rights, and is contrary to the Charter.

Every State has the duty to promote through joint and separate action universal respect for and observance of human rights and fundamental freedoms in accordance with the Charter.

The establishment of a sovereign and independent State, the free association or integration with an independent State or the emergence into any other political status freely determined by a people constitute modes of implementing the right of self-determination by that people.

Every State has the duty to refrain from any forcible action which deprives peoples referred to above in the elaboration of the present principle of their right to self-determination and freedom and independence. In their actions against, and resistance to, such forcible action in pursuit of the exercise of their right to self-determination, such peoples are entitled to seek and to receive support in accordance with the purposes and principles of the Charter.

The territory of a colony or other Non-Self-Governing Territory has, under the Charter, a status separate and distinct from the territory of the State administering it; and such separate and distinct status under the Charter shall exist until the people of the colony or Non-Self-Governing Territory have exercised their right of self-determination in accordance with the Charter, and particularly its purposes and principles.

Nothing in the foregoing paragraphs shall be construed as authorizing or encouraging any action which would dismember or impair, totally or in part, the territorial integrity or political unity of sovereign and independent States conducting themselves in compliance with the principle of equal rights and self-determination of peoples as described above and thus possessed of a government representing the whole people belonging to the territory without distinction as to race, creed or colour.

Every State shall refrain from any action aimed at the partial or total disruption of the national unity and territorial integrity of any other State or country.

(6) The principle of sovereign equality of States

All States enjoy sovereign equality. They have equal rights and duties and are equal members of the international community, notwithstanding differences of an economic, social, political or other nature.

In particular, sovereign equality includes the following elements: (a) States are judicially equal; (b) Each State enjoys the rights inherent in full sovereignty; (c) Each State has the duty to respect the personality of other States; (d) The territorial integrity and political independence of the State are inviolable; (e) Each State has the right freely to choose and develop its political, social, economic and cultural systems; (f) Each State has the duty to comply fully and in good faith with its international obligations and to live in peace with other States.

(7) The principle that States shall fulfill in good faith the obligations assumed by them in accordance with the Charter

Every State has the duty to fulfill in good faith the obligations assumed by it in accordance with the Charter of the United Nations.

Every State has the duty to fulfill in good faith its obligations under the generally recognized principles and rules of international law.

Every State has the duty to fulfill in good faith its obligations under international agreements valid under the generally recognized principles and rules of international law.

Where obligations arising under international agreements are in conflict with the obligations of Members of the United Nations under the Charter of the United Nations, the obligations under the Charter shall prevail.

2.2 The Five Principles of Peaceful Coexistence

The great idea of the Five Principles of Peaceful Coexistence, which was jointly proposed by China, India and Myanmar back in the 1950s, has been upheld by China ever since. They include: mutual respect for sovereignty and territorial integrity, mutual non-aggression, non-interference in each other's internal affairs, equality and mutual benefit, and peaceful coexistence.

2.3 Second Report on *Jus Cogens* by Dire Tladi, Special Rapporteur[①]

Para. 37 Article 53 (VCLT) sets forth two cumulative criteria for the identification of *jus cogens*. First, the relevant norm must be a norm of general international law. Second, this norm of general international law must be accepted and recognized as having certain characteristics, namely that it is one from which no derogation is permitted and one which can be modified only by a subsequent norm of *jus cogens*. Sévrine Knuchel sees article 53 as comprising three elements, namely, norm of general international law, acceptance and recognition as a norm from which no derogation is permitted and that such norms may only be modified by a subsequent norm of *jus cogens*. Yet, from a definitional perspective, the third element is, first of all, not a criterion but only describes how an existing norm of *jus cogens* can be modified. …

Para. 43 The most obvious manifestation of general international law is customary international law. Indeed many see customary international law as the most common basis for the formation of *jus cogens* norms. Gérard Cahin, for example, observes that customary international law is "a normal and common, if not exclusive, means of formation of *jus cogens* norms". The strong relationship between the rules of customary international law and norms of *jus cogens* is reflected in the Statements by States in the General Assembly over the years. The notion that norms of *jus cogens* are constituted by rules of customary international law is equally borne out in case law of both domestic and international courts. In *Questions Relating to the Obligation to Prosecute or Extradite*, the International Court of Justice recognized the prohibition of torture as "part of customary international law" that "has become a peremptory norm (*jus cogens*)". Similarly, the Court's

---

[①] UN General Assembly, Second Report on *jus cogens* by Dire Tladi, Special Rapporteur, 16 March 2017, A/CN.4/706.

description of "many of the rules of humanitarian law" as constituting "intransgressible principles of international customary law" confirms the idea that *jus cogens* norms—referred to by the Court as "intransgressible principles"—have a customary basis.

2.4 Questions and Assignment

(1) What is the relationship between the general principles and customary as sources of international law?

(2) How to understand the principle that refrains from the threat or use of force?

(3) How to regulate the use of nuclear weapons from the perspective of international law?

(4) Retreat the *Kosovo* case in Part 4 and give a case brief in English in 8-10 minutes.

3. Terminologies and Explanations

3.1 Concept and Characteristics of the Principles of International Law

There are three elements for a general principle: (1) recognized by the international society; recognized by most of the States of the international society; (2) with universal significance, and can be applied to all the fields of international law; (3) constitute the base of international law. The function of the general principle is gap-filling. It could help judges make decisions when the issues in dispute before them were not governed by any treaty or no established rule of customary law could be found to determine them. No system of law can consist solely of specific rules, covering every situation that could possibly arise. Unforeseen cases are bound to be encountered. The distinction between a rule and principle could be seen from Fitzmaurice's expression: "By a principle, or a general principle, as opposed to a rule, even a general rule, of law is meant chiefly something which is not itself a rule, but which underlies a rule, and explains or provides the reason for it. A rule answers the question 'what'; a principle in effect answers the question 'why'."①

3.2　The Principle of Sovereign Equality of States

Equality between States is a natural extension of State sovereignty. There are actually big differences between countries, and there are also significant differences in international influence. But legally, the international personality of sovereign States should be equal, for example, having equal voting rights in international organizations. The principle of equality means equality in law, not equality in fact. What we pursue is a kind of equality in essence. In other words, sovereignty does not mean that countries can do whatever they want. In international relations, no country should seek unilateral privileges and interests in form or substance. Instead, it should seek mutual benefit, mutual respect and common development.

3.3　Non-Intervention of Internal Affairs

The principle of non-interference in the internal affairs of other countries is a universally recognized basic principle of international law. It requires that no country or international organization, under any pretext or in any way, should directly or indirectly interfere in the internal affairs of another country that are essentially within the domestic jurisdiction of any country. Nor shall any State be forced by any means to accept the will of another State, or to maintain or change the social system and ideology of the interfered State.

---

① Gerald Fitzmaurice, The General Principles of International Law Considered from the Standpoint of the Rule of Law, *92 Recueil des cours* (1957).

3.4 The Principle of No Use of Force

It includes not only the prohibition of unlawful armed attacks but also the prohibition of the threat of force and the propaganda of wars of aggression. In the case of specific armed attacks, aggression is the most common. In accordance with this principle, the UN General Assembly adopted the Resolution 3314 (XXIX) — the Definition of Aggression in 1974, which enumerates seven acts of aggression exhaustively. At the same time, it stipulates that the first use of force by a State in violation of the Charter of the United Nations constitutes clear evidence of an act of aggression and shall not be justified by any reason and that an act of aggression gives rise to State responsibility.

3.5 The Principle of Peaceful Settlement of International Disputes

The principle of peaceful settlement of international disputes means that when disputes occur between countries, all countries must settle them peacefully. It is forbidden to resort to force or threat of force in the settlement process of any dispute. There are many ways to settle international disputes peacefully, and relevant countries can freely choose according to the principle of sovereign equality.

3.6 Principle of National Self-determination

The principle of national self-determination means that any oppressed nation or people have the right to get rid of the rulers of foreigners, establish their own nation-State and manage their own affairs by themselves. Any racial discrimination, racial oppression, apartheid or genocide is a violation of international law and the principle of national self-determination and is an internationally wronged act or crime.

4. Cases and Materials

Read the materials and think about the following questions:

(1) Does the international society apply the general principle consistently? Why?

(2) What is your opinion about when principles conflict with each other? Do you think there is a hierarchy between these principles?

(3) Retreat the *Kosovo Case* and find out the statement made by China.

4.1 *Kosovo Case* [①]

On 8 October 2008 (resolution 63/3), the General Assembly decided to ask the Court to render an advisory opinion on the following question: "Is the unilateral declaration of independence by the Provisional Institutions of Self-Government of Kosovo in accordance with international law?"

In its Advisory Opinion delivered on 22 July 2010, the Court concluded that "the declaration of independence of Kosovo adopted on 17 February 2008 did not violate international law". Before reaching this conclusion, the Court first addressed the question of whether it possessed jurisdiction to give the advisory opinion requested by the General Assembly. Having established that it did have jurisdiction to render the advisory opinion requested, the Court examined the question, raised by a number of participants, as to whether it should nevertheless decline to exercise that jurisdiction as a matter of discretion. It concluded that, in light of its jurisprudence, there were "no compelling reasons for it to decline to exercise its jurisdiction" in respect of the request.

With regard to the scope and meaning of the question, the Court ruled

---

[①] Accordance with International Law of the Unilateral Declaration of Independence in Respect of Kosovo, Advisory Opinion, ICJ Reports 2010, p. 403.

that the reference to the "Provisional Institutions of Self-Government of Kosovo" in the question put by the General Assembly did not prevent it from deciding for itself whether the declaration of independence had been promulgated by that body or another entity. It also concluded that it was not required by the question posed to decide whether international law conferred a positive entitlement upon Kosovo to declare independence; rather, it had to determine whether a rule of international law prohibited such a declaration.

The Court first sought to determine whether the declaration of independence was in accordance with general international law. It noted that State practice during the eighteenth, nineteenth and early twentieth centuries "points clearly to the conclusion that international law contained no prohibition of declarations of independence". In particular, the Court concluded: "the scope of the principle of territorial integrity is confined to the sphere of relations between States." It also determined that no general prohibition of declarations of independence could be deduced from Security Council resolutions condemning other declarations of independence, because those declarations of independence had been made in the context of an unlawful use of force or a violation of a *jus cogens* norm. The Court thus concluded that the declaration of independence in respect of Kosovo had not violated general international law.

The Court then considered whether the declaration of independence was in accordance with Security Council resolution 1244 (1999). It concluded that the object and purpose of that resolution "was to establish a temporary, exceptional legal régime which... superseded the Serbian legal order... on an interim basis". It then examined the identity of the authors of the declaration of independence. An analysis of the content and form of the declaration, and of the context in which it was made, led the Court to conclude that its authors were not the Provisional Institutions of Self-Government, but rather persons who "acted together in their capacity as representatives of the people of Kosovo outside the framework of the interim administration". The Court concluded that the declaration of independence did not violate resolution 1244 (1999) for two reasons. First, it emphasized the fact that the two instruments "operate on a different level": resolution 1244 (1999) was silent on the final status of Kosovo, whereas the declaration of independence was an attempt to finally determine that status. Second, it noted that resolution 1244 (1999) imposed only very limited obligations on non-State actors, none of which entailed any prohibition of a declaration of independence. Finally, in view of its conclusion that the declaration of independence did not emanate from the Provisional Institutions of Self-Government of Kosovo, the Court held that its authors were not bound by the Constitutional Framework established under resolution 1244 (1999), and thus that the declaration of independence did not violate that framework.

Consequently, the Court concluded that the adoption of the declaration of independence had not violated any applicable rule of international law. On 9 September 2010, the General Assembly adopted a resolution in which it acknowledged the content of the advisory opinion of the Court rendered in response to its request (resolution 64/298).

4.2 Crimea Voted to Join Russia

Resolution Adopted by the General Assembly on 27 March 2014 [1]

The General Assembly,

Reaffirming the paramount importance of the Charter of the United Nations in the promotion of the rule of law among nations,

Recalling the obligations of all States under Article 2 of the Charter to refrain in their international relations from the threat or use of force against the territorial integrity or political independence of any State, and to settle

---

[1] UN General Assembly, 68/262. Territorial integrity of Ukraine, https://undocs.org/en/A/RES/68/262, last visited on Jan. 8, 2022.

their international disputes by peaceful means,

Recalling also its resolution 2625 (XXV) of 24 October 1970, in which it approved the Declaration on Principles of International Law concerning Friendly Relations and Cooperation among States in accordance with the Charter of the United Nations, and reaffirming the principles contained therein that the territory of a State shall not be the object of acquisition by another State resulting from the threat or use of force, and that any attempt aimed at the partial or total disruption of the national unity and territorial integrity of a State or country or at its political independence is incompatible with the purposes and principles of the Charter,

Recalling further the Final Act of the Conference on Security and Cooperation in Europe, signed in Helsinki on 1 August 1975, the Memorandum on Security Assurances in Connection with Ukraine's Accession to the Treaty on the Non-Proliferation of Nuclear Weapons (Budapest Memorandum) of 5 December 1994,1 the Treaty on Friendship, Cooperation and Partnership between Ukraine and the Russian Federation of 31 May 1997 2 and the Alma-Ata Declaration of 21 December 1991.

Stressing the importance of maintaining the inclusive political dialogue in Ukraine that reflects the diversity of its society and includes representation from all parts of Ukraine,

......

(1) *Affirms* its commitment to the sovereignty, political independence, unity and territorial integrity of Ukraine within its internationally recognized borders;

(2) *Calls upon* all States to desist and refrain from actions aimed at the partial or total disruption of the national unity and territorial integrity of Ukraine, including any attempts to modify Ukraine's borders through the threat or use of force or other unlawful means;

(3) *Urges* all parties to pursue immediately the peaceful resolution of the situation with respect to Ukraine through direct political dialogue, to exercise

restraint, to refrain from unilateral actions and inflammatory rhetoric that may increase tensions and to engage fully with international mediation efforts;

(4) *Welcomes* the efforts of the United Nations, the Organization for Security and Cooperation in Europe and other international and regional organizations to assist Ukraine in protecting the rights of all persons in Ukraine, including the rights of persons belonging to minorities;

(5) *Underscores* that the referendum held in the Autonomous Republic of Crimea and the city of Sevastopol on 16 March 2014, having no validity, cannot form the basis for any alteration of the status of the Autonomous Republic of Crimea or of the city of Sevastopol;

(6) *Calls upon* all States, international organizations and specialized agencies not to recognize any alteration of the status of the Autonomous Republic of Crimea and the city of Sevastopol on the basis of the above-mentioned referendum and to refrain from any action or dealing that might be interpreted as recognizing any such altered status.

5. References and Recommended Reading Materials

(1) Bin Cheng, *General Principles of Law as Applied by International Courts and Tribunals*, Cambridge University Press, 1987.〔英〕郑斌:《国际法院与法庭适用的一般法律原则》,韩秀丽、蔡从燕译,法律出版社 2012 年版。

(2) Hugh Thirlway, *The Sources Of International Law*, 2nd Ed., Oxford University Press, 2019.

(3)〔美〕迈克尔·D. 贝勒斯:《法律的原则——一个规范的分析》,张文显等译,中国大百科全书出版社 1996 年版。

Chapter Ⅴ   The State

1. Introduction

Independent States remain the primary subjects of international law as they occupy the central position in the international community. As the most basic and central subject of international law, it is generally believed that the constituent elements of a State include the government and sovereignty defined by the permanent population. The accepted definition of what constitutes the criteria for Statehood is laid down in Article 1(1) of the *Montevideo Convention on the Rights and Duties of States* (1933) which includes a permanent population, a defined territory, government and capacity to enter into relations with other States.

Recognition is an important system in international law. The so-called recognition refers to a political and legal act that an existing State accepts the emergence of a new State or a new government in certain form. The objects of recognition include the new government, the rebel groups of the national liberation organization and the warring groups. The recognition of the new State is the main one, which is both a political act and a legal act. In practice, according to the specific scope and effect of recognition, it is divided into legal recognition and *de facto* recognition. Inheritance in international law refers to the change of the legal relationship caused by the transfer of international rights and obligations from one international personality to another, which is divided into the subjects of inheritance according to the inheritance of countries, governments, and international organizations, and the inheritance of treaties, national property, national debt, national archives, etc.

2. Preliminary Reading and Assignment

2.1 Montevideo Convention on the Rights and Duties of States (1933)

Article 1 The State as a person of international law should possess the following qualifications: (a) a permanent population; (b) a defined territory; (c) government; and (d) capacity to enter into relations with the other States.

Article 2 The federal State shall constitute a sole person in the eyes of international law.

Article 3 The political existence of the State is independent of recognition by the other States. Even before recognition the State has the right to defend its integrity and independence, to provide for its conservation and prosperity, and consequently to organize itself as it sees fit, to legislate upon its interests, administer its services, and to define the jurisdiction and competence of its courts. The exercise of these rights has no other limitation than the exercise of the rights of other States according to international law.

Article 4 States are juridically equal, enjoy the same rights, and have equal capacity in their exercise. The rights of each one do not depend upon the power which it possesses to assure its exercise, but upon the simple fact of its existence as a person under international law.

Article 6 The recognition of a State merely signifies that the State which recognizes it accepts the personality of the other with all the rights and duties determined by international law. Recognition is unconditional and irrevocable.

Article 9 The jurisdiction of States within the limits of national territory applies to all the inhabitants. Nationals and foreigners are under the same protection of the law and the national authorities and the foreigners may not claim rights other or more extensive than those of the nationals.

Article 10 The primary interest of States is the conservation of peace. Differences of any nature which arise between them should be settled by recognized pacific methods.

2.2 UN Convention on Jurisdictional Immunities of States and Their Property (2004)

Article 3 Privileges and immunities not affected by the present Convention

1. The present Convention is without prejudice to the privileges and immunities enjoyed by a State under international law in relation to the exercise of the functions of:

(*a*) its diplomatic missions, consular posts, special missions, missions to international organizations or delegations to organs of international organizations or to international conferences; and

(*b*) persons connected with them.

2. The present Convention is without prejudice to privileges and immunities accorded under international law to heads of State *ratione personae*.

3. The present Convention is without prejudice to the immunities enjoyed by a State under international law with respect to aircraft or space objects owned or operated by a State.

Article 5 State immunity

A State enjoys immunity, in respect of itself and its property, from the jurisdiction of the courts of another State subject to the provisions of the present Convention.

Article 6 Modalities for giving effect to State immunity

1. A State shall give effect to State immunity under article 5 by refraining from exercising jurisdiction in a proceeding before its courts against another State and to that end shall ensure that its courts determine on their own initiative that the immunity of that other State under article 5 is

respected.

2. A proceeding before a court of a State shall be considered to have been instituted against another State if that other State:

(a) is named as a party to that proceeding; or

(b) is not named as a party to the proceeding but the proceeding in effect seeks to affect the property, rights, interests or activities of that other State

Article 7 Express consent to exercise of jurisdiction

1. A State cannot invoke immunity from jurisdiction in a proceeding before a court of another State with regard to a matter or case if it has expressly consented to the exercise of jurisdiction by the court with regard to the matter or case:

(a) by international agreement;

(b) in a written contract; or

(c) by a declaration before the court or by a written communication in a specific proceeding.

2. Agreement by a State for the application of the law of another State shall not be interpreted as consent to the exercise of jurisdiction by the courts of that other State.

Article 8 Effect of participation in a proceeding before a court

1. A State cannot invoke immunity from jurisdiction in a proceeding before a court of another State if it has:

(a) itself instituted the proceeding; or

(b) intervened in the proceeding or taken any other step relating to the merits. However, if the State satisfies the court that it could not have acquired knowledge of facts on which a claim to immunity can be based until after it took such a step, it can claim immunity based on those facts, provided it does so at the earliest possible moment.

2. A State shall not be considered to have consented to the exercise of jurisdiction by a court of another State if it intervenes in a proceeding or takes any other step for the sole purpose of:

Chapter V The State 139

(a) invoking immunity; or

(b) asserting a right or interest in property at issue in the proceeding.

3. The appearance of a representative of a State before a court of another State as a witness shall not be interpreted as consent by the former State to the exercise of jurisdiction by the court.

4. Failure on the part of a State to enter an appearance in a proceeding before a court of another State shall not be interpreted as consent by the former State to the exercise of jurisdiction by the court.

Article 9 Counterclaims

1. A State instituting a proceeding before a court of another State cannot invoke immunity from the jurisdiction of the court in respect of any counterclaim arising out of the same legal relationship or facts as the principal claim.

2. A State intervening to present a claim in a proceeding before a court of another State cannot invoke immunity from the jurisdiction of the court in respect of any counterclaim arising out of the same legal relationship or facts as the claim presented by the State.

3. A State making a counterclaim in a proceeding instituted against it before a court of another State cannot invoke immunity from the jurisdiction of the court in respect of the principal claim.

Article 10 Commercial transactions

1. If a State engages in a commercial transaction with a foreign natural or juridical person and, by virtue of the applicable rules of private international law, differences relating to the commercial transaction fall within the jurisdiction of a court of another State, the State cannot invoke immunity from that jurisdiction in a proceeding arising out of that commercial transaction.

2. Paragraph 1 does not apply:

(a) in the case of a commercial transaction between States; or

(b) if the parties to the commercial transaction have expressly agreed otherwise.

3. Where a State enterprise or other entity established by a State which has an independent legal personality and is capable of:

(a) suing or being sued; and

(b) acquiring, owning or possessing and disposing of property, including property which that State has authorized it to operate or manage, is involved in a proceeding which relates to a commercial transaction in which that entity is engaged, the immunity from jurisdiction enjoyed by that State shall not be affected.

Article 11　Contracts of employment

1. Unless otherwise agreed between the States concerned, a State cannot invoke immunity from jurisdiction before a court of another State which is otherwise competent in a proceeding which relates to a contract of employment between the State and an individual for work performed or to be performed, in whole or in part, in the territory of that other State.

2. Paragraph 1 does not apply if:

(a) the employee has been recruited to perform particular functions in the exercise of governmental authority;

(b) the employee is: (i) a diplomatic agent, as defined in the Vienna Convention on Diplomatic Relations of 1961; (ii) a consular officer, as defined in the Vienna Convention on Consular Relations of 1963; (iii) a member of the diplomatic staff of a permanent mission to an international organization or of a special mission, or is recruited to represent a State at an international conference; or (iv) any other person enjoying diplomatic immunity;

(c) the subject-matter of the proceeding is the recruitment, renewal of employment or reinStatement of an individual;

(d) the subject-matter of the proceeding is the dismissal or termination of employment of an individual and, as determined by the head of State, the head of Government or the Minister for Foreign Affairs of the employer

State, such a proceeding would interfere with the security interests of that State;

(e) the employee is a national of the employer State at the time when the proceeding is instituted, unless this person has the permanent residence in the State of the forum; or

(f) the employer State and the employee have otherwise agreed in writing, subject to any considerations of public policy conferring on the courts of the State of the forum exclusive jurisdiction by reason of the subject-matter of the proceeding.

Article 18　State immunity from pre-judgment measures of constraint

No pre-judgment measures of constraint, such as attachment or arrest, against property of a State may be taken in connection with a proceeding before a court of another State unless and except to the extent that:

(a) the State has expressly consented to the taking of such measures as indicated: (i) by international agreement; (ii) by an arbitration agreement or in a written contract; or (iii) by a declaration before the court or by a written communication after a dispute between the parties has arisen; or

(b) the State has allocated or earmarked property for the satisfaction of the claim which is the object of that proceeding.

Article 19　State immunity from post-judgment measures of constraint

No post-judgment measures of constraint, such as attachment, arrest or execution, against property of a State may be taken in connection with a proceeding before a court of another State unless and except to the extent that:

(a) the State has expressly consented to the taking of such measures as indicated:(i) by international agreement;(ii) by an arbitration agreement or in a written contract; or (iii) by a declaration before the court or by a written communication after a dispute between the parties has arisen; or

(b) the State has allocated or earmarked property for the satisfaction of the claim which is the object of that proceeding; or

(c) it has been established that the property is specifically in use or intended for use by the State for other than government non-commercial purposes and is in the territory of the State of the forum, provided that post-judgment measures of constraint may only be taken against property that has a connection with the entity against which the proceeding was directed.

Article 20 Effect of consent to jurisdiction to measures of constraint

Where consent to the measures of constraint is required under articles 18 and 19, consent to the exercise of jurisdiction under article 7 shall not imply consent to the taking of measures of constraint.

Article 21 Specific categories of property

1. The following categories, in particular, of property of a State shall not be considered as property specifically in use or intended for use by the State for other than government non-commercial purposes under article 19, subparagraph (c):

(a) property, including any bank account, which is used or intended for use in the performance of the functions of the diplomatic mission of the State or its consular posts, special missions, missions to international organizations or delegations to organs of international organizations or to international conferences;

(b) property of a military character or used or intended for use in the performance of military functions;

(c) property of the central bank or other monetary authority of the State;

(d) property forming part of the cultural heritage of the State or part of its archives and not placed or intended to be placed on sale;

(e) property forming part of an exhibition of objects of scientific, cultural or historical interest and not placed or intended to be placed on sale.

2. Paragraph 1 is without prejudice to article 18 and article 19, subparagraphs (a) and (b).

2.3 Questions and Assignments

(1) What is the essence of sovereignty and jurisdiction? How to understand the relation between sovereignty and State's jurisdiction? Retreat the *Lotus Case* or *Customs Regime between Germany and Austria Case* (Part 4) and make a case brief in English.

(2) Learn about China's practice on the succession of treaties, property and debts after 1949. Give a brief description about the principles and rules in consideration of the cases involving China in this chapter *Morris Case*[①], and other cases you can find, e. g., the more famous *Jackson Case*[②].

3. Terminologies and Explanations

3.1 The Creating of Statehood

A State is a compulsory political organization with a centralized government that maintains a monopoly on the legitimate use of force within a certain geographical territory. The shortest definition of a State for present purposes is perhaps that it is a stable political community supporting a legal order to the exclusion of others in a given area. Under international law, a State is commonly defined as a community that consists of territory and population subject to an organized political authority and such a State is characterized by sovereignty.

As the most basic and main body of international law, it is generally believed that the constituent elements of a State include the permanent population, defined territory, government and capacity to enter into relations with the other States. They are recognized as legal criteria for a State.

---

① *Morris v. People's Republic of China*, 478 F. Supp. 2d 561 (S. D. N. Y. 2007).
② See *Russel Jackson, et al. v. People's Republic of China*, 794 F. 2d 1490 (11th Cir. 1986).

As to the population, defined territory and government, there is no controversy. With respect to the last one, the decisive criterion of Statehood, is more complicate for it relates closely with the State recognition.

Some writers use the term of "independence" to denote the capacity to enter relation with other States.[①] It indicates that in a particular area the State is the sole executive and legislative authority; and, the State must be independent of other State legal orders, and any interference by such legal orders, or by an international agency, must be based on a title of international law. From this interpretation, it could conclude that the independence is of the same meaning with sovereignty. And that is why Chinese international law textbooks list sovereignty as the most important element of a State.

3.2 State Recognition

The recognition in international law refers to the political and legal behavior that the subject of existing international law expresses its acceptance or willingness to develop normal relations with the new government or other situations in a certain way. As to the nature of State recognition, it can be understood from different angles that recognition is a unilateral political act of the State in terms of whether the existing State recognizes the new State. International law does not impose an obligation on States to recognize new States, nor does it give new States the right to be recognized by other States. Whether or not, a State recognizes a new State is a matter within its sovereignty and freely decided by it in accordance with the needs of international relations and foreign policy.

Recognition is a unilateral act, in which the one who accepts it has free discretion. Recognition is not only a legal act but also a political act. The political nature indicates that recognition is an act that is carried out for the

---

① See James Crawford (ed.), *Brownlie's Principles of Public International Law*, 8th Ed., Oxford University Press, 2012, pp. 128-130.

realization of some political benefits and produces expected political effects. There are two legal features of recognition of States and government in international law. While its unilateral character means that a State has discretion whether to act or not and, in making its decision, the State may take into account purely political considerations, this does not mean that its discretionary power is unfettered: a State may not use any discretionary power contrary to the rights of other States. The power might be limited by treaty but in general law, the restrictions arise in two, not wholly distinct ways.

A State is not subject to a duty to recognize another State, if a State recognizes an entity as a State, that act has legal consequences. The recognizing State accepts that relations between them are governed by international law on a State basis. While recognition implies certain substantive legal relations, it does not necessarily imply any particular diplomatic relations. The fact that the decision to recognize a State and the establishment of diplomatic relations are often simultaneous and even dealt with in the same act (sometimes called "diplomatic recognition") should not confuse the position. Recognition is discretionary; establishing diplomatic relations is also discretionary; so, even after one State has recognized another, it does not follow that there must be diplomatic relations or that they should be at any particular level or, once having been established, they may not be modified or terminated. In normal cases, there will be no reason why the establishment of relations should not be coincident with recognition.

The recognition of States is different from the recognition of government. Recognition of government occurs more often than recognition of State. It is possible that two (or more) authorities exist in a single State. In cases where the new government controls most or the vast majority of its national territory, while the old government still controls a small part of the territory, a State's recognition of the new government means that it recognizes the complete demise of the government in respect of its replacement by the new government as a representative of the State. Besides,

State recognition is often associated with territorial changes, whereas government recognition does not generally involve territorial changes.

A State can expressly recognize another State. E. g. , the intention may be expressed in a letter or a note informing the recognized party, such as China's recognition of the provisional government of Algeria. Recognition also can be implied in the following ways: (1) formal establishment of diplomatic relations; (2) establishment of consular relations and issuance of consular certificates, if the existing State formally accepts the consul sent by the new State or sends a consul to the new State; (3) enter into relevant bilateral treaties with new countries or governments, such as treaties of commerce, navigation and friendship; (4) to vote in favor of the admission of that country or that government as a member of an international organization or in its capacity to represent that country. Note that, no recognition is implied from negotiations, unofficial representation, the conclusion of a multilateral treaty to which the unrecognized entity is also a party, admission to an international organization (at least in respect to those not supporting admission), or participation with the entity concerned at an international conference.

There are at least four legal consequences of recognition: (1) Normalize relations between the recognizing and the recognized States or between the governments, end hostilities between the two parties, and establish diplomatic or consular relations; (2) Enable the recognition and the recognized States to conclude treaties and agreements in the political, economic, cultural and other fields; (3) Recognize the effectiveness of the legislative, judicial and administrative powers of the recognized State or government; (4) Recognize the administrative and judicial immunity enjoyed by the State property and conduct of the recognized State, as well as the right to dispose of property abroad.

3.3 State Succession

State succession itself may be briefly defined as the replacement of one

State by another in the responsibility for the international relations of territory. State succession is essentially an umbrella term for a phenomenon occurring upon a factual change in sovereign authority over a particular territory. In many circumstances, it is unclear as to which rights and duties will flow from one authority to another and upon which precise basis. Much will depend upon the circumstances of the particular case, for example, whether what has occurred is a merger of two States to form a new State; the absorption of one State into another, continuing State; a cession of territory from one State to another; secession of part of a State to form a new State; the dissolution or dismemberment of a State to form two or more States; or the establishment of a new State as a result of decolonization. The role of recognition and acquiescence in this process is especially important.

Succession to Treaties Treaties may fall within the following categories: multilateral treaties, including the specific category of treaties concerning international human rights; treaties concerned with territorial definition and regimes; bilateral treaties; and treaties that are treated as "political" in the circumstances.

Succession to State Property One criterion is that there is a link between the transferred State's property and its territory. The two principles are: First, the principle of transfer with the territory, that is, the national property of a country is transferred from the successor State to the successor State with the transfer of territory; Second, the principle of actual survival, that is, the transfer of State property should take into account the actual situation of the inhabitants of the territory to maintain their minimum living conditions.

Succession to State Archives Archives are State property with special characteristics. Article 20 of the 1983 Vienna Convention[①] provides that, "'State archives of the predecessor State' means all documents of whatever

---

① UN, Vienna Convention on Succession of States in respect of State Property, Archives and Debts, done at Vienna on 8 April 1983.

date and kind, produced or received by the predecessor State in the exercise of its functions which, at the date of the succession of States, belonged to the predecessor State according to its internal law and were preserved by it directly or under its control as archives for whatever purpose." While part of the territory of a State is transferred by that State to another State, the State archives for normal administration of the territory concerned, should be at the disposal of the State to which the territory is transferred, if without special agreement. In the case of "newly independent States", the same general provisions apply. Where two or more States unite to form one successor State, the State archives of the former will pass to the latter.

Succession to Public Debt In addition to State consolidation and the succession of newly independent States, the transfer of national debt is generally resolved by agreement and in accordance with the principle of equity.

4. Cases and Materials

Read the following cases in full text and think about the following questions:

(1) What is the co-relationship between sovereignty and jurisdiction?

(2) How to understand the concept of sovereignty in the interdependent international society?

(3) What is China's basic view about the issues of State recognition, immunity and succession?

(4) What is the difference between the *Morris Case* and the *Jackson Case*?

(5) What is your understanding of jurisdiction and immunity?

4.1 *Lotus Case* [①]

Facts in brief On Auguest 2nd, 1926, a collision occurred in the high seas

---

① *Lotus Case (France v. Turkey)*, PCIJ. Ser. A, No. 10 (1927).

between a French vessel and a Turkish vessel. Victims were Turkish nationals and the alleged offender was French. Could Turkey exercise its jurisdiction over this French national under international law? The question was presented before the Permanent Court of International Justice, the judicial branch of the League of Nations, the predecessor of the United Nations. The issue at stake was Turkey's jurisdiction to try Monsieur Demons, the French lieutenant on watch duty at the time of the collision. Since the collision occurred on the high seas, France claimed that the State whose flag the vessel flew had exclusive jurisdiction over the matter. France proffered case law, through which it attempted to show at least State practice in support of its position. However, those cases involved ships that both flew the flag of the same State. The Court, therefore, by a bare majority, rejected France's position stating that there was no rule to that effect in international law. This case established a principle concerning a State's jurisdiction, Lotus Principle. That is, sovereign States may act in any way they wish so long as they do not contravene an explicit prohibition. The application of this principle—an outgrowth of the *Lotus Case*—to future incidents raising the issue of jurisdiction over people on the high seas was changed by article 11 of the Convention on the High Seas (1958). The convention, held in Geneva, laid emphasis on the fact that only the flag State or the State of which the alleged offender had jurisdiction over sailors regarding incidents occurring in high seas.

International law governs relations between independent States. The rules of law binding upon States therefore emanate from their own free will as expressed in conventions or by usages generally accepted as expressing principles of law and established in order to regulate the relations between these co-existing independent communities or with a view to the achievement of common aims. Restrictions upon the independence of States cannot therefore be presumed. Now the first and foremost restriction imposed by international law upon a State is that—failing the existence of a permissive rule to the contrary—it may not exercise its power in any form in the territory of another State. In this sense jurisdiction is certainly territorial; it cannot be exercised by a State outside its territory except by virtue of a permissive rule derived from international custom or from a convention. It does not, however, follow that international law prohibits a State from exercising jurisdiction in its own territory, in respect of any case which relates to acts which have taken place abroad, and in which it cannot rely on some permissive rule of international law.

Such a view would only be tenable if international law contained a general prohibition to States to extend the application of their laws and the jurisdiction of their courts to persons, property and acts outside their territory, and if, as an exception to this general prohibition, it allowed States to do so in certain specific cases. But this is certainly not the case under international law as it stands at present. Far from laying down a general prohibition to the effect that States may not extend the application of their laws and the jurisdiction of their courts to persons, property and acts outside their territory, it leaves them in this respect a wide measure of discretion which is only limited in certain cases by prohibitive rules This discretion left to States by international law explains the great variety of rules which they have been able to adopt without objections or complaints on the part of other States.

4.2 Customs Regime between Germany and Austria [1]

The Court, composed as above, gives the following opinion:

On May 19th 1931, the Council of the League of Nations adopted the following Resolution: (1) The Council of the League of Nations has the honour to request the Permanent Court of International justice to give an advisory opinion, in accordance with Article 14 of the Covenant, on the

---

[1] *Customs Regime Between Germany and Austria*, Advisory Opinion, PCIJ, Ser. A/B, No. 41, (1931).

following question: "Would a regime established between Germany and Austria on the basis and within the limits of the principles laid down by the Protocol of March 19th, 1931, the text of which is annexed to the present request, be compatible with Article 88 of the Treaty of Saint-Germain and with the Protocol No. 1 signed at Geneva on October 4th, 1922?" (2) The Council requests that the Permanent Court will be so good as to treat the present request for an advisory opinion as a matter of urgency. (3) The Secretary-General is authorized to submit the present request to the Court, to give any assistance required in the examination of the question and, if necessary, to take steps to be represented before the Court.

Austria, owing to her geographical position in central Europe and by reason of the profound political changes resulting from the late war, is a sensitive point in the European system. Her existence, as determined by the treaties of peace concluded after the war, is an essential feature of the existing political settlement which has laid down in Europe the consequences of the break-up of the Austro-Hungarian Monarchy.

It was in view of these circumstances that the Treaty of Peace concluded at Saint-Germain on September 10th, 1919, provided as follows:

> "Article 88: The independence of Austria is inalienable otherwise than with the consent of the Council of the League of Nations. Consequently, Austria undertakes in the absence of the consent of the said Council to abstain from any act which might directly or indirectly or by any means whatever compromise her independence, particularly, and until her admission to membership of the League of Nations, by participation in the affairs of another Power."

By a Protocol drawn up at Vienna on March 19th, 1931, Germany and Austria agreed to conclude a treaty with a view to assimilating the tariff and economic policies of the two countries on the basis and principles laid down in that Protocol, thereby resulting in the establishment of a customs union regime.

Accordingly, the Court has not to consider the conditions under which the Austro-German customs union might receive the Council's consent. The only question the Court has to settle is whether, from the point of view of law, Austria could, without the consent of the Council, conclude with Germany the customs union contemplated in the Vienna Protocol of March 19th, 1931, without committing an act which would be incompatible with the obligations she has assumed under the provisions quoted above.

When—as had previously been provided in Article 80 of the Treaty of Peace concluded with Germany on June 28th, 1919—the Treaty of Saint-Germain laid down that the independence of Austria was inalienable, except with the consent of the Council of the League of Nations, that Treaty imposed upon Austria, who in principle has sovereign control over her own independence, an obligation not to alienate that independence, except with the consent of the Council of the League of Nations.

If we consider the general observations at the beginning of the present Opinion concerning Austria's present status, and irrespective of the definition of the independence of States which may be given by legal doctrine or may be adopted in particular instances in the practice of States, the independence of Austria, according to Article 88 of the Treaty of Saint-Germain, must be understood to mean the continued existence of Austria within her present frontiers as a separate State with sole right of decision in all matters economic, political, financial or other with the result that that independence is violated, as soon as there is any violation thereof, either in the economic, political, or any other field, these different aspects of independence being in practice one and indivisible.

If by the regime contemplated by the Austro-German Protocol of 1931 Austria does not alienate her independence, the Council's consent on this matter is obviously not necessary. In the other event, however, it is essential.

By "alienation", as mentioned in Article 88, must be understood any

Chapter V The State   153

voluntary act by the Austrian State which would cause it to lose its independence or which would modify its independence in that its sovereign will would be subordinated to the will of another Power or particular group of Powers, or would even be replaced by such will.

Moreover, the undertaking given by Austria to abstain from "any act which might directly or indirectly or by any means whatever compromise her independence" can only be interpreted to refer to "any act calculated to endanger" that independence, in so far, of course, as can reasonably be foreseen.

In any case, if more is wanted, the "participation in the affairs of another Power" mentioned at the end of Article 88 as an example—which ceased to be of practical application upon Austria's entry into the League of Nations—of an act which might, pending such entry, compromise her independence, cannot possibly be assimilated to an act of alienation.

By the Protocol of Vienna of 1931, the German and Austrian Governments agreed to enter into negotiations for a treaty "to assimilate the tariff and economic policies of their respective countries" on the basis and within the limits of the principles laid down in that Protocol (Preamble).

While declaring that the independence of the two States and full respect for their international engagements are to be completely maintained (Art. 1), both Governments undertook (Art. 2) to agree on a tariff law and customs tariff which are to be put into force simultaneously and concordantly in Germany and Austria and the technical execution of which shall be uniform, although each country will enforce its application by means of its own administration (Art. 5), the customs receipts being apportioned according to a quota to be fixed (Art. 6, No. 2).

As between Germany and Austria, export and import duties are in principle to be removed (Art. 3). There will be, subject to inevitable exceptions necessary for public health and security, no import, export or transit prohibitions (Art. 7, No. 1). As regards exchange of goods between the two countries, the turnover tax and commodities forming the subject of monopolies or excise duties will provisionally be regulated by agreement (Art. 4).

As regards the economic treaty regime, Article 9, while declaring that both Governments retain in principle the right to conclude commercial treaties "on their own behalf", provides on the other hand that the German and Austrian Governments will see that the interests of the other Party are not violated in contravention of the tenor and purpose of the customs union treaty, i. e. the assimilation of the tariff and economic policies of both countries; the negotiations, Article 9 continues, will, as far as possible, be conducted jointly and, notwithstanding that treaties are to be signed and ratified separately, exchanges of ratifications are to be simultaneous (Art. 9, Nos. 2 and 3).

It is not and cannot be denied that the regime thus established certainly fulfils "the requirements of a customs union: uniformity of customs law and customs tariff; unity of the customs frontiers and of the customs territory vis-à-vis third States; freedom from import and export duties in the exchange of goods between the partner States; apportionment of the duties collected according to a fixed quota" (Austrian Memorial, p. 4).

It can scarcely be denied that the establishment of this regime does not in itself constitute an act alienating Austria's independence, for Austria does not thereby cease, within her own frontiers, to be a separate State, with its own government and administration; and, in view, if not of the reciprocity in law, though perhaps not in fact, implied by the projected treaty, at all events of the possibility of denouncing the treaty, it may be said that legally Austria retains the possibility of exercising her independence.

On the other hand, it is difficult to deny that the projected regime of customs union constitutes a "special regime" and that it affords Germany, in relation to Austria, "advantages" which are withheld from third Powers.

Finally, if the regime projected by the Austro-German Protocol of Vienna in 1931 be considered as a whole from the economic standpoint adopted by the Geneva Protocol of 1922, it is difficult to maintain that this regime is not calculated to threaten the economic independence of Austria and that it is, consequently, in accord with the undertakings specifically given by Austria in that Protocol with regard to her economic independence.

The Court, by eight votes to seven, is of opinion that:

A regime established between Germany and Austria, on the basis and within the limits of the principles laid down by the Protocol of March 19th, 1931, would not be compatible with Protocol No. I signed at Geneva on October 4th, 1922.

4.3 Kosovo Case: China's Statement[①]

The Chinese Government, ··· Wishes to make the following written statement:

(1) UN Security Council Resolution 1244 (1999) has been an authoritative basis recognized by the international community for the handling of the issue of Kosovo's status. Security Council resolutions should be complied with. (a) UN Security Council Resolution 1244 (1999) sets out a political solution to the Kosovo issue and explicitly indicates that the goal of the Resolution is to enable Kosovo to "enjoy substantial autonomy within the Federal Republic of Yugoslavia. The Resolution reaffirms, in several places, the commitment to the" sovereignty and territorial integrity of the Federal Republic of Yugoslavia and the other States of the region". This resolution serves as the political and legal basis for handling the issue of Kosovo's status. ···

(2) Respect for State sovereignty and territorial integrity is a

---

[①] Written Statement of the People's Republic of China to the International Court of Justice on the Issue of Kosovo, The Hague, April 16 2009, https://www.icj-cij.org/public/files/case-related/141/15611.pdf, last visited on Jan. 8, 2022.

fundamental principle of international law. ⋯ (d) The Five Principles of Peaceful Coexistence, which were jointly initiated by China, India and Myanmar(formerly Burma) in 1954 and have ever since been consistently upheld, also contain mutual respect for sovereignty and territorial integrity.

(3) The principle of self-determination of peoples has specifically defined contents and scope of application. ⋯ (a) The principle of self-determination became a principle of international law in the course of decolonization movement. It was against such a historical background that the right to self-determination was written into the Charter of the United Nations ⋯ (b) Even after colonial rule ended in the world, the scope of application of the principle of self-determination has not changed. This can be seen in some important documents adopted by the United Nations in recent years. ⋯ (c) In the exercise of the right to self-determination, the territorial integrity of a sovereign State should be respected rather than undermined. A series of important international and regional documents, while affirming the right to self-determination, all provide for respect for State sovereignty and territorial integrity. The above principle is also reflected in State practices.

⋯⋯

4.4 Morris v. People's Republic of China[①]

Background:

These actions represent part of a concerted effort by certain American citizens to collect almost $90 billion from the People's Republic of China for the failure of the PRC to pay the principal and interest on bonds issued in 1913 by the predecessor government of Yuan Shih-Kai. The bondholders have formed the American Bondholders Foundation and are pursuing political,

---

① *Morris v. People's Republic of China*, 478 F. Supp. 2d 561 (S. D. N. Y. 2007). In this case, the Chinese Embassy in Washington, D. C. sent a memorandum to the US Department of State, reaffirming the PRC's position on absolute immunity but the memorandum was not reviewed by the court nor referred to in the judgment.

financial, and legal channels in their efforts to persuade the PRC to negotiate a settlement. Asserting their rights as American citizens, plaintiffs insist that the PRC should be held to account for its economic commitments if it wishes to partake in international financial markets.

......

Finally, in reaction to a United States district court decision rendering a default judgment against the PRC for certain defaulted bonds not including the 1913 bonds (*Jackson v. People's Republic of China*, 550 F. Supp. 869, 1982), the PRC in 1983 sent a diplomatic Aide Memoire to the United States stating that "the Chinese government recognizes no external debts incurred by the defunct Chinese governments and has no obligation to repay them". Plaintiffs now bring suit to enforce the obligations of the 1913 bonds against the PRC.

Discussion:

A. Foreign Sovereign Immunity

Until 1952, the United States held the official view that foreign sovereigns were absolutely immune from suits in the courts of the United States. At that time, the executive branch adopted a restrictive theory of immunity, under which a State would be granted immunity only for its sovereign or public acts. ⋯ This view was codified by the Foreign Sovereign Immunities Act (FSIA) in 1976, now the sole means of obtaining jurisdiction over a foreign sovereign in the United States. 28 U. S. C. §§ 1330, 1602-1611 (2006). Under the FSIA, "a foreign State is presumptively immune from the jurisdiction of United States courts" unless one of the enumerated exceptions apply. ⋯

Plaintiff invokes the "commercial activity" exception to a foreign State's immunity, which provides: A foreign State shall not be immune from the jurisdiction of courts of the United States or of the States in any case... in which the action is based (1) upon a commercial activity carried on in the United States by the foreign State; or (2) upon an act performed in the

United States in connection with a commercial activity of the foreign State elsewhere; or (3) upon an act outside the territory of the United States in connection with a commercial activity of the foreign State elsewhere and that act causes a direct effect in the United States.

In particular, plaintiff contends that the PRC is subject to suit under the third clause. For a foreign State to be subject to jurisdiction under the third clause; the lawsuit must be (1) "based... upon an act outside the territory of the United States"; (2) "that was taken in connection with a commercial activity of (the foreign State) outside this country"; and (3) "that caused a direct effect in the United States."

The parties do not dispute that the first two factors are established. ...

Thus, the only question is whether there was a "direct effect in the United States". In conducting this inquiry, the Court should balance "Congress' goal of opening the courthouse doors 'to those aggrieved by the commercial acts of a foreign sovereign'", with the requirement of "some form of substantial contact with the United States". The Court finds that there was no direct effect in the United States, and thus the PRC is entitled to sovereign immunity.

......

In sum, it is clear that foreign governments could be subject to suit since the issuance of the Tate letter in 1952 and that the commercial activity exception would have been available as a possible basis for jurisdiction regarding claims that pre- and post-date 1952. If plaintiff is correct that no court could entertain his claim against the PRC until it was officially recognized by the United States, then he is still only entitled to tolling into the 1980's. Plaintiff asserts no legitimate basis for tolling after that point. While this suit may have fared no better in the 1980's than it does here, there were certainly courts competent to hear the claim. Therefore, the statute of limitations has expired and plaintiffs claim is time-barred.

Conclusion:

For the foregoing reasons, the PRC's motion to dismiss is granted and Morris's Complaint is dismissed in its entirety. If and when service of process is effected in the action brought by plaintiffs Pons and Soria, both plaintiffs and the PRC may brief the court on why this judgment should or should not be imposed on that case as well.

5. References and Recommended Reading Materials

(1) James Crawford, *The Creation of States in International Law*, 2th Ed., Oxford University Press, 2006.

(2) M. Noortmann, A. Reinisch and C. Ryngaert (eds.), *Non-State Actors in International Law*, Oxford University Press, 2015.

(3) Roland Portmann, *Legal Personality in International Law*, Cambridge University Press, 2010.

Chapter VI   International Organization

1. Introduction

International organizations generally refer to the permanent institutions established by the governments of more than two countries through the conclusion of international treaties to seek cooperation and achieve goals in line with common interests. According to different standards, international organizations can be divided into general international organizations and specialized international organizations, global international organizations and regional international organizations, open international organizations and closed international organizations. An international organization is a subject of international law and has an international legal personality. The United Nations is the most important one among all international organizations.

Therefore, we exert some important articles reflecting its function in Part 2 and a leading case concerning its personality in Part 4. In this chapter, we also briefly explain some concepts involving international organizations, exploring the formation and institutions of an international organization.

2. Preliminary Reading and Assignment

2.1   Charter of the United Nations (UN Charter)

Article 1   The Purposes of the United Nations are:

1. To maintain international peace and security, and to that end: to take effective collective measures for the prevention and removal of threats to the

peace, and for the suppression of acts of aggression or other breaches of the peace, and to bring about by peaceful means, and in conformity with the principles of justice and international law, adjustment or settlement of international disputes or situations which might lead to a breach of the peace;

2. To develop friendly relations among nations based on respect for the principle of equal rights and self-determination of peoples, and to take other appropriate measures to strengthen universal peace;

3. To achieve international co-operation in solving international problems of an economic, social, cultural, or humanitarian character, and in promoting and encouraging respect for human rights and for fundamental freedoms for all without distinction as to race, sex, language, or religion; and

4. To be a center for harmonizing the actions of nations in the attainment of these common ends.

Article 3 The original Members of the United Nations shall be the States which, having participated in the United Nations Conference on International Organization at San Francisco, or having previously signed the Declaration by United Nations of 1 January 1942, sign the present Charter and ratify it in accordance with Article 110.

Article 4 Membership in the United Nations is open to all other peace-loving States which accept the obligations contained in the present Charter and, in the judgment of the Organization, are able and willing to carry out these obligations.

The admission of any such State to membership in the United Nations will be effected by a decision of the General Assembly upon the recommendation of the Security Council.

Article 5 A Member of the United Nations against which preventive or enforcement action has been taken by the Security Council may be suspended from the exercise of the rights and privileges of membership by the General Assembly upon the recommendation of the Security Council. The exercise of these rights and privileges may be restored by the Security Council.

Article 6 A Member of the United Nations which has persistently violated the Principles contained in the present Charter may be expelled from the Organization by the General Assembly upon the recommendation of the Security Council.

Article 7 There are established as principal organs of the United Nations: a General Assembly, a Security Council, an Economic and Social Council, a Trusteeship Council, an International Court of Justice and a Secretariat.

Such subsidiary organs as may be found necessary may be established in accordance with the present Charter.

Article 8 The United Nations shall place no restrictions on the eligibility of men and women to participate in any capacity and under conditions of equality in its principal and subsidiary organs.

Article 10 The General Assembly may discuss any questions or any matters within the scope of the present Charter or relating to the powers and functions of any organs provided for in the present Charter, and, except as provided in Article 12, may make recommendations to the Members of the United Nations or to the Security Council or to both on any such questions or matters.

Article 11 The General Assembly may consider the general principles of co-operation in the maintenance of international peace and security, including the principles governing disarmament and the regulation of armaments, and may make recommendations with regard to such principles to the Members or to the Security Council or to both.

The General Assembly may discuss any questions relating to the maintenance of international peace and security brought before it by any Member of the United Nations, or by the Security Council, or by a State which is not a Member of the United Nations in accordance with Article 35, paragraph 2, and, except as provided in Article 12, may make recommendations with regard to any such questions to the State or States concerned or to the Security Council or to both. Any such question on which action is necessary shall be referred to the Security Council by the General Assembly either before or after discussion.

The General Assembly may call the attention of the Security Council to situations which are likely to endanger international peace and security. ...

Article 12 While the Security Council is exercising in respect of any dispute or situation the functions assigned to it in the present Charter, the General Assembly shall not make any recommendation with regard to that dispute or situation unless the Security Council so requests.

The Secretary-General, with the consent of the Security Council, shall notify the General Assembly at each session of any matters relative to the maintenance of international peace and security which are being dealt with by the Security Council and shall similarly notify the General Assembly, or the Members of the United Nations if the General Assembly is not in session, immediately the Security Council ceases to deal with such matters.

Article 13 The General Assembly shall initiate studies and make recommendations for the purpose of:

a. promoting international co-operation in the political field and encouraging the progressive development of international law and its codification;

b. promoting international co-operation in the economic, social, cultural, educational, and health fields, and assisting in the realization of human rights and fundamental freedoms for all without distinction as to race, sex, language, or religion.

The further responsibilities, functions and powers of the General Assembly with respect to matters mentioned in paragraph 1 (b) above are set forth in Chapters IX and X.

Article 101 The staff shall be appointed by the Secretary-General under regulations established by the General Assembly.

Appropriate staffs shall be permanently assigned to the Economic and

Social Council, the Trusteeship Council, and, as required, to other organs of the United Nations. These staffs shall form a part of the Secretariat.

The paramount consideration in the employment of the staff and in the determination of the conditions of service shall be the necessity of securing the highest standards of efficiency, competence, and integrity. Due regard shall be paid to the importance of recruiting the staff on as wide a geographical basis as possible.

2.2 Discussion and Assignment

(1) What are the principal organs of the United Nations?

(2) How is the General Assembly organized? What are its main functions?

(3) How is the Security Council organized? What are its main functions?

(4) Retreat the Decisions made by the General Assembly and Security Council concerning the Iraq war or Syria war and make an 8-10 minutes presentation based on your understanding or comment about the UN's function to maintain peace and security.

3. Terminologies and Explanations

3.1 Concepts and Characteristics of International Organizations

International organizations generally refer to the permanent institutions established by governmental, non-governmental organizations or individuals in two or more countries through agreements for specific purposes of international cooperation. Article 2(a) of Draft Articles on the Responsibility of International Organizations 2011 provides: "international organization means an organization established by treaty or other instrument governed by international law and possessing its own international legal personality. International organizations may include as members, in addition to States, other entities." Accordingly, international organizations have the following characteristics: (1) international organizations are mainly inter-State organizations; (2) international organizations are established for international cooperation; (3) the creation of international organizations based on agreements between States; (4) the establishment of permanent bodies in international organizations; (5) International organizations have independent legal personality.

An international organization could possess personality if it fulfills the following criteria: (1) a permanent association of States, or other organizations, with lawful objects, equipped with organs; (2) distinction, in terms of legal powers and purposes, between the organization and its member States; and (3) the existence of legal powers exercisable on the international plane and not solely within the national systems of one or more States.

3.2 The Institutions and Functions of International Organizations

Most international organizations have three organs: power and decision-making bodies, executive bodies, administrative agencies. (1) Power and decision-making bodies, usually called plenary meetings of the General Assembly, are attended by representatives of all members. In some organizations, such meetings are composed or attended by heads of State or ministers of member States. E. g., Ministerial Conference in WTO. (2) Executive bodies, usually called "Executive Board" or "Executive Committee". It is composed of representatives of some member States in accordance with the constitution of the organization. It is responsible for the execution and handling of relevant matters. E. g., the General Council of WTO. (3) Administrative agencies, more commonly known as the secretariat, is mainly engaging in contact information exchange among member States internal management, and other general secretariats of daily administrative work in accordance with the relevant articles of association, engage the citizens employed personnel as an international civil servant, do not represent any country, only to accept it as neutral individual instructions, complete assigned by the work, and get paid from the organization. The administrative agency is usually led by a "Director-General" or "Secretary-General".

3.3 Votes in an International Organization

The basic documents of international organizations and the rules of procedure of their organs provide specific provisions on the voting system, including the distribution of the right to vote among members, namely, one vote for one country or more votes for one country; The number of votes cast at the time of adoption of the decision, including a unanimous simple majority, an absolute majority, a specified majority, etc. (1) Unanimity, also known as one country one vote system, requires that a bill be passed by the unanimous consent of all members. (2) Majority consent system, using one vote of one country, requires the bill to be passed by a majority with the consent of a majority of members. (3) The weighted voting system, also known as the multi-vote system of one country, has the characteristics of some joint-stock voting systems and is mainly used for financial and other economic organizations. Each member of the organization is entitled to different voting rights according to the allocation standards stipulated in the articles of association of the organization and votes on this basis. (4) Adopted by consensus. After extensive consultations among member States, a resolution shall be adopted by consensus without voting.

3.4 Members of International Organization

Members of international organizations are generally States but, in certain circumstances, national political entities that are striving for independence, and even an international organization themselves may become members of international organizations. A full member is a member who enjoys all rights and assumes all obligations in an international organization and usually participates in all activities of the organization and has full rights. Full members can be divided into the original members who participated in the establishment of the organization and the included or accessed members after the organization is in operation.

Partial members are those who are not full members of the international organization as a whole and who do not participate in the work of all organs of the international organization but only in the work of one or more organs of the organization, and who become members of a part of the organization. For example, the Palestine Liberation Organization is not a full member of the UN, but is a member of the ESCWA (The United Nations Economic and Social Commission for Western Asia, 联合国西亚经济社会委员会) and UNESCO (United Nations Educational, Scientific and Cultural Organization, 联合国教科文组织).

Contact members or associate members in international organizations have limited rights and limited liability of the members in general. It may attend and participate in discussion meeting organization, but with no right to vote or be elected. Monitors, also known as the consulting member, refers to informal members of an international organization, who shall have the ability and willingness to commit to the work of an organization. While being invited or accepted to participate in the organization's activities, its primary function is to consult but do not enjoy the voting rights and other membership rights.

4. Cases and Materials

Read the cases and materials below and thinki about the following questions:

(1) What is the difference between the international organization and State as the subject of international law?

(2) What is the contribution made by the international organization to

the development of modern international law, e. g. , in global peace keeping, global health protection or international trade?

4.1 *Reparation for Injuries Case*[①]

Background:

As a consequence of the assassination in September 1948, in Jerusalem, of Count Folke Bernadotte, the United Nations Mediator in Palestine, and other members of the United Nations Mission to Palestine, the General Assembly asked the Court whether the United Nations had the capacity to bring an international claim against the State responsible with a view to obtaining reparation for damage caused to the Organization and to the victim. If this question were answered in the affirmative, it was further asked in what manner the action taken by the United Nations could be reconciled with such rights as might be possessed by the State of which the victim was national.

The first question asked of the Court is as follows:

"In the event of an agent of the united nations in the performance of his duties suffering injury in circumstances involving the responsibility of a State, has the United Nations, as an Organization, the capacity to bring an international claim against the responsible *de jure* or *de facto* government with a view to obtaining the reparation due in respect of the damage caused (*a*) to the United Nations, (*b*) to the victim or to persons entitled through him?"

The questions asked of the Court relate to the "capacity to bring an international claim"; accordingly, we must begin by defining what is meant by that capacity, and consider the characteristics of the Organization, so as to determine whether, in general, these characteristics do, or do not, include for the Organization a right to present an international claim.

[①] *Reparation for Injuries suffered in the Service of the United Nations*, Advisory Opinion, ICJ Reports 1949, p. 174.

Competence to bring an international claim is, for those possessing it, the capacity to resort to the customary methods recognized by international law for the establishment, the presentation and the settlement of claims. Among these methods may be mentioned protest, request for an enquiry, negotiation, and request for submission to an arbitral tribunal or to the Court in so far as this may be authorized by the Statute.

This capacity certainly belongs to the State; a State can bring an international claim against another State. Such a claim takes the form of a claim between two political entities, equal in law, similar in form, and both the direct subjects of international law. It is dealt with by means of negotiation, and cannot, in the present State of the law as to international jurisdiction, be submitted to a tribunal, except with the consent of the States concerned.

When the Organization brings a claim against one of its Members, this claim will be presented in the same manner, and regulated by the same procedure. It may, when necessary, be supported by the political means at the disposal of the Organization. In these ways the Organization would find a method for securing the observance of its rights by the Member against which it has a claim.

But, in the international sphere, has the Organization such a nature as involves the capacity to bring an international claim? In order to answer this question, the Court must first enquire whether the Charter has given the Organization such a position that it possesses, in regard to its Members, rights which it is entitled to ask them to respect. In other words, does the Organization possess international personality? This is no doubt a doctrinal expression, which has sometimes given rise to controversy. But it will be used here to mean that if the Organization is recognized as having that personality; it is an entity capable of availing itself of obligations incumbent upon its Members.

To answer this question, which is not settled by the actual terms of the

Charter, we must consider what characteristics it was intended thereby to give to the Organization.

The subjects of law in any legal system are not necessarily identical in their nature or in the extent of their rights, and their nature depends upon the needs of the community. Throughout its history, the development of international law has been influenced by the requirements of international life, and the progressive increase in the collective activities of States has already given rise to instances of action upon the international plane by certain entities which are not States. This development culminated in the establishment in June 1945 of an international organization whose purposes and principles are specified in the Charter of the United Nations. But to achieve these ends the attribution of international personality is indispensable.

The Charter has not been content to make the Organization created by it merely a centre "for harmonizing the actions of nations in the attainment of these common ends" (Article 1, para. 3). It has equipped that center with organs, and has given it special tasks. It has defined the position of the Members in relation to the Organization by requiring them to give it every assistance in any action undertaken by it (Article 2, para. 5), and to accept and carry out the decisions of the Security Council; by authorizing the General Assembly to make recommendations to the Members. …

The next question is whether the sum of the international rights of the Organization comprises the right to bring the kind of international claim described in the Request for this Opinion. That is a claim against a State to obtain reparation in respect of the damage caused by the injury of an agent of the Organization in the course of the performance of his duties. Whereas a State possesses the totality of international rights and duties recognized by international law, the rights and duties of an entity such as the Organization must depend upon its purposes and functions as specified or implied in its constituent documents and developed in practice. The functions of the Organization are of such a character that they could not be effectively

Chapter VI International Organization

discharged if they involved the concurrent action, on the international plane, of fifty-eight or more Foreign Offices, and the Court concludes that the Members have endowed the Organization with capacity to bring international claims when necessitated by the discharge of its functions.

What is the position as regards the claims mentioned in the request for an opinion? Question I is divided into two points. which must be considered in turn.

Question I (a) is as follows: "In the event of an agent of the United Nations in the performance of his duties suffering injury in circumstances involving the responsibility of a State, has the United Nations, as an Organization, the capacity to bring an international claim against the responsible *de jure* or *de facto* government with a view to obtaining the reparation due in respect of the damage caused (a) to the United Nations. ... ?"

The question is concerned solely with the reparation of damage caused to the Organization when one of its agents suffers injury at the same time. It cannot be doubted that the Organization has the capacity to bring an international claim against one of its Members which has caused injury to it by a breach of its international obligations towards it. The damage specified in Question I (a) means exclusively damage caused to the interests of the Organization itself, to its administrative machine, to its property and assets, and to the interests of which it is the guardian. It is clear that the Organization has the capacity to bring a claim for this damage. As the claim is based on the breach of an international obligation on the part of the Member held responsible by the Organization, the Member cannot contend that this obligation is governed by municipal law, and the Organization is justified in giving its claim the character of an international claim.

When the Organization has sustained damage resulting from a breach by a Member of its international obligations, it is impossible to see how it can obtain reparation unless it possesses capacity to bring an international claim.

It cannot be supposed that in such an event all the Members of the Organization, Save the defendant State, must combine to bring a claim against the defendant for the damage suffered by the Organization.

The Court is not called upon to determine the precise extent of the reparation which the Organization would be entitled to recover. It may, however, be said that the measure of the reparation should depend upon the amount of the damage which the Organization has suffered as the result of the wrongful act or omission of the defendant State and should be calculated in accordance with the rules of international law. Amongst other things, this damage would include the reimbursement of any reasonable compensation which the Organization had to pay to its agent or to persons entitled through him. Again, the death or disablement of one of its agents engaged upon a distant mission might involve very considerable expenditure in replacing him. These are mere illustrations, and the Court cannot pretend to forecast all the kinds of damage which the Organization itself might sustain.

Question I (b) is as follows:

"... has the United Nations, as an Organization, the capacity to bring an international claim... in respect of the damage caused... (b) to the victim or to persons entitled through him?"

In dealing with the question of law which arises out of Question I (b), it is unnecessary to repeat the consideration which led to an affirmative answer being given to Question I (a). It can now be assumed that the Organization has the capacity to bring a claim on the international plane, to negotiate, to conclude a special agreement and to prosecute a claim before an international tribunal. The only legal question which remains to be considered is whether, in the course of bringing an international claim of this kind, the Organization can recover "the reparation due in respect of the damage caused... to the victim...".

The traditional rule that diplomatic protection is exercised by the national State does not involve the giving of a negative answer to Question I (b).

In the first place, this rule applies to claims brought by a State. But here we have the different and new case of a claim that would be brought by the organization.

In the second place, even in inter-State relations, there are important exceptions to the rule, for there are cases in which protection may be exercised by a State on behalf of persons not having its nationality.

In the third place, the rule rests on two bases. The first is that the defendant State has broken an obligation towards the national State in respect of its nationals. The second is that only the party to whom an international obligation is due can bring a claim in respect of its breach. This is precisely what happens when the Organization, in bringing a claim for damage suffered by its agent, does so by invoking the breach of an obligation towards itself. Thus, the rule of the nationality of claims affords no reason against recognizing that the Organization has the right to bring a claim for the damage referred to in Question I (b). On the contrary, the principle underlying this rule leads to the recognition of this capacity as belonging to the Organization, when the Organization invokes, as the ground of its claim, a breach of an obligation towards itself.

Nor does the analogy of the traditional rule of diplomatic protection of nationals abroad justify in itself an affirmative reply. It is not possible, by a strained use of the concept of allegiance, to assimilate the legal bond which exists, under Article 100 of the Charter, between the Organization on the one hand, and the Secretary-General and the staff on the other, to the bond of nationality existing between a State and its nationals.

The Court is here faced with a new situation. The questions to which it gives rise can only be solved by realizing that the situation is dominated by the provisions of the Charter considered in the light of the principles of international law.

The question lies within the limits already established; that is to say it presupposes that the injury for which the reparation is demanded arises from a breach of an obligation designed to help an agent of the Organization in the performance of his duties. It is not a case in which the wrongful act or omission would merely constitute a breach of the general obligations of a State concerning the position of aliens; claims made under this head would be within the competence of the national State and not, as a general rule, within that of the Organization.

The Charter does not expressly confer upon the Organization the capacity to include, in its claim for reparation, damage caused to the victim or to persons entitled through him. The Court must therefore begin by enquiring whether the provisions of the Charter concerning the functions of the Organization, and the part played by its agents in the performance of those functions, imply for the Organization power to afford its agents the limited protection that would consist in the bringing of a claim on their behalf for reparation for damage suffered in such circumstances. Under international law, the Organization must be deemed to have those powers which, though not expressly provided in the Charter, are conferred upon it by necessary implication as being essential to the performance of its duties. This principle of law was applied by the Permanent Court of International Justice to the International Labour Organization in its Advisory Opinion No. 13 of July 23rd, 1926 (Series B., No. 13, p. 18), and must be applied to the United Nations.

Having regard to its purposes and functions already referred to, the Organization may find it necessary, and has in fact found it necessary, to entrust its agents with important missions to be performed in disturbed parts of the world. Many missions, from their very nature, involve the agents in unusual dangers to which ordinary persons are not exposed. For the same reason, the injuries suffered by its agents in these circumstances will sometimes have occurred in such a manner that their national State would not be justified in bringing a claim for reparation on the ground of diplomatic protection, or, at any rate, would not feel disposed to do so. Both to ensure the efficient and independent performance of these missions and to afford effective support to its agents, the Organization must provide them with adequate protection.

This need of protection for the agents of the Organization, as a condition of the performance of its functions, has already been realized, and the Preamble to the Resolution of December 3rd, 1948, shows that this was the unanimous view of the General Assembly.

For this purpose, the Members of the Organization have entered into certain undertakings, some of which are in the Charter and others in complementary agreements. The content of these undertakings need not be described here; but the Court must stress the importance of the duty to render to the Organization "every assistance" which is accepted by the Members in Article 2, paragraph 5, of the Charter. It must be noted that the effective working of the Organization—the accomplishment of its task, and the independence and effectiveness of the work of its agents—require that these undertakings should be strictly observed. For that purpose, it is necessary that, when an infringement occurs, the Organization should be able to call upon the responsible State to remedy its default, and, in particular, to obtain from the State reparation for the damage that the default may have caused to its agent.

In order that the agent may perform his duties satisfactorily, he must feel that this protection is assured to him by the Organization, and that he may count on it. To ensure the independence of the agent, and, consequently, the independent action of the Organization itself, it is essential that in performing his duties he need not have to rely on any other protection than that of the Organization (save of course for the more direct and immediate protection due from the State in whose territory he may be). In particular, he should not have to rely on the protection of his own State. If he had to rely on that State, his independence might well be compromised, contrary to the principle applied by Article 100 of the Charter. And lastly, it is essential that—

whether the agent belongs to a powerful or to a weak State; to one more affected or less affected, by the complications of inter national life; to one in sympathy or not in sympathy with the mission of the agent—he should know that in the performance of his duties he is under the protection of the Organization. This assurance is even more necessary when the agent is stateless.

Upon examination of the character of the functions entrusted to the Organization and of the nature of the missions of its agents, it becomes clear that the capacity of the Organization to exercise a measure of functional protection of its agents arises by necessary intendment out of the Charter.

The obligations entered into by States to enable the agents of the Organization to perform their duties are undertaken not in the interest of the agents, but in that of the Organization. When it claims redress for a breach of these obligations, the Organization is invoking its own right, the right that these obligations due to it should be respected. On this ground, it asks for reparation of the injury suffered, for "it is a principle of international law that the breach of an engagement involves an obligation to make reparation in an adequate form"; … In claiming reparation based on the injury suffered by its agent, the Organization does not represent the agent, but is asserting its own right, the right to secure respect for undertakings entered into towards the Organization.

Having regard to the foregoing considerations, and to the undeniable right of the Organization to demand that its Members shall fulfil the obligations entered into by them in the interest of the good working of the Organization, the Court is of the opinion that, in the case of a breach of these obligations, the Organization has the capacity to claim adequate reparation, and that in assessing this reparation it is authorized to include the damage suffered by the victim or by persons entitled through him.

The question remains whether the Organization has "the capacity to bring an international claim against the responsible *de jure* or *de facto* government with a view to obtaining the reparation due in respect of the damage caused (a) to the United Nations, (b) to the victim or to persons entitled through him" when the defendant State is not a member of the Organization.

In considering this aspect of Question 1 (a) and (b), it is necessary to keep in mind the reasons which have the Court to give an affirmative answer to it when the defendant State is a Member of the Organization. It has now been established that the Organization has capacity to bring claims on the international plane, and that it possesses a right of functional protection in respect of its agents. Here again the Court is authorized to assume that the damage suffered involves the responsibility of a State, and it is not called upon to express an opinion upon the various ways in which that responsibility might be engaged. Accordingly the question is whether the Organization has capacity to bring a claim against the defendant State to recover reparation in respect of that damage or whether, on the contrary, the defendant State, not being a member, is justified in raising the objection that the Organization lacks the capacity to bring an international claim. On this point, the Court's opinion is that fifty States, representing the vast majority of the members of the international community, had the power, in conformity with international law, to bring into being an entity possessing objective international personality, and not merely personality recognized by them alone, together with capacity to ring international claims.

Accordingly, the Court arrives at the conclusion that ail affirmative answer should be given to Question I (a) and (b) whether or not the defendant State is a Member of the United Nations.

Question II is as follows:

"In the event of an affirmative reply on point I(b), how is action by the Unite Nations to be reconciled with such rights as may be possessed by the State of which the victim is a national?"

The affirmative reply given by the Court on point I(b) obliges it now to examine Question II. When the victim has a nationality, cases can clearly occur in which the injury suffered by him may engage the interest both of his national State and of the Organization. In such an event, competition between the State's right of diplomatic protection and the Organization's right of functional protection might arise, and this is the only case with which the Court is invited to deal.

In such a case, there is no rule of law which assigns priority to the one or to the other, or which compels either the State or the Organization to refrain from bringing an international claim. The Court sees no reason why the parties concerned should not find solutions inspired by goodwill and common sense, and as between the Organization and its Members it draws attention to their duty to render "every assistance" provided by Article 12, paragraph 5, of the Charter.

Although the bases of the two claims are different, that does not mean that the defendant State can be compelled to pay the reparation due in respect of the damage twice over. International tribunals are already familiar with the problem of a claim in which two or more national States are interested. and they know how to protect the defendant State in such a case.

The risk of competition between the Organization and the national State can be reduced or eliminated either by a general convention or by agreements entered into in each particular case. There is no doubt that in due course a practice will be developed, and it is worthy of note that already certain States whose nationals have been injured in the performance of missions undertaken for the Organization have shown a reasonable and co-operative disposition to find a practical solution.

The question of reconciling action by the organization with the rights of a national State may arise in another way; that is to say, when the agent bears the nationality of the defendant State.

The ordinary practice whereby a State does not exercise protection on behalf of one of its nationals against a State which regards him as its own national, does not constitute a precedent which is relevant here. The action of

Chapter VI   International Organization   179

the Organization is in fact based not upon the nationality of the victim but upon his status as agent of the Organization. Therefore it does not matter whether or not the State to which the claim is addressed regards him as its own national, because the question of nationality is not pertinent to the admissibility of the claim.

In law, therefore, it does not seem that the fact of the possession of the nationality of the defendant State by the agent constitutes any obstacle to a claim brought by the Organization for a breach of obligations towards it occurring in relation to the performance of his mission by that agent.

For these reasons, The Court is of opinion:

On Question I (a):

(i) unanimously: That, in the event of an agent of the United Nations in the performance of his duties suffering injury in circumstances involving the responsibility of a Member State, the United Nations as an Organization has the capacity to bring an international claim against the responsible *de jure* or *de facto* government with a view to obtaining the reparation due in respect of the damage Cause to the United Nations.

(ii) unanimously: That, in the event of an agent of the United Nations in the performance of his duties suffering injury in circumstances involving the responsibility of a State which is not a member, the United Nations as an Organization has the capacity to bring an international claim against the responsible *de jure* or *de facto* government with a view to obtaining the reparation due in respect of the damage caused to the United Nations.

On Question I (b):

(i) by eleven votes against four: That, in the event of an agent of the United Nations in the performance of his duties suffering injury in circumstances involving the responsibility of a Member State, the United Nations as an Organization has the capacity to bring an international claim against the responsible *de jure* or *de facto* government with a view to obtaining the reparation due in respect of the damage caused to the victim or to persons entitled through him.

(ii) by eleven votes against four: That, in the event of an agent of the United Nations in the performance of his duties suffering injury in circumstances involving the responsibility of a State which is not a member, the United Nations as an Organization has the capacity to bring an international claim against the responsible *de jure* or *de facto* government with a view to obtaining the reparation due in respect of the damage caused to the victim or to persons entitled through him.

On Question Ⅱ:

By ten votes against five: When the United Nations as an Organization is bringing a claim for reparation of damage caused to its agent, it can only do so by basing its claim upon a breach of obligations due to itself; respect for this rule will usually prevent a conflict between the action of the United Nations and such rights as the agent's national State may possess, and thus bring about a reconciliation between their claims; moreover, this reconciliation must depend upon considerations applicable to each particular case, and upon agreements to be made between the Organization and individual States, either generally or in each case.

4.2 WHO Constitution

Article 1

The objective of the World Health Organization (hereinafter "the Organization") shall be the attainment by all peoples of the highest possible level of health.

Article 2

In order to achieve its objective, the functions of the Organization shall be:

(a) to act as the directing and co-ordinating authority on international health work;

(b) to establish and maintain effective collaboration with the United

Nations, specialized agencies, governmental health administrations, professional groups and such other organizations as may be deemed appropriate;

(c) to assist Governments, upon request, in strengthening health services;

(d) to furnish appropriate technical assistance and, in emergencies, necessary aid upon the request or acceptance of Governments;

(e) to provide or assist in providing, upon the request of the United Nations, health services and facilities to special groups, such as the peoples of trust territories;

(f) to establish and maintain such administrative and technical services as may be required, including epidemiological and statistical services;

(g) to stimulate and advance work to eradicate epidemic, endemic and other diseases;

(h) to promote, in co-operation with other specialized agencies where necessary, the prevention of accidental injuries;

(i) to promote, in co-operation with other specialized agencies where necessary, the improvement of nutrition, housing, sanitation, recreation, economic or working conditions and other aspects of environmental hygiene;

(j) to promote co-operation among scientific and professional groups which contribute to the advancement of health;

(k) to propose conventions, agreements and regulations, and make recommendations with respect to international health matters and to perform such duties as may be assigned thereby to the Organization and are consistent with its objective;

(l) to promote maternal and child health and welfare and to foster the ability to live harmoniously in a changing total environment;

(m) to foster activities in the field of mental health, especially those affecting the harmony of human relations;

(n) to promote and conduct research in the field of health;

(o) to promote improved standards of teaching and training in the health, medical and related professions;

(p) to study and report on, in co-operation with other specialized agencies where necessary, administrative and social techniques affecting public health and medical care from preventive and curative points of view, including hospital services and social security;

(q) to provide information, counsel and assistance in the field of health;

(r) to assist in developing an informed public opinion among all peoples on matters of health;

(s) to establish and revise as necessary international nomenclatures of diseases, of causes of death and of public health practices;

(t) to standardize diagnostic procedures as necessary;

(u) to develop, establish and promote international standards with respect to food, biological, pharmaceutical and similar products;

(v) generally to take all necessary action to attain the objective of the Organization.

……

4.3 Marrakesh Declaration of 15 April 1994

……

Declaration

1. Ministers salute the historic achievement represented by the conclusion of the Round, which they believe will strengthen the world economy and lead to more trade, investment, employment and income growth throughout the world. In particular, they welcome:

—the stronger and clearer legal framework they have adopted for the conduct of international trade, including a more effective and reliable dispute settlement mechanism,

—the global reduction by 40 per cent of tariffs and wider market-opening agreements on goods, and the increased predictability and security represented by a major expansion in the scope of tariff commitments, and

—the establishment of a multilateral framework of disciplines for trade in services and for the protection of trade-related intellectual property rights, as well as the reinforced multilateral trade provisions in agriculture and in textiles and clothing.

2. Ministers affirm that the establishment of the World Trade Organization (WTO) ushers in a new era of global economic cooperation, reflecting the widespread desire to operate in a fairer and more open multilateral trading system for the benefit and welfare of their peoples. Ministers express their determination to resist protectionist pressures of all kinds. They believe that the trade liberalization and strengthened rules achieved in the Uruguay Round will lead to a progressively more open world trading environment. Ministers undertake, with immediate effect and until the entry into force of the WTO, not to take any trade measures that would undermine or adversely affect the results of the Uruguay Round negotiations or their implementation.

3. Ministers confirm their resolution to strive for greater global coherence of policies in the fields of trade, money and finance, including cooperation between the WTO, the IMF and the World Bank for that purpose.

······

5. Ministers recall that the results of the negotiations embody provisions conferring differential and more favourable treatment for developing economies, including special attention to the particular situation of least-developed countries. Ministers recognize the importance of the implementation of these provisions for the least-developed countries and declare their intention to continue to assist and facilitate the expansion of their trade and investment opportunities. They agree to keep under regular review by the Ministerial Conference and the appropriate organs of the WTO the

impact of the results of the Round on the least-developed countries as well as on the net food-importing developing countries, with a view to fostering positive measures to enable them to achieve their development objectives. Ministers recognize the need for strengthening the capability of the GATT and the WTO to provide increased technical assistance in their areas of competence, and in particular to substantially expand its provision to the least-developed countries.

……

8. With the adoption and signature of the Final Act and the opening for acceptance of the WTO Agreement, Ministers declare the work of the Trade Negotiations Committee to be complete and the Uruguay Round formally concluded.

5. References and Recommended Reading Materials

(1) C. F. Amerasinghe, *Principles of The Institutional Law Of International Organizations*, Cambridge University Press, 2005.

(2) P. Sands and P. Klein (eds.), *Bowett's Law of International Institutions*, 6th Ed., Sweet & Maxwell, 2009.

(3) J. Klabbers, *An Introduction to International Organizations Law*, 3rd Ed., Cambridge University Press, 2015.

(4) José E. Alvarez, *International Organizations as Law-Makers*, Oxford University Press, 2005.〔美〕何塞·E. 阿尔瓦雷斯:《作为造法者的国际组织》,蔡从燕等译,法律出版社 2011 年版。

Chapter Ⅶ Individual

1. Introduction

International law is traditionally a general set of principles, rules and systems with legal binding force to adjust relations between States. In the areas under State jurisdiction, to what extent do States perform their obligations of protection for foreigners and what kind of protection can be exercised by nationals in foreign countries are adjusted by corresponding rules of international law to coordinate conflicts between States in the exercise of such rights and obligations. Based on the principle of sovereign equality, equality and reciprocity, as well as in the context of human rights and humanitarian considerations, the principles, rules and systems of international law concerning individuals have evolved, including nationality, the legal status of aliens, asylum, extradition and refugees.

2. Preliminary Reading and Assignment

2.1 Convention on the Reduction of Statelessness 1961

The Contracting States:

Acting in pursuance of resolution 896 (Ⅸ), adopted by the General Assembly of the United Nations on 4 December 1954, considering it desivable to reduce statelessness by international agreement, have agreed as follows:

Article 1

1. A Contracting State shall grant its nationality to a person born in its

territory who would otherwise be Stateless. Such nationality shall be granted:

(a) at birth, by operation of law, or

(b) upon an application being lodged with the appropriate authority, by or on behalf of the person concerned, in the manner prescribed by the national law. Subject to the provisions of paragraph 2 of this article, no such application may be rejected.

A Contracting State which provides for the grant of its nationality in accordance with subparagraph (b) of this paragraph may also provide for the grant of its nationality by operation of law at such age and subject to such conditions as may be prescribed by the national law.

2. A Contracting State may make the grant of its nationality in accordance with subparagraph (b) of paragraph 1 of this article subject to one or more of the following conditions:

(a) that the application is lodged during a period, fixed by the Contracting State, beginning not later than at the age of eighteen years and ending not earlier than at the age of twenty-one years, so, however, that the person concerned shall be allowed at least one year during which he may himself make the application without having to obtain legal authorization to do so;

(b) that the person concerned has habitually resided in the territory of the Contracting State for such period as may be fixed by that State, not exceeding five years immediately preceding the lodging of the application nor ten years in all;

(c) that the person concerned has neither been convicted of an offence against national security nor has been sentenced to imprisonment for a term of five years or more on a criminal charge;

(d) that the person concerned has always been Stateless.

3. Notwithstanding the provisions of paragraphs 1 (b) and 2 of this article, a child born in wedlock in the territory of a Contracting State, whose

mother has the nationality of that State, shall acquire at birth that nationality if it otherwise would be Stateless.

4. A Contracting State shall grant its nationality to a person who would otherwise be Stateless and who is unable to acquire the nationality of the Contracting State in whose territory he was born because he had passed the age for lodging his application or has not fulfilled the required residence conditions, if the nationality of one of his parents at the time of the person's birth was that of the Contracting State first above mentioned. If his parents did not possess the same nationality at the time of his birth, the question whether the nationality of the person concerned should follow that of the father or that of the mother shall be determined by the national law of such Contracting State. If application for such nationality is required, the application shall be made to the appropriate authority by or on behalf of the applicant in the manner prescribed by the national law. Subject to the provisions of paragraph 5 of this article, such application shall not be refused.

5. The Contracting State may make the grant of its nationality in accordance with the provisions of paragraph 4 of this article subject to one or more of the following conditions:

(a) that the application is lodged before the applicant reaches an age, being not less than twenty-three years, fixed by the Contracting State;

(b) that the person concerned has habitually resided in the territory of the Contracting State for such period immediately preceding the lodging of the application, not exceeding three years, as may be fixed by that State;

(c) that the person concerned has always been Stateless.

Article 5

1. If the law of a Contracting State entails loss of nationality as a consequence of any change in the personal status of a person such as marriage, termination of marriage, legitimation, recognition or adoption, such loss shall be conditional upon possession or acquisition of another nationality.

2. If, under the law of a Contracting State, a child born out of wedlock loses the nationality of that State in consequence of a recognition of affiliation, he shall be given an opportunity to recover that nationality by written application to the appropriate authority, and the conditions governing such application shall not be more rigorous than those laid down in paragraph 2 of article 1 of this Convention.

2.2 Draft Articles on the Expulsion of Aliens[①]

Article 1 Scope

1. The present draft articles apply to the expulsion by a State of aliens present in its territory.

2. The present draft articles do not apply to aliens enjoying privileges and immunities under international law.

Article 2 Use of terms

For the purposes of the present draft articles:

(a) "expulsion" means a formal act or conduct attributable to a State by which an alien is compelled to leave the territory of that State; it does not include extradition to another State, surrender to an international criminal court or tribunal, or the non-admission of an alien to a State;

(b) "alien" means an individual who does not have the nationality of the State in whose territory that individual is present.

Commentary The definition covers both individuals with the nationality of another State and individuals without the nationality of any State, that is, Stateless persons. Based on that definition, it follows that an individual who has the nationality of the State in whose territory the individual is present cannot be considered an alien with regard to that State, even if he or she

---

[①] UN, Draft Articles on the Expulsion of Aliens, adopted by the International Law Commission at its sixty-sixth session, in 2014, https://legal.un.org/ilc/texts/instruments/english/draft_articles/9_12_2014.pdf, last visited on Jan. 8, 2022.

possesses one or more other nationalities, and even if it happens that one of those other nationalities can be considered predominant, in terms of an effective link, vis-à-vis the nationality of the State in whose territory the individual is present. The definition of "alien" for the purposes of the draft articles is without prejudice to the right of a State to accord certain categories of aliens special rights with respect to expulsion by allowing them, under its internal law, to enjoy in that regard a regime similar to or the same as that enjoyed by its nationals. Nonetheless, any individual who does not have the nationality of the State in whose territory that individual is present should be considered an alien for purposes of the draft articles, and his or her expulsion from that territory is subject to the present draft articles.

Article 3　Right of expulsion

A State has the right to expel an alien from its territory. Expulsion shall be in accordance with the present draft articles, without prejudice to other applicable rules of international law, in particular those relating to human rights.

Commentary Among the "other applicable rules of international law" to which a State's exercise of its right to expel aliens is subject and which are not addressed in specific provisions of the draft articles, it is worth mentioning in particular some of the traditional limitations that derive from the rules governing the treatment of aliens, including the prohibitions against arbitrariness, abuse of rights and denial of justice. Other applicable rules also include rules in human rights instruments concerning derogation in times of emergency. It should be emphasized in this connection that most of the obligations of States under these instruments are not absolute in nature, and that derogations are possible in certain emergency situations, for example, where there is a public emergency threatening the life of the nation.

Article 6　Rules relating to the expulsion of refugees

The present draft articles are without prejudice to the rules of international law relating to refugees, as well as to any more favorable rules or practice on refugee protection, and in particular to the following rules:

(a) a State shall not expel a refugee lawfully in its territory save on grounds of national security or public order;

(b) a State shall not expel or return (refouler) a refugee in any manner whatsoever to the frontiers of territories where the person's life or freedom would be threatened on account of his or her race, religion, nationality, membership of a particular social group or political opinion, unless there are reasonable grounds for regarding the person as a danger to the security of the country in which he or she is, or if the person, having been convicted by a final judgement of a particularly serious crime, constitutes a danger to the community of that country.

2.3 Convention Relating to the Status of Refugees and Its Protocol

(1) 1951 Convention[①]

The High Contracting Parties: ···Considering that the grant of asylum may place unduly heavy burdens on certain countries, and that a satisfactory solution of a problem of which the United Nations has recognized the international scope and nature cannot therefore be achieved without international co-operation··· Have agreed as follows:

Article 1 Definition of the Term "Refugee"

A. For the purposes of the present Convention, the term "refugee" shall apply to any person who:

(a) Has been considered a refugee under the Arrangements of 12 May 1926 and 30 June 1928 or under the Conventions of 28 October 1933 and 10 February 1938, the Protocol of 14 September 1939 or the Constitution of the International Refugee Organization;

Decisions of non-eligibility taken by the International Refugee

---

① UNHCR, 1951 Convention Relating to the Status of Refugees, https://www.unhcr.org/3b66c2aa10, last visited on Jan. 8, 2022.

Organization during the period of its activities shall not prevent the status of refugee being accorded to persons who fulfil the conditions of paragraph 2 of this section;

(b) As a result of events occurring before 1 January 1951 and owing to well-founded fear of being persecuted for reasons of race, religion, nationality, membership of a particular social group or political opinion, is outside the country of his nationality and is unable or, owing to such fear, is unwilling to avail himself of the protection of that country; or who, not having a nationality and being outside the country of his former habitual residence as a result of such events, is unable or, owing to such fear, is unwilling to return to it.

In the case of a person who has more than one nationality, the term "the country of his nationality" shall mean each of the countries of which he is a national, and a person shall not be deemed to be lacking the protection of the country of his nationality if, without any valid reason based on well-founded fear, he has not availed himself of the protection of one of the countries of which he is a national. ...

C. This Convention shall cease to apply to any person falling under the terms of section A if:

(a) He has voluntarily re-availed himself of the protection of the country of his nationality; or

(b) Having lost his nationality, he has voluntarily re-acquired it; or

(c) He has acquired a new nationality, and enjoys the protection of the country of his new nationality; or

(d) He has voluntarily re-established himself in the country which he left or outside which he remained owing to fear of persecution; or

(e) He can no longer, because the circumstances in connection with which he has been recognized as a refugee have ceased to exist, continue to refuse to avail himself of the protection of the country of his nationality; Provided that this paragraph shall not apply to a refugee falling under section

A (a) of this article who is able to invoke compelling reasons arising out of previous persecution for refusing to avail himself of the protection of the country of nationality;

(f) Being a person who has no nationality he is, because the circumstances in connexion with which he has been recognized as a refugee have ceased to exist, able to return to the country of his former habitual residence;

Provided that this paragraph shall not apply to a refugee falling under section A (a) of this article who is able to invoke compelling reasons arising out of previous persecution for refusing to return to the country of his former habitual residence.

D. This Convention shall not apply to persons who are at present receiving from organs or agencies of the United Nations other than the United Nations High Commissioner for Refugees protection or assistance.

When such protection or assistance has ceased for any reason, without the position of such persons being definitively settled in accordance with the relevant resolutions adopted by the General Assembly of the United Nations, these persons shall *ipso facto* be entitled to the benefits of this Convention.

……

F. The provisions of this Convention shall not apply to any person with respect to whom there are serious reasons for considering that:

(a) He has committed a crime against peace, a war crime, or a crime against humanity, as defined in the international instruments drawn up to make provision in respect of such crimes;

(b) He has committed a serious non-political crime outside the country of refuge prior to his admission to that country as a refugee;

(c) He has been guilty of acts contrary to the purposes and principles of the United Nations.

Article 32　Expulsion

1. The Contracting States shall not expel a refugee lawfully in their

territory save on grounds of national security or public order.

2. The expulsion of such a refugee shall be only in pursuance of a decision reached in accordance with due process of law. Except where compelling reasons of national security otherwise require, the refugee shall be allowed to submit evidence to clear himself, and to appeal to and be represented for the purpose before competent authority or a person or persons specially designated by the competent authority.

3. The Contracting States shall allow such a refugee a reasonable period within which to seek legal admission into another country. The Contracting States reserve the right to apply during that period such internal measures as they may deem necessary.

Article 33　Prohibition of Expulsion or Return ("Refoulement")

1. No Contracting State shall expel or return ("refouler") a refugee in any manner whatsoever to the frontiers of territories where his life or freedom would be threatened on account of his race, religion, nationality, membership of a particular social group or political opinion.

2. The benefit of the present provision may not, however, be claimed by a refugee whom there are reasonable grounds for regarding as a danger to the security of the country in which he is, or who, having been convicted by a final judgment of a particularly serious crime, constitutes a danger to the community of that country.

(2) *1967 Protocol* [1]

Article 1　General Provision

1. The States Parties to the present Protocol undertake to apply articles 2 to 34 inclusive of the Convention to refugees as hereinafter defined.

---

[1] UNHCR, 1967 Protocol Relating to the Status of Refugees, https://www.unhcr.org/3b66c2aa10, last visited on Jan. 8, 2022. The 1967 Protocol removed the Refugee Convention's temporal and geographical restrictions so that the Convention applied universally. The effect of the Protocol means that the Refugee Convention now applies universally amongst those States which have adopted the Protocol.

2. For the purpose of the present Protocol, the term "refugee" shall, except as regards the application of paragraph 3 of this article, mean any person within the definition of article I of the Convention as if the words "As a result of events occurring before 1 January 1951 and..." "and the words" ..."as a result of such events", in article 1 A (b) were omitted. ...

2.4 Declaration on Territorial Asylum[①]

The General Assembly, Recalling its resolutions 1839 (XVII) of 19 December 1962, 2100 (XX) of 20 December 1965 and 2203 (XXI) of 16 December 1966 concerning a declaration on the right of asylum... Adopts the following Declaration:

......

Mindful of the Universal Declaration of Human Rights, which declares in article 14 that: "1. Everyone has the right to seek and to enjoy in other countries asylum from persecution; 2. This right may not be invoked in the case of prosecutions genuinely arising from non-political crimes or from acts contrary to the purposes and principles of the United Nations."

Recalling also article 13, paragraph 2, of the Universal Declaration of Human Rights, which States: "Everyone has the right to leave any country, including his own, and to return to his country."

Recognizing that the grant of asylum by a State to persons entitled to invoke article 14 of the Universal Declaration of Human Rights is a peaceful and humanitarian act and that, as such, it cannot be regarded as unfriendly by any other State.

Recommends that, without prejudice to existing instruments dealing with asylum and the status of refugees and stateless persons, States should base

---

[①] UN General Assembly, Declaration on Territorial Asylum, 14 December 1967, A/RES/2312 (XXII), https://www.refworld.org/docid/3b00f05a2c.html, last visited on Jan. 8, 2022.

themselves in their practices relating to territorial asylum on the following principles:

Article 1

1. Asylum granted by a State, in the exercise of its sovereignty, to persons entitled to invoke article 14 of the Universal Declaration of Human Rights, including persons struggling against colonialism, shall be respected by all other States.

2. The right to seek and to enjoy asylum may not be invoked by any person with respect to whom there are serious reasons for considering that he has committed a crime against peace, a war crime or a crime against humanity, as defined in the international instruments drawn up to make provision in respect of such crimes.

3. It shall rest with the State granting asylum to evaluate the grounds for the grant of asylum.

Article 3

1. No person referred to in article 1, paragraph 1, shall be subjected to measures such as rejection at the frontier or, if he has already entered the territory in which he seeks asylum, expulsion or compulsory return to any State where he may be subjected to persecution.

2. Exception may be made to the foregoing principle only for overriding reasons of national security or in order to safeguard the population, as in the case of a mass influx of persons.

3. Should a State decide in any case that exception to the principle stated in paragraph 1 of this article would be justified, it shall consider the possibility of granting to the person concerned, under such conditions as it may deem appropriate, an opportunity, whether by way of provisional asylum or otherwise, of going to another State.

2.5 Treaty on Extradition between Canada and US[①]

Article 1

Each Contracting Party agrees to extradite to the other, in the circumstances and subject to the conditions described in this Treaty, persons found in its territory who have been charged with, or convicted of, any of the offenses covered by Article 2 of this Treaty committed within the territory of the other, or outside thereof under the conditions specified in Article 3 (3) of this Treaty.

Article 2

1. Persons shall be delivered up according to the provisions of this Treaty for any of the offenses listed in the Schedule annexed to this Treaty, which is an integral part of this Treaty, provided these offenses are punishable by the laws of both Contracting Parties by a term of imprisonment exceeding one year.

2. Extradition shall also be granted for attempts to commit, or conspiracy to commit or being a party to any of the offenses listed in the annexed Schedule.

3. Extradition shall also be granted for any offense against a federal law of the United States in which one of the offenses listed in the annexed Schedule, or made extraditable by paragraph (2) of this Article, is a substantial element, even if transporting, transportation, the use of the mails or interState facilities are also elements of the specific offense.

Article 3

······

3. When the offense for which extradition has been requested has been committed outside the territory of the requesting State, the executive or other

---

① Treaty on Extradition Between the Government of Canada and the Government of the United States of America, E101323-CTS 1976 No. 3, https://www.treaty-accord.gc.ca/text-texte.aspx?id=101323, last visited on Jan. 8, 2022.

appropriate authority of the requested State shall have the power to grant the extradition if the laws of the requested State provide for jurisdiction over such an offense committed in similar circumstances.

Article 4

1. Extradition shall not be granted in any of the following circumstances:

(a) When the person whose surrender is sought is being proceeded against, or has been tried and discharged or punished in the territory of the requested State for the offense for which his extradition is requested.

(b) When the prosecution for the offense has become barred by lapse of time according to the laws of the requesting State.

(c) When the offense in respect of which extradition is requested is of a political character, or the person whose extradition is requested proves that the extradition request has been made for the purpose of trying or punishing him for an offense of the above-mentioned character. If any question arises as to whether a case comes within the provisions of this subparagraph, the authorities of the Government on which the requisition is made shall decide.

......

Article 8

The determination that extradition should or should not be granted shall be made in accordance with the law of the requested State and the person whose extradition is sought shall have the right to use all remedies and recourses provided by such law.

Article 10

1. Extradition shall be granted only if the evidence be found sufficient, according to the laws of the place where the person sought shall be found, either to justify his committal for trial if the offense of which he is accused had been committed in its territory or to prove that he is the identical person convicted by the courts of the requesting State.

2. The documentary evidence in support of a request for extradition or copies of these documents shall be admitted in evidence in the examination of

the request for extradition when, in the case of a request emanating from Canada, they are authenticated by an officer of the Department of Justice of Canada and are certified by the principal diplomatic or consular officer of the United States in Canada, or when, in the case of a request emanating from the United States, they are authenticated by an officer of the Department of State of the United States and are certified by the principal diplomatic or consular officer of Canada in the United States.

Article 11

1. In case of urgency a Contracting Party may apply for the provisional arrest of the person sought pending the presentation of the request for extradition through the diplomatic channel. Such application shall contain a description of the person sought, an indication of intention to request the extradition of the person sought and a statement of the existence of a warrant or arrest or a judgment of conviction against that person, and such further information, if any, as would be necessary to justify the issue of a warrant of arrest had the offense been committed, or the person sought been convicted, in the territory of the requested State.

2. On receipt of such an application the requested State shall take the necessary steps to secure the arrest of the person claimed.

3. A person arrested shall be set at liberty upon the expiration of forty-five days from the date of his arrest pursuant to such application if a request for his extradition accompanied by the documents specified in Article 9 shall not have been received. This stipulation shall not prevent the institution of proceedings with a view to extraditing the person sought if the request is subsequently received.

2.6 Questions and Assignment

(1) How could an individual acquire a nationality of a State?

(2) What is the connection and difference between the regimes of diplomatic protection and asylum?

(3) What is your understanding of the concept of refugee? Are you in support of the view that those people fled from Middle East because of the war shall be treated as the refugee under 1951 convention? Do you think the refugee crisis in European is inevitable and unresolved? Why? Based on your own understanding of these questions prepare an 8-10 minites presentation in English.

3. Terminologies and Explanations

3.1 Nationality

Nationality is the link between the State and the individual for international law purposes. It refers to the legal qualification of a national or citizen belonging to a country. Nationality is not only the basis for a country to determine a person as its national or citizen and a person's legal status, but also an important basis for a country to exercise jurisdiction.

The acquisition of nationality refers to a person's acquisition of the nationality or citizenship of a certain country. Whether a person has acquired the nationality of a country or not is a domestic matter of that country. There are no general rules in international law for this, and there are mainly two ways to acquire a nationality. The other is the acquisition of national citizenship by naturalization. ICJ in the *Nottebohm Case* (see Part 4.1 below) stated that the State has the capacity to determine who are to be its nationals and this is to be recognized by other States in so far as it is consistent with international law. However, in order for other States to accept this nationality, there has to be a genuine connection between the State and the individual in question.

3.2 Treatment of Foreigner

(1) National Treatment

The treatment given to foreigners is the same as that given to nationals.

That is, under the same conditions, the rights and obligations enjoyed by foreigners and nationals are the same. The meaning of national treatment includes two aspects: First, the treatment given to foreigners by the State is no less than that given to nationals; Second, foreigners should not demand any treatment higher than that of their own citizens.

(2) *Most Favorable National Treatment*

The treatment according to an individual or legal person of a foreign State shall be no less favorable than that accorded to any individual or a legal person of third State in that State now or in the future.

(3) *Reciprocal Treatment*

Countries in accordance with the principle of equality and mutual benefit, each other give equal treatment to the citizens of the other side, such as mutual tax preferences and mutual exemption of entry visa.

(4) *Minimum Standard Treatment*

It is a norm of customary international law which governs the treatment of foreigners by providing for a minimum set of principles that States, regardless of their domestic legislation and practices, must respect when dealing with foreign nationals and their property. It is one of the most important protection standards available to non-domestic investors under international law.

3.3 Extradition

It is the act by one jurisdiction of delivering a person who has been accused of committing a crime in another jurisdiction or has been convicted of a crime in other jurisdiction into the custody of a law enforcement agency of that other jurisdiction. Extradition is usually carried out according to an extradition treaty. States are under no obligation to extradite criminals unless it is according to the obligation of the treaty. If there is no treaty, it is completely according to the sovereign free things to decide whether to extradite criminals. However, even there is a treaty, the State that received the request of extradition still withholds discretion on making a decision.

There are two interesting proceedings on this issue. One is the *Extraordinary Rendition*, which is an extrajudicial procedure in which criminal suspects, generally suspected terrorists or supporters of terrorist organizations, are transferred from one country to another. The procedure differs from extradition as the purpose of the rendition is to extract information from suspects, while extradition is used to return fugitives so that they can stand trial or fulfill their sentence. Another is about the international cooperation on anti-corruption. The United Nations Convention against Corruption requires State parties to the treaty to implement several anti-corruption measures that focus on five main areas: prevention, law enforcement, international cooperation, asset recovery, and technical assistance and information exchange. It may provide a multilateral ground for extradition.

3.4 Asylum

It is a system whereby the State grants political asylum to foreign political prisoners subjected to prosecution or political persecution and refuses to extradite them. Modern international law accepts the practice of territorial asylum, which is based on the country's territorial jurisdiction of every State. As US Immigration Council defines, "Asylum is a protection granted to foreign nationals already in the United States or at the border who meet the international law definition of a refugee." In practice, an asylum seeker must demonstrate that he or she is not barred from asylum for any of the reasons listed in the municipal immigration laws and that the decision-maker should grant asylum as a matter of discretion. It is doubtful whether there is a right of diplomatic asylum that existed in general international law. To provide diplomatic asylum is actually interference or even intervention to the receiving State's affairs. ICJ in the *Asylum Case* emphasized that a decision to grant asylum involves derogation from the sovereignty of the receiving State and constitutes an intervention in matters which are exclusively within the competence of that State.[1]

4. Cases and Materials

Read the following cases and think about the questions:

(1) Could the State enact principles and norms on nationality at wish? Please retreat the full *Nottebohm Case* and find why the Court did not support Liechtenstein's claim. Note the dissent opinion.

(2) Retreat the *Asylum Case* in Chapter Ⅱ and find that on what condition that the ICJ may support a diplomatic asylum.

(3) Making a research on the issue of EU refugee crisis and answer the question: are you in support of enlarging the scope of the concept "refugee" under current convention to provide protection for those displaced persons because of the war and other catastrophes, such as climate change? Why?

4.1 *Nottebohm Case*[2]

Fact:

Friedrich Nottebohm was born at Hamburg on September 16, 1881. He was German by birth, and still possessed German nationality when, in October 1939, he applied for naturalization in Liechtenstein.

In 1905, he moved to Guatemala, where he went into business in trade, banking, and plantations with his brothers. Nottebohm lived in Guatemala until 1943 as a permanent resident without ever acquiring Guatemalan citizenship.

In 1939, Nottebohm again visited Liechtenstein, and on October 9,

---

[1] *See Colombian-Peruvian Asylum Case*, Judgment of November 20th, 1950, ICJ Reports 1950, pp. 266, 274-275.

[2] *Nottebohm Case (Second Phase)*, Judgment of April 6th, ICJ Reports 1955, p. 4.

1939, shortly after World War II began, he applied for citizenship. His application was approved. Under German law, he lost his German citizenship.

In January 1940, he returned to Guatemala on a Liechtenstein passport and informed the local government of his change of nationality. Guatemala soon sided with the Allies and formally declared war on Germany on December 11, 1941. In spite of his Liechtenstein citizenship, the Guatemalan government treated Nottebohm as a German citizen. He was arrested by the Guatemalan government as an enemy alien in 1943, handed over to a US military base, and transferred to the US, where he was interned until 1946. The Guatemalan government confiscated all his property in the country, and the US government also seized his company's assets in the US.

In 1951, the Liechtenstein government, acting on behalf of Nottebohm, brought suit against Guatemala in the International Court of Justice for what it argued was unjust treatment of him and the illegal confiscation of his property. However, the government of Guatemala argued that Nottebohm did not gain Liechtenstein citizenship for the purposes of international law. The court agreed and stopped the case.

Judgment:

......

Since no proof has been adduced that Guatemala has recognized the title to the exercise of protection relied upon by Liechtenstein as being derived from the naturalization which it granted to Nottebohm, the Court must consider whether such an act of granting nationality by Liechtenstein directly entails an obligation on the part of Guatemala to recognize its effect, namely, Liechtenstein's right to exercise its protection. In other words, it must be determined whether that unilateral act by Liechtenstein is one which can be relied upon against Guatemala in regard to the exercise of protection. The Court will deal with this question without considering that of the validity of Nottebohm's naturalization according to the law of Liechtenstein.

It is for Liechtenstein, as it is for every sovereign State, to settle by its own legislation the rules relating to the acquisition of its nationality, and to confer that nationality by naturalization granted by its own organs in accordance with that legislation. It is not necessary to determine whether international law imposes any limitations on its freedom of decision in this domain. Furthermore, nationality has its most immediate, its most far-reaching and, for most people, its only effects within the legal system of the State conferring it. Nationality serves above all to determine that the person upon whom it is conferred enjoys the rights and is bound by the obligations which the law of the State in question grants to or imposes on its nationals. This is implied in the wider concept that nationality is within the domestic jurisdiction of the State.

But the issue which the Court must decide is not one which pertains to the legal system of Liechtenstein. It does not depend on the law or on the decision of Liechtenstein whether that State is entitled to exercise its protection, in the case under consideration. To exercise protection, to apply to the Court, is to place oneself on the plane of international law. It is international law which determines whether a State is entitled to exercise protection and to seise the Court.

The naturalization of Nottebohm was an act performed by Liechtenstein in the exercise of its domestic jurisdiction. The question to be decided is whether that act has the international effect here under consideration.

International practice provides many examples of acts performed by States in the exercise of their domestic jurisdiction which do not necessarily or automatically have international effect, which are not necessarily and automatically binding on other States or which are binding on them only subject to certain conditions…

In the present case it is necessary to determine whether the naturalization conferred on Nottebohm can be successfully invoked against Guatemala, whether, as has already been stated, it can be relied upon as against that

State, so that Liechtenstein is thereby entitled to exercise its protection in favour of Nottebohm against Guatemala.

When one State has conferred its nationality upon an individual and another State has conferred its own nationality on the same person, it may occur that each of these States, considering itself to have acted in the exercise of its domestic jurisdiction ⋯ each State remains within the limits of its domestic jurisdiction.

This situation may arise on the international plane and fall to be considered by international arbitrators or by the courts of a third State. If the arbitrators or the courts of such a State should confine themselves to the view that nationality is exclusively within the domestic jurisdiction of the State, it would be necessary for them to find that they were confronted by two contradictory assertions made by two sovereign States, assertions which they would consequently have to regard as of equal weight, which would oblige them to allow the contradiction to subsist and thus fail to resolve the conflict submitted to them.

In most cases arbitrators ⋯ but rather to determine whether the nationality invoked by the applicant State was one which could be relied upon as against the respondent State, that is to say, whether it entitled the applicant State o exercise protection. International arbitrators, having before them allegations of nationality by the applicant State which were contested by the respondent State, have sought to ascertain whether nationality had been conferred by the applicant State in circumstances such as to give rise to an obligation on the part of the respondent State to recognize the effect of that nationality. In order to decide this question arbitrators have evolved certain principles for determining whether full international effect was to be attributed to the nationality invoked. The same issue is now before the Court: it must be resolved by applying the same principles.

······

International arbitrators have decided in the same way numerous cases of dual nationality, where the question arose with regard to the exercise of protection. They have given their preference to the real and effective nationality, that which accorded with the facts, that based on stronger factual ties between the person concerned and one of the States whose nationality is involved. Different factors are taken into consideration, and their importance will vary from one case to the next: the habitual residence of the individual concerned is an important factor, but there are other factors such as the centre of his interests, his family ties, his participation in public life, attachment shown by him for a given country and inculcated in his children, etc.

……

According to the practice of States, to arbitral and judicial decisions and to the opinions of writers, nationality is a legal bond having as its basis a social fact of attachment, a genuine connection of existence, interests and sentiments, together with the existence of reciprocal rights and duties. It may be said to constitute the juridical expression of the fact that the individual upon whom it is conferred, either directly by the law or as the result of an act of the authorities, is in fact more closely connected with the population of the State conferring nationality than with that of any other State. Conferred by a State, it only entitles that State to exercise protection vis-à-vis another State, if it constitutes a translation into juridical terms of the individual's connection with the State which has made him its national.

Diplomatic protection and protection by means of international judicial proceedings constitute measures for the defence of the rights of the State. As the Permanent Court of International Justice has said and has repeated, "by taking up the case of one of its subjects and by resorting to diplomatic action or international judicial proceedings on his behalf, a State is in reality asserting its own rights-its right to ensure, in the person of its subjects, respect for the rules of international law".

The essential facts are as follows:

At the date when he applied for naturalization Nottebohm had been a German national from the time of his birth. He had always retained his connections with members of his family who had remained in Germany and he had always had business connections with that country. ⋯

He had been settled in Guatemala for 34 years. ⋯

In contrast, his actual connections with Liechtenstein were extremely tenuous. ⋯

Guatemala is under no obligation to recognlize a nationality granted in such circumstances. Liechtenstein consequently is not entitled to extend its protection to Nottebohm vis-à-vis Guatemala and its claim must, for this reason, be held to be inadmissible.

4.2 EU Refugee Crisis: UN Academic Impact [①]

The current refugee crisis is emblematic of Europe's ambivalence and failure to manage forced migrations in the present time. Despite being the cradle of human rights and of the very concept of political asylum, Europe is at the same time dominated by the securitarian logic that currently prevails on a global level. Faced with largest movement of migrants and refugees since World War Ⅱ, Europe has displayed the arbitrariness of its borders, both internal and external.

⋯⋯

⋯The situation that emerges touches upon the very cornerstone of the international system of protection given that a State-centric government system with inherent limitations must interact with a phenomenon such as forced migration, whose very nature transcends the boundaries of individual

---

① See Laura Zanfrini, Europe and the Refugee Crisis: A Challenge to Our Civilization, https://www.un.org/en/academic-impact/europe-and-refugee-crisis-challenge-our-civilization, last visited on Jan. 8, 2022.

countries. Ironically, the desperation which makes it possible to scale walls of barbed wire as well as walls created by laws and regulations, has resulted in a level of cooperation, albeit modest, that until now European countries had not been able to achieve. Finally, Europe is faced with the need to rethink the concept of border which is difficult to reconcile with the idea of universal human equality, one of the fundamental principles on which European civilization is based.

The refugee issue reveals the unavoidable gap between the inclusive logic of universal human rights and the nation State's prerogative to exclude undesirables. Indeed, as a result of a unilateral process of definition by the countries of destination, the figure of the refugee is emblematic of the contradiction of a State-centric system in response to the demands for justice and belonging in the current global society, and demonstrates the limitations of our systems for protecting the poor and vulnerable, based on the fiction of national societies delimited by national fences.

Entering more deeply in the discussion, and beyond the contrasts dividing countries, the events of these last months have revealed the main weaknesses of the European approach in this matter:

First of all, having reduced border management to a technocratic task, measured in terms of economic costs and efficiency, as is clearly demonstrated by the crude bookkeeping approach regarding expulsions whose increase is hailed as a success, Europe has discovered that it lacks convincing, persuasive and ethically based criteria for distinguishing between authentic and fictitious refugees.

At the same time, Europe has sought to contain migrant arrivals through the questionable practice of outsourcing boundaries. The need to restrain migration flows and reduce the number of refugee/asylum applications, including through agreements with countries defined as secure (that signed with Turkey is only the last in a long series), has definitely prevailed over the actual management of migratory fluxes. As a consequence, Europe has discovered that it lacks those instruments, such as humanitarian channels, which would have made it possible to manage the emergency in a way that would have been more in line with the principle of inalienable human dignity.

......

Within the current framework of human mobility the distinction between economic and humanitarian migration is increasingly shaky and uncertain, and sometimes openly questioned by those who believe in the existence of a universal right to migrate (founded on the principles of freedom of movement, the equality of all human beings, or the right to go abroad in search of dignified life conditions whenever they are not guaranteed in one's home country).

Obviously this distinction cannot be based on shallow criteria such as the country of origin, or on the prototype of the refugee as defined in the 1951 Geneva Convention, for example as a political dissident persecuted by the authorities of his own country. Today, forced migration has a collective, not individual, configuration and reflects a shared need to flee from situations of crisis whose consequences and evolution are unpredictable. The threat from which one may flee is not necessarily the State, but may be non-state actors or even family members.

The fear of persecution is not limited to imprisonment, but can include a wide range of human rights violations, including the fear of being subjected to sterilization or excision, violations of the rights of homosexuals and survival jeopardized by environmental catastrophes to name only a few. In addition, fleeing migrants do not necessarily reach a foreign territory, but often end up in one of the many overcrowded refugee camps for internally displaced persons, in locations where many of them will also end up living for years in some sort of captivity that is the very antithesis of the yearning for freedom that had once marked the journey of people migrating for humanitarian reasons. Migration is sometimes not only forced, but even compulsory, achieved through various forms of trafficking and enslavement. Finally, protection systems have been built in compliance with a male archetype, although we are now aware that the paths of forced migrants are deeply gendered, a condition that makes them inadequate to meet the needs and the specific risks posed to female migrants.

......

Immigration is a phenomenon which, by definition, challenges the borders of a community; not only the physical and political boundaries, but also those which define its identity, hence putting into question principles and values upon which a society is based, both those shaped by a shared history and those imposed by nationalistic myths. It is consequently almost inevitable that when this phenomenon appears on such a large scale and with such an unpredictable evolution, it engenders alarmist reactions. These reactions have led to various attempts to select immigrants based on arbitrary criteria. For example, there is strong pressure in several EU countries to consider the cultural and religious backgrounds of asylum applicants and migrants and favor Christian over Muslim immigrants, despite the fact that the proposal to mention the Christian roots of Europe in the EU constitution was rejected. Applying religion as a selection criterion also risks undermining the very principles on which the EU was founded, namely universalism and the dignity of all human beings. The inclusion of education and skill levels as criteria for entry has reintroduced a class-based element to membership, and while choosing more educated and skilled refugees helps with their insertion in the labor market, it is discriminatory. The consideration of country of origin under the euphemism of merit is ambiguous and could undermine protection of migrants coming from certain countries.

The application of these arbitrary criteria attempt to present immigrants as advantageous to the receiving community and mitigate fears that the new arrivals will irreparably change the features on which the process of nation building was based. In this light, we can also understand why the young

East-European democracies, fresh from a history of forced relocations and ethnic cleansings and the difficult shift to the post-communist era, are reluctant to open their frontiers to ethnic and religious minorities of whom they have no direct experience, but only a knowledge influenced by alarmist declarations and the fear of terrorism.

Given that a shared collective identity is a basic element of each political community, the problem lies, in fact, in the reluctance to include new members when a community feels it is in danger of losing its identity. However, we should not forget that it is precisely the most profound identity of Europe, the one which generated the principle of individual dignity and the idea of an institutionalized solidarity, which would be in danger of disappearing should we decide to abdicate the fundamental principles of our civilization or if the call to defend ourselves against migrants and refugees prevails over our desire to welcome them.

Finally, policies for the granting of asylum and other forms of humanitarian protection represent a conscious way of affirming principles, values and worldviews. Policies addressing humanitarian migrations, which today are often subject to security and budgetary pressures, should be an opportunity for societies to reflect on the values on which they are based and deserve to be handed down as a legacy to future generations. It is with this awareness that European societies must deal with the most severe refugee and migration crisis since World War Ⅱ.

4.3 Climate Refugees: the Landmark Case of *Teitiota v. New Zealand* [1]

Factin brief:

In 2013, Ioane Teitiota (the claimant) and his family left their home on

---

[1] *Ioane Teitiota v. New Zealand*, CCPR/C/127/D/2728/2016, UN Human Rights Committee (HRC), 7 January 2020, https://www.refworld.org/cases,HRC,5e26f7134.html, last visited on Jan. 8, 2022.

the small atoll of Tarawa, part of the Pacific nation of Kiribati, for New Zealand, where they applied for refugee status on the basis that climate change had devastated Kiribati so much so that remaining there posed a risk to their lives.

In 2015, Ioane Teitiota's asylum application in New Zealand was denied, and he was deported with his wife and children to his home country of Kiribati. He filed a complaint to the UN Human Rights Committee, arguing that by deporting him, New Zealand had violated his right to life. Mr. Teitiota argued that the rise in sea level and other effects of climate change had rendered Kiribati uninhabitable for all its residents. Violent land disputes occurred because habitable land was becoming increasingly scarce. Environmental degradation made subsistence farming difficult, and the freshwater supply was contaminated by salt water.

UN Human Rights Committee (HRC)'s Views[①]

2.10 The author also provided a copy of the decision of the Supreme Court, which denied the author's appeal of the decision of the Tribunal on 20 July 2015. The Court considered, *inter alia*, that while the Republic of Kiribati undoubtedly faced challenges, the author would not, if returned there, face serious harm. Moreover, there was no evidence that the Government of the Republic of Kiribati was failing to take steps to protect its citizens from the effects of environmental degradation to the extent that it could. The Supreme Court was also not persuaded that there was any risk that a substantial miscarriage of justice had occurred. Nevertheless, the Court did not rule out the possibility that environmental degradation resulting from climate change or other natural disasters could "create a pathway into the Refugee Convention or other protected person jurisdiction".

---

① UN Human Rights Committee, Views adopted by the Committee under article 5 (4) of the Optional Protocol, concerning communication No. 2728/2016, CCPR/C/127/D/2728/2016, adopted by the Committee at its 127th session (14 October-8 November 2019).

9.12 In the present case, the Committee accepts the author's claim that sea level rise is likely to render the Republic of Kiribati uninhabitable. However, it notes that the timeframe of 10 to 15 years, as suggested by the author, could allow for intervening acts by the Republic of Kiribati, with the assistance of the international community, to take affirmative measures to protect and, where necessary, relocate its population. The Committee notes that the State party's authorities thoroughly examined this issue and found that the Republic of Kiribati was taking adaptive measures to reduce existing vulnerabilities and build resilience to climate change-related harms. Based on the information made available to it, the Committee is not in a position to conclude that the assessment of the domestic authorities that the measures by taken by the Republic of Kiribati would suffice to protect the author's right to life under article 6 of the Covenant was clearly arbitrary or erroneous in this regard, or amounted to a denial of justice.

9.13 In the light of these findings, the Committee considers that the State party's courts provided the author with an individualized assessment of his need for protection and took note of all of the elements provided by the author when evaluating the risk he faced when the State party removed him to the Republic of Kiribati in 2015, including the prevailing conditions in Kiribati, the foreseen risks to the author and the other inhabitants of the islands, the time left for the Kiribati authorities and the international community to intervene and the efforts already underway to address the very serious situation of the islands. The Committee considers that while the author disagrees with the factual conclusions of the State party, the information made available to it does not demonstrate that the conduct of the judicial proceedings in the author's case was clearly arbitrary or amounted to a manifest error or denial of justice, or that the courts otherwise violated their obligation of independence and impartiality.

9.14 Without prejudice to the continuing responsibility of the State party to take into account in future deportation cases the situation at the time in the Republic of Kiribati and new and updated data on the effects of climate change and rising sea-levels thereupon, the Committee is not in a position to hold that the author's rights under article 6 of the Covenant were violated upon his deportation to the Republic of Kiribati in 2015.

10. The Human Rights Committee, acting under article 5 (4) of the Optional Protocol, is of the view that the facts before it do not permit it to conclude that the author's removal to the Republic of Kiribati violated his rights under article 6 (1) of the Covenant (International Covenant on Civil and Political Rights).

5. References and Recommended Reading Materials

(1) Erika Feller, *et al.*, *Refugee Protection in International Law: UNHCR's Global Consultations on International Protection*, Cambridge University Press, 2003.

(2) Thomas Gammeltoft-Hansen, *Access to Asylum: International Refugee Law and The Globalization of Migration Control*, Cambridge University Press, 2011.

(3) Rafiqul Islam and Jahid Hossain Bhuiyan (eds.), *An Introduction to International Refugee Law*, Martinus Nijhoff, 2013.

(4) Eric Fripp, *Nationality and Statelessness in the International Law of Refugee Status*, Hart Publishing, 2016.

Chapter Ⅷ Territory

1. Introduction

The concept of territory plays a central role in the international law scheme. It is generally accepted that international law is based on the concept of the State. The territory is the basic characteristic of a State. There is no State without territory.① A famous scholar gave a concise summarizing: "at the basis of international law lays the notion that a State occupies a definite part of the surface of the earth, within which it normally exercises, subject to the limitations imposed by international law, jurisdiction over persons and things to the exclusion of the jurisdiction of other States."② Since fundamental legal concepts as sovereignty and jurisdiction can only be comprehended in relation to territory, it follows that the legal nature of territory becomes a vital part of the study of international law. There are four regimes: territorial sovereignty, territory not subject to the sovereignty of any State or States and which possesses a status of its own, *res nullius*, and *res communis*, under which the States co-exist in spatial.

To better understand the essence of the concept of territory, Part 2 introduces some extracts from two classic works and a historical landmark case about territorial conflict. Part 3 makes brief explanations about the

---

① See Robert Jennings and Arthur Watts (eds.), *Oppenheim's International Law*, 9th Ed., Longman, 1996, p. 563.
② Andrew Clapham (ed.), *Brierly's Law of Nations: An Introduction to the Role of International Law in International Relations*, 7th Ed., Oxford University Press, 2012, p. 168.

concept of territory and some relevant concepts about the acquiring of territory. Part 4, focusing on the territorial dispute involving China, includes some important statements made by China on those disputes.

2. Preliminary Reading and Assignment

2.1 Territory as a Political Technology[①]

The idea of a territory as a bounded space under the control of a group of people, usually a State, is therefore historically produced. Other ways of organizing the relation between place and power have existed, were combined in diverse ways, labeled with multiple terms, argued for and against, and understood differently. Some of these ideas were reappropriated, rearranged, and revised by later thinkers. Others were abandoned along the way. Nonetheless, the notion of space that emerges in the scientific revolution is defined by extension.

Territory can be understood as the political counterpart to this notion of calculating space, and can therefore be thought of as the extension of the State's power. Equally the State in this modern form extends across Europe and from there across the globe. Therefore, from around this time we are justified in talking of the extension of the State—in this plural sense.

If the modern concept of territory is established by this time, this is not to suggest that future developments are unimportant. Far from it. Yet we should understand in what ways they are important. There are, of course, fundamental changes to particular territories, and debates about its understanding, how other political-theoretical concepts such as justice and rights apply to it, but the concept seems to be in place by then. This may partly explain the relatively unproblematic way in which the term is used and

---

① See Stuart Elden, *The Birth of Territory*, Chicago University Press, 2013, pp. 322-330.

Chapter VIII Territory 217

implicitly understood in mainstream political and geographical discussions.

Nonetheless, the historical-conceptual analysis offered here should not simply be used to support that mainstream view of territory. Territory should be understood as a political technology, or perhaps better as a bundle of political technologies. Territory is not simply land, in the political economic sense of rights of use, appropriation, and possession attached to a place; nor is it a narrowly political-strategic question that is closer to a notion of terrain. Territory comprises techniques for measuring land and controlling terrain. Measure and control—the technical and the legal—need to be thought alongside land and terrain. What is crucial in this designation is the attempt to keep the question of territory open. Understanding territory as a political technology is not to define territory once and for all; rather, it is to indicate the issues at stake in grasping how it was understood in different historical and geographical contexts.

……

Given the historical parameters of this study, the concept of the nation and the ideology of nationalism are outside its bounds. Yet it is perhaps worth underscoring that the relation between the nation and the State takes place within the spatial framework that the concept of territory produces. As Fulbrook[1] puts it: "Historically, the formation of States with a centralised government administering and controlling a clearly defined geographical territory preceded the articulation of ideas of the nation." The qualifiation to Fulbrook's point is that it was the idea of the State and territory that preceded the nation; in practice it was much more complicated and geographically variegated.

It is clear that the treaties of Westphalia and the others from the second

---

[1] Mary Jean Alexandra Fulbrook is a British academic and historian, a noted researcher in a wide range of fields, including religion and society in early modern Europe, the German dictatorships of the 20th century, Europe after the Holocaust, and historiography and social theory.

half of the 17th century did not introduce a uniform, and universally recognized, system. States, such as France, whose territory was already well established, embarked on projects of nation building within those existing borders. Breuilly notes that one of the issues behind the revolutionary wars of the late 18th century was the sovereignty of various enclaves within France that had some allegiance to the Holy Roman Empire. "The modern conception of France as a tightly bounded space within which the French State was sovereign was opposed to an older conception of power as varying bundles of privileges related to different groups and territories." Similar things happened within England somewhat earlier and the Scandinavian countries at a similar time.

Other national groups sought to create a State to represent them within defined geographical areas. These would include those like the Italian and German unification projects in the 19th century, as well as a host of independence movements across the world in the 20th and 21st centuries. While the boundaries of States in Europe continue to be an issue today—1945 was important in securing Western borders, but 1989 opened up a whole range of issues in Central and Eastern Europe—in this earlier period many of the borders were still porous and ill defined, and sovereignty was overlapping. Germany had many internal boundary disputes to solve (whether part of a State was in the confederation or not): its external boundaries were more or less secure depending on whom that boundary was with. For example, its boundary with France—"the most modern, boundary-conscious European State"—was "fixed with political administrative precision"; whereas its southern border was simply a line drawn on the map of Austria. In the north, with the disputed province of Schleswig-Holstein, "the 'boundary' dispute arose via the question of 'national sovereignty'". The way this dispute worked out only served to reinforce the notion that nation-State was a territorially sovereign State. "Boundaries came to matter more in this political conception." Breuilly notes that only with the Weimar Republic did Germany actually become a State—under Bismarck it had been a Reich, an empire: "The tragedy was that this State was also the product of defeat—its boundaries were seen as artificial and its constitution as imposed."

2.2 Land-Appropriation as a Constitutive Process of International Law[①]

The latest period of European international law, based on the great land appropriations of the 16th and 17th centuries and now coming to an end, will be discussed fully in the following chapters. The period that preceded it was based on the results of the so-called *Völkerwanderung*（民族迁徙）, which was not so much a migration of peoples as a series of great land-appropriations.

Not every invasion or temporary occupation is a land-appropriation that founds an order. In world history, there have been many acts of force that have destroyed themselves quickly. Thus, every seizure of land is not a *nomos*, although conversely, *nomos*, understood in our sense of the term, always includes a land-based order and orientation. If we add the domain of the sea, then the relation between land and sea determines the spatial order of international law. If the domination of airspace is added as a third dimension, then still other new spatial orders arise. Even then, however, a land-appropriation of the earth's soil remains fundamentally significant. For this reason, our approach to the study of international law based on the concept of land-appropriation still is meaningful.

······

In all ages, all peoples who opened up new spaces and became settled after their wanderings—Greek, Italian, Germanic, Slavic, Magyar, and other clans, tribes, and retinues—effected land-appropriations. The history of colonialism in its entirety is as well a history of spatially determined processes of settlement in which order and orientation are combined. At this origin of

---

① See Carl Schmitt, *The Nomos of the Earth: in the International Law of the Jus Dublicum Europueum*, Telos Press, 2006, pp. 80-83.

land-appropriation, law and order are one; where order and orientation coincide, they cannot be separated. Viewed in terms of legal history, if we disregard the mere acts of violence that quickly destroy themselves, there are two different types of land-appropriations: those that proceed *within* a given order of international law, which readily receive the recognition of other peoples, and *others*, which uproot an existing spatial order and establish a new *nomos* of the whole spatial sphere of neighboring peoples. A land-appropriation occurs with every territorial change. But not every land-appropriation, not every alteration of borders, not every founding of a new colony creates revolutionary change in terms of international law, i.e., is a process that constitutes a new *nomos*. In particular, it depends upon whether there is free land to be had, and whether there are accepted forms for the acquisition of non-free land. For example, Vitoria's doctrine of just war made possible the appropriation of foreign, non-free land. The many conquests, surrenders, occupations, annexations, cessions, and successions in world history either fit into an existing spatial order of international law, or exceed its framework and have a tendency, if they are not just passing acts of brute force, to constitute a new spatial order of international law.

In principle, this typical antithesis of constitutive and constituted easily is understood. The differentiation between constitutive acts and constituted institutions, the juxtaposition of *ordo ordinans*（建构的秩序）and *ordo ordinatus*（order of the ordered）, of *pouvoir constituant*（power to constitute）and *pouvoir constitué*（power to be constituted）, is generally well-known. Yet, jurists of positive law, i.e. of constituted and enacted law, have been accustomed in all times to consider only the given order and the processes that obtain within it. They have in view only the sphere of what has been established firmly, what has been constituted; in particular, only the system of a specific State legality. They are content to reject as "unjuridical" the question of what processes established this order. They find it meaningful to trace all legality back to the constitution, or to the will of the State, which is conceived of as a person. However, they have an immediate answer for the further question regarding the origin of this constitution or the origin of the State; they say it is a mere fact. In times of unproblematic security this has a certain practical rationale, when one considers that modem legality, above all, is the functional mode of a State bureaucracy, which has no interest in the right of its origin, but only in the law of its own functioning. Nevertheless, the theory of constitutive processes and power manifestations that produces constitutions also involves questions of jurisprudence. There are several types of law. There is not only State legality, but also law that precedes the State, law that is external to the State, and law among States. As for international law in particular, in every period of history there are coexisting empires, countries, and peoples that develop multifarious ways of ordering their coexistence, the most important components of which are public and private principles and procedures for territorial changes.

With this consideration of the significance of land-appropriation in international law, we have obtained the possibility of comprehending in terms of legal history and legal philosophy the basic event in the history of European international law—the land-appropriation of a new world.

2.3 *Island of Palmas case* [1]

(1) *Fact and Law at Issue*

At issue in Island of Palmas1 was the sovereignty over a miniscule island called the Island of Palmas, or the Island of Miangas, in the north of the archipelago which today constitutes Indonesia. On 21 January 1906, General Leonard Wood, US Governor of the Province of Moro, made landfall on the island, he was dismayed to find there a Dutch flag flying on the shore as well as on the dinghy that came out to greet him. This visit led to the statement

---

[1] *Island of Palmas Case (United States v. The Netherlands)*, Perm. Ct. of Arbitration, 2 U. N. Rep. Int'l Arb. Awards 829 (1928).

that the Island of Palmas (or Miangas), undoubtedly included in the "archipelago known as the Philippine Islands", as delimited by Article Ⅲ of the Treaty of Peace between the United States and Spain, dated December 10th, 1898 (Treaty of Paris), and ceded in virtue of the said article to the United States, was considered by the Netherlands as forming part of the territory of their possessions in the East Indies. There followed a diplomatic correspondence, leading up to the conclusion of the Special Agreement of January 23th 1925. In the special agreement, both parties agreed to refer the difference to the Permanent Court of Arbitration at The Hague and the arbitral tribunal shall consist of one arbitrator, Max Huber.

(2) *Judgment Made by Huber*

In the absence of an international instrument recognized by both Parties and explicitly determining the legal position of the Island of Palmas (or Miangas), the arguments of the Parties may in a general way be summed up as follows:

The United States, as successor to the rights of Spain over the Philippines, bases its title in the first place on discovery. The existence of sovereignty thus acquired is, in the American view, confirmed not merely by the most reliable cartographers and authors, but also by treaty, in particular by the Treaty of Munster, of 1648, to which Spain and the Netherlands are themselves Contracting Parties. As, according to the same argument, nothing has occurred of a nature, in international law, to cause the acquired title to disappear, this latter title was intact at the moment when, by the Treaty of December 10th, 1898, Spain ceded the Philippines to the United States. In these circumstances, it is, in the American view, unnecessary to establish facts showing the actual display of sovereignty precisely over the Island of Palmas (or Miangas). The United States Government finally maintains that Palmas (or Miangas) forms a geographical part of the Philippine group and in virtue of the principle of contiguity belongs to the Power having the sovereignty over the Philippines.

Chapter VIII Territory

According to the Netherlands Government, on the other hand, the fact of discovery by Spain is not proved, nor yet any other form of acquisition, and even if Spam had at any moment had a litle, such title had been lost. The principle of contiguity is contested.

The Netherlands Government's main argument endeavors to show that the Nelherlands, represented for this purpose in the first period of colonization by the East India Company, have possessed and exercised rights of sovereignty from 1677, or probably from a date prior even to 1648, to the present day. This sovereignty arose out of convention entered into with native princes of the Island of Sangi (the main island of the Talautse (Sangi) Isles), establishing the suzerainty of the Netherlands over the territories of these princes, including Palmas (or Miangas). The State of affairs thus set up is claimed to be validated by international treaties.

The facts alleged in support of the Netherlands arguments are, in the United State Government's view, not proved, and, even if they were proved, they would not create a title of sovereignty, or would not concern the Island of Palmas.

Before considering the Parties' argument, two point of a general character are to be dealt with, one relating to the substantive law to be applied, namely the rules on territorial sovereignty which underlie the present case, and the other relating to the rules of procedure, namely the conditions under which the Parties may, under the Special Agreement, substantiate their claims.

In the first place the Arbitrator deems it necessary to make some general remarks on *sovereignty in its relation to territory*.

···It appears to follow that sovereignty in relation to a portion of the surface of the globe is the legal condition necessary for the inclusion of such portion in the territory of any particular State. Sovereignty in relation to territory is in the present award called "territorial sovereignty".

Sovereignty in the relations between States signifies independence.

Independence in regard to a portion of the globe is the right to exercise therein, to the exclusion of any other State, the functions of a State. The development of the national organisation of States during the last few centuries and, as a corollary, the development of international law, have established this principle of the exclusive competence of the State in regard to its own territory in such a way as to make it the point of departure in settling most questions that concern international relation. ··· it may be stated that territorial sovereignty belongs always to one, or in exceptional circumstances to several States, to the exclusion of all others. ···

Territorial sovereignty is, in general, a situation recognized and delimited in space, either by so-called natural frontiers as recognised by international law or by outward signs of delimitation that are undisputed, or else by legal engagements entered into between interested neighbours, such as frontier conventions, or by acts of recognition of States within fixed boundaries. If a dispute arises as to the sovereignty over a portion of territory, it is customary to examine which of the States claiming sovereignty possesses a title—cession conquest, occupation, etc.—superior to that which the other State might possibly bring forward against it. However, if the contestation is based on the fact that the other Party has actually displayed sovereignty, it cannot be sufficient to establish the title by which territorial sovereignty was validly acquired at a certain moment; it must also be shown that the territorial sovereignty has continued to exist and did exist at the moment which for the decision of the dispute must be considered as critical. This demonstration consists in the actual display of State activities, such as belongs only to the territorial sovereign.

Titles of acquisition of territorial sovereignty in present-day international law are either based on an act of effective apprehension, such as occupation or conquest, or, like cession, presuppose that the ceding and the cessionary Powers or at least one of them, have the faculty of effectively disposing of the ceded territory. In the same way natural accretion can only be conceived of as an accretion to a portion of territory where there exists an actual sovereignty capable of extending to a spot which falls within its sphere of activity. It seems therefore natural that an element which is essential for the constitution of sovereignty should not be lading in its continuation. So true is this, that practice, as well as doctrine, recognizes—though under different legal formulae and with certain differences as to the conditions required—that the continuous and peaceful display of territorial sovereignty (peaceful in relation to other States) is as good as a title. The growing insistence with which international law, ever since the middle of the 18th century, has demanded that the occupation shall be effective would be inconceivable, if effectiveness were required only for the act of acquisition and not equally for the maintenance of the right. If the effectiveness has above all been insisted on in regard to occupation, this is because the question rarely arises in connection with territories in which there is already an established order of things. ···the fact of peaceful and continuous display is still one of the most important considerations in establishing boundaries between States.

Territorial sovereignty, as has already been said, involves the exclusive right to display the activities of a State. This right has as corollary a duty: the obligation to protect within the territory the rights of other States, in particular their right to integrity and inviolability in peace and in war, together with the rights which each State may claim for its nationals in foreign territory. Without manifesting its territorial sovereignty in a manner corresponding to circumstances, the State cannot fulfill this duty. Territorial sovereignty cannot limit itself to its negative side, i. e. to excluding the activities of other States; for it serves to divide between nation the space upon which human activities are employed, in order to assure them at all point of the minimum of protection of which international law is the guardian.

··· International law, the structure of which is not based on any super-State organisation, cannot be presumed to reduce a right such as territorial sovereignty, with which almost all international relations are bound up, to the category of an abstract right, without concrete manifestations.

The principle that continuous and peaceful display of the functions of Staie within a given region is a constituent element of territorial sovereignty is not only based on the conditions of the formation of independent States and their boundaries as well as on an international jurisprudence and doctrine widely accepted; this principle has further been recognized in more than one federal State, where a jurisdiction is established in order to apply, as need arises, rules of international law to the interstate relations of the States members. This is the more significant, in that it might well be conceived that in a federal State possessing a complete judicial system for interstate matters—far more than in the domain of international relations properly so-called—there should be applied to territorial questions the principle that, failing any specific provision of law to the contrary, a *Jus in re* once lawfully acquired shall prevail over *de facto* possession however well established.

……

The title alleged by the United States of America as constituting the immediate foundation of its claim is that of cession, brought about by the Treaty of Paris, which cession transferred all rights of sovereignty which Spain may have possessed in the region indicated in Article Ⅲ of the said Treaty and therefore also those concerning the Island of Palmas (or Miangas).

It is evident that Spain could not transfer more rights than she herself possessed. This principle of law is expressly recognized in a letter dated April 7th, 1900…

The essential point is therefore whether the Island of Palmas (or Miangas) at the moment of the conclusion and coming into force of the Treaty of Paris formed a part of the Spanish or Netherlands territory. The United States declares that Palmas (or Miangas) was Spanish territory and denies the existence of Dutch sovereignty; the Netherlands maintain the existence of their sovereignty and deny that of Spain. Only if the examination of the arguments of both Parties should lead to the conclusion that the Island of Palmas was at the *critical moment* neither Spanish nor Netherlands territory, would the question arise whether—and, if so, how—the conclusion of the Treaty of Paris and its notification to the Netherlands might have interfered with the rights which the Netherlands or the United States of America may claim over the island in dispute.

......

It is admitted by both sides that international law underwent profound modifications between the end of the Middle-Ages and the end of the 19th century as regards the rights of discovery and acquisition of uninhabited regions or regions inhabited by savages or semi-civilized peoples. Both Parties are also agreed that a juridical fact must be appreciated in the light of the law contemporary with it, and not of the law in force at the time when a dispute in regard to it arises or fall, to be settled. The effect of discovery by Spain is therefore to be determined by the rules of international law in force in the first half of the 16th century…

…International law in the 19th century… took account of a tendency already existing and especially developed since the middle of the 18th century, and laid down the principle that occupation, to constitute a claim to territorial sovereignty, must be effective, that is, offer certain guarantees to other States and their nationals. It seems therefore incompatible with this rule of positive law that there should be regions which are neither under the effective sovereignty of a State, nor without a master, but which are reserved for the exclusive influence of one State, in virtue solely of a title of acquisition which is no longer recognized by existing law, even if such a title ever conferred territorial sovereignty. For these reasons, discovery alone without any subsequent act, cannot at the present time suffice to prove sovereignty over the Island of Palmas (or Miangas);…

If on the other hand the view is adopted that discovery does not create a definitive title of sovereignty, but only an "inchoate" title, such a title exists, it is true, without external manifestation. However, according to the view that has prevailed at any rate since the 19th century, an inchoate title of discovery must be completed within a reasonable period by the effective occupation of the region claimed to be discovered. This principle must be applied in the present case, for the reasons given above in regard to the rules determining which of successive legal systems is to be applied (the so-called intertemporal Law). ⋯ But even admitting that the Spanish title still existed as inchoate in 1898 and must be considered as included in the cession under Article Ⅲ of the Treaty of Paris, an inchoate title could not prevail over the continuous and peaceful display of authority by another State; for such display may prevail even over a prior, definitive title put forward by another State. ⋯

The conclusions to be derived from the above examination of the argument of the Parties are the following:

The claim of the United States to sovereignty over the Island of Palmas (or Miangas) is derived from Spain by way of cession under the Treaty of Paris. The latter Treaty⋯has not created in favour of the United States any title of sovereignty such as was not already vested in Spain.

The United States base their claim on the titles of discovery, of recognition by treaty and of contiguity, i. e. titles relating to acts or circumstances leading to the acquisition of sovereignty; they have however not established the fact that sovereignty so acquired was effectively displayed at any time.

The Netherlands on the contrary found their claim to sovereignty essentially on the title of peaceful and continuous display of State authority over the island. Since this title would in international law prevail over a title of acquisition of sovereignty not followed by actual display of State authority, it is necessary to ascertain in the first place, whether the contention of the Netherlands is sufficiently established by evidence, and, if so, for what period of time.

In the opinion of the Arbitrator the Netherlands have succeeded in establishing the following facts: ⋯ The conditions of acquisition of sovereignty by the Netherlands are therefore to be considered as fulfilled. ⋯

2.4 Questions and Assignment

(1) What is the meaning of "the territory is a political technology"?

(2) What is your opinion about the land-appropriation after the great discovery?

(3) How many ways of acquisition were mentioned in the Island of Palmas case?

(4) Retreat the *Island of Palmas Case* and making an 8-10 minutes speech in English.

3. Terminologies and Explanations

3.1 Territory and Territorial Sovereignty

Black's Law Dictionary defines the territory as "a geography area included within a particular government's jurisdiction; the portion of the earth's surface that is in State's exclusive possession and control". The possession of a defined territory is generally identified as a fundamental prerequisite for the existence of a State. Besides Oppenheim's popular line "a State without a territory is not possible", many learned scholars echo the same views. Malcolm Shaw affirmed that "Statehood is inconceivable in the absence of a reasonably defined geographical base" in his classic textbook. It is universally accepted that one could not contemplate a State as a kind of disembodied spirit and there must be some portion of the earth's surface which its people inhabit and over which its government exercises authority. However, we should notice that international law does not prescribe a minimum area of territory necessary for a State to exist. Even a rock in the sea could establish the authority of a State.

Sovereignty is always combined with the territory to formulate an important terminology: "territorial sovereignty". Since such fundamental legal concepts as sovereignty and jurisdiction can only be comprehended in relation to territory, it follows that the legal nature of territory becomes a vital part of any the of international law. The principle of respect for the territorial integrity of States has been well-founded to prohibit interference in the internal affairs of other States. A number of factors, however, have tended to reduce the territorial exclusivity of the State in international law. Technological and economic changes have had an impact as interdependence becomes evident. And some transnational concerns, such as human rights and self-determination, have tended to undermine this exclusivity. The growth of international organizations is another relevant factor. So does the development of the "common heritage" concept in the context of the law of the sea and the air. But, we should not exaggerate the effects of such trends. Territorial sovereignty remains as a key concept in international law.

The international rules regarding territorial sovereignty are rooted in the Roman law provisions governing ownership and possession, and the classification of the different methods of acquiring territory is a direct resemblance of the Roman rules dealing with property. The essence of territorial sovereignty is contained in the notion of title. This term relates to both the factual and legal conditions under which territory is deemed to belong to one particular authority or another. In other words, it refers to the existence of those facts required under international law to entail the legal consequences of a change in the juridical status of a particular territory. [1]

Disputes over territory are always hot issues in the world. The contention may be over the status of the country itself. E.g., Arab's claims

---

[1] See Robert Y. Jennings, *The Acquisition of Territory in International Law*, Manchester University Press, 1963, p. 4.

against Israel and claims formerly pursued by Morocco against Mauritania. The dispute may refer to a certain area on the borders of two or more States. For example, Somali claims against the northeast of Kenya and southeast of Ethiopia. And, claims to territory may be based on several different grounds, ranging from the traditional method of occupation or prescription to the newer concepts such as self-determination, with various political and legal factors, for example, geographical contiguity, historical demands and economic elements, possibly being relevant.

The distinction between territorial disputes and other disputes is not straightforward: it encounters at least four problems. First, at one level, one may regard almost all disputes between States as having a territorial component. Most apparent are conflicts over the delineation of an international border or a given piece of territory, as occurred between Argentina and Chile over the Beagle Channel. More problematic are cases involving disputes over resources—for example, Iraq's complaints against Kuwait—when control over those resources is tied to control over the territory in which they are located. Even more difficult to distinguish are ethnic or religious conflicts when such differences are intimately tied to specific territories—in Jerusalem or in Kashmir, for instance. Definitions must distinguish between those disputes that are primarily over territory and those that merely have a territorial component.

3.2 Modes of Acquisition

The classical technique of categorizing the various modes of acquisition of territory is based on Roman law and is not adequate. Many of the leading cases do not specify a particular category or mode but tend to adopt an overall approach. We shall note that the transfer of territorial sovereignty is unlike the transfer of property in municipal law. It always implicates serious influences upon the people who live in the territory. They may be provided a choice to take the new nationality, but they would generally become subjects of the acquiring State.

New States pose a different problem because under classical international law, until a new State is created, there is no legal person in existence competent to hold title. None of the traditional modes of acquisition of territorial title satisfactorily resolves the dilemma. The international community has traditionally approached the problem of new States in terms of recognition rather than in terms of acquisition of title to territory. There has been relatively little discussion of the method by which the new entity itself acquires the legal rights to its lands. The stress has instead been on compliance with factual requirements as to Statehood coupled with the acceptance of this by other States. There are basically two methods by which a new entity may gain its independence as a new State: by constitutional means, that is, by agreement with the former controlling administration in an orderly devolution of power, or by non-constitutional means, usually by force, against the will of the previous sovereign.

The principle of self-determination is very relevant here. While a State gains its sovereignty in opposition to the former power by self-determination, other States will then have to decide whether or not to recognize the new State and accept the legal consequences of this new status. But, at this point, a serious problem emerges. That is the conflict between self-determination and territory integrity. The principle of the territorial integrity of States is well established and constitutes a foundational principle of international law. And, self-determination is also a principle expressed in UN Charter emphasized in the 1960 Colonial Declaration[①], the 1966 International Covenants on Human

---

① UN, Declaration on the Granting of Independence to Colonial Countries and Peoples, by General Assembly resolution 1514 (XV), 14 December 1960.

Rights[1] and the 1970 Declaration on Principles of International Law[2]. However, the principle of self-determination is only an established practice in the process of decolonization. It has been interpreted as referring only to the inhabitants of non-independent territories. The practice has not supported its application as a principle conferring the right to secede upon identifiable groups within already independent States. That is the reason why China still refuses to recognize Kosovo as an independent State.

After a territory is accepted as an independent State, the following question is how an existed State acquires additional territory. There are five traditional modes developed by international law: occupation, cession, conquest, prescription and accretion.

Occupation was a mean of acquiring territory not already forming part of the dominions of any State. That is *terra nullius*. It was accepted that the land inhabited by tribal could be seen as *terra nullius*. This view has been discredited under modern law. And after the first globalization after the industrial revolution, all the habitable areas of the earth had fallen under the control of some State or other, future titles by occupation are no longer possible. May this rule could play some role in human being outer space exploration in a remote future. For now, the law concerning occupation is still important because the occupation of the past often gives rise to the boundary disputes at present.

Cession is a transfer of the territorial sovereignty from one State to another. It is sometimes resulted from a successful war and sometimes from peaceful negotiation. Cession also could be gratuitous, an exchange, or for sale, for example, Russia's sale of the Alaskan territory in 1867 to the United

---

[1] See International Covenant on Civil and Political Rights, art. 1; International Covenant on Economic, Social and Cultural Rights, art. 1.

[2] UN, Declaration on Principles of International Law concerning Friendly Relations and Cooperation among States in accordance with the Charter of the United Nations, General Assembly 25th sess., Suppl. no. 281, 1970.

States for 7.2 million dollars. An important rule about cession is that a State cannot transfer more rights than she herself possessed.

Conquest, also known as subjugation, is the acquisition of an enemy's territory by complete and final subjugation and a declaration of the conquering State's intention to annex it. An example of conquest is that of Rumania to Bessarabia in the period between the two world wars. Today, cession by force can no longer be considered a valid way to acquire territory. This principle was first declared by Mr. Stimson's non-recognition of Japan's occupation of Northeast China, the Northeast province of China, in 1932. After World War II, this principle has been successfully written into international law and solemnly stated in the UN Charter. As Article 2(4) States: "All Members shall refrain in their international relations from the threat or use of force against the territorial integrity or political independence of any State, or in any other manner inconsistent with the Purposes of the United Nations." A treaty is void if its conclusion has been procured by the threat or use of force in violation of the principles embodied in the Charter. An established premise for today's international law is "that neither conquest nor a cession imposed by an illegal force of themselves confers the title". An important remaining question is that whether a lawful use of force in self-defense could confer a title to a territory. States always claim that their use of force is legal under the rules of self-defense. To allow for the acquisition of territory through self-defense would undermine the integrity of the not-to-use-force principle. It is a consensus that: "The territory of a State shall not be the object of acquisition by another State resulting from the threat or use of force. No territorial acquisition resulting from the threat or use of force shall be recognized as legal."

Prescription was always described as the legitimization of a doubtful title by the passage of time and presumed acquiescence of the former sovereign. In fact, the existing frontiers between States are often accepted by international law simply because they have existed *de facto* for a long time. This situation exemplifies the old maxim *e facto oritur jus*, which means the law arises from the fact. This maxim is at the root of the notion of prescription in all systems of law. For this mode, we shall note that no fixed rules as to the length of possession which will give a good title and it would be difficult to frame rules that could cover every situation.

Accretion is the addition of new territory to the existing territory of a State by operation of nature, as by the drying up of a river or the recession of the sea. This mode is of little importance in international law.

3.3 Issues in a Territory Disputes

An important issue is an effective control. This factor is both required in the occupation and prescription modes. From the *Palmas Case*, we can find that they involved contested claims by States where the parties had performed some sovereign acts. However, it is inappropriate to State that effective control should be a deciding factor. The Dutch, 5 wining the *Palmas Case* was not only because it made a public sovereign possession and exerted effective control over 200 years, but also because this control was peaceful and uninterrupted. It is universally accepted that the prescription rests vitally upon the implied consent of the former sovereign to the new State of affairs. It is a customary rule that the protests by the dispossessed sovereign could completely block any prescriptive claim over the territory.

And, in deciding rules that could conclude a judgment, the court has to ascertain a critical date to apply appropriate intertemporal law. The critical date is a determining moment at which it might be inferred that the rights of the parties have crystallized so that acts after that date cannot alter the legal position. Such a moment might be the date of a particular treaty where its provisions are at issue or the date of occupation of territory. In the *Palmas Case*, the arbitrator had to decide if Spain had title to the island in 1898 so that it could be a treaty of that year passing sovereignty to the United States. So 1898 was the critical date. However, most of the cases turn on complex facts extending over many years or centuries and it needs to ascertain more than one critical date. For example, the *Eastern Greenland Case* between Denmark and Norway, decided by the Permanent International Court of Justice in 1933.

3.4 Leases and Servitudes

Various legal rights exercisable by States over the territory of other States, which fall short of absolute sovereignty, may exist. Such rights are attached to the land and so may be enforced even though the ownership of the particular territory subject to the rights has passed to another sovereign. They are in legal terminology formulated as rights *in rem*. They constitute treaty-based regimes, dependent upon the terms of the particular treaty.

Leases of land rose into prominence in the 19th century as a way of obtaining control of usually strategic points without the necessity of actually annexing the territory. Leases were used extensively in the Far East, as for example, Britain's rights over the New Territories amalgamated with Hong Kong, and sovereignty was regarded as having passed to the lessee for the duration of the lease, upon which event it would revert to the original sovereign who made the grant.

Servitude exists where the territory of one State is under a particular restriction in the interests of the territory of another State. Such limitations are bound to the land as rights *in rem* and thus restrict the sovereignty of the State concerned, even if there is a change in control of the relevant territory, for instance, upon merger with another State or upon decolonization. Examples of servitudes would include the right to use ports or rivers in, or a right of way across, or an obligation not to fortify particular towns or areas in the territory.

4. Cases and Materials

Retreat and read the following cases and materials, then think about the following questions:

(1) What are the commons and differences between the *Eastern Greenland case* and *Palmas Case*?

(2) Based on the principles about acquisition exemplified by the cases, please make an explanation about China's absolute sovereignty over Diaoyu Dao.

(3) Retreat the history and development concerning the dispute between China and the Philippines and find out why the claims made by the Philippines are baseless under international law?

(4) What is your understanding of the Principle of "Promoting Joint Development While Shelving Differences"?

4.1 *Eastern Greenland Case* [①]

(1) Fact

In addition to claiming sovereignty over Greenland in this case on the basis of occupation, Denmark also argued that Norway had recognized Danish sovereignty over the island by the "Ihlen Declaration". Mr. Ihlen was the Norwegian Foreign Minister for Foreign Affairs. In conversations on July 14, 1919, with the Danish Minister accredited to Norway, the latter suggested to M. Ihlen that Denmark would raise no objection to any claim Norway might want to make at the Paris Peace Conference to Spitsbergen if Norway would not oppose the claim that Denmark was to make at the same Conference to the whole of Greenland. On July 22, 1919, Mr. Ihlen, in the course of further conversations with the Danish Minister, declared that "the Norwegian Government would not make any difficulty" concerning the Danish claim. These were the terms used as they were minuted by Mr. Ihlen for his

---

① *Legal Status of Eastern Greenland (Denmark v. Norway)*, PCIJ, Ser. A/B, No. 53, (1933). A contentious issue between Denmark and Norway concerning sovereignty over a swathe of Eastern Greenland was successfully resolved in 1933 through international dispute settlement. It was the only territorial dispute concerning acquisition of territorial sovereignty settled by the PICJ, which make it a historic landmark relied upon as a building-block for the international jurisprudence in this field.

Government's own purposes. Denmark argued before the Court that this undertaking was binding upon Norway.

(2) *Judgment and Key Findings*

With a majority of 10 judges against two, the Court concluded that on 10 July 1931 Denmark possessed a valid title to the sovereignty over all Greenland.

……

This declaration by M. Ihlen has been relied on by Counsel for Denmark as a recognition of an existing Danish sovereignty in Greenland. The Court is unable to accept this point of view. A careful examination of the words used and of the circumstances in which they were used, as well as of the subsequent developments, shows that M. Ihlen cannot have meant to be giving then and there a definitive recognition of Danish sovereignty over Greenland, and shows also that he cannot have been understood by the Danish Government at the time as having done so. In the text of M. Ihlen's minute, submitted by the Norwegian Government, which has not been disputed by the Danish Government, the phrase used by M. Ihlen is couched in the future tense: *"ne fera pas de difficultés"*; he had been informed that it was at the Peace Conference that the Danish Government intended to bring up the question; and two years later—when assurances had been received from the Principal Allied Powers—the Danish Government made a further application to the Norwegian Government to obtain the recognition which they desired of Danish sovereignty over all Greenland.

Nevertheless, the point which must now be considered is whether the Ihlen declaration—even if not constituting a definitive recognition of Danish sovereignty—did not constitute an engagement obliging Norway to refrain from occupying any part of Greenland.

The Danish request and M. Ihlen's reply were recorded by him in a minute, worded as follows:

The Danish Minister informed me today that his Government has heard from Paris that the question of Spitzbergen will be examined by a Commission of four members (American, British, French, Italian). If the Danish Government is questioned by this Commission, it is prepared to reply that Denmark has no interests in Spitzbergen, and that it has no reason to oppose the wishes of Norway in regard to the settlement of this question.

"Furthermore, the Danish Minister made the following statement:

The Danish Government has for some years past been anxious to obtain the recognition of all the interested Powers of Denmark's sovereignty over the whole of Greenland, and it proposes to place this question before the above-mentioned Committee at the same time. During the negotiations with the U. S. A. over the cession of the Danish West Indies, the Danish Government raised this question in so far as concerns recognition by the Government of the U. S. A., and it succeeded in inducing the latter to agree that, concurrently with the conclusion of a convention regarding the cession of the said islands, it would make a declaration to the effect that the Government of the U. S. A. would not object to the Danish Government extending their political and economic interests to the whole of Greenland.

"It is clear from the relevant Danish documents which preceded the Danish Minister's demarche at Christiania on July 14th, 1919, that the Danish attitude in the Spitzbergen question and the Norwegian attitude in the Greenland question were regarded in Denmark as interdependent, and this interdependence appears to be reflected also in M. Ihlen's minute of the interview. Even if this interdependence—which, in view of the affirmative reply of the Norwegian Government, in whose name the Minister for Foreign Affairs was speaking, would have created a bilateral engagement—is not held to have been established, it can hardly be denied that what Denmark was asking of Norway ['not to make any difficulties in the settlement of the (Greenland) question'] was equivalent to what she was indicating her readiness to concede in the Spitzbergen question (to refrain from opposing 'the wishes of Norway in regard to the settlement of this question'). What Denmark desired to obtain from Norway was that the latter should do nothing to obstruct the Danish plans in regard to Greenland. The declaration which the Minister for Foreign Affairs gave on July 22nd, 1919, on behalf of the Norwegian Government, was definitely affirmative: 'I told the Danish Minister today that the Norwegian Government would not make any difficulty in the settlement of this question.'"

The Court considers it beyond all dispute that a reply of this nature given by the Minister for Foreign Affairs on behalf of his Government in response to a request by the diplomatic representative of a foreign Power, in regard to a question falling within his province, is binding upon the country to which the Minister belongs.

······

It follows that, as a result of the undertaking involved in the Ihlen declaration of July 22nd, 1919, Norway is under an obligation to refrain from contesting Danish sovereignty over Greenland as a whole, and a fortiori to refrain from occupying a part of Greenland. ···

4.2 Diaoyu Dao, an Inherent Territory of China[①]

Foreword

Diaoyu Dao and its affiliated islands are an inseparable part of the Chinese territory. Diaoyu Dao is China's inherent territory in all historical, geographical and legal terms, and China enjoys indisputable sovereignty over Diaoyu Dao. ···

Ⅰ. Diaoyu Dao is China's Inherent Territory

Diaoyu Dao and its affiliated islands, which consist of Diaoyu Dao, Huangwei Yu, Chiwei Yu, Nanxiao Dao, Beixiao Dao, Nan Yu, Bei Yu, Fei

---

① See State Council Information Office of the People's Republic of China, Diaoyu Dao, an Inherent Territory of China (white paper), September 26, 2012.

Yu and other islands and reefs, are located to the northeast of China's Taiwan Island, in the waters between 123°20′—124°40′E (East Longitude) and 25°40′—26°00′N (North Latitude), and are affiliated to the Taiwan Island. The total landmass of these islands is approximately 5.69 square kilometers. Diaoyu Dao, situated in the western tip of the area, covers a landmass of about 3.91 square kilometers and is the largest island in the area. ⋯

1. Diaoyu Dao was first discovered, named and exploited by China ⋯

2. Diaoyu Dao had long been under China's jurisdiction

In the early years of the Ming Dynasty, China placed Diaoyu Dao under its coastal defense to guard against the invasion of Japanese pirates along its southeast coast. In 1561 (the 40th year of the reign of Emperor Jiajing of the Ming Dynasty), *An Illustrated Compendium on Maritime Security* (Chou Hai Tu Bian) compiled by Zheng Ruozeng under the auspices of Hu Zongxian, the supreme commander of the southeast coastal defense of the Ming court, included the Diaoyu Dao on the "Map of Coastal Mountains and Sands" (Yan Hai Shan Sha Tu) and incorporated them into the jurisdiction of the coastal defense of the Ming court. ⋯ Map of Fujian's Coastal Mountains and Sands (Wu Bei Zhi. Hai Fang Er. Fu Jian Yan Hai Shan Sha Tu), drawn up by Mao Yuanyi in 1621 (the first year of the reign of Emperor Tianqi of the Ming Dynasty), also included the Diaoyu Dao as part of China's maritime territory.

The Qing court not only incorporated the Diaoyu Dao into the scope of China's coastal defense as the Ming court did, but also clearly placed the islands under the jurisdiction of the local government of Taiwan. Official documents of the Qing court, such as *A Tour of Duty in the Taiwan Strait* (Tai Hai Shi Cha Lu) and *Annals of Taiwan Prefecture* (Tai Wan Fu Zhi) all gave detailed accounts concerning China's administration over Diaoyu Dao. *Volume 86 of Recompiled General Annals of Fujian* (Chong Zuan Fu Jian Tong Zhi), a book compiled by Chen Shouqi and others in 1871 (the tenth year of the reign of Emperor Tongzhi of the Qing Dynasty), included Diaoyu Dao as a strategic location for coastal defense and placed the islands under the jurisdiction of Gamalan, Taiwan (known as Yilan County today).

3. Chinese and foreign maps show that Diaoyu Dao belongs to China

......

The Map of East China Sea Littoral States created by the French cartographer Pierre Lapie and others in 1809 colored Diaoyu Dao, Huangwei Yu, Chiwei Yu and the Taiwan Island as the same. Maps such as A New Map of China from the Latest Authorities published in Britain in 1811, Colton's China published in the United States in 1859, and A Map of China's East Coast: Hongkong to Gulf of Liao-Tung compiled by the British Navy in 1877 all marked Diaoyu Dao as part of China's territory.

Ⅱ. Japan Grabbed Diaoyu Dao from China

··· Japan seized Ryukyu in 1879 and changed its name to Okinawa Prefecture. Soon after that, Japan began to act covertly to invade and occupy Diaoyu Dao and secretly "included" Diaoyu Dao in its territory at the end of the Sino-Japanese War of 1894-1895. Japan then forced China to sign the unequal Treaty of Shimonoseki and cede to Japan the island of Taiwan Region, together with Diaoyu Dao and all other islands appertaining or belonging to the said island of Taiwan Region. ···

On April 17, 1895, the Qing court was defeated in the Sino-Japanese War and forced to sign the unequal Treaty of Shimonoseki and cede to Japan "the island of Taiwan Region, together with all islands appertaining or belonging to the said island of Taiwan Region". The Diaoyu Dao were ceded to Japan as "islands appertaining or belonging to the said island of Taiwan Region".

Ⅲ. Backroom Deals between the United States and Japan Concerning Diaoyu Dao are Illegal and Invalid

Diaoyu Dao was returned to China after the Second World War. However, the United States arbitrarily included Diaoyu Dao under its trusteeship in the 1950s and "returned" the "power of administration" over Diaoyu Dao to Japan in the 1970s. The backroom deals between the United States and Japan concerning Diaoyu Dao are acts of grave violation of China's territorial sovereignty. They are illegal and invalid. They have not and cannot change the fact that Diaoyu Dao belongs to China.

......

In response to the strong opposition of the Chinese government and people, the United States had to publicly clarify its position on the sovereignty over Diaoyu Dao. In October 1971, the US administration stated that "the United States believes that a return of administrative rights over those islands to Japan, from which the rights were received, can in no way prejudice any underlying claims. The United States cannot add to the legal rights Japan possessed before it transferred administration of the islands to us, nor can the United States, by giving back what it received, diminish the rights of other claimants... The United States has made no claim to Diaoyu Dao and considers that any conflicting claims to the islands are a matter for resolution by the parties concerned."

......

Conclusion

......

China strongly urges Japan to respect history and international law and immediately stop all actions that undermine China's territorial sovereignty. The Chinese government has the unshakable resolve and will to uphold the nation's territorial sovereignty. It has the confidence and ability to safeguard China's State sovereignty and territorial integrity.

4.3 China Adheres to the Position of Settling Through Negotiation the Relevant Disputes Between China and the Philippines in the South China Sea[①]

......

[①] This is a home position paper made by the Ministry of Foreign Affairs of the People's Republic of China. To better understand the issue about South China Sea, it is necessary to read another two official statements: *the Statement of the Government of the People's Republic of China on China's Territorial Sovereignty and Maritime Rights and Interests in the South China Sea* and *the Statement of the Ministry of Foreign Affairs of the People's Republic of China on the Award of 12 July 2016 of the Arbitral Tribunal in the South China Sea Arbitration Established at the Request of the Republic of the Philippines*.

In the South China Sea, China and the Philippines are States possessing land territory with opposite coasts, the distance between which is less than 400 nautical miles. The maritime areas claimed by the two States overlap, giving rise to a dispute over maritime delimitation.

III. China and the Philippines Have Reached Consensus on Settling Their Relevant Disputes in the South China Sea

China firmly upholds its sovereignty over Nanhai Zhudao, resolutely opposes the Philippines' invasion and illegal occupation of China's islands and reefs, and resolutely opposes the unilateral acts taken by the Philippines on the pretext of enforcing its own claims to infringe China's rights and interests in waters under China's jurisdiction. ···China has conducted consultations with the Philippines on managing maritime differences and promoting practical maritime cooperation, and the two sides have reached important consensus on settling through negotiation relevant disputes in the South China Sea and properly managing relevant disputes.

······

In June 1975, China and the Philippines normalized their relations, and in the joint communiqué for that purpose, the two governments agreed to settle all disputes by peaceful means without resorting to the threat or use of force.

In fact, China's initiative of "pursuing joint development while shelving disputes" regarding the South China Sea issue was first addressed to the Philippines. In a June 1986 meeting with Philippine Vice President Salvador Laurel, Chinese leader Deng Xiaoping pointed out that Nansha Qundao belongs to China, and when referring to the matter of differences, stated that, "This issue can be shelved for now. Several years later, we can sit down and work out a solution that is acceptable to all in a calm manner. We shall not let this issue stand in the way of our friendly relations with the Philippines and with other countries." In April 1988, when meeting with Philippine President Corazón Aquino, Deng Xiaoping reiterated that "with regard to the issue concerning Nansha Qundao, China has the biggest say. Nansha Qundao has been part of China's territory throughout history, and no one has ever expressed objection to this for quite some time"; and "For the sake of the friendship between our two countries, we can shelve the issue for now and pursue joint development". ⋯

In July 1992, the 25th ASEAN Foreign Ministers Meeting held in Manila adopted the ASEAN Declaration on the South China Sea. China expressed appreciation for relevant principles outlined in that Declaration. ⋯

In August 1995, China and the Philippines issued the Joint Statement Between the People's Republic of China and the Republic of the Philippines concerning Consultations on the South China Sea and on Other Areas of Cooperation in which they agreed that "disputes shall be settled by the countries directly concerned" and that "a gradual and progressive process of cooperation shall be adopted with a view to eventually negotiating a settlement of the bilateral disputes". Subsequently, China and the Philippines reaffirmed their consensus on settling the South China Sea issue through bilateral negotiation and consultation in a number of bilateral documents, such as the March 1999 Joint Statement of the China-Philippines Experts Group Meeting on Confidence-Building Measures and the May 2000 Joint Statement between the Government of the People's Republic of China and the Government of the Republic of the Philippines on the Framework of Bilateral Cooperation in the Twenty-First Century.

⋯⋯

Afterwards, China and the Philippines reaffirmed this solemn commitment they had made in the DOC in a number of bilateral documents, such as the September 2004 Joint Press Statement Between the Government of the People's Republic of China and the Government of the Republic of the Philippines and the September 2011 Joint Statement Between the People's Republic of China and the Republic of the Philippines. ⋯

V. China's Policy on the South China Sea Issue

China⋯ respects and acts in accordance with international law. While firmly safeguarding its territorial sovereignty and maritime rights and interests, China adheres to the position of settling disputes through negotiation and consultation and managing differences through rules and mechanisms. ...

China is firm in upholding its sovereignty over Nanhai Zhudao and their surrounding waters. ...

China has spared no efforts to settle, on the basis of respecting historical facts, relevant disputes with the Philippines and other countries directly concerned, through negotiation in accordance with international law.

......

China maintains that the issue of maritime delimitation in the South China Sea should be settled equitably through negotiation with countries directly concerned in accordance with international law, including UNCLOS. Pending the final settlement of this issue, all relevant parties must exercise self-restraint in the conduct of activities that may complicate or escalate disputes and affect peace and stability.

When ratifying UNCLOS in 1996, China stated that, "The People's Republic of China will effect, through consultations, the delimitation of the boundary of the maritime jurisdiction with the States with coasts opposite or adjacent to China respectively on the basis of international law and in accordance with the principle of equitability." China's positions in this regard are further elaborated in the 1998 Law of the People's Republic of China on the Exclusive Economic Zone and the Continental Shelf. This Law provides that, "The People's Republic of China shall determine the delimitation of its exclusive economic zone and continental shelf in respect of the overlapping claims by agreement with the States with opposite or adjacent coasts, in accordance with the principle of equitability and on the basis of international law", and that...

In keeping with international law and practice, pending final settlement of maritime disputes, the States concerned should exercise restraint and make every effort to enter into provisional arrangements of a practical nature, including establishing and improving dispute management rules and mechanisms, engaging in cooperation in various sectors, and promoting joint development while shelving differences, so as to uphold peace and stability in the South China Sea region and create conditions for the final settlement of disputes. Relevant cooperation and joint development are without prejudice to the final delimitation.

······

China is committed to upholding the freedom of navigation and overflight enjoyed by all States under international law, and ensuring the safety of sea lanes of communication.

······

China maintains that, when exercising freedom of navigation and overflight in the South China Sea, relevant parties shall fully respect the sovereignty and security interests of coastal States and abide by the laws and regulations enacted by coastal States in accordance with UNCLOS and other rules of international law.

······

China pursues peaceful development and adheres to a defense policy that is defensive in nature. China champions a new security vision featuring mutual trust, mutual benefit, equality and coordination, and pursues a foreign policy of building friendship and partnership with its neighbors and of fostering an amicable, secure and prosperous neighborhood based on the principle of amity, sincerity, mutual benefit and inclusiveness. China is a staunch force for upholding peace and stability and advancing cooperation and development in the South China Sea. China is committed to strengthening good-neighborliness and promoting practical cooperation with its neighbors and regional organizations including ASEAN to deliver mutual benefit.

··· To realize peace, stability, prosperity and development in the South China Sea region is the shared aspiration and responsibility of China and

ASEAN Member States, and serves the common interests of all countries.

5. References and Recommended Reading Materials

(1) Robert Y. Jennings, *The Acquisition of Territory in International Law*, Manchester University Press, 1963.〔英〕罗伯特·詹宁斯:《国际法上的领土取得》,孔令杰译,商务印书馆2018年版。

(2) Stuart Elden, *The Birth of Territory*, Chicago University Press, 2013.〔英〕斯图尔特·埃尔登:《领土论》,冬初阳译,时代文艺出版社2017年版。

(3) Carl Schmitt, *The Nomos of The Earth: in the International Law of Jus Publicum Europaeum*, Telos Press, 2006.〔德〕卡尔·施米特:《大地的法》,刘毅、张陈果译,上海人民出版社2017年版。

Chapter IX   Law of the Sea

1. Introduction

The law of the sea is complex and fascinating. The sea has played two important functions for the States and the international society. First, as a medium of communication, it provides passage and channels for transboundary people, cargo and information. Second, it is a vast of resources, both living and non-living, creating fortunes for human being and serve as an integrated part of the ecosystem.

Two competing basic principles have been developed. One is "the land dominates the sea", which underlies rules on coastal State's sovereignty or jurisdiction over the sea, exploiting resources or taking responsibility to protect the environment. The other is "freedom of the high seas", ensuring that the sea could provide free transit of ship and aircraft or installation of submarine cable. Those rules concerning the function of marine transit usually constitute exception to the rules of coastal States' sovereignty and jurisdiction.

This chapter is to provide an overview of this increasingly important plane of international law under development. Part 2 provides some classic articles and important conventions to illustrate the historical development; Part 3 provides a brief definition and discussion about those basic principles and important concepts, such as territorial sea, exclusive economic zone, continental shelf, etc. ; Part 4 includes some cases to show the complex practice.

2. Preliminary Reading and Assignment

2.1 Grotius' Idea about the Sea[①]

Chapter 1: *By the law of nations navigation is free for any to whomsoever*

Our purpose is shortly and clearly to demonstrate that it is lawful for the Hollanders, that is the subjects of the confederate States of the Low Countries, to sail to the Indians as they do and entertain traffic with them. We will lay this certain rule of the law of nations (which they call primary) as the foundation, the reason whereof is clear and immutable: that it is lawful for any nation to go to any other and to trade with it. …

They, therefore, that take away this, take away that most laudable society of mankind; they take away the mutual occasions of doing good and, to conclude, violate nature herself. For even that ocean wherewith God hath compassed the Earth is navigable on every side round about, and the settled or extraordinary blasts of wind, not always blowing from the same quarter, and sometimes from every quarter, do they not sufficiently signify that nature hath granted a passage from all nations unto all? This Seneca think the greatest benefit of nature, that even by the wind she hath mingled nations scattered in regard of place and hath so divided all her goods into countries that mortal men must needs traffic among themselves. This right therefore equally appertained to all nations, which the most famous lawyers enlarge so far that they deny any commonwealth or prince to be able wholly to forbid others to come unto their subjects and trade with them.

[①] See Hugo Grotius, *The Free Sea*, translated by Richard Hakluyt, Liberty Fund, 2004, pp. 10-11.

2.2 Anglo-Norwegian Fisheries Case [①]

Judgment of The Court:

On September 28th, 1949, the Government of the United Kingdom of Great Britain and Northern Ireland filed in the Registry an Application instituting proceedings before the Court against the Kingdom of Norway, the subject of the proceedings being the validity or otherwise, under international law, of the lines of delimitation of the Norwegian fisheries zone laid down by the Royal Decree of July 12th, 1935, as amended by a Decree of December 10th, 1937, for that part of Norway which is situated northward of 66°28.8' (or 66°28' 48") N. latitude. The Application refers to the Declarations by which the United Kingdom and Norway have accepted the compulsory jurisdiction of the Court in accordance with Article 36, paragraph 2, of the Statute.

This Application asked the Court:

(a) to declare the principles of international law to be applied in defining the base-lines, by reference to which the Norwegian Government is entitled to delimit a fisheries zone, extending to seaward 4 sea miles from those lines and exclusively reserved for its own nationals, and to define the said base-lines in so far as it appears necessary, in the light of the arguments of the Parties, in order to avoid further legal differences between them;

(b) to award damages to the Government of the United Kingdom in respect of all interferences by the Norwegian authorities with British, fishing vessels outside the zone…

At the end of his argument, the Agent of the United Kingdom

[①] See *Fisheries Case* (*United Kingdom v. Norway*), Judgment of December 18, 1951, ICJ Reports 1951, p. 116.

Government presented the following submissions:

The United Kingdom submits that the Court should decide that the maritime limits which Norway is entitled to enforce as against the United Kingdom should be drawn in accordance with the following principles:

(1) That Norway is entitled to a belt of territorial waters of fixed breadth—the breadth cannot, at a maximum, exceed 4 sea miles.

(2) That, in consequence, the outer limit of Norway's territorial waters must never be more than 4 sea miles from some point on the base-line.

(3) That, subject to (4) (9) and (10) below, the base-line must be low-water mark on permanently dry land (which is part of Norwegian territory) or the proper closing line of (see (7) below) Norwegian internal waters.

(4) That, where there is a low-tide elevation situated within 4 sea miles of permanently dry land, or of the proper closing line of Norwegian internal waters, the outer limit of territorial waters may be 4 sea miles from the outer edge (at low tide) of this low-tide elevation. In no other case may a low-tide elevation be taken into account.

(5) That Norway is entitled to claim as Norwegian internal waters, on historic grounds, all fjords and sands which fall within the conception of a bay as defined in international law, whether the proper entrance to the indentation is more or less than 10 sea miles wide.

(6) That the definition of a bay in international law is a well-marked indentation, whose penetration inland is in such proportion to the width of its mouth as to constitute the indentation more than a mere curvature of the coast.

(7) That, where an area of water is a bay, the principle which determines where the closing line should be drawn, is that the closing line should be drawn between the natural geographical entrance points

where the indentation ceases to have the configuration of a bay.

(8) That a legal strait is any geographical strait which connects two portions of the high seas.

(9) That Norway is entitled to claim as Norwegian territorial waters, on historic grounds, all the waters of the fjords and sands which have the character of a legal strait. Where the maritime belts, drawn from each shore, overlap at each end of the strait, the limit of territorial waters is formed by the outer rims of these two maritime belts. Where, however, the maritime belts so drawn do not overlap, the limit follows the outer rims of each of these two maritime belts, until they intersect with the straight line, joining the natural entrance points of the strait, after which inter section the limit follows that straight line.

(10) That, in the case of the Vestfjord, the outer limit of Norwegian territorial waters, at the south-westerly end of the fjord, is the pecked green line shown on Charts Nos. 8 and 9 of Annex 35 of the Reply.

(11) That Norway, by reason of her historic title to fjords and sands, is entitled to claim, either as territorial or as internal waters, the areas of water lying between the island fringe and the mainland of Norway. In order to determine what areas must be deemed to lie between the islands and the mainland, and whether these area are territorial or internal waters, recourse must be had to Nos. (6) and (8) above, being the definitions of a bay and of a legal strait.

(12) That Norway is not entitled, as against the United Kingdom, to enforce any claim to waters not covered by the preceding principles. As between Norway and the United Kingdom, waters off the coast of Norway north of parallel 66° 28. 8′ N., which are not Norwegian by virtue of the above-mentioned principles, are high seas.

……

The Court has no difficulty in finding that, for the purpose of measuring the breadth of the territorial sea, it is the low-water mark as opposed to the high-water mark, or the mean between the two tides, which has generally been adopted in the practice of States. This criterion is the most favorable to the coastal State and clearly shows the character of territorial waters as appurtenant to the land territory. The Court notes that the Parties agree as to this criterion, but that they differ as to its application.

……

The principle that the belt of territorial waters must follow the general direction of the coast makes it possible to fix certain criteria valid for any delimitation of the territorial sea; these criteria will be elucidated later. The Court will confine itself at this stage to noting that, in order to apply this principle, several States have deemed it necessary to follow the straight baselines method and that they have not encountered objections of principle by other States. …

In these Circumstances the Court deems it necessary to point out that although the ten-mile rule has been adopted by certain States both in their national law and in their treaties and conventions, and although certain arbitral decisions have applied it as between these States, other States have adopted a different limit. Consequently, the ten-mile rule has not acquired the authority of a general rule of international law.

……

The Court must ascertain precisely what this alleged system of delimitation consists of, what is its effect in law as against the United Kingdom, and whether it was applied by the 1935 Decree in a manner which conformed to international law.

……

The Court is thus led to conclude that the method of straight lines, established in the Norwegian system, was imposed by the peculiar geography of the Norwegian coast; that even before the dispute arose, this method had been consolidated by a constant and sufficiently long practice, in the face of which the attitude of governments bears witness to the fact that they did not consider it to be contrary to international law.

......

In the absence of convincing evidence to the contrary, the Court cannot readily find that the lines adopted in these circumstances by the 1935 Decree are not in accordance with the traditional Norwegian system. ...

Individual Opinion of Judge Alvarez: [1]

......

The present litigation is of great importance, not only to the Parties to the case, but also to all other States.

At the beginning of his address to the Court, the Attorney-General said: "It is common ground that this case is not only a very important one to the United Kingdom and to Norway, but that the decision of the Court on it will be of the very greatest importance to the world generally as a precedent, since the Court's decision in this case must contain important pronouncements concerning the rules of international law relating to coastal waters. The fact that so many governments have asked for copies of Our Pleadings in this case is evidence that this is the general view."

In considering the present case, I propose to follow a method different from that which is customarily adopted, particularly with regard to the law. It consists of bringing to light and retaining the principal facts, then of considering the points of law dominating the whole case and, finally, those which relate to each important question.

The application of this method may, at first sight, appear to be somewhat academic; but it is essentially practical, since it has as its object the furnishing of direct answers to be given on the questions submitted to the

---

[1] See *Anglo-Norwegian Fisheries* (U. K. v. Norway), Order, ICJ 117, Jan. 18, 1951, http://www.worldcourts.com/icj/eng/decisions/1951.12.18_fisheries.htm, last visited on Jan. 8, 2022.

Court.

Moreover, this method is called for by reason of the double task which the Court now has: the resolution of cases submitted to it and the development of the law of nations.

······

These changes have underlined the importance of the Court's second function. For it now happens with greater frequency than formerly that, on a given topic, no applicable precepts are to be found, or that those which do exist present lacunae or appear to be obsolete, that is to say, they no longer correspond to the new conditions of the life of peoples. In all such cases, the Court must develop the law of nations, that is to say, it must remedy its shortcomings, adapt existing principles to these new conditions and, even if no principles exist, create principles in conformity with such conditions. ···

The adaptation of the law of nations to the new conditions of international life, which is to-day necessary, is something quite different from the "Restatement" advocated by Anglo-Saxon jurists as a means of ending the crisis in international law, which consists merely of stating the law as it has been established and applied up to the present, without being too much concerned with any changes that it may recently have undergone or which it may undergo in the future.

···In the following pages I shall concentrate only on the questions of law raised by the present case.

For centuries, because of the vastness of the sea and the limited relations between States, the use of the sea was subject to no rules; every State could use it as it pleased.

From the end of the 18th century, publicists proclaimed, and the law of nations recognized as necessary for States, the exercise of sovereign powers by States over an area of the sea bordering their shores. The extent of this sea area, which was known as the territorial sea, was first fixed at the range of the contemporary cannon, and later at 3 sea miles. The question indeed was

Chapter IX Law of the Sea   257

one for the domestic law of each country. Several of the countries of Latin America incorporated provisions relating to this question in their civil codes.

As the result of the growing importance of the question of the territorial sea, a World Conference was convened at The Hague in 1930 for the purpose of providing rules governing certain of its aspects and to deal with two other matters. This Conference, in which such great hopes had been reposed, did not establish any precept relating to the territorial sea. It made it clear that no well-defined rules existed on this subject, that there were merely a number of conventions between certain States, certain trends and certain usages and practices. ...

What should be the position adopted by the Court, in these circumstances, to resolve the present dispute?

The Parties, in their Pleadings and in their Oral Arguments, have advanced a number of theories, as well as systems, practices and, indeed, rules which they regarded as constituting international law. The Court thought that it was necessary to take them into consideration. These arguments, in my opinion, marked the beginning of a serious distortion of the case.

In accordance with uniformly accepted doctrine, international judicial tribunals must, in the absence of principles provided by conventions, or of customary principles on a given question, apply the general principles of law. This doctrine is expressly confirmed in Article 38 of the Statute of the Court.

......

What are the principles of international law which the Court must have recourse to and, if necessary, adapt? And what are the principles which it must in reality create?

......

These are the new elements on which the new international law, still in the process of formation, will be founded. This law will, consequently, have a character entirely different from that of traditional or classical international law, which has prevailed to the present time.

......

What are the principles which, in accordance with the foregoing, the Court must bring to light, adapt if necessary, or even create, with regard to the maritime domain and, in particular, the territorial sea? They may be stated as follows:

(1) Having regard to the great variety of the geographical and economic conditions of States, it is not possible to lay down uniform rules, applicable to all, governing the extent of the territorial sea and the way in which it is to be reckoned.

(2) Each State may therefore determine the extent of its territorial sea and the way in which it is to be reckoned, provided it does so in a reasonable manner, that it is capable of exercising supervision over the zone in question and of carrying out the duties imposed by international law, that it does not infringe rights acquired by other States, that it does no harm to general interests and does not constitute an *abus de droit*. In fixing the breadth of its territorial sea, the State must indicate the reasons, geographic, economic, etc., which provide the justification therefor. In the light of this principle, it is no longer necessary to debate questions of base-lines, straight lines, closing lines of ten sea miles for bays, etc., as has been done in this case. Similarly, if a State adopts too great a breadth for its territorial sea, having regard to its land territory and to the needs of its population, or if the base-lines which it indicates appear to be arbitrarily selected, that will constitute an *abus de droit*.

(3) States have certain rights over their territorial sea, particularly rights to the fisheries; but they also have certain duties, particularly those of exercising supervision off their coasts, of facilitating navigation by the construction of lighthouses, by the dredging of certain areas of sea, etc.

(4) States may alter the extent of the territorial sea which they have fixed, provided that they furnish adequate grounds to justify the change.

(5) States may fix a greater or lesser area beyond their territorial sea over which they may reserve for themselves certain rights: customs, police rights, etc.

(6) The rights indicated above are of great weight if established by a group of States, and especially by all the States of a continent. ...

(7) Any State directly concerned may raise an objection to another State's decision as to the extent of its territorial sea or of the area beyond it, if it alleges that the conditions set out above for the determination of these areas have been violated. Disputes arising out of such objections must be resolved in accordance with the provisions of the Charter of the United Nations.

(8) Similarly, for the great bays and Straits, there can be no uniform rules. The international status of every great bay and strait must be determined by the coastal States directly concerned, having regard to the general interest. The position here must be the same as in the case of the great international rivers: each case must be subject to its own special rules. ...

(9) A principle which must receive special consideration is that relating to prescription. This principle, under the name of historic rights, was discussed at length in the course of the hearings. The concept of prescription in international law is quite different from that which it has in domestic law. As a result of the important part played by force in the formation of States, there is no prescription with regard to their territorial status. ...

(10) It is also necessary to pay special attention to another principle which has been much spoken of: the right of States to do everything which is not expressly forbidden by international law. This principle, formerly correct, in the days of absolute sovereignty, is no longer so at the present day. ...

(11) Any State alleging a principle of international law must prove its existence; and one claiming that a principle of international law has been abrogated or has become ineffective and requires to be renewed, must likewise

provide proof of this claim.

......

2.3 Convention on the Territorial Sea and the Contiguous Zone (1958)

Article 1

1. The sovereignty of a State extends, beyond its land territory and its internal waters, to a belt of sea adjacent to its coast, described as the territorial sea.

2. This sovereignty is exercised subject to the provisions of these articles and to other rules of international law.

Article 2

The sovereignty of a coastal State extends to the air space over the territorial sea as well as to its bed and subsoil.

Article 4

1. In localities where the coastline is deeply indented and cut into, or if there is a fringe of islands along the coast in its immediate vicinity, the method of straight baselines joining appropriate points may be employed in drawing the baseline from which the breadth of the territorial sea is measured.

2. The drawing of such baselines must not depart to any appreciable extent from the general direction of the coast, and the sea areas lying within the lines must be sufficiently closely linked to the land domain to be subject to the regime of internal waters.

3. Baselines shall not be drawn to and from low-tide elevations, unless lighthouses or similar installations which are permanently above sea level have been built on them.

4. Where the method of straight baselines is applicable under the provisions of paragraph 1, account may be taken, in determining particular baselines, of economic interests peculiar to the region concerned, the reality and the importance of which are clearly evidenced by a long usage.

5. The system of straight baselines may not be applied by a State in such a manner as to cut off from the high seas the territorial sea of another State.

......

Article 14

1. Subject to the provisions of these articles, ships of all States, whether coastal or not, shall enjoy the right of innocent passage through the territorial sea.

2. Passage means navigation through the territorial sea for the purpose either of traversing that sea without entering internal waters, or of proceeding to internal waters, or of making for the high seas from internal waters.

3. Passage includes stopping and anchoring, but only insofar as the same are incidental to ordinary navigation or are rendered necessary by force majeure or by distress.

4. Passage is innocent so long as it is not prejudicial to the peace, good order or security of the coastal State. Such passage shall take place in conformity with these articles and with other rules of international law.

5. Passage of foreign fishing vessels shall not be considered innocent if they do not observe such laws and regulations as the coastal State may make and publish in order to prevent these vessels from fishing in the territorial sea.

6. Submarines are required to navigate on the surface and to show their flag.

Article 15

1. The coastal State must not hamper innocent passage through the territorial sea.

2. The coastal State is required to give appropriate publicity to any dangers to navigation, of which it has knowledge, within its territorial sea.

Article 16

1. The coastal State may take the necessary steps in its territorial sea to prevent passage which is not innocent.

2. In the case of ships proceeding to internal waters, the coastal State shall also have the right to take the necessary steps to prevent any breach of the conditions to which admission of those ships to those waters is subject.

······

Article 17

Foreign ships exercising the right of innocent passage shall comply with the laws and regulations enacted by the coastal State in conformity with these articles and other rules of international law and, in particular, with such laws and regulations relating to transport and navigation.

2.4 Questions and Assignment

Read the materials and think about the following questions:

(1) How has the law of the sea developed to balance the sovereignty or sovereign interests of coastal States and freedom of the sea?

(2) How many zones with different statuses under modern law of the sea, specifically, the United Nations Convention on the Law of the Sea (UNCLOS) 1982?

(3) Prepare a 5-10 minutes English speech about your understanding of a case brief of the *Anglo-Norwegian Fisheries Case* (1951) or any case mentioned in this chapter.

3. Terminologies and Discussions

3.1 Development of Law of the Sea

The development of the law of the sea is a process of interaction between two competing beliefs: that the sea is free and that the seas are capable of subjection to national sovereignties. In the 17th century, the Portuguese proclaimed huge tracts of the high seas as part of their territorial domain. These claims were responded to by Grotius's doctrine of the open seas, whereby the oceans are *res communis*, accessible to all nations. It is recognized that the freedom of the high sea became a basic principle of international law. However, it is also accepted that the coastal State could exert sovereignty or jurisdiction over a maritime belt around its coastline. Grounded on the principle that the land dominates the sea, the coastal States can now exercise jurisdiction in the contiguous zone, exclusive economic zone, and continental shelf. The enlargement of the coastal States' right over a particular portion of the sea parallels the movement proclaiming a common heritage of humankind regime of the seabed of the high seas. Besides, the protection of the environment also plays a vital role in shaping the law of the sea. The law of the sea has developed subject to these conflicting principles, maintaining a sophisticated balance among State sovereignty and jurisdiction, free transit of the passage and sustainable development of the vast ocean.

The UNCLOS repeated principles enshrined in the earlier instruments and proposed many new rules, e. g. , the exclusive economic zone, landlocked and geographically disadvantaged States, archipelagic States, the International Seabed Area and environment protection and scientific research. Some rules have become customary rules in the field, which caused a complicated series of relationships between various States that exist in this field, based on customary rules and treaty rules. For example, the United States, not a party to this convention, have always proclaimed that it complies with the customary rules to navigate free in the Pacific Ocean. This complicated relationship between States may contribute to the inconsistent State practice and those maritime disputes. These disputes are mainly concerned with the divided oceans with conflicting delimitation rules.

3.2 Key Concepts Formulating the Basic Regime

(1) *Territorial Sea: Legal Status and Innocent Passage*

The territorial sea is a marine space under the territorial sovereignty of the coastal State up to a limit not exceeding twelve nautical miles measured from baselines. The territorial sea comprises the seabed and its subsoil, the adjacent waters, and its airspace. The landward limit of the territorial sea is the baseline. In the case of archipelagic States, the inner boundary of the territorial sea is the archipelagic baseline. The outer limit of the territorial sea is the line, every point of which is at a distance from the nearest point of the baseline equal to the breadth of the territorial sea. The baseline from which the breadth of the territorial sea is measured is normally the coastal low-water line.①

There is no doubt that the territorial sea is under the territorial sovereignty of the coastal State. As explained earlier, territorial sovereignty in international law is characterized by completeness and exclusiveness. The coastal State can exercise complete legislative and enforcement jurisdiction over all matters and all people in an exclusive manner unless international law provides otherwise. As provided by the Article 17 of the UNCLOS, coastal States' sovereignty over the territorial sea is restricted by the right of innocent passage for foreign vessels. This right is based on the freedom of navigation as an essential means to accomplish freedom of trade. It is important to note that the right of innocent passage does not comprise the freedom of over-flight. Under Article 18(1) of the UNCLOS, innocent passage comprises lateral passage and inward/outward-bound passage. The lateral passage is the passage traversing the territorial sea without entering internal waters or calling at a roadstead or port facility outside internal waters. Inward/outward-bound passage concerns the passage proceeding to or from internal waters or a call at such roadstead or port facility.

As to the innocent passage, there are several rules. First, the passage shall be continuous and expeditious, which means that ships are required to proceed with due speed regarding safety and other relevant factors. Second,

---

① See Yoshifumi Tanaka, *The International Law of The Sea*, 2nd Ed., Cambridge University Press, 2015, pp. 264-276.

submarines and other underwater vehicles must navigate on the surface and show their flags in the territorial sea. Third, foreign ships exercising the right of innocent passage through the territorial sea shall comply with all such laws and regulations and all generally accepted international regulations relating to preventing collisions at sea. Fourth, the following acts are presumed prejudice, such as any threat or use of force, any exercise with weapons of any kind, spying, any act of propaganda, the launching, landing or taking on board of any aircraft or military device, the loading or unloading of any commodity, currency or person contrary to the customs, fiscal, immigration or sanitary laws of the coastal State, any act of willful and serious pollution, fishing activities, research activities, interference with coastal communications or any other facilities, and any other activity not having a direct bearing on passage.

Another complex issue is whether a warship could claim innocent passage across the coastal State's territorial sea. Some may think that the right of innocent passage of warships is of paramount importance for major naval powers in order to secure global naval mobility. However, the passage of foreign warships through the territorial sea may be a threat to the security of the coastal State. Based on the status of the territorial sea and the aim of granting innocent passage for ships, it is quite clear that no reason for freedom of innocent passage of vessels of war. In the 1930 Hague Codification Conference, Articles 12 and 13 of the Legal Status of the Territorial Sea provided that, "The coastal State has the right to regulate the conditions of such passage. Submarines shall navigate on the surface. If a foreign warship passing through the territorial sea does not comply with the regulations of the coastal State and disregards any request for compliance which may be brought to its notice, the coastal State may require the warship to leave the territorial sea". In the 1949 *Corfu Channel Case* (in Chapter XIII), the ICJ did not directly address the question of whether foreign warships have the same right of innocent passage in the territorial sea. The customary law is obscure on this matter. As to the treaty law, UNCLOS contains no explicit provision concerning the right of innocent passage of foreign warships in the territorial sea. However, the articles concerned overall imply a restricted right of innocent passage of foreign warships. It shall note that the State practice is not uniform. Developing countries, including China, require prior notification or prior authorization of warships through their territorial sea. Some States, mostly the developed States, e. g., the United States, Germany and the United Kingdom, expressed that claims to prior authorization and prior notification were at variance with UNCLOS. It was accepted that the right of innocent passage of foreign warships and the requirement of prior notification of the coastal State could be compatible. It appears that the legality of prior authorization remains a matter for further discussion. However, since the UNCLOS has no clear provision expressly grants warship innocent passage and the coastal State has sovereignty over the territorial sea, it is permissible to enact domestic law applying specifically to warship based on national security concerns. Technically, going through the territorial sea without authorization constitutes the use of force or exercise with weapons, except that the warships do not carry any kind of weapons.

Delimitation of territorial sea between States opposite or adjacent to each other is primarily governed by Article 15 of the UNCLOS, which is virtually identical to Article 12(1) of the Convention on the Territorial Sea and the Contiquous Zone (1958) and is considered reflective of customary international law. It provides that, "Where the coasts of two States are opposite or adjacent to each other, neither of the two States is entitled, failing agreement between them to the contrary, to extend its territorial sea beyond the median line every point of which is equidistant from the nearest points on the baselines from which the breadth of the territorial seas of each of the two States is measured. The above provisions of this paragraph shall not apply, however, where it is necessary by reason of historic title or other special circumstances to delimit the territorial seas of the two States in a way which is at variance with this provision."

(2) *Contiguous Zone*

The contiguous zone is a marine space contiguous to the territorial sea, in which the coastal State may exercise the control necessary to prevent and punish infringement of its customs, fiscal, immigration or sanitary laws and regulations within its territory or territorial sea. The landward limit of the contiguous zone is the seaward limit of the territorial sea. Under Article 33 (2) of the UNCLOS, the maximum breadth of the contiguous zone is 24 nautical miles. And, the contiguous zone is part of the EEZ where the coastal State claims the zone. Where the coastal State does not claim its EEZ, the contiguous zone is part of the high seas.

Article 33(1) of the UNCLOS defines the legal status of the contiguous zone by specifying the coastal State jurisdiction over it. Accordingly, the coastal State may exercise the control necessary to (a) prevent infringement of its customs, fiscal, immigration or sanitary laws and regulations within its territory or territorial sea; (b) punish infringement of the above laws and regulations committed within its territory or territorial sea.

(3) *Exclusive Economic Zone* (*EEZ*)

According to articles 55 and 57 of the UNCLOS, the EEZ is an area beyond and adjacent to the territorial sea, not extending beyond 200 nautical miles from the baselines of the territorial sea. The origin of the concept of the EEZ may go back to the practice of the Latin American States after World War Ⅱ. The figure of 200 nautical miles relied on scientific facts: it would enable the Andean States to reach the Peruvian and the Humboldt Currents, which were particularly rich in living species. [1] The coastal State must claim the zone in order to establish an EEZ. The ICJ, in the *Continental Shelf Case* of 1985 (see Part 4.1 in this chapter), stated that: "The institution of the

---

[1] See Yoshifumi Tanaka, *The International Law of The Sea*, 2nd Ed., Cambridge University Press, 2015, p. 350.

exclusive economic zone, with its rule on entitlement by reason of distance, is shown by the practice of States to have become a part of customary law."①

The concept of the EEZ comprises the seabed and its subsoil, the waters superjacent to the seabed as well as the airspace above the waters. With respect to the seabed and its subsoil, Article 56(1) of the UNCLDS provides that, "In the exclusive economic zone, the coastal State has (a) sovereign rights for the purpose of exploring and exploiting, conserving and managing the natural resources, whether living or non-living, of the waters superjacent to the seabed and of the seabed and its subsoil". Article 58(1) of the UNCLDS stipulates that, "In the exclusive economic zone, all States, whether coastal or land-locked, enjoy, subject to the relevant provisions of this Convention, the freedoms referred to in article 87 of navigation and overflight". It is important to note that the sovereign rights of the coastal State over the EEZ are essentially limited to economic exploration and exploitation. In this respect, the concept of sovereign rights must be distinguished from territorial sovereignty, which is comprehensive unless international law provides otherwise.

(4) *Continental Shelf*

Geologically, the continental shelf is an area adjacent to a continent or around an island extending from the low-water line to the depth at which there is usually a marked increase of slope to a greater depth. The landward limit of the continental shelf, in the legal sense, is the seaward limit of the territorial sea. In this respect, Article 1 of the Convention on the Continental Shelf (1958) stipulates that the continental shelf is the seabed and subsoil of the submarine areas adjacent to the coast but outside the area of the territorial sea. Similarly, Article 76(1) of the UNCLOS stipulates that "the continental shelf of a coastal State comprises the seabed and subsoil of the submarine areas that extend beyond its territorial sea". It follows that the continental

---

① *Continental Shelf* (*Libyan v. Malta*), Judgment, ICJ Reports 1985, para. 34.

shelf, in a legal sense, does not include the seabed of the territorial sea. The Article 76(1) provides two alternative criterias determining the outer limits of the continental shelf beyond 200 nautical miles: (a) the limit of the outer edge of the continental margin (geological criterion) or (b) a distance of 200 nautical miles (distance criterion).

The coastal State exercises sovereign rights over the continental shelf for the purpose of exploring and exploiting its natural resources in accordance with Article 77(1) of the UNCLOS. The principal features of the sovereign rights can be summarized in the following points: (a) the sovereign rights of the coastal State over the continental shelf are inherent rights, and do not depend on occupation, effective or notional, or on any express proclamation; (b) non-natural resources are not included in the ambit of sovereign rights of the coastal State; (c) natural resources basically consist of the mineral and other non-living resources of the seabed and subsoil; (d) the sovereign rights include legislative and enforcement jurisdiction with a view to exploring and exploiting natural resources; (e) the sovereign rights of the coastal State are exercisable over all people or vessels regardless of their nationalities; and,(f) the rights are exclusive in the sense that if the coastal State does not explore the continental shelf or exploit its natural resources, no one may undertake these activities without the express consent of the coastal State.

Delimitation of the continental shelf is usually done in three stages. First, the relevant tribunal establishes a provisional delimitation line based on methods that are geometrically objective and also appropriate for the geography of the area in which the delimitation is to take place. This provisional delimitation line is an equidistance line in the case of two adjacent coasts and a median line when two opposite coasts are concerned. Second, the tribunal considers whether there are "relevant circumstances" calling for the adjustment or shifting of the provisional equidistance line in order to achieve an equitable result. Third, the tribunal verifies that the delimitation line as it stands does not lead to an inequitable result by reason of any marked disproportion between the ratio of the respective coastal lengths and the ratio between the relevant maritime area of each State.

(5) *Archipelagic State*

Article 46(a) of the UNCLOS defines "archipelagic State" as "a State constituted wholly by one or more archipelagos and may include other islands". States possessing territory in a continent are not archipelagic States, i.e., Greece. For the key concept "archipelago", Article 46(b) of the UNCLOS defines it as "a group of islands, including parts of islands, interconnecting waters and other natural features which are so closely interrelated that such islands, waters and other natural features form an intrinsic geographical, economic and political entity, or which historically have been regarded as such". There are 22 States that claim this status. They are Antigua and Barbuda, Bahamas, Cape Verde, Comoros, Dominican Republic, Fiji, Grenada, Indonesia, Jamaica, Kiribati, Maldives, Marshall Islands, Mauritius, Papua New Guinea, Philippines, Saint Vincent and the Grenadines, São Tomé e Principe, Seychelles, Solomon Islands, Trinidad and Tobago, Tuvalu and Vanuatu. As clearly stated in Article 49(1) and (2) of the LOSC, archipelagic waters are under the territorial sovereignty of the archipelagic State.

(6) *Strait*

In light of the paramount importance of international straits for sea communication, the freedom of navigation through straits has attracted much attention in the international community. A question is whether or not foreign vessels enjoy the right of innocent passage through international straits between one part of the high seas and another under customary law. The ICJ, in the 1949 *Corfu Channel Case*, gave a positive answer to this question. The UNCLOS establishes the right of transit based on this case for the strait. Article 38(2) of the UNCLOS defines transit passage as "the exercise in accordance with this Part Ⅲ of the freedom of navigation and overflight solely for the purpose of continuous and expeditious transit of the strait between one part of the high seas or an exclusive economic zone and another part of the high seas or an exclusive economic zone".

(7) *High Seas*

Under Article 86 of the UNCLOS, the high seas are defined as "all parts of the sea that are not included in the EEZ, in the territorial sea or in the internal waters of a State, or in the archipelagic waters of an archipelagic State". Where a coastal State has established its EEZ, the landward limit of the high seas is the seaward limit of the EEZ. Where the coastal State has not claimed its EEZ, the landward limit of the high seas is the seaward limit of the territorial sea. In this case, the seabed of the high seas is the continental shelf of the coastal State up to the limit fixed by the international law of the sea. The seabed and subsoil beyond the outer limits of the continental shelf are the Area, which is the common heritage of mankind. The superjacent waters above the Area are always the high seas. Where the continental shelf extends beyond the limit of 200 nautical miles, the superjacent waters and the airspace above those waters are the high seas.

The principle of the freedom of the high seas has two basic meanings. First, the freedom of the high seas means that the high seas are free from national jurisdiction. It has been made clear in Article 89 of the UNCLOS, "No State may validly purport to subject any part of the high seas to its sovereignty." Second, the freedom of the high seas means the freedom of activities there. Consequently, each and every State has an equal right to enjoy the freedom to use the high seas in conformity with international law.

Another important principle about high seas is the flag State, namely, the State which has granted a ship the right to sail under its flag has exclusive jurisdiction over vessels flying its flag. The flag State jurisdiction comprises both legislative and enforcement jurisdiction over its ships on the high seas.

This enforcement jurisdiction applies to all peoples within its ships flying its flag regardless of their nationalities. The principle of the exclusive jurisdiction of the flag State plays a dual role. First, this principle prevents any interference by other States with vessels flying its flag on the high seas. In so doing, the principle of the exclusive jurisdiction of the flag State ensures the freedom of activity of vessels on the high seas. Second, under this principle, the flag State has a responsibility to ensure compliance with national and international laws concerning the activities of ships flying its flag on the high seas.

(8) *The Area: International Seabed*

The limits of the Area are the seaward limit of the continental shelf in the legal sense. It follows that the limits of the Area consist in at the maximum the 200 nautical miles from the baseline or the limit of the continental margin where it extends beyond 200 nautical miles.

The Area is governed by the principle of the common heritage of mankind. This principle had already been introduced into space law. All rights in the resources of the Area are vested in mankind as a whole, on whose behalf the Authority shall act by virtue of Article 137(2) of the UNCLOS. Under Artide 133 of the UNCLOS, the resources mean "all solid, liquid or gaseous mineral resources *in situ* in the Area at or beneath the seabed, including polymetallic nodules". The principle of the common heritage of humankind could be interpreted in the following three elements. The first is the non-appropriation of the Area as well as its natural resources. The second concerns the benefit of mankind as a whole. Article 140(1) of the UNCLOS explicitly provides that activities in the Area shall be carried out for the benefit of mankind as a whole. The third pertains to the peaceful use of the Area.

UNCLOS established a special mechanism for promoting the benefit of the Area. Article 153(1) provides that activities in the Area shall be organized, carried out and controlled by the Authority on behalf of mankind as a whole. All States Parties to the UNCLOS are *ipso facto* members of the Authority. And the Authority comprises three principal organs, that is to say, an Assembly, a Council and a Secretariat. The Assembly, which consists of all the members of the Authority, is the supreme organ of the Authority to which the other principal organs shall be accountable. The Council, which consists of thirty-six members of the Authority, is the executive organ of the Authority. The Secretariat of the Authority comprises a Secretary-General and such staff as the Authority may require. In the performance of their duties, the Secretary-General and the staff shall not seek or receive instructions from any government or from any other source external to the Authority.

4. Cases and Materials

Read the following cases and materials and think about the following questions:

(1) What are the features of marine disputes and their solutions?

(2) What are the factors having been taken into account by the Court during marine delimitation to ensure an equitable result required by the UNCLOS?

(3) Supposing you are a famous publicist being consulted about the solution of marine disputes involving China, what are your explanations of China's right over the South China Sea to counter back other countries' illegal claims?

4.1 *Continental Shelf Case* [1]

(1) *Special Agreement*

The Government of the Republic of Malta and the Government of the Libyan Arab Republic agree to recourse to the International Court of Justice as follows:

Article I The Court is requested to decide the following question: What principles and rules of international law are applicable to the

---

[1] *Continental Shelf* (*Libyan v. Malta*), Judgment, ICJ Reports 1985, p. 13.

delimitation of the area of the continental shelf which appertains to the Republic of Malta and the area of continental shelf which appertains to the Libyan Arab Republic, and how in practice such principles and rules can be applied by the two Parties in this particular case in order that they may without difficulty delimit such areas by an agreement as provided in Article Ⅲ.

......

(2) *Judgment*

A. The applicable principles and rules of international law (Paras. 26-35)

26. The Parties are broadly in agreement as to the sources of the law applicable in this case. Malta is a party to the 1958 Geneva Convention on the Continental Shelf, while Libya is not; the Parties agree that the Convention, and in particular the provisions for delimitation in Article 6, is thus not as such applicable in the relations between them. Both Parties have signed the 1982 United Nations Convention on the Law of the Sea, but that Convention has not yet entered into force, and is therefore not operative as treaty-law; the Special Agreement contains no provisions as to the substantive law applicable. Nor are there any other bilateral or multilateral treaties claimed to be binding on the Parties. The Parties thus agree that the dispute is to be governed by customary international law. ···

27. It is of course axiomatic that the material of customary international law is to be looked for primarily in the actual practice and *opinio Juris* of States, even though multilateral conventions may have an important role to play in recording and defining rules deriving from custom, or indeed in developing them. There has in fact been much debate between the Parties in the present case as to the significance, for the delimitation of—and indeed entitlement to—the continental shelf, of State practice in the matter, and this will be examined further at a later stage in the present judgment. Nevertheless, it cannot be denied that the 1982 Convention is of major importance, having been adopted by an overwhelming majority of States;

hence it is clearly the duty of the Court, even independently of the references made to the Convention by the Parties, to consider in what degree any of its relevant provisions are binding upon the Parties as a rule of customary international law. In this context particularly, the Parties have laid some emphasis on a distinction between the law applicable to the basis of entitlement to areas of continental shelf—the rules governing the existence, "*ipso jure* and *ab initio*", and the exercise of sovereign rights of the coastal State over areas of continental shelf situate off its coasts—and the law applicable to the delimitation of such areas of shelf between neighboring States. The first question is dealt with in Article 76 of the 1982 Convention, and the second in Article 83 of the Convention. ⋯

29. In the present case, both Parties agree that, whatever the status of Article 83 of the 1982 Convention, which refers only to the "solution" as being equitable, and does not specifically mention the application of equitable principles, both these requirements form part of the law to be applied. In the first of Libya's submissions, the Court is asked to declare that, "The delimitation is to be effected by agreement in accordance with equitable principles and taking account of all relevant circumstances in order to achieve an equitable result." The first submission of Malta reads: "the principles and rules of international law applicable to the delimitation of the areas of the continental shelf which appertain to Malta and Libya are that the delimitation shall be effected on the basis of international law in order to achieve an equitable result."⋯

31. In this connection the question arises of the relationship, both within the context of the 1982 Convention and generally, between the legal concept of the continental shelf and that of the exclusive economic zone. Malta relies on the genesis of the exclusive economic zone concept, and its inclusion in the 1982 Convention, as confirming the importance of the "distance principle" in the law of the continental shelf and the detachment of the concept of the shelf from any criterion of physical prolongation. Malta has submitted that, in the

present delimitation, account must be taken of the rules of customary law reflected in Article 76 of the Convention in the light of the provisions of the Convention concerning the exclusive economic zone. … For Malta, the "distance principle", referred to also by the Court itself, is accordingly included among the principles and rules of customary international law and should be taken into account. …

32. Libya, on the other hand, points out that this case is concerned only with the delimitation of the continental shelf, and emphasizes that the 1982 Convention has not yet come into force and is not binding as between the Parties to the present case. It contends that the "distance principle" is not a rule of positive international law with regard to the continental shelf, and that the "distance criterion", which may be applicable to the definition of the outer limit of the continental shelf in certain circumstances, if it applies at all to delimitation, is inappropriate for application in the Mediterranean. It is Libya's contention that the continental shelf has not been absorbed by the concept of the exclusive economic zone under present international law; and that the establishment of fishery zones and exclusive economic zones has not changed the law of maritime zone delimitation, or given more prominence to the criterion of distance from the coast. …

33. In the view of the Court, even though the present case relates only to the delimitation of the continental shelf and not to that of the exclusive economic zone, the principles and rules underlying the latter concept cannot be left out of consideration. As the 1982 Convention demonstrates, the two institutions—continental shelf and exclusive economic zone—are linked together in modern law. Since the rights enjoyed by a State over its continental shelf would also be possessed by it over the seabed and subsoil of any exclusive economic zone which it might proclaim, one of the relevant circumstances to be taken into account for the delimitation of the continental shelf of a State is the legally permissible extent of the exclusive economic zone appertaining to that same State. This does not mean that the concept of the

continental shelf has been absorbed by that of the exclusive economic zone; it does however signify that greater importance must be attributed to elements, such as distance from the coast, which are common to both concepts.

34. For Malta, the reference to distance in Article 76 of the 1982 Convention represents a consecration of the "distance principle"; for Libya, only the reference to natural prolongation corresponds to customary international law. It is in the Court's view incontestable that, apart from those provisions, the institution of the exclusive economic zone, with its rule on entitlement by reason of distance, is shown by the practice of States to have become a part of customary law; in any case, Libya itself seemed to recognize this fact when, at one stage during the negotiation of the Special Agreement, it proposed that the extent of the exclusive economic zone be included in the reference to the Court. ··· It follows that, for juridical and practical reasons, the distance criterion must now apply to the continental shelf as well as to the exclusive economic zone; and this quite apart from the provision as to distance in paragraph 1 of Article 76. This is not to suggest that the idea of natural prolongation is now superseded by that of distance. What it does mean is that where the continental margin does not extend as far as 200 miles from the shore, natural prolongation, which in spite of its physical origins has throughout its history become more and more a complex arid juridical concept, is in part defined by distance from the shore, irrespective of the physical nature of the intervening seabed and subsoil. The concepts of natural prolongation and distance are therefore not opposed but complementary; and both remain essential elements in the juridical concept of the continental shelf. As the Court has observed, the legal basis of that which is to be delimited cannot be other than pertinent to the delimitation; the Court is thus unable to accept the Libyan contention that distance from the coast is not a relevant element for the decision of the present case.

35. It will now be convenient in view of this conclusion to examine two important and opposed arguments of the Parties: first the Libyan "rift zone"

argument, which depends upon giving primacy to the idea of natural prolongation, in the physical sense; and second, the argument of Malta that, on the contrary, it is distance that is now the prime element; and that, in consequence of this, equidistance, at least between opposite coasts, is virtually a required method, if only as the first stage in a delimitation.

B. The Libyan "Rift Zone" Argument

39. The Court however considers that since the development of the law enables a State to claim that the continental shelf appertaining to it extends up to as far as 200 miles from its coast, whatever the geological characteristics of the corresponding seabed and subsoil, there is no reason to ascribe any role to geological or geophysical factors within that distance either in verifying the legal title of the States concerned or in proceeding to a delimitation as between their claims. This is especially clear where verification of the validity of title is concerned, since, at least in so far as those areas are situated at a distance of under 200 miles from the coasts in question, title depends solely on the distance from the coasts of the claimant States of any areas of seabed claimed by way of continental shelf, and the geological or geomorphological characteristics of those areas are completely immaterial. It follows that, since the distance between the coasts of the Parties is less than 400 miles, so that no geophysical feature can lie more than 200 miles from each coast, the feature referred to as the "rift zone" cannot constitute a fundamental discontinuity terminating the southward extension of the Maltese shelf and the northward extension of the Libyan as if it were some natural boundary.

41. ···The Court is unable to accept the position (rift zone) that in order to decide this case. It must first make a determination upon a disagreement between scientists of distinction as to the more plausibly correct interpretation of apparently incomplete scientific data; for a criterion that depends upon such a judgment or estimate having to be made by a court, or perhaps also by negotiating governments, is clearly inapt to a general legal rule of delimitation. For all the above reasons, the Court, therefore, rejects the so-

Chapter IX Law of the Sea 279

called "rift zone" argument of Libya.

C. Malta's Argument Respecting the Primacy of Equidistance

42. Neither, however, is the Court able to accept the argument of Malta—almost diametrically opposed to the Libyan rift zone argument—that the new importance of the idea of distance from the coast has, at any rate for delimitation between opposite coasts, in turn conferred a primacy on the method of equidistance. ···Malta does not assert that the equidistance method is fundamental, or inherent, or has a legally obligatory character. It does argue that the legal basis of continental shelf rights requires that as a starting point of the delimitation process consideration must be given to a line based on equidistance; though it is only to the extent that this primary delimitation produces an equitable result by a balancing up of the relevant circumstances that the boundary coincides with the equidistance line. As a provisional point of departure, consideration of equidistance "is required" on the basis of the legal title.

43. The Court is unable to accept that, even as a preliminary and provisional step towards the drawing of a delimitation line, the equidistance method is one which must be used, or that the Court is "required, as a first step, to examine the effects of a delimitation by application of the equidistance method".

44. ···Even the existence of such a rule as is contended for by Malta, requiring equidistance simply to be used as a first stage in any delimitation, but subject to correction, cannot be supported solely by the production of numerous examples of delimitations using equidistance or modified equidistance, though it is impressive evidence that the equidistance method can in many different situations yield an equitable result.

D. Equitable Principle

45. Judicial decisions are at one in holding that the delimitation of a continental shelf boundary must be effected by the application of equitable principles in all the relevant circumstances in order to achieve an equitable

result. …

46. The normative character of equitable principles applied as a part of general international law is important because these principles govern not only delimitation by adjudication or arbitration, but also, and indeed primarily, the duty of Parties to seek first a delimitation by agreement, which is also to seek an equitable result. That equitable principles are expressed in terms of general application, is immediately apparent from a glance at some well-known examples: the principle that there is to be no question of refashioning geography, or compensating for the inequalities of nature; the related principle of non-encroachment by one party on the natural prolongation of the other, which is no more than the negative expression of the positive rule that the coastal State enjoys sovereign rights over the continental shelf off its coasts to the full extent authorized by international law in the relevant circumstances; the principle of respect due to all such relevant circumstances; the principle that although all States are equal before the law and are entitled to equal treatment, "equity does not necessarily imply equality" nor does it seek to make equal what nature has made unequal; and the principle that there can be no question of distributive justice.

47. The nature of equity is nowhere more evident than in these wellestablished principles. In interpreting them, it must be borne in mind that the geography which is not to be refashioned means those aspects of a geographical situation most germane to the legal institution of the continental shelf; …

E. The relevant circumstances

48. The application of equitable principles thus still leaves the Court with the task of appreciation of the weight to be accorded to *the relevant circumstances* in any particular case of delimitation. … Yet although there may be no legal limit to the considerations which States may take account of, this can hardly be true for a court applying equitable procedures. For a court, although there is assuredly no closed list of considerations, it is evident that

Chapter IX Law of the Sea 281

only those that are pertinent to the institution of the continental shelf as it has developed within the law, and to the application of equitable principles to its delimitation, will qualify for inclusion. ···

49. It was argued by Libya that the relevant geographical considerations include the landmass behind the coast, in the sense that landmass provides in Libya's view the factual basis and legal justification for the State's entitlement to continental shelf rights, a State with a greater landmass having a more intense natural prolongation. The Court is unable to accept this as a relevant consideration. Landmass has never been regarded as a basis of entitlement to continental shelf rights, and such a proposition finds no support in the practice of States, in the jurisprudence, in doctrine···

50. It was argued by Malta, on the other hand, that the considerations that may be taken account of include economic factors and security. Malta has contended that the relevant equitable considerations, employed not to dictate a delimitation but to contribute to assessment of the equitableness of a delimitation otherwise arrived at, include the absence of energy resources on the island of Malta, its requirements as an island developing country, and the range of its established fishing activity. The Court does not however consider that a delimitation should be influenced by the relative economic position of the two States in question, in such a way that the area of continental shelf regarded as appertaining to the less rich of the two States would be somewhat increased in order to compensate for its inferiority in economic resources. Such considerations are totally unrelated to the underlying intention of the applicable rules of international law. ···

51. Malta contends that the "equitable consideration" of security and defense interests confirms the equidistance method of delimitation, which gives each party a comparable lateral control from its coasts. Security considerations are of course not unrelated to the concept of the continental shelf. They were referred to when this legal concept first emerged, particularly in the Truman Proclamation. However, in the present case

neither Party has raised the question whether the law at present attributes to the coastal State particular competences in the military field over its continental shelf, including competence over the placing of military devices. ...

54. Malta has also invoked the principle of sovereign equality of States as an argument in favour of the equidistance method pure and simple, and as an objection to any adjustment based on length of coasts or proportionality considerations. It has observed that since all States are equal and equally sovereign, the maritime extensions generated by the sovereignty of each State must be of equal juridical value, whether or not the coasts of one State are longer than those of the other. The first question is whether the use of the equidistance method or recourse to proportionality considerations derive from legal rules accepted by States. If, for example, States had adopted a principle of apportionment of shelf on a basis of strict proportionality of coastal lengths (which the Court does not consider to be the case), their consent to that rule would be no breach of the principle of sovereign equality between them. Secondly, it is evident that the existence of equal entitlement, *ipso jure* and *ab initio*, of coastal States, does not imply an equality of extent of shelf, whatever the circumstances of the area; ... The principle of equality of States has therefore no particular role to play in the applicable law.

·······

The Court, by fourteen votes to three, finds that, with reference to the areas of continental shelf between the coasts of the Parties within the limits defined in the present Judgment, namely the meridian 13°50′ E and the Meridian 15°10′E:

A. The principles and rules of international law applicable for the delimitation, to be effected by agreement in implementation of the present Judgment, of the areas of continental shelf appertaining to the Socialist People's Libyan Arab Jamahiriya and to the Republic of Malta respectively are as follows:

(1) the delimitation is to be effected in accordance with equitable

principles and taking account of all relevant circumstances, so as to arrive at an equitable result;

(2) the area of continental shelf to be found to appertain to either Party not extending more than 200 miles from the coast of the Party concerned, no criterion for delimitation of shelf areas can be derived from the principle of natural prolongation in the physical sense.

B. The circumstances and factors to be taken into account in achieving an equitable delimitation in the present case are the following:

(1) the general configuration of the coasts of the Parties, their oppositeness, and their relationship to each other within the general geographical context;

(2) the disparity in the lengths of the relevant coasts of the Parties and the distance between them;

(3) the need to avoid in the delimitation any excessive disproportion between the extent of the continental shelf areas appertaining to the coastal State and the length of the relevant part of its coast, measured in the general direction of the coastlines.

4.2 Black Sea Case 2009[①]

Judgment

1. On 16 September 2004, Romania filed in the Registry of the Court an Application dated 13 September 2004, instituting proceedings against Ukraine concerning the delimitation of the continental shelf and the exclusive economic zones of Romania and Ukraine in the Black Sea.

......

31. Both Romania and Ukraine are parties to the 1982 United Nations Convention on the Law of the Sea (UNCLOS). Romania deposited its

---

① See *Maritime Delimitation in the Black Sea (Romania v. Ukraine)*, Judgment, ICJ Reports 2009, p. 61.

instrument of ratification on 17 December 1996 and Ukraine on 26 July 1999.

Articles 74 and 83 of UNCLOS are relevant for the delimitation of the exclusive economic zone and the continental shelf, respectively. Their texts are identical, the only difference being that Article 74 refers to the exclusive economic zone and Article 83 to the continental shelf. These Articles provide as follows: ...

32. Romania States that the Parties concur in the view that the Procès-Verbaux concluded between Romania and the USSR in 1949, 1963 and 1974 are agreements which are legally binding on the Parties. Romania contends that these agreements, which establish the initial segment of the maritime boundary, should be taken into account as agreements relating to the delimitation within the meaning of Articles 74, paragraph 4, and 83, paragraph 4, of UNCLOS. Another such agreement is the 2003 State Border Régime Treaty which delimited the maritime boundary up to the outer limit of the territorial sea at the point of intersection of Romania's territorial sea with the 12-nautical mile arc drawn around Serpents' Island. ...

33. Romania argues that the principles recognized by the Parties in the 1997 Additional Agreement are applicable both to the diplomatic negotiations between the two States and for the purposes of any eventual settlement of the dispute by the Court. These principles are listed in paragraph 4 of the 1997 Additional Agreements as follows:

(a) the principle stated in article 121 of the United Nations Convention on the Law of the Sea of December 10, 1982, as applied in the practice of States and in international case jurisprudence;

(b) the principle of the equidistance line in areas submitted to delimitation where the coasts are adjacent and the principle of the median line in areas where the coasts are opposite;

(c) the principle of equity and the method of proportionality, as they are applied in the practice of States and in the decisions of international

Chapter IX Law of the Sea 285

courts regarding the delimitation of continental shelf and exclusive economic zones;

(d) the principle according to which neither of the Contracting Parties shall contest the sovereignty of the other Contracting Party over any part of its territory adjacent to the zone submitted to delimitation;

(e) the principle of taking into consideration the special circumstances of the zone submitted to delimitation

......

36. Ukraine contends that the Court is obliged to decide disputes in accordance with international law, as laid down in Article 38, paragraph 1, of the Statute. In relation to maritime delimitation and as between the Parties to the present case, "that applicable body of rules of international law comprises principally the provisions of UNCLOS and certain specific rules which have become well established in the jurisprudence of the Court".

37. According to Ukraine, the 1997 Additional Agreement is an international treaty binding upon the Parties, however … but they were not agreed by the Parties as applying to the subsequent judicial proceedings. … some of these principles may be relevant as part of the established rules of international law which the Court will apply but not as part of any bilateral agreement.

38. Ukraine further argues that the 1949, 1963 and 1974 Procès-Verbaux and the 1997 Additional Agreement do not constitute agreements mentioned in Articles 74, paragraph 4, and 83, paragraph 4, of UNCLOS…

40. In deciding what will be a single maritime delimitation line, the Court will duly take into account the agreements in force between the Parties. Whether the Procès-Verbaux concluded between Romania and the USSR in 1949, 1963 and 1974 constitute agreements relating to the delimitation within the meaning of Articles 74, paragraph 4, and 83, paragraph 4, of UNCLOS, depends on the conclusion the Court will reach on Romania's contention that

they establish the initial segment of the maritime boundary which the Court has to determine. ···

41. With respect to the principles listed in subparagraphs 4(a) to (e) of the Additional Agreement, the Court is of the view ··· that these principles were intended by the Parties to be taken into account in their negotiations on the maritime delimitation, but do not constitute the law to be applied by the Court. This does not necessarily mean that these principles would *per se* be of no applicability in the present case; they may apply to the extent that they are part of the relevant rules of international law. ···

Relevant Circumstances

155. As the Court indicated above (paragraphs 120-121), once the provisional equidistance line has been drawn, it shall "then (consider) whether there are factors calling for the adjustment or shifting of that line in order to achieve an 'equitable result'". Such factors have usually been referred to in the jurisprudence of the Court, since the *North Sea Continental Shelf (Federal Republic of Germany/Denmark; Federal Republic of Germany/Netherlands) Cases*, as the relevant circumstances. Their function is to verify that the provisional equidistance line, drawn by the geometrical method from the determined base points on the coasts of the Parties is not, in light of the particular circumstances of the case, perceived as inequitable. If such would be the case, the Court should adjust the line in order to achieve the "equitable solution" as required by Articles 74, paragraph 1, and 83, paragraph 1, of UNCLOS.

156. The Parties suggested and discussed several factors which they consider as the possible relevant circumstances of the case. They arrive at different conclusions. Romania argues that its provisional equidistance line achieves the equitable result and thus does not require any adjustment. Ukraine, on the other hand, submits that there are relevant circumstances which call for the adjustment of its provisional equidistance line "by moving the provisional line closer to the Romanian coast".

157. ··· the Court wishes to recall that the provisional equidistance line it has drawn in Section 8 above does not coincide with the provisional lines drawn either by Ukraine or Romania. Therefore, it is this line, drawn by the Court, and not by Romania or Ukraine, which will be in the focus of the Court's attention when analysing what the Parties consider to be the relevant circumstances of the case.

(1) Disproportion between Lengths of Coasts

158. The circumstance which Ukraine invokes in order to justify its claim that the provisional equidistance line should be adjusted by moving the delimitation line closer to Romania's coast is the disparity between the length of the Parties' coasts abutting on the delimitation area.

159. ···However, with regard specifically to any disproportion between the lengths of the Parties' coasts, Romania notes that in a maritime delimitation it is rare for the disparities between the Parties' coasts to feature as a relevant circumstance. Moreover, in the present case, there is no manifest disparity in the respective coastal lengths of Romania and Ukraine.

163. The Court observes that the respective length of coasts can play no role in identifying the equidistance line which has been provisionally established. ···

164. Where disparities in the lengths of coasts are particularly marked, the Court may choose to treat that fact of geography as a relevant circumstance that would require some adjustments to the provisional equidistance line to be made.

166. In the case concerning *Maritime Delimitation in the Area between Greenland and Jan Mayen (Denmark v. Norway)*, the Court found that the disparity between the lengths of the coasts of Jan Mayen and Greenland (approximately 1 : 9) constituted a "special circumstance" requiring modification of the provisional median line··· In the latter case[1], the Court

---

[1] See *Continental Shelf (Libyan v. Malta) Case*, Judgment, ICJ Reports 1985, p. 45, para. 58.

was of the view that the difference in the lengths of the relevant coasts of Malta and Libya (being in ratio 1∶8) "is so great as to justify the adjustment of the median line". ⋯

168. In the present case, however the Court sees no such particularly marked disparities between the relevant coasts of Ukraine and Romania. ⋯

(2) *The Enclosed Nature of the Black Sea and the Delimitations Already Effected*

169. Romania notes that the enclosed nature of the Black Sea is also a relevant circumstance as part of the wider requirement to take account of the geographical context of the area to be delimited. According to Romania, in considering the equitable nature of an equidistance line, the "general maritime geography" of the Black Sea must be assessed. ⋯

170. Romania contends that all the delimitation agreements concluded in the Black Sea used equidistance as the method for the delimitation of the continental shelf and the exclusive economic zones. ⋯

171. Romania concludes that the Black Sea's nature as an enclosed sea and its rather small size, together with the agreed solutions established in the delimitation agreements in force, constitute a relevant circumstance which must be taken into account in the delimitation process for Romania's and Ukraine's maritime areas.

In Ukraine's view, there is "no support in law or in the factual context" for Romania's arguments regarding the characterization of the Black Sea as an enclosed sea and the importance of maritime delimitation agreements previously concluded between certain States bordering the Black Sea. ⋯

173. Ukraine further notes that ⋯ the existing maritime delimitation agreements in the Black Sea cannot influence the present dispute. ⋯ The presence of third States may be relevant only to the extent that the Court may have to take precautions in identifying a precise endpoint of the delimitation line so as to avoid potential prejudice to States situated on the periphery of the delimitation area.

Chapter IX Law of the Sea 289

174. The Court recalls that it has intimated earlier, when it briefly described the delimitation methodology, that it would establish a provisional equidistance line. ⋯

175. Two delimitation agreements concerning the Black Sea were brought to the attention of the Court. The first agreement, the Agreement concerning the Delimitation of the Continental Shelf in the Black Sea, was concluded between Turkey and the USSR on 23 June 1978. ⋯

176. The second agreement is the Agreement between Turkey and Bulgaria on the determination of the boundary in the mouth area of the Rezovska/Mutludere River and delimitation of the maritime areas between the two States in the Black Sea, signed on 4 December 1997. ⋯

177. The Court will bear in mind the agreed maritime delimitations between Turkey and Bulgaria, as well as between Turkey and Ukraine, when considering the endpoint of the single maritime boundary it is asked to draw in the present case.

178. The Court nevertheless considers that, in the light of the abovementioned delimitation agreements and the enclosed nature of the Black Sea, no adjustment to the equidistance line as provisionally drawn is caued for.

(3) *The Presence of Serpents' Island in the Area of Delimitation*

179. The Parties disagree as to the proper characterization of Serpents' Island and the role this maritime feature should play in the delimitation of the continental shelf and the Parties' exclusive economic zones in the Black Sea.

180. Romania maintains that Serpents' Island is entitled to no more than a 12-nautical-mile territorial sea, and that it cannot be used as a base point in drawing a delimitation line beyond the 12-mile limit. Romania claims that Serpents' Island is a rock incapable of sustaining human habitation or economic life of its own, and therefore has no exclusive economic zone or continental shelf, as provided for in Article 121, paragraph 3, of the 1982 UNCLOS. ⋯

181. Romania further argues that Serpents' Island does not form part of the coastal configuration of the Parties and that its coast cannot therefore be included among Ukraine's relevant coasts for purposes of the delimitation.

183. Ukraine argues that Serpents' Island has a baseline which generates base points for the construction of the provisional equidistance line. Thus, in Ukraine's view, the coast of the island constitutes part of Ukraine's relevant coasts for purposes of the delimitation and cannot be reduced to just a relevant circumstance to be considered only at the second stage of the delimitation process after the provisional equidistance line has been established.

184. According to Ukraine, Serpents' Island is indisputably an "island" under Article 121, paragraph 2, of UNCLOS, rather than a "rock". Ukraine contends that the evidence shows that Serpents' Island can readily sustain human habitation and that it is well established that it can sustain an economic life of its own. In particular, the island has vegetation and a sufficient supply of fresh water. …Ukraine also argues that paragraph 3 of Article 121 is not relevant to this delimitation because that paragraph is not concerned with questions of delimitation but is, rather, an entitlement provision that has no practical application with respect to a maritime area that is, in any event, within the 200-mile limit of the exclusive economic zone and continental shelf of a mainland coast.

185. …In this phase, the Court may be called upon to decide whether this line should be adjusted because of the presence of small islands in its vicinity. As the jurisprudence has indicated, the Court may on occasion decide not to take account of very small islands or decide not to give them their full potential entitlement to maritime zones, should such an approach have a disproportionate effect on the delimitation line under consideration.

186. The Court recalls that it has already determined that Serpents' Island cannot serve as a base point for the construction of the provisional equidistance line between the coasts of the Parties, that it has drawn in the first stage of this delimitation process, since it does not form part of the

Chapter IX Law of the Sea 291

general configuration of the coast. The Court must now, at the second stage, ascertain whether the presence of Serpents' Island in the maritime delimitation area constitutes a relevant circumstance calling for an adjustment of the provisional equidistance line.

187. ··· The Court observes that Serpents' Island is situated approximately 20 nautical miles to the east of Ukraine's mainland coast in the area of the Danube delta. Given this geographical configuration and in the context of the delimitation with Romania, any continental shelf and exclusive economic zone entitlements possibly generated by Serpents' Island could not project further than the entitlements generated by Ukraine's mainland coast because of the southern limit of the delimitation area as identified by the Court. Further, any possible entitlements generated by Serpents' Island in an eastward direction are fully subsumed by the entitlements generated by the western and eastern mainland coasts of Ukraine itself. ···the Court concludes that the presence of Serpents' Island does not call for an adjustment of the provisional equidistance line. ···

(4) *The Conduct of the Parties (Oil and Gas Concessions Fishing Activities and Naval Patrols)*

189. Ukraine suggests that State activities in the relevant area "constitute a relevant circumstance which operates in favour of the continental shelf/EEZ claim line proposed by Ukraine". ···

190. Ukraine argues that in 1993, 2001 and 2003 it licensed activities relating to the exploration of oil and gas deposits within the continental shelf/exclusive economic zone area claimed by Ukraine in the current case. It asserts that the existence of these licences demonstrates that Ukraine, both before and after the 1997 Additional Agreement, authorized activities relating to the exploration of oil and gas deposits in areas of the continental shelf to which Romania lays claim in these proceedings. ···

191. Ukraine further argues that the exclusive economic zone and continental shelf boundary it claims furthermore corresponds generally to the limit of the Parties

exclusive fishing zones "as respected by both Romania and Ukraine in their administration of fishing in the north-west part of the Black Sea". ···

193. Romania does not consider that State activities in the relevant area, namely licences for the exploration and exploitation of oil and gas and fishing practices, constitute relevant circumstances. ···

198. The Court does not see, in the circumstances of the present case, any particular role for the State activities invoked above in this maritime delimitation. ··· With respect to fisheries, the Court adds that no evidence has been submitted to it by Ukraine that any delimitation line other than that claimed by it would be "likely to entail catastrophic repercussions for the livelihood and economic well-being of the population". ···

(5) *Any Cutting Off Effect*

199. Romania contends that its proposed maritime boundary does not cut off the entitlements to the continental shelf and to the exclusive economic zone of either Romania or Ukraine. The area attributed to each Party does not encroach on the natural prolongation of the other.

Romania argues that Ukraine's delimitation line leads to a cut-off of Romania's maritime entitlements ···

200. ··· Ukraine argues that "Romania's versions of equidistance produce a marked cut-off effect of the projection of Ukraine's coastal front north of the land boundary". ··· Ukraine argues that its line fully respects the principle of non-encroachment. ···

201. The Court observes that the delimitation lines proposed by the Parties, in particular their first segments, each significantly curtail the entitlement of the other Party to the continental shelf and the exclusive economic zone. ··· the provisional equidistance line drawn by the Court avoids such a drawback as it allows the adjacent coasts of the Parties to produce their effects, in terms of maritime entitlements, in a reasonable and mutually balanced way. That being so, the Court sees no reason to adjust the provisional equidistance line on this ground.

(6) *The Security Considerations of the Parties*

202. Romania asserts that there is no evidence to suggest that the delimitation advanced by it would adversely affect Ukraine's security interests, including Serpents' Island, which has a belt of maritime space of 12 nautical miles.

In Romania's view, Ukraine's delimitation line runs unreasonably close to the Romanian coast and thus encroaches on the security interests of Romania.

203. Ukraine claims that its line in no way compromises any Romanian security interests because Ukraine's delimitation line accords to Romania areas of continental shelf and exclusive economic zone off its coastline. In this regard Ukraine refers to "the predominant interest Ukraine has for security and other matters as a function of its geographical position along this part of the Black Sea on three sides of the coast" and maintains that Ukraine has been the only Party to police the area and to prevent illegal fishing and other activities in that area. According to Ukraine, its claim is consistent with this aspect of the conduct of the Parties, whereas Romania's claim is not.

204. The Court confines itself to two observations. First, the legitimate security considerations of the Parties may play a role in determining the final delimitation line. Second, in the present case however, the provisional equidistance line it has drawn substantially differs from the lines drawn either by Romania or Ukraine. The provisional equidistance line determined by the Court fully respects the legitimate security interests of either Party. ...

The Disproportionality Test

210. The Court now turns to check that the result thus far arrived at, so far as the envisaged delimitation line is concerned, does not lead to any significant disproportionality by reference to the respective coastal lengths and the apportionment of areas that ensue. ...

211. The continental shelf and exclusive economic zone allocations are not to be assigned in proportion to length of respective coastlines. Rather, the Court will check, *ex post facto*, on the equitableness of the delimitation line it has constructed.

212. This checking can only be approximate. Diverse techniques have in the past been used for assessing coastal lengths, with no clear requirements of international law having been shown as to whether the real coastline should be followed, or baselines used, or whether or not coasts relating to internal waters should be excluded.

213. The Court cannot but observe that various tribunals, and the Court itself, have drawn different conclusions over the years as to what disparity in coastal lengths would constitute a significant disproportionality which suggested the delimitation line was inequitable and still required adjustment. This remains in each case a matter for the Court's appreciation…

214. In the present case the Court has measured the coasts according to their general direction. It has not used baselines suggested by the Parties for this measurement. … These measurements are necessarily approximate given that the purpose of this final stage is to make sure there is no significant disproportionality.

215. It suffices for this third stage for the Court to note that the ratio of the respective coastal lengths for Romania and Ukraine, measured as described above, is approximately 1∶2.8 and the ratio of the relevant area between Romania and Ukraine is approximately 1∶2.1.

216. The Court is not of the view that this suggests that the line as constructed, and checked carefully for any relevant circumstances that might have warranted adjustment, requires any alteration.

5. References and Recommended Reading Materials

（1）中国国际法学会编：《南海仲裁案裁决之批判》（中、英文版），外文出版社2018年版。

（2）Hugo Grotius, *The Free Sea*, translated by Richard Hakluyt, Liberty Fund, 2004.〔荷〕格劳秀斯：《论海洋自由：或荷兰参与东印度贸易的权利》，马忠法译，上海人民出版社2005年版。

Chapter X   International Space Law

1. Introduction

The space law is synonyms for Outer Space Law in some textbooks. International space law is usually defined as a branch of general (public) international law, a subset of rules, rights and obligations of States within the latter specifically related to outer space and activities in or with respect to that realm. ① In China, the space law includes the law of airspace and the law of outer space. The two bodies of rules concerning the earth's envelope differ fundamentally in their basic legal regime. As to the airspace, the State can extend sovereignty to it. It is an established principle that every State has complete and exclusive sovereignty over the airspace above its territory. As the ICJ noted in the *Nicaragua Case*, "The principle of respect for territorial sovereignty is also directly infringed by the unauthorized over-flight of a State's territory by aircraft belonging to or under the control of the government of another State."②There is no right of innocent passage through the airspace of a State. Aircraft may only traverse the airspace of States with the agreement of those States. As to outer space, States have agreed to apply the international law principles of *res communis*, so that no portion of outer

---

① See Frans von der Dunk and Fabio Tronchetti (eds.), *Handbook of Space Law*, Edward Elgar Publishing, 2015, p. 29.

② *Military and Paramilitary Activities in and against Nicaragua (Nicaragua v. United States of America)*, Judgment. ICJ Reports 1986, pp. 14, 128.

space may be appropriated to the sovereignty of individual States. It was made evident in several General Assembly resolutions following the advent of the satellite era in the late 1950s. For instance, UN General Assembly resolution 1962 (XVIII), adopted in 1963 and entitled the Declaration of Legal Principles Governing the Activities of States in the Exploration and Use of Outer Space, lays down a series of applicable legal principles which include the provisions that outer space and celestial bodies were free for exploration and use by all States on the basis of equality and in accordance with international law, and that outer space and celestial bodies were not subject to national appropriation by any means.

This chapter is mainly about the outer space since the rules on the airspace are covered by the international economic law. To avoid repetition and save space, this chapter will list only some provisions about the State's sovereignty over its airspace. As to the outer space law, it addresses a variety of matters, such as, the preservation of the space and earth environment, liability for damages caused by space objects, the settlement of disputes, the rescue of astronauts, the sharing of information about potential dangers in outer space, the use of space-related technologies, and international cooperation. A number of fundamental principles guide the conduct of space activities, including the notion of space as the province of all humankind, the freedom of exploration and use of outer space by all States without discrimination, and the principle of non-appropriation of outer space.

2. Preliminary Reading and Assignment

2.1 Convention on International Civil Aviation

Convention on International Civil Aviation (also known as Chicago

Convention), was signed on 7 December 1944 by 52 States. Pending ratification of the Convention by 26 States, the Provisional International Civil Aviation Organization (PICAO) was established. ICAO came into being on 4 April 1947. In October of the same year, ICAO became a specialized agency of the United Nations Economic and Social Council (ECOSOC).

Article 1　Sovereignty

The contracting States recognize that every State has complete and exclusive sovereignty over the airspace above its territory.

Article 2　Territory

For the purposes of this Convention the territory of a State shall be deemed to be the land areas and territorial waters adjacent thereto under the sovereignty, suzerainty, protection or mandate of such State.

Article 3　Civil and State aircraft

a. This Convention shall be applicable only to civil aircraft, and shall not be applicable to State aircraft.

b. Aircraft used in military, customs and police services shall be deemed to be State aircraft.

c. No State aircraft of a contracting State shall fly over the territory of another State or land thereon without authorization by special agreement or otherwise, and in accordance with the terms thereof.

d. The contracting States undertake, when issuing regulations for their State aircraft, that they will have due regard for the safety of navigation of civil aircraft.

Article 3bis. [1]

a. The contracting States recognize that every State must refrain from resorting to the use of weapons against civil aircraft in flight and that, in case

---

[1] Added by amendment 1984-05-10, entered into force 1998-10-01.

of interception, the lives of persons on board and the safety of aircraft must not be endangered. This provision shall not be interpreted as modifying in any way the rights and obligations of States set forth in the Charter of the United Nations.

b. The contracting States recognize that every State, in the exercise of its sovereignty, is entitled to require the landing at some designated airport of a civil aircraft flying above its territory without authority or if there are reasonable grounds to conclude that it is being used for any purpose inconsistent with the aims of this Convention; it may also give such aircraft any other instructions to put an end to such violations. For this purpose, the contracting States may resort to any appropriate means consistent with relevant rules of international law, including the relevant provisions of this Convention, specifically paragraph a) of this Article. Each contracting State agrees to publish its regulations in force regarding the interception of civil aircraft.

c. Every civil aircraft shall comply with an order given in conformity with paragraph b) of this Article. To this end each contracting State shall establish all necessary provisions in its national laws or regulations to make such compliance mandatory for any civil aircraft registered in that State or operated by an operator who has his principal place of business or permanent residence in that State. Each contracting State shall make any violation of such applicable laws or regulations punishable by severe penalties and shall submit the case to its competent authorities in accordance with its laws or regulations.

d. Each contracting State shall take appropriate measures to prohibit the deliberate use of any civil aircraft registered in that State or operated by an operator who has his principal place of business or permanent residence in that State for any purpose inconsistent with the aims of this Convention. This provision shall not affect paragraph a or derogate from paragraphs b and c of this Article.

......

2.2 Outer Space Treaty (1967)[①]

Article I

The exploration and use of outer space, including the moon and other celestial bodies, shall be carried out for the benefit and in the interests of all countries, irrespective of their degree of economic or scientific development, and shall be the province of all mankind.

Outer space, including the moon and other celestial bodies, shall be free for exploration and use by all States without discrimination of any kind, on a basis of equality and in accordance with international law, and there shall be free access to all areas of celestial bodies.

There shall be freedom of scientific investigation in outer space, including the moon and other celestial bodies, and States shall facilitate and encourage international co-operation in such investigation.

Article II

Outer space, including the moon and other celestial bodies, is not subject to national appropriation by claim of sovereignty, by means of use or occupation, or by any other means.

Article III

States Parties to the Treaty shall carry on activities in the exploration and

---

[①] The Treaty on Principles Governing the Activities of States in the Exploration and Use of Outer Space, Including the Moon and Other Celestial Bodies, which is usually called the Outer Space Treaty, is one of the most significant law-making treaties concluded in the second half of the 20th century. It was adopted by the United Nations General Assembly on 19 December 1966 (resolution 2222 (XXI)), opened for signature at London, Moscow and Washington on 27 January 1967, and entered into force on 10 October 1967. The Outer Space Treaty laid down the foundations of international regulation of space activities and thus established the framework of the present legal regime of outer space and celestial bodies.

use of outer space, including the moon and other celestial bodies, in accordance with international law, including the Charter of the United Nations, in the interest of maintaining international peace and security and promoting international co-operation and understanding.

Article IV

States Parties to the Treaty undertake not to place in orbit around the earth any objects carrying nuclear weapons or any other kinds of weapons of mass destruction, install such weapons on celestial bodies, or station such weapons in outer space in any other manner.

The moon and other celestial bodies shall be used by all States Parties to the Treaty exclusively for peaceful purposes. The establishment of military bases, installations and fortifications, the testing of any type of weapons and the conduct of military manoeuvres on celestial bodies shall be forbidden. The use of military personnel for scientific research or for any other peaceful purposes shall not be prohibited. The use of any equipment or facility necessary for peaceful exploration of the moon and other celestial bodies shall also not be prohibited.

Article V

States Parties to the Treaty shall regard astronauts as envoys of mankind in outer space and shall render to them all possible assistance in the event of accident, distress, or emergency landing on the territory of another State Party or on the high seas. When astronauts make such a landing, they shall be safely and promptly returned to the State of registry of their space vehicle.

In carrying on activities in outer space and on celestial bodies, the astronauts of one State Party shall render all possible assistance to the astronauts of other States Parties.

States Parties to the Treaty shall immediately inform the other States Parties to the Treaty or the Secretary-General of the United Nations of any phenomena they discover in outer space, including the moon and other celestial bodies, which could constitute a danger to the life or health of astronauts.

Article VI

States Parties to the Treaty shall bear international responsibility for national activities in outer space, including the moon and other celestial bodies, whether such activities are carried on by governmental agencies or by non-governmental entities, and for assuring that national activities are carried out in conformity with the provisions set forth in the present Treaty. The activities of non-governmental entities in outer space, including the moon and other celestial bodies, shall require authorization and continuing supervision by the appropriate State Party to the Treaty. When activities are carried on in outer space, including the moon and other celestial bodies, by an international organization, responsibility for compliance with this Treaty shall be borne both by the international organization and by the States Parties to the Treaty participating in such organization.

Article VII

Each State Party to the Treaty that launches or procures the launching of an object into outer space, including the moon and other celestial bodies, and each State Party from whose territory or facility an object is launched, is internationally liable for damage to another State Party to the Treaty or to its natural or juridical persons by such object or its component parts on the Earth, in air or in outer space, including the moon and other celestial bodies.

Article VIII

A State Party to the Treaty on whose registry an object launched into outer space is carried shall retain jurisdiction and control over such object, and over any personnel thereof, while in outer space or on a celestial body. Ownership of objects launched into outer space, including objects landed or constructed on a celestial body, and of their component parts, is not affected by their presence in outer space or on a celestial body or by their return to the Earth. Such objects or component parts found beyond the limits of the State Party to the Treaty on whose registry they are carried shall be returned to that State Party, which shall, upon request, furnish identifying data prior to their return.

Article IX

In the exploration and use of outer space, including the moon and other celestial bodies, States Parties to the Treaty shall be guided by the principle of co-operation and mutual assistance and shall conduct all their activities in outer space, including the moon and other celestial bodies, with due regard to the corresponding interests of all other States Parties to the Treaty. States Parties to the Treaty shall pursue studies of outer space, including the moon and other celestial bodies, and conduct exploration of them so as to avoid their harmful contamination and also adverse changes in the environment of the Earth resulting from the introduction of extraterrestrial matter and, where necessary, shall adopt appropriate measures for this purpose. If a State Party to the Treaty has reason to believe that an activity or experiment planned by it or its nationals in outer space, including the moon and other celestial bodies, would cause potentially harmful interference with activities of other States Parties in the peaceful exploration and use of outer space, including the moon and other celestial bodies, it shall undertake appropriate international consultations before proceeding with any such activity or experiment. A State Party to the Treaty which has reason to believe that an activity or experiment planned by another State Party in outer space, including the moon and other celestial bodies, would cause potentially harmful interference with activities in the peaceful exploration and use of outer space, including the moon and other celestial bodies, may request consultation concerning the activity or experiment.

Article X

In order to promote international co-operation in the exploration and use of outer space, including the moon and other celestial bodies, in conformity with the purposes of this Treaty, the States Parties to the Treaty shall consider on a basis of equality any requests by other States Parties to the

Treaty to be afforded an opportunity to observe the flight of space objects launched by those States. The nature of such an opportunity for observation and the conditions under which it could be afforded shall be determined by agreement between the States concerned.

Article XI

In order to promote international co-operation in the peaceful exploration and use of outer space, States Parties to the Treaty conducting activities in outer space, including the moon and other celestial bodies, agree to inform the Secretary-General of the United Nations as well as the public and the international scientific community, to the greatest extent feasible and practicable, of the nature, conduct, locations and results of such activities. On receiving the said information, the Secretary-General of the United Nations should be prepared to disseminate it immediately and effectively.

Article XII

All stations, installations, equipment and space vehicles on the moon and other celestial bodies shall be open to representatives of other States Parties to the Treaty on a basis of reciprocity. Such representatives shall give reasonable advance notice of a projected visit, in order that appropriate consultations may be held and that maximum precautions may betaken to assure safety and to avoid interference with normal operations in the facility to be visited.

2.3 Assignment and questions

(1) Retreat the full text of the Rescue Agreement 1967, Convention on International Liability for Damage Caused by Space Objects 1971 and the Moon Agreement 1979.

(2) Reading the treaties and making a brief about the basic regime of the outer space law in English (8-10 minutes).

(3) Based on the provisions of those treaties and conventions, do you agree with the view that deploying military weapon in Moon and Mars is illegal under international law? Why?

3. Terminologies and Explanations

3.1 International Aviation Law

Aviation law is the law about aircrafts, including their passengers and cargo. The law governs their transit above States and other governed territories. Aviation law is considered international law in many cases due to the nature of air travel. Airplanes flying through international skies are subject to international aviation law. They are in no way the equivalent of instrumentalities of commerce that travel exclusively between the various States of one country. Because of the international nature of air travel, countries have entered into conventions to standardize the laws regulating airlines. The conventions also set forth the rights of passengers.

There are many important conventions on public international air laws. Such as, *Convention Relating to the Regulation of Aerial Navigation (Paris Convention, 1919)*, *Convention on International Civil Aviation (Chicago Convention, 1944)*, *International Air Services Transit Agreement (1944)*, *International Air Transport Agreement (1944)*, *Multilateral Agreement on Commercial Rights of Non-Scheduled Air Services among the Association of South-East Asian Nations (1971)*, *Memorandum of Understanding Between the Governments of Indonesia, Malaysia and Thailand on Expansion of Air Linkages (IMT-GT, 2021)*, *General Agreement on Tariffs and Trade (1947)*, *General Agreement on Trade in Services* and *Agreement on Trade in Civil Aircraft (1994)*.

An International Commission for Aerial Navigation (ICAN) was created under *the Paris Convention (1919)*. Additionally, *the Warsaw Convention 1929*, short of *the Convention for the Unification of Certain Rules Relating to International Carriage by Air*, limits the liability of airlines for accidents on international flights except when the airline engages in willful misconduct.

The Montreal Convention 1999 amended the important provisions of the Warsaw Convention's articles regulating compensation for the victims of air disasters.

International aviation laws are enforced through a set of institutions. Among them, ICAO, a branch of the United Nations, provides general rules and mediates international concerns to an extent regarding aviation law. The European Aviation Safety Agency (EASA) is an agency responsible for the certification of new aircraft. The EASA has specific regulatory and executive tasks in the field of civilian aviation safety. The Joint Aviation Authorities (JAA) represents the civil aviation regulatory authorities of a number of European States who have agreed to cooperate in developing and implementing common safety regulatory standards and procedures.

International policies are introduced through open skies agreements to liberalize the rules for international aviation markets, to minimize government intervention, and to adjust the rules under which military and other State-based flights are permitted.

3.2 Special Legal Problems

(1) *The boundary between airspace and outer space*

The Outer Space Treaty laid down for outer space an international legal status quite different from the status of air space, the latter being under the sovereignty of the underlying State. However, no agreement exists as to where the regime of airspace ends and that of outer space begins. There are at least 35 theories on precisely where outer space begins. None of these theories has received general acceptance among jurists or States. From a legal point of view, two schools of thought emerged at an early stage: that of the functionalists, who consider the nature of the activity of a space vehicle rather than the physical location of its activities to be crucial, and the specialists, who more traditionally pointed to the acknowledged territorial sovereignty of States. In 1979, the Soviet Union submitted a working paper to COPUOS suggesting *inter alia* that the region above an altitude of 100 (110) km should be deemed to be outer space. Several countries, including the United States and the United Kingdom, opposed this proposal and argued that a demarcation line was unnecessary and could possibly interfere with current and future space activities. The question of the definition of outer space has become more controversial as a result of the position of several equatorial States that have declared the geostationary orbit, because of its dependence on the earth's gravity, to be under the sovereignty of the subjacent States. This position has been widely rejected. Had an international agreement on the definition of outer space existed, the equatorial States might not have advanced their claim. While the debate continues as to whether delimitation is possible or necessary, the issue has acquired a new dimension with the advent of the space shuttle which performs its mission as a spacecraft but returns to the earth through airspace as a glider. The solution to the problem of delimitation remains elusive.

(2) *Protection of the space environment*

More than five thousand space objects have been tracked in outer space. Congestion of the near-earth space, space debris, damage to the atmosphere and ionosphere by rocket propellants and the danger of radioactive contamination are the most obvious risks involved in the growing utilization of outer space. The open nature of the space environment, as well as experience with pollution problems on the surface of the earth, are indicative of the need for effective legal protection of space.

Space environmental law will have to deal with both space debris and space pollution. Rules will be needed on the removal of inactive satellites and generally on the reduction of space debris. In the near future, a large assembly of orbital stations in outer space can be expected, further adding to the density of traffic. Future space activities will have to be subjected to limitations on pollution in an effective way, as they may affect the entire globe. Another area of concern involves the dangers connected with the use of nuclear power sources (NPS) in space (Nuclear Energy, Peaceful Uses). Attention was drawn to this issue following the disintegration in 1978 of a Soviet surveillance satellite, Cosmos 954, over Canada's Arctic territory. This incident drew attention to the longstanding practice of space powers of launching into outer space, without any international controls, vehicles carrying radioactive materials. It is estimated that about 25 to 100 satellites equipped with NPS have been placed by the United States and the Soviet Union in the earth's orbit. Guidelines to ensure that NPS be used in outer space as safely as possible are needed. These could cover radiation levels, protection standards, assistance to States, orbital prediction and notification requirements.

(3) *Commercial space activities*

Human's activities in space have gone from scientific exploration to commercial utilization. At present, all national economies are cutting down on budgets. This situation, together with the high costs of future space activities, will necessitate financial help from States and governments. The commercialization of satellite services and the commercial availability of the Space Shuttle are indicative of this approach. Existing rules of space law must take into account the economic and technical background which characterize the growing commercialization of space activities. The role of private enterprises in space activities can also be expected to develop considerably both in volume and in the relative share of space activities compared to those of States. The legal framework of such commercial activities of private enterprises will require clarification.

(4) *Militarization of outer space*

The growing danger of militarization of outer space can hardly be overestimated. The Outer Space Treaty provides only to the partial demilitarization of outer space. The advent of new technologies, such as antisatellites (ASATs), ballistic missile defense (BMO) and strategic defense initiative (SOl) systems, will require not only clarification of existing rules but also the elaboration of new legal instruments IS alternatives and possible compromises to limit and reduce such activities.

4. Further Reading Materials

Read the following materials and think about the questions below:

(1) What do you think about the Space Force launched by Trump's administration? How to interpret and apply the phrase "exclusively for peaceful purposes" used in the conventions?

(2) What is your attitude towards the exploitation of Mars by private companies?

(3) Do you agree that these new State practices will alternate the current legal regime of the outer space framed by the conventions and treaties enacted by the UN? Learn about the history of the US Strategic Defense Initiative (SDI), nicknamed the "Star Wars program". What is your opinion about the US' new Defense Space Strategy? How to counter its threat and risk against international security?

(4) "You want to wake up in the morning and think the future is going to be great—and that's what being a spacefaring civilization is all about. It's about believing in the future and thinking that the future will be better than the past. And I can't think of anything more exciting than going out there and being among the stars." This is a statement made by Elon Musk, CEO of SpaceX, a leading company in the commercial exploitation of Mars. What do you think about the prospect of human space exploitation? Will it change the current legal regime and human civilization? What guidelines do these commercial exploitations shall follow according to the concerned international law?

4.1 US National Aeronautics and Space Act of 1958

Declaration of Policy and Purpose: Section 102

(a) The Congress hereby declares that it is the policy of the United

States that activities in space should be devoted to peaceful purposes for the benefit of all mankind.

(b) The Congress declares that the general welfare and security of the United States require that adequate provision be made for aeronautical and space activities. The Congress further declares that such activities shall be the responsibility of, and shall be directed by, a civilian agency exercising control over aeronautical and space activities sponsored by the United States, except that activities peculiar to or primarily associated with the development of weapons systems, military operations, or the defense of the United States (including the research and development necessary to make effective provision for the defense of the United States) shall be the responsibility of, and shall be directed by, the Department of Defense (DOD); and that determination as to which such agency has responsibility for and direction of any such activity shall be made by the President in conformity with section 201 (e).

(c) The aeronautical and space activities of the United States shall be conducted so as to contribute materially to one or more of the following objectives:

(1) The expansion of human knowledge of phenomena in the atmosphere and space;

(2) The improvement of the usefulness, performance, speed, safety, and efficiency of aeronautical and space vehicles;

(3) The development and operation of vehicles capable of carrying instruments, equipment, supplies and living organisms through space;

(4) The establishment of long-range studies of the potential benefits to be gained from, the opportunities for, and the problems involved in the utilization of aeronautical and space activities for peaceful and scientific purposes;

(5) The preservation of the role of the United States as a leader in aeronautical and space science and technology and in the application thereof to the conduct of peaceful activities within and outside the atmosphere;

(6) The making available to agencies directly concerned with national defenses of discoveries that have military value or significance, and the furnishing by such agencies, to the civilian agency established to direct and control nonmilitary aeronautical and space activities, of information as to discoveries which have value or significance to that agency;

(7) Cooperation by the United States with other nations and groups of nations in work done pursuant to this Act and in the peaceful application of the results, thereof; and

(8) The most effective utilization of the scientific and engineering resources of the United States, with close cooperation among all interested agencies of the United States in order to avoid unnecessary duplication of effort, facilities, and equipment.

(d) It is the purpose of this Act to carry out and effectuate the policies declared in subsections (a), (b), and (c).

4.2 Presidential Directive on National Space Policy 1988[①]

Fact Sheet

The President approved on January 5, 1988, a revised national space policy that will set the direction of U.S. efforts in space for the future. The policy is the result of a five-month interagency review which included a thorough analysis of previous Presidential decisions, the National Commission on Space report, and the implications of the Space Shuttle and expendable

---

① See Presidential Directive on National Space Policy, February 11, 1988, https://spp.fas.org/military/docops/national/policy88.htm, last visited on Jan. 8, 2022. Between the issuance of the first Reagan administration space policy statement in July 1982 and 1987, there were a number of significant changes, including the Challenger accident, increased emphasis on the commercial uses of space, and the report of the blue ribbon National Commission on Space. A five-month SIG (Space) review during the second half of 1987 resulted in a new statement of national space policy reflecting these and other changes. President Reagan approved the new policy statement on January 5, but witheld its release until a parallel review of commercial space policy initiatives being conducted by the Economic Policy Council was completed. The policy statement itself was classified; this unclassified summary was all that was publicly released.

launch vehicle accidents. The primary objective of this review was to consolidate and update Presidential guidance on U.S. space activities well into the future.

The resulting Presidential Directive reaffirms the national commitment to the exploration and use of space in support of our national well being. It acknowledges that United States space activities are conducted by three separate and distinct sectors: two strongly interacting governmental sectors (Civil, and National Security) and a separate, non-governmental Commercial Sector. Close coordination, cooperation, and technology and information exchange will be maintained among sectors to avoid unnecessary duplication and promote attainment of United States space goals.

Goals and Principles

The directive states that a fundamental objective guiding United States space activities has been, and continues to be, space leadership. Leadership in an increasingly competitive international environment does not require United States preeminence in all areas and disciplines of space enterprise. It does require United States preeminence in key areas of space activity critical to achieving our national security, scientific, technical, economic, and foreign policy goals.

The overall goals of United States space activities are: (1) to strengthen and security of the United States; (2) to obtain scientific, technological, and economic benefits for the general population and to improve the quality of life on Earth through space-related activities; (3) to encourage continuing United States private-sector investment in space and related activities; (4) to promote international cooperative activities taking into account United States national security, foreign policy, scientific, and economic interests; (5) to cooperate with other nations in maintaining the freedom of space for all activities that enhance the security and welfare of mankind; and, as a long-range goal, (6) to expand human presence and activity beyond Earth orbit into the solar system.

The directive states that United States space activities shall be conducted in accordance with the following principles:

(1) The United States is committed to the exploration and use of outer space by all nations for peaceful purposes and for the benefit of all mankind. "Peaceful purposes" allow for activities in pursuit of national security goals.

(2) The United States will pursue activities in space in support of its inherent right of self-defense and its defense commitments to its allies.

(3) The United States rejects any claims to sovereignty by any nation over outer space or celestial bodies, or any portion thereof, and rejects any limitations on the fundamental right of sovereign nations to acquire data from space.

(4) The United States considers the space systems of any nation to be national property with the right of passage through and operations in space without interference. Purposeful interference with space systems shall be viewed as an infringement on sovereign rights.

(5) The United States shall encourage and not preclude the commercial use and exploitation of space technologies and systems for national economic benefit without direct Federal subsidy. These commercial activities must be consistent with national security interests, and international and domestic legal obligations.

(6) The United States shall encourage other countries to engage in free and fair trade in commercial space goods and services.

(7) The United States will conduct international cooperative space-related activities that are expected to achieve sufficient scientific, political, economic, or national security benefits for the nation. The United States will see mutually beneficial international participation in its space and space-related programs.

Civil Space Policy

The directive states that:

The United States civil space sector activities shall contribute significantly to enhancing the Nation's science, technology, economy, pride, sense, of well-being and direction, as well as United States world prestige and leadership. Civil sector activities shall comprise a balanced strategy of research, development, operations, and technology for science, exploration, and appropriate applications.

The objectives of the United States civil space activities shall be (1) to expand knowledge of the Earth, its environment, the solar system, and the universe; (2) to create new opportunities for use of the space environment through the conduct of appropriate research and experimentation in advanced technology and systems; (3) to develop space technology for civil applications and, wherever appropriate, make such technology available to the commercial sector; (4) to preserve the United States preeminence in critical aspects of space science, applications, technology, and manned space flight; (5) to establish a permanently manned presence in space; and (6) to engage in international cooperative efforts that further United States space goals.

Commercial Space Policy

The directive states that the United States government shall not preclude or deter the continuing development of a separate, non-governmental Commercial Space Sector. Expanding private sector investment in space by the market-driven Commercial Sector generates economic benefits for the Nation and supports governmental Space Sectors with an increasing range of space goods and services. Governmental Space Sectors shall purchase commercially available space goods and services to the fullest extent feasible and shall not conduct activities with potential commercial applications that preclude or deter Commercial Sector space activities except for national security or public safety reasons. Commercial Sector space activities shall be supervised or regulated only to the extent required by law, national security, international obligations, and public safety.

Inter-Sector Policies

This section contains policies applicable to, and binding on, the national security and civil space sectors:

The United States Government will maintain and coordinate separate national security and civil operational space systems where differing needs of the sectors dictate.

Survivability and endurance of national security space systems, including all necessary system elements, will be pursued commensurate with their planned use in crisis and conflict, with the threat, and with the availability of other assets to perform the mission.

Government sectors shall encourage, to the maximum extent feasible, the development and use of Unites States private sector space capabilities without direct Federal subsidy.

The directive states that the United States Government will: (1) encourage the development of commercial systems which image the Earth from space competitive with or superior to foreign-operated civil or commercial systems; (2) discuss remote sensing issues and activities with foreign governments operating or regulating the private operation of remote sensing systems; and (3) continue a research and development effort for future advanced, remote sensing technologies. Commercial applications of such technologies will not involve direct Federal subsidy.

The directive further states that assured access to space, sufficient to achieve all United States space goals, is a key element of national space policy. United States space transportations systems, must provide a balanced, robust, and flexible capability with sufficient resiliency to allow continued operations despite failures in any single system. The goals of United States space transportation policy are: (1) to achieve and maintain safe and reliable access to transportation in, and return from, space; (2) to exploit the unique attributes of manned and unmanned launch and recovery systems; (3) to encourage to the maximum extent feasible, the development and use of United States private sector space transportation capabilities without direct Federal subsidy; and (4) to reduce the costs of space transportation and related services.

The directive also states that communications advancements are critical to all United States space sectors. To ensure necessary capabilities exits, the directive states that the United States Government will continue research and development efforts for future advanced space communications technologies. These technologies, when utilized for commercial purposes, will be without direct Federal subsidy.

The directive states that it is the policy of the United States to control or prohibit, as appropriate, exports of equipment and/or technology that would make an significant contribution to a foreign country's strategic military missile programs. Certain United States friends and allies will be exempted from this policy, subject to appropriate non-transfer and end-use assurances.

The directive also states that the United States will consider and, as appropriate, formulate policy positions on arms control measures governing activities in space, and will conduct negotiations on such measures only if they are equitable, effectively verifiable, and enhance the security of the United States and its allies.

The directive further States that all space sectors will seek to minimize the creation of space debris. Design and operations of space tests, experiments and systems will strive to minimize or reduce accumulation of space debris consistent with mission requirements and cost effectiveness.

Civil Space Sector Guidelines

The directive specifies that in conjunction with other agencies: NASA will continue the lead role within the Federal Government for advancing space science, exploration, and appropriate applications through the conduct of activities for research, technology, development and related operations; the National Oceanic and Atmospheric Administration will gather data, conduct research, and make predictions about the Earth's environment; DOT will license and promote commercial launch operations which support civil sector operations.

Space Science. NASA, with the collaboration of other appropriate agencies, will conduct a balanced program to support scientific research, exploration, and experimentation to expand understanding of: (1) astrophysical phenomena and the origin and evolution of the universe; (2) the Earth, its environment and its dynamic relationship with the Sun; (3) the origin and evolution of the solar system; (4) fundamental physical, chemical, and biological processes; (5) the effects of the space environment on human beings; and (6) the factors governing the origin and spread of life in the universe.

Space Exploration. In order to investigate phenomena and objects both within and beyond the solar system, the directive States that NASA will conduct a balanced program of manned and unmanned exploration.

......

Commercial Space Sector Guidelines

The directive states that NASA, and the Departments of Commerce, Defense, and Transportation will work cooperatively to develop and implement specific measures to foster the growth of private sector commercial use of space. A high-level focus for commercial space issues has been created through establishment of a Commercial Space Working Group of the Economic Policy Council. SIG (Space) will continue to coordinate the development and implementation of national space policy.

To stimulate private sector investment, ownership, and operation of space assets, and directive provides that the United States Government will facilitate private sector access to appropriate U.S. space-related hardware and facilities, and encourage the private sector to undertake commercial space ventures. The directive states that Governmental Space Sectors shall, without providing direct Federal subsidies:

(a) Utilize commercially available goods and services to the fullest extent feasible, and avoid actions that may preclude or deter commercial space sector activities except as required by national security or public safety. A space good or service is "commercially available" if it is currently offered commercially, or if it could be supplied commercially in response to a government service procurement request. "Feasible" means that such goods or services meet mission requirements in a cost-effective manner.

(b) Enter into appropriate cooperative agreements to encourage and advance private sector basic research, development, and operations while protecting the commercial value of the intellectual property developed;

(c) Provide for the use of appropriate Government facilities on a reimbursable basis;

(d) Identify, and eliminate or propose for elimination, applicable portions of United States laws and regulations that unnecessarily impede commercial space sector activities;

(e) Encourage free trade in commercial space activities. The United States Trade Representative will consult, or, as appropriate, negotiate with other countries to encourage free trade in commercial space activities. In entering into space-related technology development and transfer agreements with other countries, Executive Departments and agencies will take into consideration whether such countries practice and encourage free and fair trade in commercial space activities.

(f) Provide for the timely transfer of Government-developed space technology to the private sector in such a manner as to protect its commercial value, consistent with national security.

······

(g) The directive also states that the Department of Commerce (DOC) will commission a study to provide information for future policy and program decisions on options for a commercial advanced earth remote sensing system. This study, to be conducted in the private sector under DOC direction with input from Federal Agencies, will consist of assessments of the following elements: (1) domestic and international markets for remote sensing data; (2) financing options, such as cooperative opportunities between government and industry in which the private sector contributes substantial financing to the venture, participation by other government agencies, and international cooperative partnerships; (3) sensor and data processing technology; and (4) spacecraft technology and launch options. The results of this study will include an action plan on the best alternatives identified during the study.

National Security Space Sector Guidelines

......

Force Enhancement. The directive states that the national security space sector will develop, operate, and maintain space systems and develop plans and architectures to meet the requirements of operational land, sea, and air forces through all levels of conflict commensurate with their intended use.

Space Control. The directive also states that:

(1) The DOD will develop, operate, and maintain enduring space systems to ensure its freedom of action in space. This requires an integrated combination of antisatellite, survivability, and surveillance capabilities.

(2) Antisatellite (ASAT) Capability. DOD will develop and deploy a robust and comprehensive ASAT capability with programs as required and with initial operational capability at the earliest possible date.

(3) DOD space programs will pursue a survivability enhancement program with long-term planning for future requirements. The DOD must provide for the survivability of selected, critical national security space assets (including associated terrestrial components) to a degree commensurate with the value and utility of the support they provide to national-level decision functions, and military operational forces across the spectrum of conflict.

(4) The United States will develop and maintain an integrated attack warning, notification, verification, and contingency reaction capability which can effectively detect and react to threats to United States space systems.

Force Application. The directive states that the DOD will, consistent will treaty obligations, conduct research, development, and planning to be prepared to acquire and deploy space weapons systems for strategic defense should national security conditions dictate.

4.3 US Defense Space Strategy 2020[①]

......

Space is vital to our Nation's security, prosperity, and scientific achievement. Space-based capabilities are integral to modern life in the United States and around the world and are an indispensable component of U.S. military power. Ensuring the availability of these capabilities is fundamental to establishing and maintaining military superiority across all domains and to advancing U.S. and global security and economic prosperity. Space, however, is not a sanctuary from attack and space systems are potential targets at all levels of conflict. In particular, China and Russia present the greatest strategic threat due to their development, testing, and deployment of counterspace capabilities and their associated military doctrine for employment in conflict extending to space. China and Russia each have weaponized space as a means to reduce U.S. and allied military effectiveness and challenge our freedom of operation in space.

Rapid increases in commercial and international space activities worldwide add to the complexity of the space environment. Commercial space activities provide national and homeland security benefits with new technologies and services and create new economic opportunities in established and emerging markets. The same activities, however, also create challenges in protecting critical technology, ensuring operational security, and maintaining strategic advantages. Internationally, allies and partners also recognize the benefits of space for military operations, and increasingly understand the threats to those space activities. Allies and partners who are actively expanding their defense space programs, present novel opportunities

---

[①] See US Department of Defense, Defense Space Strategy Summary, June 2020, https://media.defense.gov/2020/Jun/17/2002317391/-1/-1/1/2020_DEFENSE_SPACE_STRATEGY_SUMMARY.PDF, last visited on Jan. 8, 2022.

to increase defense collaboration and cooperation.

In response to this new security environment, and in accordance with the 2018 National Strategy for Space (NSfS) and the 2018 National Defense Strategy (NDS), this Defense Space Strategy (DSS) provides guidance to DOD for achieving desired conditions in space over the next 10 years. The DOD desires a secure, stable, and accessible space domain, whose use by the United States and our allies and partners is underpinned by comprehensive, sustained military strength. The strategy includes a phased approach for the defense enterprise to move with purpose and speed across four lines of effort (LOEs): (1) build a comprehensive military advantage in space; (2) integrate space into national, joint, and combined operations; (3) shape the strategic environment; and (4) cooperate with allies, partners, industry, and other U. S. Government departments and agencies.

The Department is taking innovative and bold actions to ensure space superiority and to secure the Nation's vital interests in space now and in the future. Establishing the U. S. Space Force (USSF) as the newest branch of our Armed Forces and the U. S. Space Command (USSPACECOM) as a unified combatant command, as well as undertaking significant space acquisition reform across the DOD, has set a strategic path to expand spacepower for the Nation. It is a path that embraces space as a unique domain of national military power that, together with the other domains, underpins multi-domain joint and combined military operations to advance national security.

......

To achieve these desired conditions, DOD will advance spacepower through the pursuit of the following defense objectives:

Maintain Space Superiority DOD will establish, maintain, and preserve U. S. freedom of operations in the space domain. DOD will be prepared to protect and defend U. S. and, as directed, allied, partner, and commercial space capabilities and to deter and defeat adversary hostile use of space.

Provide Space Support to National, Joint, and Combined Operations DOD space forces will deliver advanced space capabilities and effects to enable national, joint, and combined operations in any domain through sustained, comprehensive space military advantages. DOD will leverage and bolster a thriving domestic civil and commercial space industry.

Ensure Space Stability In cooperation with allies and partners, DOD will maintain persistent presence in space in order to: deter aggression in space; provide for safe transit in, to, and through space; uphold internationally accepted standards of responsible behavior as a good steward of space; and support U. S. leadership in space traffic management and the long-term sustainability of outer space activities.

......

Great power competition defines the strategic environment. Space is both a source of and conduit for national power, prosperity, and prestige. As a result, space is a domain that has reemerged as a central arena of great power competition, primarily with China and Russia.

......

Threats China and Russia present the most immediate and serious threats to U. S. space operations, although threats from North Korea and Iran are also growing. Chinese and Russian strategic intentions and capabilities present urgent and enduring threats to the ability of the Department to achieve its desired conditions in space. China and Russia have analyzed U. S. dependencies on space and have developed doctrine, organizations, and capabilities specifically designed to contest or deny U. S. access to and operations in the domain. Concurrently, their use of space is expanding significantly. Both countries consider space access and denial as critical components of their national and military strategies. Specifically, Chinese and Russian military doctrines indicate that they view space as important to modern warfare and consider the use of counterspace capabilities as a means for reducing U. S., allied, and partner military effectiveness and for winning future wars. China and Russia have weaponized space as a way to deter and counter a possible U.S. intervention during a regional military conflict.

……

DOD will develop an agile space enterprise that can take advantage of emerging technological and commercial innovation in order to continually outpace adversary threats. Space superiority will be achieved through on-orbit, multi-domain, and cross-component operations that are fully integrated with our allies and partners. The establishment of the USSF as a new branch of the Armed Forces offers a historic and immediate opportunity to rapidly transform the enterprise to achieve space superiority. Additionally, the creation of a new ASAF (A&I) and SFAC will further unify DOD space acquisition efforts, improving the synchronization of space systems and programs and ensuring integration across the national security space enterprise. DOD components will prioritize necessary resources for this LOE for the duration of the DSS timeframe. Specific objectives include:

(1) Build out the U.S. Space Force.

(2) Develop and document doctrinal foundations of military space power.

(3) Develop and expand space war fighting expertise and culture.

(4) Field assured space capabilities.

(5) Develop and field capabilities that counter hostile use of space.

(6) Improve intelligence and command and control (C2) capabilities that enable military advantage in the space domain.

5. References and Recommended Reading Materials

(1) Frans G. von der Dunk and Fabio Tronchetti (eds.), *Handbook of Space Law*, Edward Elgar Publishing, 2015.

(2) T. L. Masson-Zwaan and S. Hobe, *The Law of Outer Space*, The Hague, 2010.

Chapter XI Treaty Law

1. Introduction

States transact a vast amount of work by using the device of treaty. For instance, wars will be terminated, disputes settled, territory acquired, special interests determined, alliances established and international organizations created, all by means of treaties. Treaty is of paramount importance to the evolution of international law. E. g., most of those international organizations, including the United Nations, have their legal basis in multilateral treaties; networks of bilateral treaties regulate such matters as aviation, boundaries, extradition, investment protection, and shared natural resources.[①]

The most important formal source of law about the treaty is the Vienna Convention on the Law of Treaties (VCLT), known as the "treaty on treaties". This convention establishes comprehensive rules, procedures, and guidelines for how treaties are defined, drafted, amended, interpreted, and generally operated. The VCLT is considered a codification of customary international law and state practice concerning treaties. Even those countries that have not ratified it recognize its significance, such as United States. The VCLT provides rules for the main legal issues concerning treaties. It includes rules about conclusion and entry into force of treaties, observance,

---

① See James Crawford (ed.), *Brownlie's Principles of Public International Law*, 8th Ed., Oxford University Press, 2012, p. 367.

application and interpretation of treaties, amendment and modification of treaties, invalidity, termination and suspension of the operation of treaties.

To better understand treaty law, Part 2 introduces some historical discussions about the treaty made by Grotius and, some selected articles from conventions reflecting the historical development of the treaty, especially the practice involving China. Part 3 discusses some basic concepts. Part 4 includes some cases to illustrate how treaty is to be applied in practice.

2. Preliminary Reading and Assignment

2.1 Peace and Friendship Treaty of Utrecht between France and Great Britain (1713)[①]

I. That there be an universal perpetual peace, and a true and sincere friendship, between the most Serene and most Potent Princess Anne, Queen of Great Britain, and the most Serene and most Potent Prince Lewis XIV, the most Christian King, and their Heirs and Successors, as also the Kingdoms, States, and Subjects of both, as well without as within Europe; and that the same be so sincerely and inviolably preserved and cultivated, that the one do promote the interest, honour, and advantage of the other; and that a faithful neighbourhood on all sides, and a secure cultivating of peace and friendship do daily flourish again and increase.

IV. Furthermore, for adding a greater strength to the peace which is restored, and to the faithful friendship which is never to be violated, and for cutting off all occasions of distrust, which might at any time arise from the

---

[①] The Peace of Utrecht is a series of peace treaties signed by the belligerents in the War of the Spanish Succession, in the Dutch city of Utrecht between April 1713 and February 1715. It is considered as the first political treaty that had a global impact. It not only ended a European-wide war, but also led to a cessation of hostilities on the American continent and India subcontinent. See Inken Schmidt-Voges and Ana Crespo Solana (eds.), *New Worlds? Transformations in the Culture of International Relations around the Peace of Utrecht*, Routledge, 2017, pp. 1-3.

established right and order of the hereditary succession to the Crown of Great Britain, and the limitation thereof by the laws of Great Britain (made and enacted in the reigns of the late King William the Third, of glorious Memory, and of the present Queen) to the issue of the abovesaid Queen, and in default thereof, to the most Serene Princess Sophia, Dowager of Brunswick Hannover, and her heirs in the Protestant line of Hannover: That therefore the said succession may remain safe and secure, the most Christian King sincerely and solemnly acknowledges the abovesaid limitation of the succession to the Kingdom of Great Britain, and on the faith and word of a king, on the pledge of his own and his successors honour, he does declare and engage, that he accepts and approves the same, and that his heirs and successors do and shall accept and approve the same for ever. And under the same obligation of the word and honour of a king, the most Christian King promises, that no one besides the Queen herself, and her Successors, according to the series of the said limitation, shall ever by him, or by his heirs or successors, be acknowledged, or reputed to be King of Queen of Great Britain. And for adding more ample credit to the said acknowledgement and promises, the most Christian King does engage, that whereas the person who, in the life-time of the late King James the Second, did take upon him the title of Prince of Wales, and since his decease that of King of Great Britain, is lately gone, of his own accord, out of the Kingdom of France, to reside in some other place, he the aforesaid most Christian King, his heirs and successors, will take all possible care that he shall not at any time hereafter, or under any pretence whatsoever, return into the Kingdom of France, or any the dominions thereof.

V. Moreover, the most Christian King promises, as well in his own name, as in that of his heirs and successors, that they will at no time whatever disturb, or give any molestation to the Queen of Great Britain, her heirs and successors, descended from the aforesaid Protestant line, who possess the Crown of Great Britain, and the dominions belonging thereunto.

Neither will the aforesaid most Christian King, or any one of his heirs, give at any time any aid, succour, favour, or counsel, directly or indirectly, by land of by sea, in money, arms, ammunition, warlike provision, ships, soldiers, seamen, or any other way, to any person or persons, whosoever they be, who for any cause, or under any pretext whatsoever, should hereafter endeavour to oppose the said succession, either by open war, or by fomenting seditions, and forming conspiracies against such Prince or Princess who are in possession of the Throne of Great Britain, by virtue of the Acts of Parliament aforementioned; or against that Prince or Princess, to whom the succession to the Crown of Great Britain shall be open according to the said Acts of Parliament.

2.2 Treaty of TienTsin (1858)[①]

Ⅰ. The Treaty of Peace and Amity between the two nations, signed at Nanking on the 29th day of August, in the year 1842, is hereby renewed and confirmed.

The Supplementary Treaty and General Regulations of Trade having been amended and improved, and the substance of their provisions having been incorporated in this Treaty, the said Supplementary Treaty and General Regulations of Trade are hereby abrogated.

Ⅹ. British merchant ships shall have authority to trade upon the Great River (Yangytsze). The Upper and Lower Valley of the river being, however, disturbed by outlaws, no port shall be for the present opened to trade, with the exception of Chinkiang, which shall be opened in a year from the date of the signing of this Treaty.

So soon as peace shall have been restored, British vessels shall also be

---

① See Treaty-of Peace, Friendship and Commerce, Between Great Britain and China, Signed at TienTsin, 26th June, 1858, https://oelawhk.lib.hku.hk/items/show/1025, last visited on Jan. 8, 2022.

admitted to trade at such ports as far as Nanking, not exceeding three in number, as the British Minister, after consultation with the Chinese Secretary of State, may determine shall be ports of entry and discharge.

XI. In addition to the cities and towns of Canton, Amoy, Fuchow, Ningpo, and Shanghai, opened by the Treaty of Nanking, it is agreed that British subjects may frequent the cities and ports of Yingkou, Taiwan Region, etc.

They are permitted to carry on trade with whomsoever they please, and to proceed to and fro at pleasure with their Vessels and Merchandise.

They shall enjoy the same privileges, advantages, and immunities, at the said towns and Ports, as they enjoy at the Ports already opened to trade, including the right of residence, of buying or renting Houses, of leasing Land therein, and of building Churches, Hospitals, and Cemeteries.

XVI. Chinese subjects who may be guilty of any criminal act towards British subjects shall be arrested and punished by the Chinese authorities according to the Laws of China.

British subjects who may commit any crime in China shall be tried and punished by the Consul, or other public functionary authorized thereto, according to the Laws of Great Britain.

Justice shall be equitably and impartially administered on both sides.

2.3 The Joint Declaration (1984)①

The Government of the United Kingdom of Great Britain and Northern Ireland and the Government of the People's Republic of China have reviewed with satisfaction the friendly relations existing between the two Governments and peoples in recent years and agreed that a proper negotiated settlement of

---

① See Joint Declaration of the Government of the United Kingdom of Great Britain and Northern Ireland and the Government of the People's Republic of China on the Question of Hong Kong, https://www.cmab.gov.hk/en/issues/jd2.htm, last visited on Jan. 8, 2022.

the issue of Hong Kong, which is left over from the past, is conducive to the maintenance of the prosperity and stability of Hong Kong and to the further strengthening and development of the relations between the two countries on a new basis. To this end, they have, after talks between the delegations of the two Governments, agreed to declare as follows:

1. The Government of the People's Republic of China declares that to recover the Hong Kong area (including Hong Kong Island, Kowloon and the New Territories, hereinafter referred to as Hong Kong) is the common aspiration of the entire Chinese people, and that it has decided to resume the exercise of sovereignty over Hong Kong with effect from 1 July 1997.

3. The Government of the People's Republic of China declares that the basic policies of the People's Republic of China regarding Hong Kong are as follows:

(1) Upholding national unity and territorial integrity and taking account of the history of Hong Kong and its realities, the People's Republic of China has decided to establish, in accordance with the provisions of Article 31 of the Constitution of the People's Republic of China, a Hong Kong Special Administrative Region upon resuming the exercise of sovereignty over Hong Kong.

(2) The Hong Kong Special Administrative Region will be directly under the authority of the Central People's Government of the People's Republic of China. The Hong Kong Special Administrative Region will enjoy a high degree of autonomy, except in foreign and defence affairs which are the responsibilities of the Central People's Government.

(3) The Hong Kong Special Administrative Region will be vested with executive, legislative and independent judicial power, including that of final adjudication. The laws currently in force in Hong Kong will remain basically unchanged.

(4) The Government of the Hong Kong Special Administrative Region will be composed of local inhabitants. The chief executive will be appointed

by the Central People's Government on the basis of the results of elections or consultations to be held locally. Principal officials will be nominated by the chief executive of the Hong Kong Special Administrative Region for appointment by the Central People's Government. Chinese and foreign nationals previously working in the public and police services in the government departments of Hong Kong may remain in employment. British and other foreign nationals may also be employed to serve as advisers or hold certain public posts in government departments of the Hong Kong Special Administrative Region.

(5) The current social and economic systems in Hong Kong will remain unchanged, and so will the life-style. Rights and freedoms, including those of the person, of speech, of the press, of assembly, of association, of travel, of movement, of correspondence, of strike, of choice of occupation, of academic research and of religious belief will be ensured by law in the Hong Kong Special Administrative Region. Private property, ownership of enterprises, legitimate right of inheritance and foreign investment will be protected by law.

······

2.4 Discussion and Assignment

Read the materials and think about the following questions:

(1) What function does the treaty play in the world order?

(2) How has the treaty practice of China changed to keep in line with China's status in history and today?

(3) Report the codification history and content of VCLT briefly in a 5-10 minutes speech in English.

3. Key Concepts and Discussions

3.1 What is Treaty?

A treaty is an agreement of a suitable formal character, designed to give rise to legal rights and obligations, operating within the sphere of international law, and concluded by two or more parties possessing legal personality under international law. The International Law Commission (ILC) defined treaty as "any international agreement in written form, concluded between two or more States or other subjects of international law and governed by international law, whether embodied in a single instrument or in two or more related instruments and whatever its particular designation, such as a treaty, convention, protocol, covenant, charter, statute, act, declaration, concordat, exchange of notes, agreed minute, memorandum of agreement, or any other appellation". Simply, a treaty is an agreement between parties on the international scene. It is usual that many agreements between States are merely statements of commonly held principles or objectives and are not intended to establish binding obligations. To ascertain whether a particular agreement amount to a treaty, all facts around the situation have to be examined carefully.

3.2 The Making of Treaty

This question could be divided into three parts: who can represent a State to enter a treaty, how to make consent to the rules or obligation stipulated in the treaty, and how to make a treaty enter into force.

(1) Who can represent a State to enter a treaty? This question is essentially about the capacity to conclude treaties. It is about the first step of making a treaty, the negotiating. The States and those international organizations comprised by them could conduct in the negotiation of a treaty.

In modern practice, full powers are given the bearer authority to negotiate, sign and seal a treaty. VCLT provides a definition of full power as follow: document emanating from the competent authority of a State designating a person or persons to represent the State for negotiating, adopting or authenticating the text of a treaty, for expressing the consent of a State to be bound by a treaty, or for accomplishing any other act with respect to a treaty.

There are three categories of persons who are each subject to a distinct legal regime as to the issue to decide who is entitled to negotiate and sign on behalf of a State. The first category is those so-called "Big Three". According to article 7 of VCLT 1969, which reflects in this point, customary international law, the Head of State, the Head of Government (Prime Minister) and the Minister of Foreign Affairs possess an inherent right to negotiate for the State and to engage in international agreements. The ICJ in *Land and Maritime Boundary Between Cameroon and Nigeria* confirmed that the full powers afforded to a head of State derive from their position at the top of a State's hierarchy. In the *Genocide Case*, the Court repeated that "every Head of State is presumed to be able to act on behalf of the State in its international relations". Notice, however, that the inherent powers of the head of the diplomatic mission are only for the adoption of the text, not for the ratification of it. The second category traditionally concerns all other persons. These persons have no inherent power to represent the State. They need a specific appointment under letters of "full powers" in order to be entitled to negotiate and sign treaty commitments. The third category was added by ICJ from practice, notably the other State Ministers, such as the minister of commerce or minister of defense. It is increasingly frequent that such persons directly engage the State in treaties concerning their sphere of competence. In the *Armed Activities Case* (*DRC v. Rwanda*, 2006), the ICJ suggested that international law had evolved so as to allow such ministers and their personnel (through full powers delivered by their minister) to negotiate and conclude treaties in their sphere of competence.

(2) How to make consent to the rules or obligation is about the way of adopting a treaty text. That is the procedure of expressing the State's consent by vote or signature to adopt and authenticate the treaty text or provisions. If the negotiating has been successful and the States were able to enter an agreement on something, as to those multilateral treaties, the text will be adopted by a vote in the conference. And, then, it will be authenticated by initialing each page or signing the document. The authentication is important because it could avoid any ambiguity on which text was finally adopted. The adoption of the treaty marks the end of the negotiating phase. From that moment onwards, the treaty text can no longer be changed unless by the agreement of all the former negotiating States. In addition, the treaty is deemed to have been concluded at the time of adoption or at the time it is opened to a signature, whichever is the latter.

(3) How to make a treaty enter into force? A member State makes consent to be bound by the treaty by ratifying it according to the procedure stipulated in its municipal law. Only in the case of bilateral agreements, the State could sign and ratify an international agreement. This is the so-called short procedure to conclude treaties, skipping any supplementary phase of ratification. A State can always decide to sign and ratify at the same time, but from the standpoint of municipal law, this is not always the case. Treaties on certain subject matters must be submitted to the parliament or even to the popular vote. The representative will have to respect these restrictions of internal law and meet a two-tier process of conclusion, with separate signature and ratification. Under this situation, the effects of signature are mainly the two following ways: Firstly, entry into force of transitory provisions; Secondly, obligation to abstain from acts which would frustrate the object and purpose of the treaty once entered into force. This is regulated in Article 18 of VCLT, grounded on the principle of good faith. The parties signing the adopted treaty owe to each other a minimum of fair dealing so as not to frustrate the common procedure, which is linked with legitimate

expectations.

The ratification is the term used to indicate the consent to be bound, given by a signatory State. It usually consists of a letter written by some members of the foreign ministry to the depository where it is set out that the State consents to be bound by the treaty. Only States having signed the treaty may ratify it. Ratification cannot be conditional but must be unconditional. However, the State may make reservations. If a State has not yet made up its mind sufficiently, it must wait for ratification or postpone the effect of its ratification. The way of ratification is described in article 16 of VCLT. For ratification, full powers are needed unless one of the Big Three performs it. The depository will circulate the ratification instrument to the former negotiating States, including signatory States and States entitled to become parties to the treaty. What are the reasons for a ratification procedure separate from a signature? This reason lies in most cases in the democratic structure of a series of States. The treaty is negotiated by the executive branch and its ratification is again performed by the executive. If there were no consultation of parliament, the executive branch could undertake obligations of the greatest reach for a State, such as the cession of some of its territory, without the democratically legitimized organ having had control and say. For democratic States, it is, therefore, necessary to have a time for reflection and for consulting parliament or the people. This is the main reason why ratification is postponed. Note that the act of parliament to authorize the treaty laid before it is purely a domestic matter, having no impact on international law. When parliament has said "yes" to the treaty, it is still not internationally binding on the State since it is still not actually ratified. As long as the ratification instrument has not been received by the depository or the other States Parties, the consent to be bound has not been given. Another important point is that could ratification be withdrawn after it has been made but before the treaty enters into force? According to the practice of the UN as a treaty depository, a ratification instrument may be withdrawn before entry into force of the treaty.

Another important issue about making of treaty or putting a State under a treaty is accession. It differs from ratification on account of the entitlement to become a party to the treaty. Ratification is performed by the States that have participated in the negotiation of the treaty and then have signed it. For those States, ratification is a subjective right. They are entitled to become parties to the treaty. In contrast, accession concerns the position of third States, not having participated in the negotiation and not having signed the treaty. To what extent can such a third State become a party to a treaty? If it contains accession clauses, the third State will be able to become a party on the conditions setting out there. If there is no accession clause, the third State still could become a party provided that all the State parties impliedly intended to allow accession. And, the accession also happens when all the State parties have subsequently agreed to allow it. Therefore, accession is not a subjective right of the third State. It will be able to accede only if and under the conditions allowed by the parties to the treaty. There are treaties that are normally closed and to which accession is impossible: this is the mast frequent case first of all for bilateral treaties, where accession clauses are rare. Some other treaties are relatively closed, for example, political and military alliances, such as NATO. However, most of the multilateral treaties are open to access for all States or any States, such as the VCLT of 1969. Once performed, accession is treated in wholly the same way as ratification. Notice that the law of treaties knows of no distinction in status between States having ratified and those having acceded. Both are treated as treaty parties with exactly the same rights and obligations.

3.3 Reservation

According to a report on reservation prepared by the International Law Commission (ILC) in 2011, "reservation" means a unilateral statement, however, phrased or named, made by a State or an international organization when signing, ratifying, formally confirming, accepting, approving or acceding to a treaty, or by a State when making a notification of succession to a treaty, whereby the State or organization purports to exclude or to modify the legal effect of certain provisions of the treaty in their application to that State or to that international organization.

Reservation is a device to facilitate the conclusion of a treaty where the State is satisfied with most of the terms of a treaty but is unhappy about particular provisions. If a State has to accept a treaty entirely, it is more difficult to enter an agreement of a multilateral treaty. Therefore, reservation has beneficial results by inducing as many States as possible to adhere to the proposed treaty. To some extent, it is a means of encouraging harmony among States of widely differing social, economic and political systems by concentrating upon the agreed, basic issues and accepting disagreement on certain other matters.

There are two distinct purported effects of reservations: either to exclude the application of a provision completely; or to maintain the provision but to modify it in some regard. Notice that there is a difference between a reservation and an understanding or an interpretative declaration. These forms of State declaration are used to designate a statement that is not intended to modify or limit any of the treaty provisions. The understanding purports to clarify the meaning or scope of treaty provisions. It does not have the effect of altering a provision by changing the applicable rights and obligations. In practice, a State is entitled to formulate as many reservations as it wants. But there are limitations on that right to formulate reservations, such as the treaty itself may prohibit certain reservations or certain general rules of treaty law may operate significant restrictions.

3.4 Third party

The issue of treaties and third States is regulated in Articles 34 to 38 of VCLT. A Third State is a State not being a party to the treaty. The main principle is that a treaty does not create either obligations or rights for a third State without its consent. It means that a State cannot invoke rights deriving from a treaty to which it is not a party, and neither can it have obligations under such a treaty imposed upon it. This relativity principle is a deduction of the principle of sovereignty of States. A State does not intend to be bound without its consent to any treaty rights or obligations. However, we shall notice that a treaty concluded between some States may affect and even heavily affect a given third State. If a military alliance is concluded by its surrounding States, this fact will importantly impact the situation and policy of the encircled third State.

3.5 Application and Observance

In the absence of contrary intention, a treaty will not operate retroactively so that its provisions will not bind a party as regards any facts, acts or situations prior to that State's acceptance of the treaty. Unless a different intention appears from the treaty or is otherwise established, Article 29 of VCLT provides that a treaty is binding upon each party in respect of its entire territory. This is the general rule, but it is possible for a State to stipulate that an international agreement will apply only to part of its territory.

Article 30 of VCLT deals with the problem of the application of successive treaties. This problem is becoming serious because of the growth in the number of States and the increasing number of treaties entered into, and the added complication of enhanced activity at the regional level. The relation of treaties between the same parties and with overlapping provisions is primarily a matter of interpretation. That is how to resolve the conflict of norms in treaties applicable to the same State and to the same set of facts. There is a general rule under international law whereby the interpreter tries to smooth out or even to avoid conflicts by way of a "harmonizing interpretation", the presumption of non-conflict. This rule is based on the assumption that when States wanted different rules to be applicable, they could not at the same time have wanted normative contradiction. If there were such a contradiction, this would lead at the end of the day to the sacrifice of one rule to the other. It is more reasonable to presume that the legislator wants both rules to apply. Another point about this issue is that a conflict will disappear if all the contracting States to the treaty agree on an interpretation that ensures compatibility or agree on a modification of the treaty so as to ensure compatibility. It is presumed that a later treaty prevails over an earlier treaty concerning the same subject matter. A treaty may provide that it is to prevail over subsequent incompatible treaties; Article 103 of the UN Charter goes further by providing that in the case of conflict, obligations under the Charter prevail over obligations arising under any other international agreement.

As to the observance or implementation, any State parties shall observe and implement the treaty applied to him. It is because of the obligatory character of treaty commitments indicated from a legal maxim, the *pacta sunt servanda*. It is a general principle of international law: a treaty in force is binding upon the parties and must be performed by them in good faith. When the municipal law of the State does not allow proper treaty performance, the State must either change its internal law before or after ratifying or acceding to the treaty or withdraw from the treaty. It is important to emphasize that treaties are concluded on behalf of States, not of governments. The latter acts in the name of the State; the State is the treaty party. This implies that a change of government does not have any impact on the validity of treaties. This remains true even if the change is revolutionary and entails a complete political and social change.

Another important principle is provided in Article 27 of VCLT. That is the internal law may not be invoked to justify a failure to perform a treaty. This rule is closely linked with *pacta sunt servanda*. If a State could invoke with success its internal law so as to override the treaty, the binding nature of the commitment would wholly disappear. The State could at any time change its internal law in order to be freed from its treaty obligations. In other words, a State could liberate itself from the commitment by its own action. It is clear that for the purposes of Article 27 of VCLT all sources of municipal law are included, from the tiniest legal regulation to the most eminent constitutional law. Note that it applies only to inter-State relations, not to the rank of an international law norm in the municipal legal order.

In international law, the principle of supremacy of the international legal norm over the municipal legal norm is valid without exceptions. If a State breaches this commitment, it will be responsible under the law of State responsibility. However, a State may well give precedence to its municipal law within its own municipal legal order. For example, a constitutional norm will prevail over a treaty norm in the Supreme Court of the United States. The point is that when a State has recourse to such primacy of internal law within its legal order, it will have to face international responsibility (including the duty to make reparation and, possibly, to suffer countermeasures) and the embarrassment of its foreign relations with the aggrieved State. Taking the United States as an example, the Trump administration decided to apply its own internal foreign trade law to levy an additional duty to goods imported from European Union. This makes its internal law prevail over the WTO rules. The European Union could adopt countermeasures under customary international law. This could explain why we adopted retaliating tariffs against goods imported from the United States during the trade frictions last year.

A State may not observe the treaty as it should. They could even mistrust themselves. This situation arises when one State behaves in bad faith and when States parties differ in conceptions of the content of the treaty and of its interpretation. There are some old-fashioned instruments for securing performance. Some of them are now illegal or in dispute, such as the taking of hostages, charges on revenues of another State, occupation of territory, and guarantees by third States. The most frequent current mechanisms are special and general monitoring proceedings. For example, the WTO provides a trade policy review mechanism to strengthen its observance. This is a kind of special proceedings in which a treaty sets up its own machinery for supervision and control. The general proceedings are the procedures of peaceful settlement of disputes under international law, such as clauses whereby States accept the jurisdiction of the ICJ.

3.6 Treaty Interpretation

Treaty interpretation is probably the most crucial issue in the treaty law. Interpretation is not limited to situations where the sense and scope of a provision are not clear. It extends to any application of the law. In a broader sense, it seeks to understand the legal meaning of a provision in order to be able to apply it. In a narrower sense, it seeks to ascertain the legal sense of a provision in case of doubts on the meaning. The VCLT regulates the issue in Articles 31 to 33. These are often regarded as being among the most successful provisions of the VCLT. They strike a proper and felicitous balance between sobriety, flexibility and normative guidelines. There are three important questions to be answered here: the subject of interpretation, the object of interpretation and the method of interpretation.

The first question is about who is entitled to interpret. Primarily, the parties bound by or subjected to legal rules are the main interpreters. This is called self-interpretation. As in a contract, when we conclude it, we are called in the first place to read, understand and apply it according to our own judgment. In international law, States and other subjects themselves interpret their legal obligations. The main difference is that in the realm of international relations, there is no judge with compulsory jurisdiction. This self-interpretation may result in a risk of self-interested manipulations of the legal texts and the practice of excessive subjectivism. A more objective interpretation is third-party interpretation, in particular judicial interpretation. Third-party interpretation can be made by a political organ, such as the UN General Assembly, when hearing a dispute under Chapter Ⅵ of the UN Charter. Judicial interpretation, which is performed by professional lawyers who have no direct interest in the outcome of the case, is at the other extreme from self-interpretation. Such an interpretation best ensures the equality of the parties and the proper performance of the treaty.

The second question is about what to be interpreted. There is on this question a great divide between the objective and the subjective schools of thought. The former relies on the "text"; the latter prefer the "common intention." The former consequently tends towards an evolutionary interpretation; the latter tends towards a historical interpretation. The argument of the former text is the only objective common denominator that can be externally ascertained by any party to the treaty and which therefore ensures an appreciable degree of legal certainty. The main argument of the latter is that the text is but a vehicle to express an intention. Thus, the interpretation should not take the means for the end. The VCLT has made a clear choice in favor of the objective method concentrating on the text.

The third question is about how to interpret. VCLT adopts an objective method to set the principle of interpretation. It provides a progressive way to stipulate provisions on the interpretive process. Based on the rules in Articles 31 and 32 of VCLT, there are two main methods of treaty interpretation. One is Grammatical Interpretation; the other is Systematic Interpretation. Article 31.1 provides that "a treaty shall be interpreted in good faith in accordance with the ordinary meaning to be given to the terms of the treaty in their context and in the light of its object and purpose". This is the primary method of interpretation. Since the parties carefully negotiate the text of the treaty, which is meant to express their intentions, it is therefore reasonable that the interpreter should analyze the text in the first place. The text is the vehicle for the necessary legal certainty and the expression of the parties' intent. The meaning of the terms is to be construed in the most "usual" sense, that is, according to what is reasonable in the circumstances. The issue is one of the objectively legitimate expectations: it is attached to what the parties could and should have understood by the terms used. No party should be taken by surprise with an unexpected, idiosyncratic or aberrational sense of a word or term. Note that the reasonable sense of the terms depends on the context, object and purpose of the treaty. It is not a statistical issue. In a treaty on civil aviation, it is to be expected that words are used according to the usual sense in this branch of human activities, not a special meaning from Star Wars. The reason to make context interpretation or systematic interpretation is also easy to understand. The word cannot be understood in isolation from the sentence it is inserted in; nor the paragraph in isolation from the provision of which it forms part; and so on. An interpreter always has to look at the whole of the treaty in order to properly understand the true meaning of its parts. Each part of the treaty may shed light on some other elements of that treaty.

3.7 Amendment and Modification, Termination, and Suspension

Amendment and modification share the same aim in revising a treaty. But they are separate activities and may be accomplished in different manners. Amendments refer to the formal alteration of treaty provisions, affecting all the parties to the particular agreement, while modifications relate to variations of certain treaty terms between particular parties only.

As to the formal amendment and modification, VCLT makes a different requirement for multilateral treaties and bilateral treaties. For bilateral treaties, the amending agreement can be concluded in any form, for example, by an exchange of letters. Even if the treaty contains a formal amendment clause, the parties remain free to change the treaty by any other agreed means. This is true because the parties are the *domini negotii*. As they agreed on the formal clause, they can now agree on another course to be taken. For multilateral treaties, there are two sets of situations. In the first, the treaty contains specific clauses for its amendment. In the second, the treaty is silent on an amendment so that the residual rules of the VCLT are applicable. In the first situation, the express rules adopted will normally be followed. But the parties remain free, by common consent to modify the treaty in any other way they see fit. Acquiescence and subsequent practice are also sufficient. In the second situation, There are again two situations to be distinguished: (i) "objective amendments" in Article 40, where the original treaty is amended for all treaty parties; and (ii) "subjective amendments" in Article 41, where a treaty is simply modified by a separate treaty of rather limited personal reach, with effect only among certain parties.

Termination and suspension are often used together to describe the operation of a valid treaty after its entry into force. A treaty may specify the conditions of its termination and may provide for denunciation by the parties. There are two series of circumstances that can give rise to the termination, suspension or withdrawal from a treaty. The first series of circumstances is based on the will of the parties as manifested in the treaty itself or as crystallized later. These are thus "subjective" grounds for termination. The second series of circumstances is based on events beyond the intention of the parties, sometimes even contrary to their legitimate expectations. These events are objective legal facts, which entail a right to terminate, suspend or withdraw. These are "objective" grounds for termination.

The "subjective grounds" of termination include the following instances:

(i) Consent to terminate expressed outside the treaty.

(ii) Resolutory clauses, as stated in Article 54(a) of VCLT, termination of the treaty can also take place "in conformity with the provisions of the treaty".

(iii) Subsequent abrogative treaty with identical parties. Article 59.1 of VCLT provides that: A treaty shall be considered as terminated if all the parties to it conclude a later treaty relating to the same subject matter and: (a) it appears from the later treaty or is otherwise established that the parties

Chapter XI Treaty Law 343

intended that the matter should be governed by that treaty; or (b) the provisions of the later treaty are so far incompatible with those of the earlier one that the two treaties are not capable of being applied at the same time.

(iv) Denunciation or withdrawal. The two words are taken here as being synonymous: a State seeks to be released from the treaty obligations by a unilateral act whereby it declares its intention to no longer be a party to the treaty. State party withdraws from a treaty may either terminate the treaty or restrict its personal scope of application.

The objective grounds of termination are those circumstances independent from the will of the parties. These are material breach, a fundamental change of circumstances, supervening impossibility of performance, *jus cogens* supervenient, severance of diplomatic or consular relations, international armed conflict and State succession.

The legal consequences of the termination of a treaty are set out in Article 70 of VCLT. The main principle is that unless the treaty otherwise provides, the parties are released from the duty of performance. As from the date of termination, and that the rights acquired when the treaty was in force remain unaffected. The main difference to the situation in case of invalidity of a treaty is that the rights acquired are now deprived of their legal basis since invalidity retroacts. Contrariwise, in the case of termination, the effect is from a prospective date onwards. The validity of the treaty in the past is not cast into doubt.

4. Cases and Materials

Read the following cases and think about the following questions:

(1) Could you give an example of China's practice of making a reservation to a treaty? Why did China make the reservation and what was its effect on China's relationship with other parties?

(2) How do international tribunals interpret the treaty in practice?

4.1 Genocide Case[①]

On November 16th, 1950, the General Assembly of the United Nations adopted the following resolution:

The General Assembly … Requests the International Court of Justice to give an Advisory Opinion on the following questions: In so far as concerns the Convention on the Prevention and Punishment of the Crime of Genocide in the event of a State ratification or acceding to the Convention subject to a reservation made either on ratification or on accession, or on signature followed by ratification:

Ⅰ. Can the reserving State be regarded as being a party to the Convention while still maintaining its reservation if the reservation is objected to by one or more of the parties to the Convention but not by others?

Ⅱ. If the answer to Question Ⅰ is in the affirmative, what is the effect of the reservation as between the reserving State and:

(a) The parties which object to the reservation?

(b) Those which accept it?

Ⅲ. What would be the legal effect as regards the answer to Question Ⅰ if an objection to a reservation is made:

(a) By a signatory which has not yet ratified?

(b) By a State entitled to sign or accede but which has not yet done so?

……

The Court observes that the three questions which have been referred to it for an Opinion have certain common characteristics.

All three questions are expressly limited by the terms of the Resolution

---

① See *Reserations to the Convention on Genocide*, Advisory Opinion, ICJ Reports 1951, p. 15.

Chapter XI   Treaty Law   345

of the General Assembly to the Convention on the Prevention and Punishment of the Crime of Genocide and the same Resolution invites the International Law Commission to study the general question of reservations to multilateral conventions both from the point of view of codification and from that of the progressive development of international law. The questions thus having a clearly defined object, the replies which the Court is called upon to give to them are necessarily and strictly limited to that Convention. The Court will seek these replies in the rules of law relating to the effect to be given to the intention of the parties to multilateral conventions.

Question I is······ The Court observes that this question refers, not to the possibility of making reservations to the Genocide Convention, but solely to the question whether a contracting State which has made a reservation can, while still maintaining it, be regarded as being a party to the Convention, when there is a divergence of views between the contracting parties concerning this reservation, some accepting the reservation, others refusing to accept it.

It is well established that in its treaty relations a State cannot be bound without its consent, and that consequently no reservation can be effective against any State without its agreement thereto. It is also a generally recognized principle that a multilateral convention is the result of an agreement freely concluded upon its clauses and that consequently none of the contracting parties is entitled to frustrate or impair, by means of unilateral decisions or particular agreements, the purpose and *raison d'etre* of the convention. To this principle was linked the notion of the integrity of the convention as adopted, a notion which in its traditional concept involved the proposition that no reservation was valid unless it was accepted by all the contracting parties without exception, as would have been the case if it had been stated during the negotiations.

This concept ··· is of undisputed value as a principle. However, as regards the Genocide Convention, it is proper to refer to a variety of circumstances which would lead to a more flexible application of this principle. ··· Extensive participation in conventions of this type has already given rise to greater flexibility in the international practice concerning multilateral conventions. More general resort to reservations, very great allowance made for tacit assent to reservations, the existence of practices which go so far as to admit that the author of reservations which have been rejected by certain contracting parties is nevertheless to be regarded as a party to the convention in relation to those contracting parties that have accepted the reservations—all these factors are manifestations of a new need for flexibility in the operation of multilateral conventions.

It must also be pointed out that although the Genocide Convention was finally approved unanimously, it is nevertheless the result of a series of majority votes. The majority principle, while facilitating the conclusion of multilateral conventions, may also make it necessary for certain States to make reservations. This observation is confirmed by the great number of reservations which have been made of recent years to multilateral conventions.

In this State of international practice, it could certainly not be inferred from the absence of an article providing for reservations in a multilateral convention that the contracting States are prohibited from making certain reservations. Account should also be taken of the fact that the absence of such an article or even the decision not to insert such an article can be explained by the desire not to invite a multiplicity of reservations. The character of a multilateral convention, its purpose, provisions, mode of: preparation and adoption, are factors which must be considered m determining, in the absence of any express provision on the subject, the possibility of making reservations, as well as their validity and effect.

······

The Court recognizes that an understanding was reached within the General Assembly on the faculty to make reservations to the Genocide Convention and that it is permitted to conclude therefrom that States becoming parties to the Convention gave their assent thereto. It must now determine what kind of reservations may be made and what kind of objections may be taken to them.

The solution of these problems must be found in the special characteristics of the Genocide Convention. The origins and character of that Convention, the objects pursued by the General Assembly and the contracting parties, the relations which exist between the provisions of the Convention, *inter se*, and between those provisions and these objects, furnish elements of interpretation of the will of the General Assembly and the parties. The origins of the Convention show that it was the intention of the United Nations to condemn and punish genocide as "a crime under international law" involving a denial of the right of existence of entire human groups, a denial which shocks the conscience of mankind and results in great losses to humanity, and which is contrary to moral law and to the spirit and aims of the United Nations (Resolution 96 (I) of the General Assembly, December 11th 1946). The first consequence arising from this conception is that the principles underlying the Convention are principles which are recognized by civilized nations as binding on States, even without any conventional obligation. A second consequence is the universal character both of the condemnation of genocide and of the co-operation required "in order to liberate mankind from such an odious scourge" (Preamble to the Convention). The Genocide Convention was therefore intended by the General Assembly and by the contracting parties to be definitely universal in scope. ⋯

The objects of such a convention must also be considered. The Convention was manifestly adopted for a purely humanitarian and civilizing purpose. It is indeed difficult to imagine a convention that might have this dual character to a greater degree, since its object on the one hand is to safeguard the very existence of certain human groups and on the other to confirm and endorse the most elementary principles of morality. In such a convention the contracting States do not have any interests of their own; they merely have, one and all, a common interest, namely, the accomplishment of those high purposes which are the *raison d'etre* of the convention. Consequently, in a convention of this type one cannot speak of individual advantages or disadvantages to States, or of the maintenance of a perfect contractual balance between rights and duties. The high ideals which inspired the Convention provide, by virtue of the common will of the parties, the foundation and measure of all its provisions.

The foregoing considerations, when applied to the question of reservations, and more particularly to the effects of objections to reservations, lead to the following conclusions.

The object and purpose of the Genocide Convention imply that it was the intention of the General Assembly and of the States which adopted it that as many States as possible should participate. The complete exclusion from the Convention of one or more States would not only restrict the scope of its application, but would detract from the authority of the moral and humanitarian principles which are its basis. It is inconceivable that the contracting parties readily contemplated that an objection to a minor reservation should produce such a result. But even less could the contracting parties have intended to sacrifice the very object of the Convention in favor of a vain desire to secure as many participants as possible. The object and purpose of the Convention thus limit both the freedom of making reservations and that of objecting to them. It follows that it is the compatibility of a reservation with the object and purpose of the Convention that must furnish the criterion for the attitude of a State in making the reservation on accession as well as for the appraisal by a State in objecting to the reservation. Such is the rule of conduct which must guide every State in the appraisal which it must make, individually and from its own standpoint, of the admissibility of any reservation.

……

4.2 Territorial Dispute Case[①]

......

46. In support of its interpretation of the Treaty, Libya has drawn attention to the fact that Article 3 of the Treaty mentions "the frontiers" in the plural. It argues from this that the parties had in view delimitation of some of their frontiers, not that of the whole of the frontier. The use of the plural is, in the view of the Court, to be explained by the fact that there were differences of legal status between the various territories bordering on Libya for whose international relations France was at the time responsible, and their respective frontiers had been delimited by different agreements. ⋯ In this context the use of the plural is clearly appropriate, and does not have the significance attributed to it by Libya. Moreover, it is to be noted that the parties referred to a frontier between French Equatorial Africa and Libya.

48. The Court considers that Article 3 of the 1955 Treaty was aimed at settling all the frontier questions, and not just some of them. The manifest intention of the parties was that the instruments referred to in Annex I would indicate, cumulatively, all the frontiers between the parties, and that no frontier taken in isolation would be left out of that arrangement. In the expression "the frontiers between the territories⋯", the use of the definite article is to be explained by the intention to refer to all the frontiers between Libya and those neighboring territories for whose international relations France was then responsible. Article 3 does not itself define the frontiers but refers to the instruments mentioned in Annex I. The list in Annex I was taken by the parties as exhaustive as regards delimitation of their frontiers.

[①] See *Territorial Dispute (Libyun Aruh Jamuhiriyu/Chad)*, Judgment, I C J Reports 1994, p. 6. The dispute revolved around whether a boundary between Libya and Chad had been settled by a treaty in 1955 between Libya and France (the former colonial power in Chad). The Court held, by 16 votes to 1, that the 1955 treaty did indeed define the boundary. In reaching this conclusion it noted that Article 31 of VCLT reflected customary international law.

51. The parties could have indicated the frontiers by specifying in words the course of the boundary, or by indicating it on a map, by way of illustration or otherwise; or they could have done both. They chose to proceed in a different manner and to establish, by agreement, the list of international instruments from which the frontiers resulted, but the course for which they elected presents no difficulties of interpretation. That being so, the Court's task is clear. ···

The text of Article 3 clearly conveys the intention of the parties to reach a definitive settlement of the question of their common frontiers. Article 3 and Annex I are intended to define frontiers by reference to legal instruments which would yield the course of such frontiers. Any other construction would be contrary to one of the fundamental principles of interpretation of treaties, consistently upheld by international jurisprudence, namely that of effectiveness.

······

4.3 Costa Rica v. Nicaragua[1]

······

48. In the second place, the Court is not convinced by Nicaragua's argument that Costa Rica's right of free navigation should be interpreted narrowly because it represents a limitation of the sovereignty over the river conferred by the Treaty on Nicaragua, that being the most important principle set forth by Article Ⅵ.

While it is certainly true that limitations of the sovereignty of a State over its territory are not to be presumed, this does not mean that treaty

---

[1] See *Dispute Regarding Navigational and Related Rights* (*Costa Rica v. Nicaragua*), Judgment, ICJ Reports 2009, p. 213. In determining the types of navigation conferred on Costa Rica by the 1958 Treaty of Limits between the States, the ICJ was required to interpret the phrase "*con objectos de comercio*" in the treaty. Nicaragua argued for a narrow interpretation of the phrase, so that navigation rights only extended to vessels carrying commercial objects, as opposed to journeys for the purpose of commerce.

provisions establishing such limitations, such as those that are in issue in the present case, should for this reason be interpreted *a priori* in a restrictive way. A treaty provision which has the purpose of limiting the sovereign powers of a State must be interpreted like any other provision of a treaty, i. e. in accordance with the intentions of its authors as reflected by the text of the treaty and the other relevant factors in terms of interpretation.

A simple reading of Article VI shows that the Parties did not intend to establish any hierarchy as between Nicaragua's sovereignty over the river and Costa Rica's right of free navigation, characterized as "perpetual", with each of these affirmations counter-balancing the other. Nicaragua's sovereignty is affirmed only to the extent that it does not prejudice the substance of Costa Rica's right of free navigation in its domain, the establishment of which is precisely the point at issue; the right of free navigation, albeit "perpetual", is granted only on condition that it does not prejudice the key prerogatives of territorial sovereignty.

There are thus no grounds for supposing, *a priori*, that the words "libre navegación... con objetos de comercio" should be given a specially restrictive interpretation, any more than an extensive one.

50. It is now appropriate to consider the issue of the meaning of the phrase *"con objetos de"* as used in Article VI of the 1858 Treaty, specifically whether it means "for the purposes of"—as Costa Rica contends—or "with articles of"—as Nicaragua contends.

51. It should first be observed that the Spanish word *"objetos"* can, depending on its context, have either of the two meanings put forward. Thus, the context must be examined to ascertain the meaning to be ascribed here. The two meanings—one concrete and the other abstract—are sufficiently different that examination of the context will generally allow for a firm conclusion to be reached.

52. Having conducted this examination, the Court is of the view that the interpretation advocated by Nicaragua cannot be upheld.

The main reason for this is that ascribing the meaning "with goods" or "with articles" to the phrase "*con objetos*" results in rendering meaningless the entire sentence in which the phrase appears.

The part of Article Ⅵ which is relevant in this connection reads: "Costa Rica tendrá... los derechos perpetuos de libre navegación... , *con objetos de comercio*, ya sea con Nicaragua ó al interior de Costa Rica."

If Nicaragua's interpretation were to be accepted, there would be no intelligible relationship between the clause following the phrase "*con objetos de comercio*", i. e., "ya sea con Nicaragua ó al interior de Costa Rica" ("whether with Nicaragua or with the interior of Costa Rica"), and the preceding part of the sentence.

Either the words "with Nicaragua" would relate to "*objetos de comercio*", which would hardly make sense, since it would not be meaningful to speak of "goods (or articles) of trade with Nicaragua"; or these words relate to "navegación" and that would make even less sense, because the expression "navegación... con Nicaragua" would simply be incomprehensible.

By contrast, Costa Rica's interpretation of the words "*con objetos*" allows the entire sentence to be given coherent meaning. If the phrase means "purposes of commerce", then the immediately following clause, "ya sea con Nicaragua...", plainly relates to "*comercio*" ("for the purposes of commerce with Nicaragua..."), and the sentence then conveys a perfectly comprehensible idea.

Thus, in the present instance a literal analysis of the sentence containing the words requiring interpretation leads to one of the proposed meanings being preferred over the other.

62. In respect of the narrow interpretation advanced by Nicaragua, the Court observes that it is supported mainly by two arguments: the first is based on the Respondent's interpretation of the phrase "*con objetos*", which has just been rejected; the second is based on the assertion that "commerce" should be given the narrow meaning it had when the Treaty was entered into.

63. The Court does not agree with this second argument. It is true that the terms used in a treaty must be interpreted in light of what is determined to have been the parties' common intention, which is, by definition, contemporaneous with the treaty's conclusion. That may lead a court seised of a dispute, or the parties themselves, when they seek to determine the meaning of a treaty for purposes of good-faith compliance with it, to ascertain the meaning a term had when the treaty was drafted, since doing so can shed light on the parties' common intention. The Court has so proceeded in certain cases requiring it to interpret a term whose meaning had evolved since the conclusion of the treaty at issue, and in those cases the Court adhered to the original meaning ⋯

64. This does not however signify that, where a term's meaning is no longer the same as it was at the date of conclusion, no account should ever be taken of its meaning at the time when the treaty is to be interpreted for purposes of applying it.

On the one hand, the subsequent practice of the parties, within the meaning of Article 31 (3) (b) of the Vienna Convention, can result in a departure from the original intent on the basis of a tacit agreement between the parties. On the other hand, there are situations in which the parties' intent upon conclusion of the treaty was, or may be presumed to have been, to give the terms used—or some of them—a meaning or content capable of evolving, not one fixed once and for all, so as to make allowance for, among other things, developments in international law. In such instances it is indeed in order to respect the parties' common intention at the time the treaty was concluded, not to depart from it, that account should be taken of the meaning acquired by the terms in question upon each occasion on which the treaty is to be applied.

······

4.4 *China-Auto Parts Case*[①]

151. We have already stated that the task of the treaty interpreter is to ascertain the meaning of particular treaty terms using the tools set out in Articles 31 and 32 of the Vienna Convention. The realm of context as defined in Article 31(2) is broad. "Context" includes all of the text of the treaty—in this case, the WTO Agreement—and may also extend to "any agreement relating to the treaty which was made between all the parties in connection with the conclusion of the treaty" and "any instrument which was made by one or more parties in connection with the conclusion of the treaty and accepted by the other parties as an instrument related to the treaty". Yet context is relevant for a treaty interpreter to the extent that it may shed light on the interpretative issue to be resolved, such as the meaning of the term or phrase at issue. Thus, for a particular provision, agreement or instrument to serve as relevant context in any given situation, it must not only fall within the scope of the formal boundaries identified in Article 31(2), it must also have some pertinence to the language being interpreted that renders it capable of helping the interpreter to determine the meaning of such language. Because WTO Members' Schedules of Concessions were constructed using the nomenclature of the Harmonized System, the Harmonized System is apt to shed light on the meaning of terms used in these Schedules. It does not, however, automatically follow that the Harmonized System was context relevant to the interpretative question faced by the Panel in its analysis of the threshold issue in this dispute.

[①] The Appellate Body was called upon to consider the context in interpreting a treaty, in this case whether a description and coding system under another treaty could be taken into account as part of the context of the treaty. See China-Measures Affecting Imports of Automobile Parts, WT/DS342/AB/R, Para. 151.

5. References and Recommended Reading Materials

(1) Anthony Aust, *Modern Treaty Law And Practice*, 2nd Ed., Cambridge University Press, 2007.〔英〕安托尼·奥斯特:《现代条约法与实践》,江国青译,中国人民大学出版社 2005 年版。

(2) 李浩培:《条约法概论》,法律出版社 2003 年版。

(3) 李育民:《晚清中外条约关系研究》,法律出版社 2018 年版。

Chapter XII   Diplomacy and Immunity

1. Introduction

Rules regulating the various aspects of diplomatic relations constitute one of the earliest expressions of international law. Throughout history, there has been a group of independent States co-existing. As a result, particular customs have developed on how other States' ambassadors and other special representatives were to be treated.

Diplomacy as a method of communication between various parties, including negotiations between recognized agents, is an ancient institution and international legal provisions governing its manifestations result from centuries of State practices. The special privileges and immunities related to diplomatic personnel of various kinds grew up partly as a consequence of sovereign immunity and the independence and equality of States and partly as an essential requirement of an international system. States must negotiate and consult with each other and with international organizations, in order to do so they need diplomatic staff. Since these persons represent their States in various ways, they thus benefit from the legal principle of State sovereignty.

With the growth of trade and commercial intercourse, the office of consul was established and expanded. In addition, the development of speedy communications stimulated the creation of special missions designed to be sent to particular areas for specific purposes, often with the head of State or government in charge. To some extent, however, the establishment of telephone, telegraph, telex and fax services has lessened the importance of the traditional diplomatic personnel by strengthening the centralizing process. Nevertheless, diplomats and consuls do retain some valuable functions in collecting information and in pursuit of friendly relations and providing a permanent presence in foreign States, with all that implies for commercial and economic activities. The field of diplomatic immunities is one of the most accepted and uncontroversial international law topics, as it is ultimately in the interest of all States to preserve an even tenor of diplomatic relations.

2. Preliminary Reading and Assignment

2.1 Vienna Convention on Diplomatic Relations (1961)

Article 1

For the purpose of the present Convention, the following expressions shall have the meanings hereunder assigned to them:

(a) The "head of the mission" is the person charged by the sending State with the duty of acting in that capacity;

(b) The "members of the mission" are the head of the mission and the members of the staff of the mission;

(c) The "members of the staff of the mission" are the members of the diplomatic staff, of the administrative and technical staff and of the service staff of the mission;

(d) The "members of the diplomatic staff" are the members of the staff of the mission having diplomatic rank;

(e) A "diplomatic agent" is the head of the mission or a member of the diplomatic staff of the mission;

(f) The "members of the administrative and technical staff" are the members of the staff of the mission employed in the administrative and technical service of the mission;

(h) A "private servant" is a person who is in the domestic service of a member of the mission and who is not an employee of the sending State;

(i) The "premises of the mission" are the buildings or parts of buildings and the land ancillary thereto, irrespective of ownership, used for the purposes of the mission including the residence of the head of the mission.

Article 3

1. The functions of a diplomatic mission consist, *inter alia*, in:

(a) Representing the sending State in the receiving State;

(b) Protecting in the receiving State the interests of the sending State and of its nationals, within the limits permitted by international law;

(c) Negotiating with the Government of the receiving State;

(d) Ascertaining by all lawful means conditions and developments in the receiving State, and reporting thereon to the Government of the sending State;

(e) Promoting friendly relations between the sending State and the receiving State, and developing their economic, cultural and scientific relations;

2. Nothing in the present Convention shall be construed as preventing the performance of consular functions by a diplomatic mission.

Article 4

1. The sending State must make certain that the agreement of the receiving State has been given for the person it proposes to accredit as head of the mission to that State.

2. The receiving State is not obliged to give reasons to the sending State for a refusal of agreement.

Article 9

1. The receiving State may at any time and without having to explain its decision, notify the sending State that the head of the mission or any member of the diplomatic staff of the mission is persona non grata or that any other member of the staff of the mission is not acceptable. In any such case, the sending State shall, as appropriate, either recall the person concerned or

terminate his functions with the mission. A person may be declared non grata or not acceptable before arriving in the territory of the receiving State.

2. If the sending State refuses or fails within a reasonable period to carry out its obligations under paragraph 1 of this article, the receiving State may refuse to recognize the person concerned as a member of the mission.

Article 21

1. The receiving State shall either facilitate the acquisition on its territory, in accordance with its laws, by the sending State of premises necessary for its mission or assist the latter in obtaining accommodation in some other way.

2. It shall also, where necessary, assist missions in obtaining suitable accommodation for their members.

Article 22

1. The premises of the mission shall be inviolable. The agents of the receiving State may not enter them, except with the consent of the head of the mission.

2. The receiving State is under a special duty to take all appropriate steps to protect the premises of the mission against any intrusion or damage and to prevent any disturbance of the peace of the mission or impairment of its dignity.

3. The premises of the mission, their furnishings and other property thereon and the means of transport of the mission shall be immune from search, requisition, attachment or execution.

Article 26

Subject to its laws and regulations concerning zones entry into which is prohibited or regulated for reasons of national security, the receiving State shall ensure to all members of the mission freedom of movement and travel in its territory.

Article 29

The person of a diplomatic agent shall be inviolable. He shall not be liable to any form of arrest or detention. The receiving State shall treat him with due respect and shall take all appropriate steps to prevent any attack on his person, freedom or dignity.

Article 31

1. A diplomatic agent shall enjoy immunity from the criminal jurisdiction of the receiving State. He shall also enjoy immunity from its civil and administrative jurisdiction, except in the case of:

(a) A real action relating to private immovable property situated in the territory of the receiving State, unless he holds it on behalf of the sending State for the purposes of the mission;

(b) An action relating to succession in which the diplomatic agent is involved as executor, administrator, heir or legatee as a private person and not on behalf of the sending State;

(c) An action relating to any professional or commercial activity exercised by the diplomatic agent in the receiving State outside his official functions. ……

Article 32

1. The immunity from jurisdiction of diplomatic agents and of persons enjoying immunity under article 37 may be waived by the sending State.

2. Waiver must always be express.

3. The initiation of proceedings by a diplomatic agent or by a person enjoying immunity from jurisdiction under article 37 shall preclude him from invoking immunity from jurisdiction in respect of any counterclaim directly connected with the principal claim.

4. Waiver of immunity from jurisdiction in respect of civil or administrative proceedings shall not be held to imply waiver of immunity in respect of the execution of the judgement, for which a separate waiver shall be necessary.

Article 39

1. Every person entitled to privileges and immunities shall enjoy them

from the moment he enters the territory of the receiving State on proceeding to take up his post or, if already in its territory, from the moment when his appointment is notified to the Ministry for Foreign Affairs or such other ministry as may be agreed.

2. When the functions of a person enjoying privileges and immunities have come to an end, such privileges and immunities shall normally cease at the moment when he leaves the country, or on expiry of a reasonable period in which to do so, but shall subsist until that time, even in case of armed conflict. However, with respect to acts performed by such a person in the exercise of his functions as a member of the mission, immunity shall continue to subsist.

3. In case of the death of a member of the mission, the members of his family shall continue to enjoy the privileges and immunities to which they are entitled until the expiry of a reasonable period in which to leave the country.

......

2.2 Vienna Convention on Consular Relations (1963)

Article 2 Establishment of Consular Relations

1. The establishment of consular relations between States takes place by mutual consent.

2. The consent given to the establishment of diplomatic relations between two States implies, unless otherwise stated, consent to the establishment of consular relations.

3. The severance of diplomatic relations shall not *ipso facto* involve the severance of consular relations.

Article 3 Exercise of Consular Functions

Consular functions are exercised by consular posts. They are also exercised by diplomatic missions in accordance with the provisions of the present Convention.

Article 4　Establishment of a Consular Post

1. A consular post may be established in the territory of the receiving State only with that State's consent.

2. The seat of the consular post, its classification and the consular district shall be established by the sending State and shall be subject to the approval of the receiving State.

3. Subsequent changes in the seat of the consular post, its classification or the consular district may be made by the sending State only with the consent of the receiving State.

4. The consent of the receiving State shall also be required if a consulate general or a consulate desires to open a vice-consulate or a consular agency in a locality other than that in which it is itself established.

5. The prior express consent of the receiving State shall also be required for the opening of an office forming part of an existing consular post elsewhere than at the seat thereof.

Article 5　Consular Functions

Consular functions consist in:

(a) protecting in the receiving State the interests of the sending State and of its nationals, both individuals and bodies corporate, within the limits permitted by international law;

(b) furthering the development of commercial, economic, cultural and scientific relations between the sending State and the receiving State and otherwise promoting friendly relations between them in accordance with the provisions of the present Convention;

(c) ascertaining by all lawful means conditions and developments in the commercial, economic, cultural and scientific life of the receiving State, reporting thereon to the Government of the sending State and giving information to persons interested;

(d) issuing passports and travel documents to nationals of the sending State, and visas or appropriate documents to persons wishing to travel to the sending State;

(e) helping and assisting nationals, both individuals and bodies corporate, of the sending State;

(f) acting as notary and civil registrar and in capacities of a similar kind, and performing certain functions of an administrative nature, provided that there is nothing contrary thereto in the laws and regulations of the receiving State;

(g) safeguarding the interests of nationals, both individuals and bodies corporate, of the sending State in cases of succession mortis causa in the territory of the receiving State, in accordance with the laws and regulations of the receiving State;

(h) safeguarding, within the limits imposed by the laws and regulations of the receiving State, the interests of minors and other persons lacking full capacity who are nationals of the sending State, particularly where any guardianship or trusteeship is required with respect to such persons;

(i) subject to the practices and procedures obtaining in the receiving State, representing or arranging appropriate representation for nationals of the sending State before the tribunals and other authorities of the receiving State, for the purpose of obtaining, in accordance with the laws and regulations of the receiving State, provisional measures for the preservation of the rights and interests of these nationals, where, because of absence or any other reason, such nationals are unable at the proper time to assume the defence of their rights and interests;

(j) transmitting judicial and extra-judicial documents or executing letters regatory or commissions to take evidence for the courts of the sending State in accordance with international agreements in force or, in the absence of such international agreements, in any other manner com patible with the laws and regulations of the receiving State;

(k) exercising rights of supervision and inspection provided for in the laws and regulations of the sending State in respect of vessels having the nationality of the sending State, and of aircraft registered in that State, and in respect of their crews;

(l) extending assistance to vessels and aircraft mentioned in sub-paragraph (k) of this Article and to their crews, taking Statements regarding the voyage of a vessel, examining and stamping the ship's papers, and, without prejudice to the powers of the authorities of the receiving State, conduct ing investigations into any incidents which occurred during the voyage, and settling disputes of any kind between the master, the officers and the seamen in so far as this may be authorized by the laws and regulations of the sending State;

(m) performing any other functions entrusted to a consular post by the sending State which are not prohibited by the laws and regulations of the receiving State or to which no objection is taken by the receiving State or which are referred to in the international agreements in force between the sending State and the receiving State.

……

2.3 Questions and Assignment

(1) Retreat the full articles of Vienna Convention on Consular Relations (1963) and Vienna Convention on Diplomatic Relations (1961). Compare the two conventions and answer the question: what are the key differences between them?

(2) What are the privileges and immunities enjoyed by the diplomats?

(3) Why should the privileges and immunities of diplomats be guaranteed?

(4) Make a comment on the US's rejection of diplomats from Iran and Russia and find out whether the US is in violation of rules concerned. Prepare an 8-10 minutes speech in English on this question.

3. Terminologies and Explanations

3.1 Diplomatic Law and Basic Questions

The Vienna Convention on Diplomatic Relations and the *Vienna Convention on Consular Relations* codify the existing laws and established State practices concerning diplomacy. Questions not expressly regulated by the Conventions continue to be governed by the rules of customary international law. There are six basic legal questions to be clarified based on *the Vienna Convention on Diplomatic Relations* ("the Convention").

First, mutual consent is the only legal ground to establish formal diplomatic relations. The Convention provides that: "The establishment of diplomatic relations between States, and permanent diplomatic missions, takes place by mutual consent." They must be sovereign States and must recognize each other as such. Recognition is usually soon followed by the establishment of diplomatic relations, sometimes the establishment of relations constitutes the act of recognition. There is no right of legation in general international law, though all States can establish diplomatic relations. Accordingly, the Convention specifies in Article 4 that the sending State must ensure that the consent of the receiving State has been given for the proposed head of its mission, and reasons for any refusal of consent do not have to be given.

Similarly, by Article 9, the receiving State may declare any member of the diplomatic mission *persona non grata* without having to explain its decision and thus obtain the removal of that person. Since diplomatic relations are consensual, they may be terminated by withdrawing the mission by either the sending or receiving State. The sending State may terminate the functions of individual staff members on notification to the receiving State for its own practical or political reasons.

Second, the members of a diplomatic mission are the head of mission, the diplomatic staff, the administrative and technical staff, and the service staff. The head of mission and the diplomatic staff of the mission are defined in Article 1 (e) as "diplomatic agents" and enjoy the highest privileges and immunities; the other members of the mission are on lower scales of privileges and immunities. Members of the diplomatic staff should be nationals of the sending State. Exceptionally, they can be nationals of the receiving State if the latter agrees.

The head of the mission has to be expressly accepted by the receiving State before taking up his post, which is done by obtaining the *agrément* of the receiving State. No reasons have to be given for refusing *agrément*. The sending State may "freely appoint" the other members of the mission, who also do not have to be members of the diplomatic service. There is no requirement for prior or subsequent approval by the receiving State. The foreign ministry of the receiving State must be notified, in advance where possible, of all appointments and the arrivals and departures of members of the mission. The engagement and discharge of local staff must also be notified. Notifications should clearly indicate whether the person is a diplomatic agent, a member of the administrative and technical staff, or service staff by describing the post, such as first secretary, communications officer, driver. Members of the family and private servants must also be notified. Failure to inform a person entitled to privileges and immunities will not affect the person's entitlement, which takes effect automatically on arrival in the receiving State to take up the post. Nevertheless, since the freedom of a sending State to appoint the members of its mission requires the receiving State to exempt the arriving members from immigration restrictions, failure to notify in advance could result in inconvenience.

Third, the main functions of the diplomat's mission are representation and protection of the interests and nationals of the sending State and the promotion of information and friendly relations. The Convention specifies this in Article 3 by a non-exhaustive list. It provides that the functions of a diplomatic mission consist of representing the sending State in the receiving State, protecting in the receiving State the interests of the sending State and of its nationals, negotiating with the government of the receiving State, ascertaining by all lawful means conditions and developments in the receiving State and reporting thereon to the Government of the sending State, promoting friendly relations between the sending State and the receiving State, and developing their economic, cultural and scientific relations. Article 41(1) also emphasizes the duty of all persons enjoying privileges and immunities to respect the laws and regulations of the receiving State and the obligation not to interfere in the internal affairs of that State.

Fourth, the rationale of privileges and immunities. The special privileges and immunities related to diplomatic personnel of various kinds grew up partly as a consequence of sovereign immunity and the independence and equality of States and partly as an essential requirement of an international system. Since these persons represent their States in various ways, they thus benefit from the legal principle of State sovereignty. It is also an issue of practical convenience. Having agreed to the establishment of diplomatic relations, the receiving State must enable the sending State to benefit from the content of the license. Doing so results in a body of privileges and immunities. One explanation is that the diplomatic agent and the mission premises were "exterritorial", legally assimilated to the territorial jurisdiction of the sending State. The Convention rests on a combination of functional and representative theories, emphasizing the functional necessity of diplomatic privileges and immunities for the efficient conduct of international relations and pointing to the character of the diplomatic mission as representing its State. Under the functional theory, firstly, immunity is a statement recognizing the sovereign and independent status of the sending State and the public nature of a diplomat's acts and their consequent immunity from the receiving State's jurisdiction. And, secondly, the immunities are to protect the diplomatic mission and staff and ensure the efficient performance of functions designed to preserve international order and maintain communication between States.

Fifth, the fulfillment of duties by the receiving State. Immunities and privileges enjoyed by the missions from sending States mean that the receiving States shall take some legal duties. Appropriate care must be shown in providing police protection for personnel and premises and the State will incur responsibility if the judiciary fails to maintain the necessary privileges and immunities.

Sixth, the abuse of diplomatic immunities. Serious breaches of diplomatic immunity are rare. But there have been serious abuses. The most recent case was *Jamal Khashoggi* incident, who was murdered brutally in the Consulate of Saudi Arabia in Turkey. Another famous case was that a Nigerian former minister was found drugged in a "diplomatic bag" at Stansted Airport. An institution, the House of Commons Foreign Affairs Committee concluded that any attempt to alter the balance of rights and duties so as to further require protected individuals to respect the laws of the receiving State was undesirable.

3.2 Inviolability of the Mission and Diplomatic Immunity

The inviolability of the mission, which is to facilitate the operations of normal diplomatic activities, extends to the premises, archives, documents, official correspondence and diplomatic agents.

First, the inviolability of the premises. The "premises of the mission" include all the buildings and land used for the mission, including the residence of the head of mission, which today is usually physically separated from the chancery. The receiving State must either "facilitate the acquisition, under its laws, by the sending State of premises necessary for its mission or assist the latter in obtaining accommodation in some other way". Article 22 of the Convention provides the basic rule concerned. It states that the premises of the mission are inviolable and that agents of the receiving State are not to enter them without the consent of the mission. It flows from the concept of diplomatic immunity. The Convention also requires the receiving State to take all appropriate steps to protect the mission's premises against intrusion or damage and prevent any disturbance of its peace or impairment of its dignity. Inviolability is an absolute rule since any exception to it could be abused by a receiving State.

In contrast to consular premises, the prohibition on entry applies even in an emergency. If an ambassador would insist his embassy burn down rather than call in the local fire service, all the receiving State can do is try to persuade him to let them in. Diplomatic missions with chanceries and residences in historic buildings in prime locations can now be an obstacle to the building of highways and shopping malls. The mission cannot be required to move. Even if negotiations with the receiving State do not resolve the matter, inviolability means that the mission cannot be made to move or to give up part of its land even if suitable alternatives are offered free.

Second, the inviolability of the archives, documents, and official correspondence. The Convention establishes the inviolability of the archives and documents of the mission "at any time and wherever they may be", as well as official correspondence. It provides simply that "the diplomatic bag shall not be opened or detained". A significant breach of this obligation was the subject of Tehran Hostages before the International Court. Recent examples of a breach were that the United States to open the diplomatic bags belonging to China in July 2018 and January 2020. The evidence of abuse of the diplomatic bag in the form of drug trafficking or involvement in terrorist activities has led the UK government to scan bags where there are strong grounds of suspicion. A member of the relevant mission is invited to be present. In 1989 the ILC adopted a set of more precise rules concerning diplomatic bags and diplomatic couriers, but no agreement could be reached in the General Assembly.

Third, the inviolability of the diplomatic agent. Article 29 of the

Convention provides that: "The person of a diplomatic agent shall be inviolable. He shall not be liable to any form of arrest or detention. The receiving State shall treat him with due respect and shall take all appropriate steps to prevent any attack on his person, freedom or dignity." This inviolability is distinct from immunity from criminal jurisdiction. As with inviolability of the mission premises, there is no express reservation for action in cases of emergency, for example, a drunken diplomat with a loaded gun in a public place. Article 30 provides that the private residence, including a temporary residence, of a diplomatic agent, is likewise inviolable. So are the agent's papers, correspondence, and property. There is no jurisdictional immunity in case of a real action concerning the immovable property. It has recently been suggested that the scope of the duty in Article 29 should include indirect attacks on a diplomat's dignity or even events in general that may embarrass or offend a diplomat. A related legal issue with inviolability is about the police action of receiving State. From the 1960s, there have been examples of police entering diplomatic missions without permission in pursuance of their normal duties, in particular pursuing suspected criminals. Even if the police were unaware of the status of the premises, the intrusion would amount to a breach of its inviolability. However, there is a possibility that in very exceptional circumstances, the police may enter the premises without consent if its occupants, whether diplomats or terrorists, clearly pose a real and immediate danger to human life outside the premises.

Compared with inviolability, the immunities of diplomatic agents concern mainly with their privileges from the judicial jurisdiction of receiving State. It includes the diplomatic agents' immunities from the jurisdiction of criminal, civil and administrative actions, not an exemption from the substantive law. The immunity can be waived, and the local law may then be applied. Article 41(1) stipulates that "it is the duty of all persons enjoying such privileges and immunities to respect the laws and regulations of the receiving State", though without prejudice to those privileges or immunities. Article 31(1) provides without qualification that "a diplomatic agent shall enjoy immunity from the criminal jurisdiction of the receiving State". A diplomatic agent, guilty of severe or persistent breaches of the law, may be declared *persona non grata* but is immune from prosecution while in the post, irrespective of the character of the crime or its relation to the functions or work of the mission. Immunity covers not only direct claims against a diplomat and his or her property but also family law claims, including proceedings to protect children and other family members.

Article 31(1) also confers immunity on the diplomatic agent from the local civil and administrative jurisdiction, except in the case of (a) a real action relating to private immovable property in the territory of the receiving State, unless held on behalf of the sending State for the purposes of the mission; (b) an action relating to succession in which the agent is involved as executor, administrator, heir, or legatee in his or her capacity as a private individual; and (c) any professional or commercial activity by the diplomatic agent outside his or her official duties.

The exceptions to this form of immunity represent a modern development in the law and reflect the principle that the personal immunities of diplomatic agents should not be unqualified. Note that, even if immunity from jurisdiction has been waived, a judgment cannot be enforced by execution against the person, private residence or private property of the immune person.

The last question is about the waiver of immunity. The purpose of diplomatic immunity is to ensure the efficient performance of the functions of a diplomatic mission. It is not for personal benefit. Therefore, immunity cannot be validly waived by the person enjoying it. It can be waived only by or on behalf of the sending State. The law of the receiving State must determine whether immunity has been waived, and particular care must be taken with criminal proceedings since the accused diplomat might challenge the waiver. The waiver by the head of mission will normally be regarded as valid unless it purports to be of his own immunity. And most governments require a head of mission to seek authority before waiving the immunity of any of his staff. Waiver of diplomatic immunity must be express. If a person enjoying immunity takes part in civil or criminal proceedings as a defendant but without an express waiver, the proceedings will be void. Informal or voluntary cooperation with proceedings does not amount to waiver. If a person enjoying immunity initiates civil proceedings, he cannot invoke his immunity in respect of any counter-claim directly connected with his claim.

3.3 Consular Relations

Consuls are, in principle, distinct in function and legal status from diplomatic agents. They are not accorded the type of immunity from the laws and enforcement jurisdiction of the receiving State enjoyed by diplomatic agents. Since the 18th century, the status of consuls has been based upon general usage rather than law. The Vienna Convention on Consular Relations (1963) follows the pattern of the 1961 Diplomatic Convention, drawing heavily on established practices.

The establishment of diplomatic relations implies consent to consular relations too. Today, most embassies also carry out consular functions. But there is still a need for States to establish "consular posts" (not missions) separate from their diplomatic missions. The establishment of each post requires the receiving State's consent, including its location and the district that it will cover. A consul may not act outside his district. Consular posts are headed by a consul-general, consul, vice-consul or consular agent. The appointment must first be approved by the receiving State through an *exequatur*, although the consul may be allowed to exercise his functions on a provisional basis.

4. Cases and Materials

Read the cases and think about the following queseions:

(1) What kind of obligation shall the receiving State bear towards the embassy under international law?

(2) How to understand the immunity and inviolability enjoyed by the diplomatic premises?

(3) Retreat the case of *Equatorial Guinea v. France* on the ICJ website and find out: why the ICJ declined to accept the request made by Equatorial Guinea? Do you agree with the decision made by the Court? Check the dissent opinion made by the vice president of the Court.

4.1 *Tehran Case* [1]

(1) *Procedures Before the Court (Paras. 1-10)*

On 29 November 1979, the Legal Adviser of the Department of State of the United States of America handed to the Registrar an Application instituting proceedings against the Islamic Republic of Iran in respect of a dispute concerning the seizure and holding as hostages of members of the United States diplomatic and consular staff and certain other United States nationals.

Pursuant to Article 40, paragraph 2, of the Statute and Article 38, paragraph 4, of the Rules of Court, the Application was at once communicated to the Government of Iran. In accordance with Article 40, paragraph 3, of the Statute and Article 42 of the Rules of Court, the Secretary-General of the United Nations, the Members of the United Nations, and other States entitled to appear before the Court were notified of

---

[1] See *United States Diplomatic and Consular Staff in Tehran (United States of America v. Iran)*, Judgment, ICJ Reports 1980, p. 3.

the Application.

On the same day, the Government of the United States filed in the Registry of the Court a request for the indication of provisional measures under Article 41 of the Statute and Article 73 of the Rules of Court. By an Order dated 15 December 1979, and adopted unanimously, the Court indicated provisional measures in the case.

By an Order made by the President of the Court dated 24 December 1979, 15 January 1980 was fixed as the time-limit for the filing of the Memorial of the United States, and 18 February 1980 as the time-limit for the Counter-Memorial of Iran, with liberty for Iran, if it appointed an Agent for the purpose of appearing before the Court and presenting its observations on the case, to apply for reconsideration of such time-limit. The Memorial of the United States was filed…no Counter-Memorial was filed by the Government of Iran, nor was any agent appointed or any application made for reconsideration of the time-limit.

The case thus became ready for hearing on 19 February 1980, the day following the expiration of the time-limit fixed for the Counter-Memorial of Iran. …he Government of Iran was not represented at the hearings. …

On 6 December 1979, the Registrar addressed the notifications provided for in Article 63 of the Statute of the Court to the States which according to information supplied by the Secretary-General of the United Nations as depositary were parties to one or more of the following Conventions and Protocols: (a) the Vienna Convention on Diplomatic Relations of 1961; (b) the Optional Protocol to that Convention concerning the Compulsory Settlement of Disputes; (c) the Vienna Convention on Consular Relations of 1963; (d) the Optional Protocol to that Convention concerning the Compulsory Settlement of Disputes; (e) the Convention on the Prevention and Punishment of Crimes against Internationally Protected Persons, including Diplomatic Agents, of 1973.

The Court, after ascertaining the views of the Government of the United

Chapter XII Diplomacy and Immunity   375

States on the matter, and affording the Government of Iran the opportunity of making its views known…

In the course of the written proceedings the following submissions were presented on behalf of the Government of the United States of America:

in the Application:

The United States requests the Court to adjudge and declare as follows:

(a) That the Government of Iran, in tolerating, encouraging, and failing to prevent and punish the conduct described in the preceding statement of Facts, violated its international legal obligations to the United States as provided by:

- Articles 22, 24, 25, 27, 29, 31, 37 and 47 of the Vienna Convention on Diplomatic Relations,

- Articles 28, 31, 33, 34, 36 and 40 of the Vienna Convention on Consular Relations,

- Articles 4 and 7 of the Convention on the Prevention and Punishment of Crimes against Internationally Protected Persons, including Diplomatic Agents, and

- Articles II (4), XIII, XVIII and XIX of the Treaty of Amity, Economic Relations, and Consular Rights between the United States and Iran, and

- Articles 2 (3), 2 (4) and 33 of the Charter of the United Nations;

(b) That pursuant to the foregoing international legal obligations, the Government of Iran is under a particular obligation immediately to secure the release of all United States nationals currently being detained within the premises of the United States Embassy in Tehran and to assure that all such persons and all other United States nationals in Tehran are allowed to leave Iran safely;

(c) That the Government of Iran shall pay to the United States, in its own right and in the exercise of its right of diplomatic protection of its nationals, reparation for the foregoing violations of Iran's international legal obligations to the United States, in a sum to be determined by the Court; and

(d) That the Government of Iran submit to its competent authorities for the purpose of prosecution those persons responsible for the crimes committed against the premises and staff of the United States Embassy and against the premises of its Consulates;…

in the Memorial:

"The Government of the United States respectively requests the Court adjudge and declare as follows:

(a) that the Government of the Islamic Republic of Iran, in permitting, tolerating, encouraging, adopting, and endeavoring to exploit, as well as in failing to prevent and punish, the conduct described in the statement of the Facts, violated its international legal obligations to the United States as provided by: …

(b) That, pursuant to the foregoing international legal obligations:

i. the Government of the Islamic Republic of Iran shall immediately ensure that the premises at the United States Embassy, Chancery and Consulates are restored to the possession of the United States authorities under their exclusive control, and shall ensure their inviolability and effective protection as provided for by the treaties in force between the two States, and by general international law;

ii. the Government of the Islamic Republic of Iran shall ensure the immediate release, without any exception, of all persons of United States nationality who are or have been held in the Embassy of the United States of America or in the Ministry of Foreign Affairs in Tehran, or who are or have been held as hostages elsewhere, and afford full protection to all such persons, in accordance with the treaties in force between the two States, and with general international law;

iii. the Government of the Islamic Republic of Iran shall, as from that moment, afford to all the diplomatic and consular personnel of the United States the protection, privileges and immunities to which they are entitled under the treaties in force between the two States, and under general international law, including immunity from any form of criminal jurisdiction and freedom and facilities to leave the territory of Iran;

iv. the Government of the Islamic Republic of Iran shall, in affording the diplomatic and consular personnel of the United States the protection, privileges and immunities to which they are entitled, including immunity from any form of criminal jurisdiction, ensure that no such personnel shall be obliged to appear on trial or as a witness, deponent, source of information, or in any other role, at any proceedings, whether formal or informal, initiated by or with the acquiescence of the Iranian Government, whether such proceedings be denominated a ' trial ', ' grand jury ', ' international commission ' or otherwise;

v. the Government of the Islamic Republic of Iran shall submit to its competent authorities for the purpose of prosecution, or extradite to the United States, those persons responsible for the crimes committed against the personnel and premises of the United States Embassy and Consulates in Iran;
……"

No pleadings were filed by the Government of Iran, which also was not represented at the oral proceedings, and no submissions were therefore presented on its behalf. The position of that Government was, however, defined in two communications addressed to the Court by the Minister for Foreign Affairs of Iran… reads as follows:

"The Government of the Islamic Republic of Iran wishes to express its respect for the International Court of Justice … and respectfully draws the attention of the Court to the deep-rootedness and the essential character of the Islamic Revolution of Iran, a revolution of a whole oppressed nation against its oppressors and their masters, the examination of whose numerous repercussions is essentially and directly a matter within the national sovereignty of Iran.

"Iran considers that the Court cannot and should not take cognizance of the case which the Government of the United States of America has submitted to it, and in the most significant fashion, a case confined to what is called the question of the 'hostages of the American Embassy in Tehran'.

"For this question only represents a marginal and secondary aspect of an overall problem, one such that it cannot be studied separately, and which involves, *inter alia*, more than 25 years of continual interference by the United States in the internal affairs of Iran, the shameless exploitation of our country, and numerous crimes perpetrated against the Iranian people, contrary to and in conflict with all international and humanitarian norms.

"The problem involved in the conflict between Iran and the United States is thus not one of the interpretation and the application of the treaties upon which the American Application is based, but results from an overall situation containing much more fundamental and more complex elements. Consequently, the Court cannot examine the American Application divorced from its proper context, namely the whole political dossier of the relations between Iran and the United States over the last 25 years.

"With regard to the request for provisional measures, as formulated by the United States, it in fact implies that the Court should have passed judgment on the actual substance of the case submitted to it, which the Court cannot do without breach of the norms governing its jurisdiction. Furthermore, since provisional measures are by definition intended to protect the interest of the parties, they cannot be unilateral, as they are in the request submitted by the American Government." (*Translated from French*)

(2) *Facts and Jurisdiction* (*Paras. 11-44*)

The position taken up by the Iranian Government in regard to the present proceedings brings into operation Article 53 of the Statute, under which the Court is required *inter alia* to satisfy itself that the claims of the Applicant are well founded in fact. As to this article the Court pointed out in the *Corfu Channel Case* that this requirement is to be understood as applying within certain limits: "While Article 53 thus obliges the Court to consider the submissions of the Party which appears, it does not compel the Court to examine their accuracy in all their details; for this might in certain unopposed cases prove impossible in practice. It is sufficient for the Court to convince itself by such methods as it considers suitable that the submissions are well founded."

In the present case, the United States has explained that, owing to the events in Iran of which it complains, it has been unable since then to have access to its diplomatic and consular representatives, premises and archives in Iran. ···

The essential facts of the present case are, for the most part, matters of public knowledge which have received extensive coverage in the world press and in radio and television broadcasts from Iran and other countries. ···

Four instruments having Been cited by the United States as bases for the Court's jurisdiction to deal with its claims, the Court finds that three, namely the Optional Protocol to the two Vienna Conventions of 1961 and 1963 on, respectively, Diplomatic and Consular Relations, and the 1955 Treaty of Amity, Economic Relations, and Consular Rights between the United States and Iran, do in fact provide such foundations. The Court, however, does not find it necessary in the present Judgment to enter into the question whether Article 13 of the fourth instrument so cited, namely the 1973 Convention on the Prevention and Punishment of Crimes Against Internationally Protected Persons Including Diplomatic Agents, provides a basis for the exercise of its jurisdiction with respect to the United States' claims thereunder.

······

(3) *Violation by Iran of Certain Obligations* (Paras. 56-94)

The first phase of the events underlying the Applicant's claims covers the armed attack on the United States Embassy carried out on 4 November 1979 by Muslim Student Followers of the Imam's Policy (further referred to as "the militants" in the Judgment), the overrunning of its premises, the seizure of its inmates as hostages, the appropriation of its property and archives, and the conduct of the Iranian authorities in the face of these occurrences. ···

The Court points out that the conduct of the militants on that occasion could be directly attributed to the Iranian State only if it were established that they were in fact acting on its behalf. The information before the Court did not suffice to establish this with due certainty. However, the Iranian State—which, as the State to which the mission was accredited, was under obligation to take appropriate steps to protect the United States Embassy—did nothing to prevent the attack, stop it before it reached its completion or oblige the militants to withdraw from the premises anti release the hostages. This inaction was in contrast with the conduct of the Iranian authorities on several similar occasions at the same period, when they had taken appropriate steps. It constituted, the Court finds, a clear and serious violation of Iran's obligations to the United States under Articles 22 (2), 24,25,26, 27 amd 29 of the 1961 Vienna Convention on Diplomatic Relations, of Articles 5 and 36 of the 1963 Vienna Convention on Consular Relations, and of Article II (4) of the 1955 Treaty of Amity, Economic Relations, and Consular Rights. Further breaches of the 1963 Convention had been involved in failure to protect the Consulates at Tabriz and Shiraz. …

The second phase of the events underlying the United States' claims comprises the whole series; of facts which occurred following the occupation of the Embassy by the militants. Though it was the duty of the Iranian Government to take every appropriate step to end the infringement of the inviolability of the Embassy premises and staff, and to offer reparation for the damage, it did nothing of the kind. Instead, expressions of approval were immediately heard from numerous Iranian authorities. Above all, the Ayatollah Khomeini himself proclaimed the Iranian State's endorsement of both the seizure of the premises and the detention of the hostages. He described the Embassy as a "center of espionage", declared that the hostages would (with some exceptions) remain "under arrest" until the United States had returned the former Shah and his property to Iran, and forbade all negotiation with the United States on the subject. Once organs of the Iranian

State had thus given approval to the acts complained of and decided to perpetuate them as a means of pressure on the United States, those acts were transformed into acts of the Iranian State: the militants became agents of that State, which itself became internationally responsible for their acts. During the six months which ensued, the situation underwent no material change: the Court's Order of 19 December 1979 was publicly rejected by Iran, while the Ayatollah declared that the detention of the hostages would continue until the new Iranian parliament had taken a decision as to their fate. The Iranian authorities' decision to continue the subjection of the Embassy to occupation, and of its staff to detention as hostages, gave rise to repeated and multiple breaches of Iran's treaty obligations, additional to those already committed at the time of the seizure of the Embassy.

The Court considers that it should examine the question whether the conduct of the Iranian Government might be justified by the existence of special circumstances, for the Iranian Mister for Foreign Affairs had alleged in his two letters to the Court that the United States had carried out criminal activities in Iran. The Court considers that, even if these alleged activities could be considered as proven, they would not constitute a defense to the United States' claims, since diplomatic law provides the possibility of breaking off diplomatic relations, or of declaring *persona non grata* members of diplomatic or consular missions who may be carrying on illicit activities. The Court concludes that the Government of Iran had recourse to coercion against the United States Embassy and its staff instead of making use of the normal means at its disposal. ⋯

The Court :

By thirteen votes to two,

decides that the Islamic Republic of Iran, by the conduct which the Court has; set out in this Judgment, has violated in several respects, and is still violating, obligations owed by it to the United States of America under international conventions in force between the two countries, as well as under long-established rules of general international law;

......

4.2 Immunities and Criminal Proceedings Case[1]

(1) Proceedings

On 13 June 2016, the Government of the Republic of Equatorial Guinea (hereinafter "Equatorial Guinea") filed in the Registry of the Court an Application instituting proceedings against the French Republic (hereinafter "France") with regard to a dispute concerning "the immunity from criminal jurisdiction of the Second Vice-President of the Republic of Equatorial Guinea in charge of Defense and State Security (Mr. Teodoro Nguema Obiang Mangue), and the legal status of the building which houses the Embassy of Equatorial Guinea, both as premises of the diplomatic mission and as State property".

In the application, Equatorial Guinea requested the Court:

(a) With regard to the French Republic's failure to respect the sovereignty of the Republic of Equatorial Guinea: to adjudge and declare that the French Republic has breached its obligation to respect the principles of the sovereign equality of States and non interference in the internal affairs of another State, owed to the Republic of Equatorial Guinea in accordance with international law, by permitting its courts to initiate criminal legal proceedings against the Second Vice-President of Equatorial Guinea for alleged offences which, even if they were established, *quod non*, would fall solely within the jurisdiction of the courts of Equatorial Guinea, and by allowing its courts to order the attachment of a building belonging to the Republic of Equatorial Guinea and used for the purposes of that country's diplomatic mission in France;

---

[1] See *Immunities and Criminal Proceedings* (*Equatorial Guinea v. France*), Preliminary Objections, Judgment, ICJ Reports 2018, p. 292.

(b) With regard to the Second Vice-President of the Republic of Equatorial Guinea in charge of Defence and State Security,

i. to adjudge and declare that, by initiating criminal proceedings against the Second Vice-President of the Republic of Equatorial Guinea in charge of Defence and State Security, His Excellency Mr. Teodoro Nguema Obiang Mangue, the French Republic has acted and is continuing to act in violation of its obligations under international law, notably the United Nations Convention against Transnational Organized Crime and general international law;

ii. to order the French Republic to take all necessary measures to put an end to any ongoing proceedings against the Second Vice-President of the Republic of Equatorial Guinea in charge of Defence and State Security;

iii. to order the French Republic to take all necessary measures to prevent further violations of the immunity of the Second Vice-President of Equatorial Guinea in charge of Defence and State Security and to ensure, in particular, that its courts do not initiate any criminal proceedings against the Second Vice-President of the Republic of Equatorial Guinea in the future;

(c) With regard to the building located at 42 Avenue Foch in Paris,

i. to adjudge and declare that, by attaching the building located at 42 Avenue Foch in Paris, the property of the Republic of Equatorial Guinea and used for the purposes of that country's diplomatic mission in France, the French Republic is in breach of its obligations under international law, notably the Vienna Convention on Diplomatic Relations and the United Nations Convention, as well as general international law;

ii. to order the French Republic to recognize the status of the building located at 42 Avenue Foch in Paris as the property of the Republic of Equatorial Guinea, and as the premises of its diplomatic mission in Paris, and, accordingly, to ensure its protection as required by international law;

(d) In view of all the violations by the French Republic of international obligations owed to the Republic of Equatorial Guinea,

i. to adjudge and declare that the responsibility of the French Republic is engaged on account of the harm that the violations of its international obligations have caused and are continuing to cause to the Republic of Equatorial Guinea;

ii. to order the French Republic to make full reparation to the Republic of Equatorial Guinea for the harm suffered, the amount of which shall be determined at a later stage.

In its Application, Equatorial Guinea seeks to found the Court's jurisdiction, first, on Article 35 of the United Nations Convention against Transnational Organized Crime of 15 November 2000 (hereinafter "Palermo Convention"), and, second, on Article I of the Optional Protocol to the Vienna Convention on Diplomatic Relations concerning the Compulsory Settlement of Disputes of 18 April 1961 (hereinafter the "Optional Protocol to the Vienna Convention").

On 29 September 2016, Equatorial Guinea submitted a Request for the indication of provisional measures, asking the Court "pending its judgment on the merits, to indicate the following provisional measures:

(a) that France suspend all the criminal proceedings brought against the Vice-President of the Republic of Equatorial Guinea, and refrain from launching new proceedings against him, which might aggravate or extend the dispute submitted to the Court;

(b) that France ensure that the building located at 42 avenue Foch in Paris is treated as premises of Equatorial Guinea's diplomatic mission in France and, in particular, assure its inviolability, and that those premises, together with their furnishings and other property thereon, or previously thereon, are protected from any intrusion or damage, any search, requisition, attachment or any other measure of constraint;

(c) that France refrain from taking any other measure that might cause prejudice to the rights claimed by Equatorial Guinea and/or aggravate or extend the dispute submitted to the Court, or compromise the implementation of any decision which the Court might render".

On 31 March 2017, France raised preliminary objections to the jurisdiction of the Court, claimed that: (a) The Court's lack of jurisdiction on the basis of the United Nations Convention against Transnational Organized Crime; (b) The Court's lack of jurisdiction on the basis of the Vienna Convention on Diplomatic Relations.

(2) *Fact and Jurisdiction*

The Court explains that, beginning in 2007, a number of associations and private individuals lodged complaints with the Paris public prosecutor against certain African Heads of State and members of their families in respect of allegations of misappropriation of public funds in their country of origin, the proceeds of which had allegedly been invested in France.

One of these complaints, filed on 2 December 2008 by the association Transparency International France, was declared admissible by the French courts, and a judicial investigation was opened in respect of "handling misappropriated public funds", "complicity in handling misappropriated public funds, complicity in the misappropriation of public funds, money laundering, complicity in money laundering, misuse of corporate assets, complicity in misuse of corporate assets, breach of trust, complicity in breach of trust and concealment of each of these offences". …

The investigation focused, in particular, on the methods used to finance the acquisition of movable and immovable assets in France by several individuals, including Mr. Teodoro Nguema Obiang Mangue, the son of the President of Equatorial Guinea, who was at the time Ministre d'Etat for Agriculture and Forestry of Equatorial Guinea.

The investigation more specifically concerned the way in which Mr. Teodoro Nguema Obiang Mangue acquired various objects of considerable value and a building located at 42 Avenue Foch in Paris. In 2011 and 2012, that building was the subject of an attachment order (saisie pénale immobilière) and various objects found on the premises were seized, following a finding by the French courts that the building had been wholly or partly paid for out of the proceeds of the offences under investigation and that its real owner was Mr. Teodoro Nguema Obiang Mangue. Equatorial Guinea systematically objected to those actions, claiming that it had previously acquired the building in question and that it constituted part of the premises of its diplomatic mission in France.

The Court notes that Mr. Teodoro Nguema Obiang Mangue, who became Second Vice-President of Equatorial Guinea in charge of Defence and State Security on 21 May 2012, challenged the measures taken against him and on several occasions invoked the immunity from jurisdiction to which he believed he was entitled on account of his functions. Nevertheless, he was indicted by the French judiciary in March 2014. All the legal remedies taken by Mr. Teodoro Nguema Obiang Mangue against that indictment were rejected, as were Equatorial Guinea's diplomatic protests. At the end of the investigation, Mr. Teodoro Nguema Obiang Mangue—who had been appointed as the Vice-President of Equatorial Guinea in charge of National Defence and State Security on June 2016—was referred for trial before the *Tribunal correctionnel de Paris* for alleged money-laundering offences committed in France between 1997 and October 2011.

The hearings on the merits of the case before the *Tribunal correctionnel de Paris* were held from 19 June to 6 July 2017. The tribunal delivered its judgment on 27 October 2017, in which it found Mr. Teodoro Nguema Obiang Mangue guilty of the offences. He was sentenced to a three-year suspended prison term and a suspended fine of €30 million. The tribunal also ordered the confiscation of all the assets seized during the judicial investigation and of the attached building at 42 Avenue Foch in Paris. Regarding the confiscation of this building, the tribunal, referring to the Court's Order of 7 December 2016 indicating provisional measures, stated that "the... proceedings (pending before the International Court of Justice) make the execution of any measure of confiscation by the French State impossible, but not the imposition of that penalty".

Following delivery of the judgment, Mr. Teodoro Nguema Obiang Mangue lodged an appeal against his conviction with the *Cour d'appel de Paris*. This appeal having a suspensive effect, no steps have been taken to enforce the sentences handed down to Mr. Teodoro Nguema Obiang Mangue.

For Equatorial Guinea's claims based on the Palermo Convention:

After review France's First Objection, the Court noted that Article 4 (1) imposes an obligation on States parties and that it is not preambular in character and does not merely formulate a general aim. However, Article 4 is not independent of the other provisions of the Convention. Its purpose is to ensure that the States parties to the Convention perform their obligations in accordance with the principles of sovereign equality, territorial integrity and non-intervention in the domestic affairs of other States. The Court notes that Article 4 does not refer to the customary international rules, including State immunity, that derive from sovereign equality but to the principle of sovereign equality itself. Article 4 refers only to general principles of international law. The Court considers that, in its ordinary meaning, Article 4 (1) does not impose, through its reference to sovereign equality, an obligation on States parties to act in a manner consistent with the many rules of international law which protect sovereignty in general, as well as all the qualifications to those rules. With regard to context, it notes that none of the provisions of the Palermo Convention relates expressly to the immunities of States and State officials. The Court concludes that, in its ordinary meaning, Article 4, read in its context and in light of the object and purpose of the Convention, does not incorporate the customary international rules on immunities of States and State officials. …

For Equatorial Guinea's claims based on the Vienna Convention:

The Court further observes that the aspect of the dispute for which Equatorial Guinea invokes the Optional Protocol to the Vienna Convention as the title of jurisdiction involves two claims on which the Parties have expressed differing views. First, they disagree on whether the building at 42 Avenue Foch in Paris constitutes part of the premises of the mission of Equatorial Guinea in France and is thus entitled to the treatment afforded for such premises under Article 22 of the Vienna Convention. They also disagree on whether France, by the action of its authorities in relation to the building, is in breach of its obligations under Article 22. The Court States that it will ascertain whether this aspect of the dispute between the Parties is capable of falling within the Vienna Convention and, consequently, whether it is one which the Court has jurisdiction to entertain under the Optional Protocol to the Vienna Convention.

The Second Preliminary Objection

The Court observes that ··· In order to establish jurisdiction over this aspect of the dispute, it is required determine whether this aspect of the dispute is one that arises out of the interpretation or application of the Vienna Convention, as required by the provisions of Article I of the Optional Protocol to the Vienna Convention. Making that determination requires an analysis of the relevant terms of the Vienna Convention in accordance with the rules of customary international law on the interpretation of treaties.

The Court notes that Article 1 (i) of the Vienna Convention is prefaced by the following sentence: "For the purpose of the present Convention, the following expressions shall have the meanings hereunder assigned to them." Article 1 (i) of the Vienna Convention thus does no more than to define what constitutes "premises of the mission", a phrase used later in Article 22. For the purposes of the Vienna Convention, a building or part of a building "used for the purposes of (a diplomatic) mission", including the residence of the head of mission, is considered "premises of the mission", regardless of ownership.

The Court next notes that Article 22 of the Vienna Convention provides a régime of inviolability, protection and immunity for "premises of (a diplomatic) mission" by obligating the receiving State, *inter alia*, to refrain from entering such premises without the consent of the head of mission, and to protect those premises against intrusion, damage or disturbance of the peace of the mission by agents of the receiving State. The Article also guarantees immunity from search, requisition, attachment or execution for the premises of the mission, their furnishings and other property thereon, as well as means of transportation of the mission.

According to the Court, where, as in this case, there is a difference of opinion as to whether or not the building at 42 Avenue Foch in Paris, which Equatorial Guinea claims is "used for the purposes of its diplomatic mission", qualifies as "premises of the mission" and, consequently, whether it should be accorded or denied protection under Article 22, this aspect of the dispute can be said to "arise out of the interpretation or application of the Vienna Convention" within the meaning of Article I of the Optional Protocol to the said Convention. The Court therefore finds that this aspect of the dispute falls within the scope of the Vienna Convention and that it has jurisdiction under Article I of the Optional Protocol to the Vienna Convention to entertain it. It then remains for the Court to determine the extent of its jurisdiction.

It notes that, under Article 22 (3) of the Vienna Convention, it is not only the premises of the mission but also "their furnishings and other property thereon and the means of transport of the mission" that are immune from search, requisition, attachment or execution. The Court concludes that any claims relating to movable property present on the premises at 42 Avenue Foch in Paris and resulting from the alleged violation of the immunity to which the building is said to be entitled, fall within the subject-matter of the dispute and that, as such, the Court is competent to entertain them. The Court thus concludes that it has jurisdiction to entertain the aspect of the dispute relating to the status of the building, including any claims relating to the furnishings and other property present on the premises at 42 Avenue Foch in Paris. France's second preliminary objection is consequently dismissed.

(3) *Judgment of the Court made on December 2020*

As to the Vienna Convention's object and purpose, the preamble specifies the Convention's aim to "contribute to the development of friendly relations among nations". This is to be achieved by according sending States and their representatives' significant privileges and immunities. …

The Court considers that the Vienna Convention cannot be interpreted so as to allow a sending State unilaterally to impose its choice of mission premises upon the receiving State where the latter has objected to this choice. …

The Court considers that if the receiving State may object to the sending State's choice of premises, it follows that it may choose the modality of such objection. …

The Court emphasizes, however, that the receiving State's power to object to a sending State's designation of the premises of its diplomatic mission is not unlimited. … Further, in accordance with Article 47 of the Vienna Convention, this objection must not be discriminatory in character. In any event, the receiving State remains obliged under Article 21 of the Vienna Convention to facilitate the acquisition on its territory, in accordance with its laws, by the sending State of the premises necessary for its diplomatic mission, or otherwise assist the latter in obtaining accommodation in some other way.

Given the above considerations, the Court concludes that—where the receiving State objects to the designation by the sending State of certain property as forming part of the premises of its diplomatic mission, and this objection is communicated in a timely manner and is neither arbitrary nor discriminatory in character—that property does not acquire the status of "premises of the mission" within the meaning of Article 1 (i) of the Vienna Convention, and therefore does not benefit from protection under Article 22 of the Convention. Whether or not the aforementioned criteria have been met is a matter to be assessed in the circumstances of each case.

······

On the basis of all of the above considerations, the Court considers that France objected to Equatorial Guinea's designation of the building as premises of its diplomatic mission in a timely manner, and that this objection was neither arbitrary nor discriminatory in character.

For all these reasons, the Court concludes that the building at 42 avenue Foch in Paris has never acquired the status of "premises of the mission" within the meaning of Article 1 (i) of the Convention.

As the Court concluded that the building at 42 avenue Foch in Paris has never acquired the status of "premises of the mission" under the Vienna Convention, the acts complained of by Equatorial Guinea cannot constitute a breach by France of its obligations under that Convention. Consequently, the Court cannot uphold Equatorial Guinea's submission that the Court declare that France has an obligation to make reparation for the harm suffered by Equatorial Guinea.

The Court recalls that an objection by a receiving State to the designation of property as forming part of the premises of a foreign diplomatic mission prevents that property from acquiring the status of the "premises of the mission", within the meaning of Article 1 (i) of the Vienna Convention, provided that this objection is communicated in a timely manner and is neither arbitrary nor discriminatory in character. The Court has found that the objection by France in the present case meets these conditions. In the light of the above conclusions, the Court cannot uphold the submission of Equatorial Guinea that it declare that France must recognize the status of the said building as premises of the diplomatic mission of Equatorial Guinea.

······

5. References and Recommended Reading Materials

(1) Eileen Denza, *Diplomatic Law*, 4th Ed., Oxford University Press, 2016.

(2) Luke T. Lee and John Quigley, *Consular Law and Practice*, 3rd Ed. Oxford University Press, 2008.

(3) Sir Ivor Roberts (ed.), *Satow's Diplomatic Practice*, 7th Ed. Oxford University Press, 2017.

Chapter XIII The Law of Responsibility

1. Introduction

　　As James Crawford pointed out, responsibility was ignored or touched on only incidentally in international law doctrine for a long time. ① After the late 19th century, the codification work on responsibility has become an important project in dynamic international law. The codification work has lasted nearly half a century before the publishing of Draft Articles on Responsibility of State for Internationally Wrongful Acts (2001) ("ARSIWA"). After the ARSIWA, ILC continued to make contributions to the law of responsibility. It codified the ILC Articles on Diplomatic Protection of 2006 and Draft Articles on the Responsibility of International Organizations 2011.

　　This chapter is mainly on State responsibility. Note that other international law subjects also take responsibility if they are in breach of international law. As to the responsibility of individuals under international law, it is mainly about rules on individuals' criminal liability resulting from committing international crimes, such as aggression, genocide, or crimes against humanity. After enacting the *Rome Statute*, these rules have developed into the well-established rules and principles of international criminal law. Most textbooks compile a single chapter on this issue. To make readers notice that the responsibility under international law shall include the

---

　　① See James Crawford, *State Responsibility: The General Part*, Cambridge Uiniversity Press, 2013, p. 3.

criminal liability of individuals, we put the rules on State responsibility and international criminal justice together and name this chapter as "the law of responsibility".

2. Preliminary Reading and Assignment

2.1 ARSIWA (2001)

Article 1   Responsibility of a State for its internationally wrongful acts

Every internationally wrongful act of a State entails the international responsibility of that State.

Article 2   Elements of an internationally wrongful act of a State

There is an internationally wrongful act of a State when conduct consisting of an action or omission: (a) is attributable to the State under international law; and (b) constitutes a breach of an obligation of the State.

Article 3   Characterization of an act of a State as internationally wrongful

The characterization of an act of a State as internationally wrongful is governed by international law. Such characterization is not affected by the characterization of the same act as lawful by internal law.

Article 12   Existence of a breach of an international obligation

There is a breach of an international obligation by a State when an act of that State is not in conformity with what is required of it by that obligation, regardless of its origin or character.

Article 14   Extension in time of the breach of an international obligation

1. The breach of an international obligation by an act of a State not having a continuing character occurs at the moment when the act is performed, even if its effects continue.

2. The breach of an international obligation by an act of a State having a continuing character extends over the entire period during which the act continues and remains not in conformity with the international obligation.

3. The breach of an international obligation requiring a State to prevent a given event occurs when the event occurs and extends over the entire period during which the event continues and remains not in conformity with that obligation.

Article 20   Consent

Valid consent by a State to the commission of a given act by another State precludes the wrongfulness of that act in relation to the former State to the extent that the act remains within the limits of that consent.

Article 21   Self-defence

The wrongfulness of an act of a State is precluded if the act constitutes a lawful measure of self-defence taken in conformity with the Charter of the United Nations.

Article 22   Countermeasures in respect of an internationally wrongful act

The wrongfulness of an act of a State not in conformity with an international obligation towards another State is precluded if and to the extent that the act constitutes a countermeasure taken against the latter State in accordance with chapter Ⅱ of Part three.

Article 23   Force majeure

1. The wrongfulness of an act of a State not in conformity with an international obligation of that State is precluded if the act is due to *force majeure*, that is the occurrence of an irresistible force or of an unforeseen event, beyond the control of the State, making it materially impossible in the circumstances to perform the obligation.

2. Paragraph 1 does not apply if: (a) the situation of force majeure is due, either alone or in combination with other factors, to the conduct of the State invoking it; or (b) the State has assumed the risk of that situation occurring.

Article 24   Distress

1. The wrongfulness of an act of a State not in conformity with an international obligation of that State is precluded if the author of the act in question has no other reasonable way, in a situation of distress, of saving the author's life or the lives of other persons entrusted to the author's care.

2. Paragraph 1 does not apply if: (a) the situation of distress is due, either alone or in combination with other factors, to the conduct of the State invoking it; or (b) the act in question is likely to create a comparable or greater peril.

Article 25　Necessity

1. Necessity may not be invoked by a State as a ground for precluding the wrongfulness of an act not in conformity with an international obligation of that State unless the act: (a) is the only way for the State to safeguard an essential interest against a grave and imminent peril; and (b) does not seriously impair an essential interest of the State or States towards which the obligation exists, or of the international community as a whole.

2. In any case, necessity may not be invoked by a State as a ground for precluding wrongfulness if: (a) the international obligation in question excludes the possibility of invoking necessity; or (b) the State has contributed to the situation of necessity.

Article 27　Consequences of invoking a circumstance precluding wrongfulness

The invocation of a circumstance precluding wrongfulness in accordance with this chapter is without prejudice to: (a) compliance with the obligation in question, if and to the extent that the circumstance precluding wrongfulness no longer exists; (b) the question of compensation for any material loss caused by the act in question.

Article 32　Irrelevance of internal law

The responsible State may not rely on the provisions of its internal law as justification for failure to comply with its obligations under this part.

Article 42　Invocation of responsibility by an injured State

A State is entitled as an injured State to invoke the responsibility of another State if the obligation breached is owed to: (a) that State individually; or (b) a group of States including that State, or the international community as a whole, and the breach of the obligation: (i) specially affects that State; or (ii) is of such a character as radically to change the position of all the other States to which the obligation is owed with respect to the further performance of the obligation.

Article 44 Admissibility of claims

The responsibility of a State may not be invoked if: (a) the claim is not brought in accordance with any applicable rule relating to the nationality of claims; (b) the claim is one to which the rule of exhaustion of local remedies applies and any available and effective local remedy has not been exhausted.

Article 48 Invocation of responsibility by a State other than an injured State

1. Any State other than an injured State is entitled to invoke the responsibility of another State in accordance with paragraph 2 if: (a) the obligation breached is owed to a group of States including that State, and is established for the protection of a collective interest of the group; or (b) the obligation breached is owed to the international community as a whole.

2. Any State entitled to invoke responsibility under paragraph 1 may claim from the responsible State: (a) cessation of the internationally wrongful act, and assurances and guarantees of non-repetition in accordance with article 30; and (b) performance of the obligation of reparation in accordance with the preceding articles, in the interest of the injured State or of the beneficiaries of the obligation breached.

3. The requirements for the invocation of responsibility by an injured State under articles 43, 44 and 45 apply to an invocation of responsibility by a State entitled to do so under paragraph 1.

......

2.2 Draft Articles on the Responsibility of International Organizations (2011)[①]

Article 1 Scope of the present draft articles

1. The present draft articles apply to the international responsibility of

---

① Adopted by the International Law Commission at its sixty-third session, in 2011, and submitted to the General Assembly as a part of the Commission's report covering the work of that session (A/66/10, para. 87), Yearbook of the International Law Commission, 2011, vol. Ⅱ, Part Two.

an international organization for an internationally wrongful act.

2. The present draft articles also apply to the international responsibility of a State for an internationally wrongful act in connection with the conduct of an international organization.

Article 4　Elements of an internationally wrongful act of an international organization

There is an internationally wrongful act of an international organization when conduct consisting of an action or omission: (a) is attributable to that organization under international law; and (b) constitutes a breach of an international obligation of that organization.

Article 6　Conduct of organs or agents of an international organization

1. The conduct of an organ or agent of an international organization in the performance of functions of that organ or agent shall be considered an act of that organization under international law, whatever position the organ or agent holds in respect of the organization.

2. The rules of the organization apply in the determination of the functions of its organs and agents.

Article 8　Excess of authority or contravention of instructions

The conduct of an organ or agent of an international organization shall be considered an act of that organization under international law if the organ or agent acts in an official capacity and within the overall functions of that organization, even if the conduct exceeds the authority of that organ or agent or contravenes instructions.

Article 10　Existence of a breach of an international obligation

1. There is a breach of an international obligation by an international organization when an act of that international organization is not in conformity with what is required of it by that obligation, regardless of the origin or character of the obligation concerned.

2. Paragraph 1 includes the breach of any international obligation that may arise for an international organization towards its members under the

rules of the organization.

Article 43　Invocation of responsibility by an injured State or international organization

A State or an international organization is entitled as an injured State or an injured international organization to invoke the responsibility of another international organization if the obligation breached is owed to: (a) that State or the former international organization individually; (b) a group of States or international organizations including that State or the former international organization, or the international community as a whole, and the breach of the obligation: (i) specially affects that State or that international organization; or (ii) is of such a character as radically to change the position of all the other States and international organizations to which the obligation is owed with respect to the further performance of the obligation.

2.3　Rome Statute

Article 1　The Court

An International Criminal Court ("the Court") is hereby established. It shall be a permanent institution and shall have the power to exercise its jurisdiction over persons for the most serious crimes of international concern, as referred to in this Statute, and shall be complementary to national criminal jurisdictions. The jurisdiction and functioning of the Court shall be governed by the provisions of this Statute.

Article 2　Relationship of the Court with the United Nations

The Court shall be brought into relationship with the United Nations through an agreement to be approved by the Assembly of States Parties to this Statute and thereafter concluded by the President of the Court on its behalf.

Article 4　Legal status and powers of the Court

1. The Court shall have international legal personality. It shall also have such legal capacity as may be necessary for the exercise of its functions and

the fulfilment of its purposes.

2. The Court may exercise its functions and powers, as provided in this Statute, on the territory of any State Party and, by special agreement, on the territory of any other State.

Article 5　Crimes within the jurisdiction of the Court

The jurisdiction of the Court shall be limited to the most serious crimes of concern to the international community as a whole. The Court has jurisdiction in accordance with this Statute with respect to the following crimes: (a) The crime of genocide; (b) Crimes against humanity; (c) War crimes; (d) The crime of aggression.

Article 6　Genocide

For the purpose of this Statute, "genocide" means any of the following acts committed with intent to destroy, in whole or in part, a national, ethnical, racial or religious group, as such: (a) Killing members of the group; (b) Causing serious bodily or mental harm to members of the group; (c) Deliberately inflicting on the group conditions of life calculated to bring about its physical destruction in whole or in part; (d) Imposing measures intended to prevent births within the group; (e) Forcibly transferring children of the group to another group.

Article 7　Crimes against humanity

1. For the purpose of this Statute, "crime against humanity" means any of the following acts when committed as part of a widespread or systematic attack directed against any civilian population, with knowledge of the attack: (a) Murder; (b) Extermination; (c) Enslavement; (d) Deportation or forcible transfer of population; (e) Imprisonment or other severe deprivation of physical liberty in violation of fundamental rules of international law; (f) Torture; (g) Rape, sexual slavery, enforced prostitution, forced pregnancy, enforced sterilization, or any other form of sexual violence of comparable gravity; (h) Persecution against any identifiable group or collectivity on political, racial, national, ethnic, cultural, religious, gender

as defined in paragraph 3, or other grounds that are universally recognized as impermissible under international law, in connection with any act referred to in this paragraph or any crime within the jurisdiction of the Court; (i) Enforced disappearance of persons; (j) The crime of apartheid; (k) Other inhumane acts of a similar character intentionally causing great suffering, or serious injury to body or to mental or physical health.

2. For the purpose of paragraph 1:

(a) "Attack directed against any civilian population" means a course of conduct involving the multiple commission of acts referred to in paragraph 1 against any civilian population, pursuant to or in furtherance of a State or organizational policy to commit such attack;

(b) "Extermination" includes the intentional infliction of conditions of life, *inter alia* the deprivation of access to food and medicine, calculated to bring about the destruction of part of a population;

(c) "Enslavement" means the exercise of any or all of the powers attaching to the right of ownership over a person and includes the exercise of such power in the course of trafficking in persons, in particular women and children;

(d) "Deportation or forcible transfer of population" means forced displacement of the persons concerned by expulsion or other coercive acts from the area in which they are lawfully present, without grounds permitted under international law;

(e) "Torture" means the intentional infliction of severe pain or suffering, whether physical or mental, upon a person in the custody or under the control of the accused; except that torture shall not include pain or suffering arising only from, inherent in or incidental to, lawful sanctions;

(f) "Forced pregnancy" means the unlawful confinement of a woman forcibly made pregnant, with the intent of affecting the ethnic composition of any population or carrying out other grave violations of international law. This definition shall not in any way be interpreted as affecting national laws relating to pregnancy;

(g) "Persecution" means the intentional and severe deprivation of fundamental rights contrary to international law by reason of the identity of the group or collectivity;

(h) "The crime of apartheid" means inhumane acts of a character similar to those referred to in paragraph 1, committed in the context of an institutionalized regime of systematic oppression and domination by one racial group over any other racial group or groups and committed with the intention of maintaining that regime;

(i) "Enforced disappearance of persons" means the arrest, detention or abduction of persons by, or with the authorization, support or acquiescence of, a State or a political organization, followed by a refusal to acknowledge that deprivation of freedom or to give information on the fate or whereabouts of those persons, with the intention of removing them from the protection of the law for a prolonged period of time.

Article 8　War crimes

1. The Court shall have jurisdiction in respect of war crimes in particular when committed as part of a plan or policy or as part of a large-scale commission of such crimes.

2. For the purpose of this Statute, "war crimes" means:

(a) Grave breaches of the Geneva Conventions of 12 August 1949, namely, any of acts against persons or property protected under the provisions of the relevant Geneva Convention:…

(b) Other serious violations of the laws and customs applicable in international armed conflict, within the established framework of international law, namely, any of the following acts:…

(c) In the case of an armed conflict not of an international character, serious violations of article 3 common to the four Geneva Conventions of 12 August 1949, namely, any of the following acts committed against persons taking no active part in the hostilities, including members of armed forces who have laid down their arms and those placed hors de combat by sickness, wounds, detention or any other cause;…

Article 8 bis Crime of aggression

1. For the purpose of this Statute, "crime of aggression" means the planning, preparation, initiation or execution, by a person in a position effectively to exercise control over or to direct the political or military action of a State, of an act of aggression which, by its character, gravity and scale, constitutes a manifest violation of the Charter of the United Nations.

2. For the purpose of paragraph 1, "act of aggression" means the use of armed force by a State against the sovereignty, territorial integrity or political independence of another State, or in any other manner inconsistent with the Charter of the United Nations. Any of the following acts, regardless of a declaration of war, shall, in accordance with United Nations General Assembly resolution 3314 (XXIX) of 14 December 1974, qualify as an act of aggression: (a) The invasion or attack by the armed forces of a State of the territory of another State, or any military occupation, however temporary, resulting from such invasion or attack, or any annexation by the use of force of the territory of another State or part thereof; (b) Bombardment by the armed forces of a State against the territory of another State or the use of any weapons by a State against the territory of another State; (c) The blockade of the ports or coasts of a State by the armed forces of another State; (d) An attack by the armed forces of a State on the land, sea or air forces, or marine and air fleets of another State; (e) The use of armed forces of one State which are within the territory of another State with the agreement of the receiving State, in contravention of the conditions provided for in the agreement or any extension of their presence in such territory beyond the termination of the agreement; (f) The action of a State in allowing its territory, which it has placed at the disposal of another State, to be used by that other State for perpetrating an act of aggression against a third State; (g) The sending by or on behalf of a State of armed bands, groups, irregulars or mercenaries, which carry out acts of armed force against another State of such gravity as to

amount to the acts listed above, or its substantial involvement therein.

......

2.4 Discussion and Assignment

(1) Retrieving the full text of the ARSIWA and Draft Articles on The Responsibility of International Organizations 2011, including the commentary made by the ILC, and finding out the difference between the rules concerning State responsibility and international organization responsibility under international law.

(2) The Jessup Moot Court Competition proposed an interesting legal issue in 2021 that a State R may be responsible for another State A's economic losses resulting from R's entry restriction to preventing spreading of a virus causing a pandemic, for the entry regulation chilled the tourist from R's territory to A's famous scenic spots. Would you please make a 5-10 minutes speech on why R is not responsible for A's loss grounded on the provisions of ARSIWA and the *International Health Regulation 2005*?

(3) The ICC Moot Court in 2019 is about the aggression. State Astipur launched airstrikes against three targets after the Bravos government fired bombs to rioters and the Security Council made no effective decision about this humanitarian crisis. Before this airstrike, the President of Astipur consulted a legal professor majoring in international law, who explained that no applied laws prohibiting the airstrike based on human intervention. So the questions are: whether the airstrike constitutes a crime of aggression and whether the ICC could interrogate the professor since this State is a member State?

3. Terminologies and Explanations

3.1 State Responsibility: Wrongful Act and Elements of Responsibility

State responsibility is a fundamental principle of international law. It provides that international responsibility is established whenever one State commits an internationally unlawful act against another State. According to ARSIWA, every internationally wrongful act of a State entails the international responsibility of that State.

According to the ARSIWA, fault or delict is not needed to constitute wrongfulness. Generally, there are two circumstances that a State could breach its obligation under international law. The first is that the State is in breach of an obligation provided by a treaty. ICJ emphasizes that in a famous case, *Factory at Chorzów*: "it is a principle of international law, and even a general conception of law, that any breach of an engagement involves an obligation to make reparation." The Court has already said that reparation is the indispensable complement of a failure to apply a convention, and there is no necessity for this to be stated in the convention itself. [1]

The second circumstance is about the obligation established by customary international law or general principles. One example is the *Corfu Channel Case* (in Part 4. 1). In that case, the Albanian Government deployed mines into a passage within its territorial sea. They caused the death of the crew to a UK warship. The Court judged that, since the Albanian Government had a duty to notify the risk under customary law for those who are predictable to be the victims. The rationale underlined this judgment is that people who conduct dangerous behavior shall have a duty of care to warn of the danger. Since the incident happened in the territory of Albanian, the government was liable for the consequences of mine-laying, based on knowledge possessed by that State as to the presence of such mines, even though it had not laid the mines.

It is necessary to prove that the wrongful act shall attribute to the State if it is to make a State responsible for a wrongful act. Every breach of duty on the part of States must arise by reason of the act or omission of one or more

---

[1] See *Factory at Chorzów* (*Germ. v. Pol.*), PCIJ, Ser. A, No. 9 (1927), p. 21.

organs or agents. According to the ARSIWA, the following acts could attribute to the State:

(i) **Wrongful act of a State organ.** Article 4 provides that "the conduct of any State organ shall be considered an act of that State under international law", regardless of the character of that organ and whatever functions it exercises. These conducts may be done by executive and administration officials, armed force, federal units, provinces and other internal divisions or an act of "denial of justice" by judicial organs.

(ii) *Ultra vires* **or unauthorized acts.** In international law, there is an apparent reason for disregarding a plea of unlawfulness under domestic law: the lack of express authority cannot be decisive as to the State's responsibility. It is well established that States may be responsible for *ultra vires* acts of their officials committed within their apparent authority or general scope of authority. The State also bears international responsibility for all acts committed by its officials or its organs which are delictual according to international law, regardless of whether the official or organ has acted within the limits of his competency or has exceeded those limits. It is not difficult to find cases in which the acts of State agents were clearly *ultra vires* and yet responsibility has been affirmed. The principle that the State shall be responsible for unauthorized acts of its organs is of particular importance in relation to administrative practices involving violations of human rights, as well as for the conduct of armed forces during the conflict.

(iii) **Mob violence, insurrection, revolution, and civil war.** A principle that applies to these situations is that a State on whose territory an insurrection occurs is not responsible for loss or damage sustained by a foreigner unless it can be shown that the government of that State was negligent in the use of, or in the failure to use, the forces at its disposal for the prevention or suppression of the insurrection. There is no modern example of a State being held responsible for negligent failure to suppress insurgents. The ILC made the point that "the general principle that the conduct of an insurrectional or other movement is not attributable to the State... on the assumption that the structures and organization of the movement are and remain independent of those of the State. Exceptional cases may occur where the State was in a position to adopt measures of vigilance, prevention or punishment in respect of the movement's conduct but improperly failed to do so"[1].

(iv) **Approval or adoption by a State of wrongful acts.** A wrongful act conducted by a private person or entity may invoke the responsibility of a State if a State accepts or otherwise adopts it. The International Court applied this principle to the actions of the militants in *Tehran Hostages Case*. Article 11 of the Draft specifies that the State only becomes responsible "if and to the extent that the State acknowledges and adopts the conduct in question as its own".

There are some circumstances precluding wrongfulness under international law. They are "excuses" "defenses" and "exceptions". That is, justifications available to States which exclude responsibility. The ILC included five types of circumstances. They are consent, self-defense, countermeasures, force majeure, distress, and necessity. Note that the proponents of defenses shall bear the burden of proof. E. g., in a case adjudicated by WTO Appellate Body, "the complaining party bears the burden of establishing that a challenged measure is inconsistent with the provision permitting particular behavior only where one of the provisions suggests that the obligation does not apply to the said measure. Otherwise, the permissive provision has been characterized as an exception or defense, and the onus of invoking it and proving the consistency of the measure with its requirements has been placed on the responding party."[2]

---

[1] ARSIWA, Art. 10 & commentary, § § 4, 15.
[2] *European Communities-Conditions for the Granting of Tariff Preferences to Developing Countries (EC-Tariff Preferences)*, WT/DS246/AB/R, para. 88.

3.2 Consequences: Cessation, Reparation, and Invocation

The responsibility of a State will cause consequences. These consequences may be done by invoking the responsibilities of the wrongdoer in the forms of cessation, reparation or countermeasures. ARSIWA deals with these issues in Part 2 and Part 3. Cessation and reparation are obligations that arose by the operation of law. The countermeasures are different. They are ultimate remedies that an injured State may take after efforts to obtain cessation and reparation have failed.

"Cessation" refers to the basic obligation of compliance with international law, which in principle remains due in spite of any breaches. Cessation is required, not as a means of reparation but as an independent obligation, whenever the obligation in question continues to exist. Since wrongful acts of a continuing character are quite common, cessation is often the main demand by the injured State, reparation being a secondary consideration. In some cases, cessation may shade into restitution, such as the return of stolen objects. An assurance or guarantee of non-repetition, with perhaps a promise to repeal objectionable legislation, may overlap with satisfaction.

About the basic principle applied to the reparation, we shall refer to *the Factory at Chorzów Case*. The ICJ stated that "the essential principle contained in the actual notion of an illegal act-a principle which seems to be established by international practice and in particular by the decisions of arbitral tribunals-is that reparation must, as far as possible, wipe out all the consequences of the illegal act and re-establish the situation which would, in all probability, have existed if that act had not been committed."[①] ARSIWA restates this principle in Article 31 of its draft, providing that the responsible State is obligated to make full reparation for the injury caused by the internationally wrongful act and that injury includes any damage, whether

---

① *Factory at Chorzów* (*Germ. v. Pol.*), Merits, PCIJ, Ser. A, No. 17 (1928), p. 48.

material or moral caused by the internationally wrongful act of a State. Furthermore, Article 34 provides that full reparation for the injury caused by the internationally wrongful act shall take the form of restitution, compensation and satisfaction, either singly or in combination. Therefore, the term "reparation" is used in international law to refer to all measures which may be expected from the responsible State, over and above cessation, it includes restitution, compensation, and satisfaction.

"Restitution" refers to restitution in kind, a withdrawal of the wrongful measure or the return of persons or assets seized illegally. Restitution and cessation may sometimes overlap. "Compensation" will be used to describe reparation in the narrow sense of the payment of money in the measure of the wrong done. The award of compensation, sometimes described as "moral" or "political" reparation, terms connected with concepts of "moral" and "political" injury, creates confusion. Satisfaction refers to means of redressing a wrong other than by restitution or compensation. It may take a variety of forms, including an apology, trial and punishment of the individuals responsible, taking steps to prevent a recurrence of the breach, and so on. The aim of restitution is to re-establish the situation which existed before the wrongful act was committed. Like the specific performance in the contract, the restitution is rarer to be applied today. A large number of cases now involve expropriation disputes, where it is politically difficult for the State concerned to return the expropriated property to multinational companies. Recognizing some of these problems, Article 35 provides for restitution as long as and to the extent that: "it is not materially impossible; does not involve a burden out of all proportion to the benefit deriving from restitution instead of compensation."

The compensation has been more and more usually used to make complementary for the restitution. As ICJ held that it was a "well-established rule of international law that an injured State is entitled to obtain compensation from the State which has committed an internationally wrongful act for the damage caused by it"①. Article 36(1) provides that in so far as damage caused by an internationally wrongful act is not made good by restitution, the State responsible is under an obligation to give compensation. Article 36(2) states that the compensation to be provided shall cover any financially assessable damage, including loss of profits in so far as this is established. The aim is to deal with the economic losses actually caused. Compensation is usually assessed on the basis of the fair market value of the property lost, although the method used to calculate this may depend upon the type of property involved. Loss of profits may also be claimed where, for example, there has been an interference with use and enjoyment or unlawful taking of income-producing property or in some cases with regard to loss of future income. Damage includes both material and non-material (or moral) damage. Monetary compensation may thus be paid for individual pain and suffering and insults.

As to satisfaction, another form of reparation, it is a remedy long-established as a practice done by States and international courts in a situation that moral or legal damage had been done directly to the State. In the *Rainbow Warrior* arbitration, it concluded that the public condemnation of France for its breaches of treaty obligations to New Zealand made by the Tribunal constituted "appropriate satisfaction". The Tribunal also made an interesting "Recommendation" that the two States concerned to establish a fund to promote close relations between their respective citizens and additionally recommended that the French government "make an initial contribution equivalent to US dollars 2 million to that fund"②. In some cases, a party to a dispute will simply seek a declaration that the activity complained

---

① *Gabčikovo-Nagymaros Project (Hungary/Slovakia)*, Judgment, ICJ Reports 1997, p. 81.

② Reports of International Arbitral Awards, Case concerning the difference between New Zealand and France concerning the interpretation or application of two agreements, concluded on 9 July 1986 between the two States and which related to the problems arising from the Rainbow Warrior Affair, Volume XX, 1990, pp. 274.

of is illegal. In territorial disputes, for example, such declarations may be of particular significance. Article 37 of ARSIWA provides that a State responsible for a wrongful act is obliged to give satisfaction for the injury thereby caused in so far as it cannot be made good by restitution or compensation.

The general principle about who can invoke the responsibility of a State is provided in Articles 42 and 48 of the ARSIWA. Article 42 stipulates that an injured State is entitled to invoke the responsibility of another State if the obligation breached is owed to that State individually or a group of States, including that State or the international community as a whole, and the breach of the obligation ⋯ Article 48 provides rules for those uninjured States. It envisages a much more limited scope of action. Responsibility may only be invoked in the circumstances that the beached obligation is owned to a group of States, to protect a collective interest of the group, or because it is an *erga omnes* obligation. This terminology is used to refer to the obligations of a State towards the international community as a whole as distinct from those owed to another State.

3.3 International Criminal Justice: General Introduction and Jurisdiction

Nuremberg and Tokyo Trial opened the era to impose responsibility directly on individuals and punish violations through international mechanisms. This body of international criminal law is still evolving and is not yet uniform. The rapid development of the international criminal law field has not been without pitfalls. The operation of the international criminal tribunals has been far more expensive and time-consuming than anticipated, and the conduct of proceedings has generated controversy, particularly in cases involving high-profile figures. Most importantly, questions remain about the broad goals of this field. Although the prosecution of individuals responsible for the commission of international crimes may be justified on the basis of retribution and deterrence, a balance between national and international processes and between peacemaking or post-conflict reconciliation and the reduction of impunity has proved elusive. Before establishing the International Criminal Court ("ICC") by the Rome Statute, there were some codification works and foundations of *ad hoc* Tribunals to formulate the general conception about international crime and law.

The codification was within the function of the United Nations. After the Nuremberg judgment, The General Assembly unanimously affirmed "the principles of international law recognized by the Charter of the Nuremberg Tribunal and the Judgment of the Tribunal". The ILC was directed to formulate the principles of international law recognized in the Tribunal's judgment and prepare a draft code of offenses against the peace and security of humankind. It listed some "crimes under international law", such as crimes against peace, war crimes, and crimes against humanity. After two separate phases of drafting between 1947-1954 and 1982-1996, the ILC in 1996 adopted 20 draft articles constituting "a Code of Crimes against the Peace and Security of Mankind". The Code was never implemented, being superseded by the Rome Statute. Besides, ILC also concluded the Genocide Convention in 1948 and the "grave breaches" provisions of the 1949 Geneva Convention.

After the end of the Cold War, the Security Council acted under Chapter VII of the UN Charter to establish an international tribunal in Hague for the "purpose of prosecuting persons responsible for serious violations of international humanitarian law" committed in the former Yugoslavia after January 1, 1991. There was controversy about whether the Security Council could create a criminal tribunal, but the International Criminal Tribunal for the former Yugoslavia (ICTY) upheld its own constitutionality, relying in part on the parallel support of the General Assembly. The Statue as annexation to SC Resolution 827 grants the ICTY the power to prosecute persons for violations of the laws or customs of war, genocide, and crimes against humanity. There are three main organs of the ICTY, the Registry, the Office of the Prosecutor and the Chambers. Although the ICTY and national courts have concurrent jurisdiction, the ICTY has primacy, and in its early years, the tribunal requested that national courts defer to its competence in situations where both were seeking to exercise jurisdiction.

The Rwanda Tribunal was established in the background of the assassination of Rwandan President Habyarimana, which ignited the slaughter of Tutsi and moderate Hutus, resulting in the deaths of approximately 800,000 persons over the course of several months. In November 1994, after an ineffectual response to the genocide itself, the Security Council created the International Criminal Tribunal for Rwanda (ICTR), located in Arusha, Tanzania. It shares Appeals Chamber with the ICTY. The ICTY Statute provided a model for the Statute of the ICTR, which similarly endows the ICTR with "the power to prosecute persons responsible for serious violations of international humanitarian law". There are differences between the Statutes, such as the omission of an article in the ICTR Statute for prosecution for grave breaches of the 1949 Geneva Convention. It is because of the non-international character of the armed conflict in Rwanda. Instead, the ICTR Statute provides for jurisdiction over violations of Article 3 common to the 1949 Geneva Convention and of Additional Protocol II, which apply in non-international armed conflicts. In addition, the ICTR Statute requires a discriminatory motive as an element of crimes against humanity, although it has been held that this is not a requirement under customary international law. The ICTR also began operations quite slowly, but it initially gained custody of indictees more successfully than did the ICTY. The *Akayesu Case* was the first to go to trial at the ICTR and has been seminal, representing the first conviction by an international tribunal for genocide, as well as the first time that rape in the war was held to constitute genocide.

Emerging from the way paved by the failures of ILC, the ICC's Stature was finalized at a five-week conference in 1998. The ICC, located in the Hague, began its work in 2003. Its jurisdiction is limited to "the most serious crimes of concern to the international community as a whole". They are genocide, crimes against humanity, war crimes, and the crime of aggression. The Assembly of States Parties also adopted *the Elements of Crimes*, intended to assist the Court in the interpretation and application of these crimes.

The ICC's temporal jurisdiction does not extend to offenses committed prior to the entry into force of the Statute. Its territorial jurisdiction extends to the territory of States parties. Its personal jurisdiction covers nationals of those States. The ICC may also exercise its jurisdiction with respect to the territory and nationals of a State not party to the Rome Statute if that State has accepted the ICC's jurisdiction under Article 12(3). This article provides that a State not a party to the Statute may accept the ICC's jurisdiction by a declaration lodged with the Registrar. It is also possible for the ICC to exercise jurisdiction over nationals of third States if the conduct in question occurred on the territory of a State party, a possibility that has given rise to significant objections on the part of the US.

The ICC's exercise of jurisdiction may be triggered in three different ways. First, a State party may refer to the ICC as a situation where one or more crimes within the Court's jurisdiction appear to have been committed. Uganda, the Democratic Republic of Congo, and the Central African Republic have referred such situations to the ICC. The prosecutor initiated investigations in all of them. Second, the Security Council may refer a situation to the prosecutor. The Security Council did so in 2005 concerning the situation in Darfur, Sudan, and in 2011 concerning the situation in Libya. Third, the prosecutor may initiate an investigation independently. In March 2010, Pre-Trial Chamber II granted the prosecution's request to open an investigation into the post-election violence in Kenya in late 2007 and early 2008. Recently, the ICC authorized an investigation into possible war crimes in Afghanistan, including those that may have been committed by the US military, which could lead to the indictment of US military and intelligence personnel. Unlike the ICTY and ICTR which had primacy of jurisdiction, the ICC's jurisdiction is "complementary". It means that if there are, or have been, genuine domestic proceedings in a specific case, the case is inadmissible before the ICC, it should be stressed that it is cases that are inadmissible, not situations. It is one of the weaknesses of the complementarity regime: in situations of mass crime, the prosecutor will almost always be able to find a case that has not been prosecuted domestically.

The ICC has to rely entirely on the international community to arrest suspects for trial and imprison them on conviction for the enforcement issue. Therefore, Part 9 of the Rome Statute requires States Parties to cooperate with the Court in providing various forms of assistance such as the taking of evidence and the tracing of assets. Article 89(1) imposes the all-important obligation to surrender any person found within a State's territory when the Court so requests. Article 98 provides limitations on the Court in making such requests where the person concerned enjoys immunity or a relevant international agreement. International organizations may also be requested to provide information or any other form of assistance to the ICC. Regarding sentences of imprisonment imposed by the ICC, there is no obligation on States to provide prison facilities, and sentences will be served in a State selected by the ICC from a list of those that have declared their willingness to accept sentenced persons. If a State party fails to comply with a request to cooperate from the ICC, which is a breach of its obligations under the Statute, the court may refer the matter to the Assembly of States Parties or the Security Council.

There is still some opposition to the ICC even it has enjoyed strong support from much of the international community. The United States is by no means the only State to oppose the creation of the court. It has been the most open and vocal in expressing its opposition and taking action pursuant to its views against the ICC. The United States, under the Clinton administration, signed the Statute on December 31, 2001, the last day that it was possible to do so. Its signature may be attributed to the fact that the US was not in principle opposed to creating a new court to dispense international criminal justice. With the advent of the Bush administration came fiercer opposition to the ICC and, to avoid the obligation under Article 18, the US made clear its intention not to ratify the Statute in a communication to the UN Secretariat on 6 May 2002. The principal objection made against the ICC on legal grounds is that under Article 12, ICC may take jurisdiction over nationals of a State not a party to the Statute without that State's consent. They claim that this is contrary to that international law is made first by referencing the VCLT. Article 34 of that convention provides: "A treaty does not create either obligations or rights for a third State without its consent." Other arguments are from a more general mistrust of the ICC. They include the concern that States with effective legal systems cannot be sure that the court will not take over their nationals' prosecutions because the Statute leaves it to the court itself to judge whether the national court is "unable or unwilling" genuinely to deal with a case. On this view, the complementarity principle is not a reliable safeguard since the ICC cannot be trusted to apply it without political bias. A further concern is that the prosecutor, unlike national prosecutors, is accountable to no outside agency or authority in exercising his power of initiating investigations.

The US opposition to the ICC has led them to make various attempts to prevent the possibility of US nationals being tried by the court. It is doubtful whether the US believes in the practical likelihood of ICC proceedings in every case they seek an impediment to such proceedings. Their action on the international front has been supported and partially instigated by domestic legislation. The American Service members' Protection Act prohibits various forms of US cooperation with the ICC, provides for the cessation of military and other aid to States Parties that do not sign a non-surrender agreement with the US, and authorizes the use of "all means necessary, including military force" to release persons arrested by the ICC.

4. Cases and Materials

Read the following cases and think about the following questions:

(1) Compare the following three cases, and find out the different features of the wrongfulness of the acts resulting in the respondents' responsibility, respectively.

(2) A scholar made a ridiculous claim that a State where the pandemic broke firstly should be liable to other States grounded on the rule established by the *Corfu Channel Case* and *Trail Smelter Case*. Read carefully and find out why the two cases are not appropriate to support this kind of view.

4.1 *Corfu Channel Case* [1]

The Court was notified ⋯ as follows: The Government of the People's Republic of Albania and the Government of the United Kingdom of Great Britain and Northern Ireland have accepted the present Special Agreement, which has been drawn up as a result of the Resolution of the Security Council of the 9th April, 1947, for the purpose of submitting to the International Court of Justice for decision the following questions:

(1) Is Albania responsible under international law for the explosions which occurred on the 22nd October 1946 in Albanian waters and for the damage and loss of human life which resulted from them and is there any duty to any compensation?

(2) Has the United Kingdom under mternational law violated the sovereignty of the Albanian People's Republic by reason of the acts of the Royal Navy in Albanian waters on the 22nd October and on the I2th and 13th November 1946 and is there any duty to give satisfaction?

---

[1] See *Corfu Channel Case*, Judgment of April 9th, ICJ Reports 1949, p. 4. The *Corfu Channel Case* was the first public international law case heard before the ICJ between 1947 and 1949.

......

On behalf of the Albanian Government: "…(2) It has not been proved that the mines which caused the accidents of October 22nd, 1946, were laid by Albania; (3) It has not been proved that these mines were laid by a third Power on behalf of Albania; (4) It has not been proved that these mines were laid with the help or acquiescence of Albania; (5) It has not been proved that Albania knew, before the incidents of October 22nd, 1946, that these mines were in her territorial waters; (6) Consequently, Albania cannot be declared responsible, under international law, for the explosions which occurred on October 22nd, 1946, in Albanian waters, and for the damage and loss of human life which resulted from them. Albania owes no compensation to the United Kingdom Government."

......

On the evidence produced, the Court finds that the following facts are established:

In October, 1944, the North Corfu Channel was swept by the British Navy and no mines were found in the channel thus swept, whereupon the existence of a safe route through the Channel was announced in November 1944. In January and February, 1945, the Channel was check-swept by the British Navy with negative results. That the British Admiralty must have considered the Channel to be a safe route for navigation is shown by the fact that on May 15th 1946, it sent two British cruisers and on October 22nd a squadron through the Channel without any special measures of precaution against danger from moored mines. It was in this swept channel that the minefield was discovered on November 13th, 1946.

......

It is established by the evidence of witnesses that the minefield consisted of moored contact mines of the German GY type. It is further shown by the nature of the damage sustained by the two ships, and confirmed by witnesses and experts, that it could not have been caused by floating mines, magnetic ground mines, magnetic moored mines, or German GR mines. The experts of the Court have stated that the nature of the damage excludes the faintest possibility of its cause being a floating mine; nor could it have been caused by a ground mine. They also expressed the view that the damage must have been caused by the explosion of moored contact mines, each having a charge of approximately 600 lbs. of explosives, and that the two ships struck mines of the same type as those which were swept on November 13th, 1946.

The Albanian Government put forward a suggestion that the minefield discovered on November 13th may have been laid after October 22nd, so that the explosions that occurred on this latter date would not have been caused by mines from the field in question. But it brought no evidence in support of this supposition. As it has been established that the explosions could only have been due to moored mines having an explosive charge similar to that contained in GY mines, there would, if the Albanian contention were true, have been at least two mines of this nature in the channel outside the Bay of Saranda, in spite of the sweep in October 1944 and the check-sweeps in January and February 1945; and these mines would have been struck by the two vessels at points fairly close to one another on October 22nd, 1946. Such a supposition is too improbable to be accepted.

The Court consequently finds that the following facts are established. The two ships were mined in Albanian territorial waters in a previously swept and check-swept channel just at the place where a newly laid minefield consisting of moored contact German GY mines was discovered three weeks later. The damage sustained by the ships was inconsistent with damage which could have been caused by floating mines, magnetic ground mines, magnetic moored mines, or German GR mines, but its nature and extent were such as would be caused by mines of the type found in the minefield. In such circumstances the Court arrives at the conclusion that the explosions were due to mines belonging to that minefield.

Such are the facts upon which the Court must, in order to reply to the first question of the Special Agreement, give judgment as to Albania's responsibility for the explosions on October 22nd, 1946, and for the damage and loss of human life which resulted, and for the compensation, if any, due in respect of such damage and loss.

······

The Court considered first the various grounds for responsibility alleged in this submission.

In fact, although the United Kingdom Government never abandoned its contention that Albania herself laid the mines, very little attempt was made by the Government to demonstrate this point. In the written Reply, the United Kingdom Government takes note of the Albanian Government's formal statement that it did not lay the mines, and was not in a position to do so, as Albania possessed no navy; and that, on the whole Albanian littoral, the Albanian authorities only had a few launches and motor boats. In the light of these Statements, the Albanian Government was called upon, in the Reply, to disclose the circumstances in which two Yugoslav war vessels, the *Mijet* and the *Meljine*, carrying contact mines of the GY type, sailed southward from the port of Sibenik on or about October 18th, and proceeded to the Corfu Channel. The United Kingdom Government, having thus indicated the argument upon which it was thenceforth to concentrate, stated that it proposed to show that the said warships, with the knowledge and connivance of the Albanian Government, laid mines in the Corfu Channel just before October 22nd, 1946. ···

······

The Court now comes to the second alternative argument of the United Kingdom Government, namely, that the minefield was laid with the connivance of the Albanian Government. According to this argument, the mine laying operation was carried out by two Yugoslav warships at a date prior to October 22nd, but very near that date. This would imply collusion between the Albanian and the Yugoslav Governments, consisting either of a request by the Albanian Government to the Yugoslav Government for assistance, or of acquiescence by the Albanian authorities in the laying of the mines.

······

The Court considers that, even in so far as the facts are established, they lead to no firm conclusion. It has not been legally established that Yugoslavia possessed any GY mines, and the origin of the mines laid in Albanian territorial waters remains a matter for conjecture. It is clear that the existence of a treaty, such as that of July 9th, 1946, however close may be the bonds uniting its signatories, in no way leads to the conclusion that they participated in a criminal act.

······

The Court need not dwell on the assertion of one of the Counsel for the Albanian Government that the minefield might have been laid by the Greek Government. It is enough to say that this was a mere conjecture which, as Counsel himself admitted, was based on no proof.

In the light of the information now available to the Court, the authors of the minelaying remain unknown. In any case, the task of the Court, as defined by the Special Agreement, is to decide whether Albania is responsible, under international law, for the explosions which occurred on October 22nd, 1946, and to give judgment as to the compensation, if any.

Finally, the United Kingdom Government put forward the argument that, whoever the authors of the mine-laying were, it could not have been done without the Albanian Government's knowledge.

It is clear that knowledge of the minelaying cannot be imputed to the Albanian Government by reason merely of the fact that a minefield discovered in Albanian territorial waters caused the explosions of which the British warships were the victims. It is true, as international practice shows, that a State on whose territory or in whose waters an act contrary to international law has occurred, may be called upon to give an explanation. It is also true that that State cannot evade such a request by limiting itself to a reply that it is ignorant of the circumstances of the act and of its authors. The State may, up to a certain point, be bound to supply particulars of the use made by it of the means of information and inquiry at its disposal. But it cannot be concluded from the mere fact of the control exercised by a State over its territory and waters that that State necessarily knew, or ought to have known, of any unlawful act perpetrated therein, nor yet that it necessarily knew, or should have known, the authors. This fact, by itself and apart from other circumstances, neither involves *prima facie* responsibility nor shifts the burden of proof.

On the other hand, the fact of this exclusive territorial control exercised by a State within its frontiers has a bearing upon the methods of proof available to establish the knowledge of that State as to such events. By reason of this exclusive control, the other State, the victim of a breach of international law, is often unable to furnish direct proof of facts giving rise to responsibility. Such a State should be allowed a more liberal recourse to inferences of fact and circumstantial evidence. This indirect evidence is admitted in all systems of law, and its use is recognized by international decisions. It must be regarded as of special weight when it is based on a series of facts linked together and leading logically to a single conclusion.

The Court must examine therefore whether it has been established by means of indirect evidence that Albania has knowledge of minelaying in her territorial waters independently of any connivance on her part in this operation. The proof may be drawn from inferences of fact, provided that they leave no room for reasonable doubt. The elements of fact on which these inferences can be based may differ from those which are relevant to the question of connivance.

In the present case, two series of facts, which corroborate one another, have to be considered: the first relates to Albania's attitude before and after the disaster of October 22nd, 1946; the other concerns the feasibility of observing minelaying from the Albanian coast.

(1) It is clearly established that the Albanian Government constantly kept a close watch over the waters of the North Corfu Channel, at any rate after May 1946. This vigilance is proved by the declaration of the Albanian Delegate in the Security Council on February 19th, 1947, and especially by the diplomatic notes of the Albanian Government concerning the passage of foreign ships through its territorial waters.

......

As the Parties agree that the minefield had been recently laid, it must be concluded that the operation was carried out during the period of close watch by the Albanian authorities in this sector. This conclusion renders the Albanian Government's assertion of ignorance *a priori* somewhat improbable.

......

Another indication of the Albanian Government's knowledge consists in the fact that Government did not notify the presence of mines in its waters, at the moment when it must have known this, at the latest after the sweep on November 13th, and further, whereas the Greek Government immediately appointed a Commission to inquire into the events of October 22nd, the Albanian Government took no decision of such a nature, nor did it proceed to the judicial investigation incumbent, in such a case, on the territorial sovereign.

This attitude does not seem reconcilable with the alleged ignorance of the Albanian authorities that the minefield had been laid in Albanian territorial waters. It could be explained if the Albanian Government, while knowing of the minelaying, desired the circumstances of the operation to remain secret.

(2) As regards the possibility of observing minelaying from the Albanian coast, the Court regards the following facts, relating to the technical conditions of a secret minelaying and to the Albanian surveillance, as particularly important.

The Bay of Saranda and the channel used by shipping through the Strait are, from their geographical configuration, easily watched; the entrance of the bay is dominated by heights offering excellent observation points, both over the bay and over the Strait; whilst the channel throughout is close to the Albanian coast. The laying of a minefield in these waters could hardly fail to have been observed by the Albanian coastal defences.

......

The facilities for observation from the coast are confirmed by the two following circumstances: the distance of the nearest mine from the coast was only 500 meters; the minelayers must have passed at not more than about 500 meters from the coast between Denta Point and St. George's Monastery.

Being anxious to obtain any technical information that might guide it in its search for the truth, the Court submitted the following question to the Experts appointed by it: ···

The Experts' Report on this visit stated that: "The Experts consider it to be indisputable that if a normal look-out was kept at Cape Kiephali, Denta Point, and St. George's Monastery, and if the look-outs were equipped with binoculars as has been stated, under normal weather conditions for this area, the minelaying operations shown in Annex 9 to the United Kingdom Memorial must have been noticed by these coastguards."

......

From all the facts and observations mentioned above, the Court draws the conclusion that the laying of the minefield which caused the explosions on October 22nd, 1946, could not have been accomplished without the knowledge of the Albanian Government.

The obligations resulting for Albania from this knowledge are not disputed between the Parties. Counsel for the Albanian Government expressly recognized that (translation) "if Albania had been informed of the operation before the incidents of October 22nd, and in time to warn the British vessels and shipping in general of the existence of mines in the Corfu Channel, her responsibility would be involved…"

The obligations incumbent upon the Albanian authorities consisted in notifying, for the benefit of shipping in general, the existence of a minefield in Albanian territorial waters and in warning the approaching British warships of the imminent danger to which the minefield exposed them. Such obligations are based, not on the Hague Convention of 1907, No. VIII, which is applicable in time of war, but on certain general and well-recognized principles, namely: elementary considerations of humanity, even more exacting in peace than in war; the principle of the freedom of maritime communication; and every State's obligation not to allow knowingly its territory to be used for acts contrary to the rights of other States.

In fact, Albania neither notified the existence of the minefield, nor warned the British warships of the danger they were approaching. But Albania's obligation to notify shipping of the existence of mines in her waters depends on her having obtained knowledge of that fact in sufficient time before October 22nd; and the duty of the Albanian coastal authorities to warn the British ships depends on the time that elapsed between the moment that these ships were reported and the moment of the first explosion.

……

In fact, nothing was attempted by the Albanian authorities to prevent the disaster. These grave omissions involve the international responsibility of Albania.

The Court therefore reaches the conclusion that Albania is responsible under international law for the explosions which occurred on October 22nd, 1946, in Albanian waters, and for the damage and loss of human life which resulted from them, and that there is a duty upon Albania to pay compensation to the United Kingdom.

……

4.2 *Trail Smelter Case* [1]

Case brief

In 1935 a Canadian based corporation (defendant) owned a smelter plant which emitted hazardous fumes (sulfur dioxide) that caused damage to plant life, forest trees, soil, and crop yields accross the border in Washington State in the United States (plaintiff). The United States took Canada to court. The same year a Convention established an arbitral tribunal consisting of two national members and a neutral chairman. The Tribunal was aided by scientific experts appointed by the governments. In its first decision, 1938, the Tribunal concluded that harm had occurred between 1932 and 1937 and ordered the payment of an indemnity of ＄78,000 as the "complete and final indemnity and compensation for all damage which occurred between such dates". The Tribunal's second decision (1941), was concerned with the final three questions presented by the 1935 Convention, namely, responsibility for, and the appropriate mitigation and indemnification of, future harm. The Tribunal concluded, that, "no State has the right to use or permit the use of its territory in such a manner as to cause injury by fumes in or to the territory of another or the properties or persons therein, when the case is of serious consequence and the injury is established by clear and convincing evidence".

This Tribunal is constituted under, and its powers are derived from and limited by, the Convention between the United States of America and the Dominion of Canada signed at Ottawa, April 15, 1935, duly ratified by the two parties, and ratifications exchanged at Ottawa, August 3, 1935 (hereinafter termed "the Convention").

Article Ⅳ

The Tribunal shall apply the law and practice followed in dealing with

---

[1] See UN Reports of International Arbitral Awards, *Trail Smelter Case* (*United States*, *Canada*), 16 April 1938 and 11 March 1941, Vol. Ⅲ. pp. 1905-1982.

Chapter XIII The Law of Responsibility   427

cognate questions in the United States of America as well as international law and practice, and shall give consideration to the desire of the high contracting parties to reach a solution just to all parties concerned.

......

The duty imposed upon the Tribunal by the Convention was to "finally decide" the following questions:

(1) Whether damage caused by the Trail Smelter in the State of Washington has occurred since the first day of January, 1932, and, if so, what indemnity should be paid therefor?

(2) In the event of the answer to the first part of the preceding question being in the affirmative, whether the Trail Smelter should be required to refrain from causing damage in the State of Washington in the future and, if so, to what extent?

(3) In the light of the answer to the preceding question, what measures or regime, if any, should be adopted or maintained by the Trail Smelter?

(4) What indemnity or compensation, if any, should be paid on account of any decision or decisions rendered by the Tribunal pursuant to the next two preceding questions?

......

The controversy is between two Governments involving damage occurring in the territory of one of them (the United States of America) and alleged to be due to an agency situated in the territory of the other (the Dominion of Canada), for which damage the latter has assumed by the Convention an international responsibility. In this controversy, the Tribunal is not sitting to pass upon claims presented by individuals or on behalf of one or more individuals by their Government, although individuals may come within the meaning of "parties concerned", in Article IV and of "interested parties", in Article VIII of the Convention and although the damage suffered by individuals may, in part, "afford a convenient scale for the calculation of the reparation due to the State".

......

Comments made by Duncan French[1]

This case would undoubtedly be characterised as a landmark case, particularly if the principal criterion for such status is subsequent repetition leading to widespread and near-universal endorsement. In addition to its specific focus on responsibility for transboundary air pollution—which has subsequently developed into a more general rule of customary international environmental law. ··· Particularly unclear is on what basis a State owes this responsibility—purely because harm occurred (a form of strict liability) or because it has failed to adequately prevent it (the idea of a failure of due diligence upon the State). The Tribunal itself confuses this question by going on to note that "Canada is responsible in international law for the conduct of the Trail Smelter"; an unfortunate statement that in later decades would similarly cause ambiguity in the work of the International Law Commission on State liability for "acts not prohibited by international law".

4.3 *Gabčíkovo-Nagymaros Project Case*[2]

(1) *Jurisdiction: Special Agreement*

By a letter dated 2 July 1993, filed in the Registry of the Court on the same day, the Ambassador of Hungary ··· notified to the Court a Special Agreement in English. ··· The Court is requested to decide on the basis of the Treaty and rules and principles of general international law, as well as such other treaties as the Court may find applicable,

---

① See Eirik Bjorge and Cameron Miles (eds.), *Landmark Cases in Public International Law*, Hart Publishing, 2017, p. 174.
② See *Gabčíkovo-Nagymaros Project (Hungary/Slovakia)*, Judgment, ICJ Reports 1997, p. 7. This case has, like a prism, refracted the international law on environmental protection as well as on fundamental fields of general international law such as State responsibility, the law of treaties and the law of international watercourses. It is a landmark decision. Some scholars commented that Gabčíkovo-Nagymaros was the first case before the ICJ to be concerned with international environmental law in such a comprehensive manner, and in many ways the ICJ clarified this field of law.

Chapter XIII　The Law of Responsibility　　　　　429

(a) whether the Republic of Hungary was entitled to suspend and subsequently abandon, in 1989, the works on the Nagymaros Project and on the part of the Gabčíkovo Project for which the Treaty attributed responsibility to the Republic of Hungary;

(b) whether the Czech and Slovak Federal Republic was entitled to proceed, in November 1991, to the "provisional solution" and to put into operation from October 1992 this system, described in the Report of the Working Group of Independent Experts of the Commission of the European Communities, the Republic of Hungary and the Czech and Slovak Federal Republic dated 23 November 1992 (damming up of the Danube at river kilometre 1851. 7 on Czechoslovak territory and resulting consequences on water and navigation course);

(c) what are the legal effects of the notification, on 19 May 1992, of the termination of the Treaty by the Republic of Hungary.

The Court is also requested to determine the legal consequences…

(2) *Fact at issue* (Paras. 15-26)

15. The present case arose out of the signature, on 16 September 1977, by the Hungarian People's Republic and the Czechoslovak People's Republic, of a treaty "concerning the construction and operation of the Gabcilcovo-Nagymaros System of Locks" (hereinafter called the "1977 Treaty"). The names of the two contracting States have varied over the years; they are referred to as Hungary and Czechoslovakia. The 1977 Treaty entered into force on 30 June 1978.

It provides for the construction and operation of a System of Locks by the parties as a "joint investment". According to its Preamble, the system was designed to attain "the broad utilization of the natural resources of the Bratislava-Budapest section of the Danube river for the development of water resources, energy, transport, agriculture and other sectors of the national economy of the Contracting Parties".

The joint investment was thus essentially aimed at the production of hydroelectricity, the improvement of navigation on the relevant section of the Danube and the protection of the areas along the banks against flooding. At the same time, by the terms of the Treaty, the contracting parties undertook to ensure that the quality of water in the Danube was not impaired as a result of the Project, and that compliance with the obligations for the protection of nature arising in connection with the construction and operation of the System of Locks would be observed.

16. The Danube … the sector of with which this case is concerned is a stretch of approximately 200 kilometres between Bratislava in Slovakia and Budapest in Hungary. … The boundary between the two States is constituted, in the major part of that region, by the main channel of the river. … Cunovo and, further downstream, Gabčíkovo, are situated in this sector of the river on Slovak territory, Cunovo on the right bank and Gabčíkovo on the left. Further downstream, after the confluence of the various branches, the river enters Hungarian territory and the topography becomes hillier. Nabyrnaros lies in a narrow valley at a bend in the Danube just before it turns south, enclosing the large river island of Szentendre before reaching Budapest.

18. Article 1, Paragraph 1, of the 1977 Treaty describes the principal works to be constructed in pursuance of the Project. It provided for the building of two series of locks, one at Gabčíkovo (in Czechoslovak territory) and the other at Nagymaros (in Hungarian territory), to constitute "a single arid indivisible operational system of works".

Article 1, paragraph 4, of the Treaty further provided that the technical specifications concerning the system would be included in the "Joint Contractual Plan" which was to be drawn up in accordance with the Agreement signed by the two Governments for this purpose on 6 May 1976… It also provided for the construction, financing and management of the works on a joint basis in which the Parties participated in equal measure.

19. The Joint Contractual plan, referred to in the previous paragraph, set forth, on a large number of points, both the objectives of the system and

the characteristics of the works.

It also contained "Preliminary Operating and Maintenance Rules", Article 23 of which specified that "The final operating rules (should) be approved within a year of' the setting into operation of the system".

20. Thus, the Project was to have taken the form of an integrated joint project with the two contracting parties on an equal footing in respect of the financing, construction and operation of the works. Its single and indivisible nature was to have been realized through the Joint Contractual Plan which complemented the Treaty. In particular, Hungary would have had control of the sluices at Dunakiliti and the works at Nagymaros, whereas Czechoslovakia would have had control of the works at Gabčíkovo.

21. The schedule of work had for its part been fixed in an Agreement on mutual assistance signed by the two parties on 16 September 1977, at the same time as the Treaty itself. The Agreement made some adjustments to the allocation of the works between the parties as laid down by the Treaty.

Work on the Project started in 1978. On Hungary's initiative, the two partier first agreed, by two Protocols signed on 10 October 1983, to slow the work down and to postpone putting into operation the power plants, and then, by a Protocol signed on 6 February 1989, to accelerate the Project.

22. As a result of intense criticism which the Project had generated in Hungary, the Hungarian Government decided on 13 May 1989 to suspend the works at Nagymaros pending the completion of various studies which the competent authorities were to finish before 31 July 1989. On 21 July 1989, the Hungarian Government extended the suspension of the works at Nagymaros until 31 October 1989, and, in addition, suspended the works at Dunakiliti until the same date. Lastly, on 27 October 1989, Hungary decided to abandon the works at Nagymaros and to maintain the *status quo* at Dunakiliti.

23. During this period, negotiations took place between the parties. Czechoslovakia also started investigating alternative solutions. One of them,

an alternative solution subsequently known as "Variant C", entailed a unilateral diversion of the Danube by Czechoslovakia on its territory some 10 kilometres upstream of Dunakiliti. In its final stage, Variant C included the construction at Cunovo of an overflow dam and a levee linking that dam to the south bank of the bypass canal. ···Provision was made for ancillary works···

On 23 July 1991, the Slovak Government decided "to begin, in September 1991, construction to put the Gabčíkovo Project into operation by the provisional solution". ··· Work on Variant C began in November 1991. Discussions continued between the two parties but to no avail, and, on 19 May 1992, the Hungarian Government transmitted to the Czechoslovak Government a Note Verbale terminating the 1977 Treaty with effect from 25 May 1992. On 15 October 1992, Czechoslovakia began work to enable the Danube to be closed and, starting on 23 October, proceeded to the damming of the river.

The Court finally takes note of the fact that on 1 January 1993 Slovakia became an independent State; that in the Special Agreement thereafter concluded between Hungary and Slovakia the Parties agreed to establish and implement a temporary water management regime for the Danube; and that finally they concluded an Agreement in respect of it on 19 April 1995, which would come to an end 14 days after the Judgment of the Court. The Court also observes that not only the 1977 Treaty, but also the "related instruments" are covered in the preamble to the Special Agreement and that the Parties, when concentrating their reasoning on the 1977 Treaty, appear to have extended their arguments to the "related instruments".

(3) *Treaty and Responsibility issues* (Paras. *27-59*)

27. The Court ··· is requested to decide first, "whether the Republic of Hungary was entitled to suspend and subsequently abandon, in 1989, the works on the Nagymaros Project and on the part of the Gabčíkovo Project for which the Treaty attributed responsibility to the Republic of Hungary".

33. On 13 May 1989, the Government of Hungary adopted a resolution

to suspend works at Nagymaros, and ordered "the Ministers concerned to commission further studies in order to place the Council of Ministers in a position where it can make well-founded suggestions to the Parliament in connection with the amendment of the international treaty on the investment. In the interests of the above, we must examine the international and legal consequences, the technical considerations, the obligations related to continuous navigation on the Danube and the environmental/ecological and seismic impacts of the eventual stopping of the Nagymaros investment. To be further examined are the opportunities for the replacement of the lost electric energy and the procedures for mini-mising claims for compensation". ⋯

37. In the ensuing period, negotiations were conducted at various levels between the two States, but proved fruitless. Finally, by a letter dated 4 October 1989, the Hungarian Prime Minister formally proposed to Czechoslovakia that the Nagymaros sector of the Project be abandoned and that an agreement be concluded with a view to reducing the ecological risks associated with the Gabcikovo sector of the Project. He proposed that that agreement should be concluded before 30 July 1990.

The two Heads of Government met on 26 October 1989, and were unable to reach agreement. ⋯

38. During winter 1989-1990, the political situation in Czechoslovakia and Hungary alike was transformed, and the new Governments were confronted with many new problems.

In spring 1990 the new Hungarian Government, in presenting its National Renewal Programme, announced that the whole of the Gabčíkovo-Nagymaros ProJect was a "mistake" and that it would initiate negotiations as soon as possible with the Czechoslovak Government "on remedying and sharing the damages". ⋯ On 15 February 1991, the Czechoslovak President declared that the Gabcikovo-Nagymaros Project constituted a "totalitarian, gigomaniac monument which is against nature" ⋯ but that, if there were "many reasons to change, modify the treaty⋯it was not acceptable to cancel the treaty…and negotiate lateron".

39. The two Parties to this case concur in recognizing that the 1977 Treaty, the above-mentioned Agreement on mutual assistance of 1977 and the Protocol of 1989 were validly concluded and were duly in force when the facts recounted above took place.

Further, they do not dispute the fact that, however flexible they may have been, these texts did not envisage the possibility of the signatories unilaterally suspending or abandoning the work provided for therein, or even carrying it out according to a new schedule not approved by the two partners.

40. Hungary contended that, although it did suspend or abandon certain works, on the contrary, it never suspended the application of the 1977 Treaty itself. To justify its conduct, it relied essentially on a "State of ecological necessity". …

41. Hungary also accused Czechoslovakia of having violated various provisions of the 1977 Treaty from before 1989—in particular Articles 15 and 19 relating, respectively, to water quality and nature protection—in refusing to take account of the now evident ecological dangers and insisting that the works be continued, notably at Nagymaros. …

42. Hungary moreover contended from the outset that its conduct in the present case should not be evaluated only in relation to the law of treaties. It also observed that, in accordance with the provisions of Article 4, the Vienna Convention of 23 May 1969 on the Law of Treaties could not be applied to the 1977 Treaty, which was concluded before that Convention entered into force as between the parties. Hungary has indeed acknowledged, with reference to the jurisprudence of the Court, that in many respects the Convention reflects the existing customary law. …

43. Slovakia, for its part, denied that the basis for suspending or abandoning the performance of a treaty obligation can be found outside the law of treaties. It acknowledged that the 1969 Vienna Convention could not be applied as such to the 1977 Treaty, but at the same time stressed that a

Chapter XIII   The Law of Responsibility   435

number of its provisions are a reflection of pre-existing rules of customary international law and specified that this is, in particular, the case with the provisions of Part V relating to invalidity termination and suspension of the operation of treaties. ···

45. Slovakia moreover denied that in any way breached the 1977 Treaty ··· it reproached Hungary with having adopted its unilateral measures of suspension and abandonment of the works in violation of the provisions of Article 27 of the 1977 Treaty, which it submits required prior recourse to the machinery for dispute settlement provided for in that Article.

46. The Court has no need to dwell upon the question of the applicability in the present case of the Vienna Convention of 1969 on the Law of Treaties. It needs only to be mindful of the fact that it has several times had occasion to hold that some of the rules laid down in that Convention might be considered as a codification of existing customary law. ···

Neither has the Court lost sight of the fact that the Vienna Convention is in any event applicable to the Protocol of 6 February 1989 whereby Hungary and Czechoslovakia agreed to accelerate completion of the works relating to the Gabcikovo-Nagymaros Project.

47. Nor does the Court need to dwell upon the question of the relationship between the law of treaties and the law of State responsibility, to which the Parties devoted lengthy arguments, as those two branches of international law obviously have a scope that is distinct. A determination of whether a convention is or is not in force, and whether it has or has not been properly suspended or denounced, is to be made pursuant to the law of treaties. On the other hand, an evaluation of the extent to which the suspension or denunciation of a convention, seen as incompatible with the law of treaties, involves the responsibility of the State which proceeded to it, is to be made under the law of State responsibility.

Thus the Vienna Convention of 1969 on the Law of Treaties confines itself to defining the conditions in which a treaty may lawfully be denounced or suspended; while the effects of a denunciation or suspension seen as not meeting those conditions are, on the contrary, expressly excluded from the scope of the Convention by operation of Article 73. ···

48. The Court cannot accept Hungary's argument to the effect that, in 1989, in suspending and subsequently abandoning the works for which it was still responsible at Nagymaros and at Dunakiliti, it did not, for all that, suspend the application of the 1977 Treaty itself or then reject that Treaty. The conduct of Hungary at that time can only be interpreted as an expression of its unwillingness to comply with at least some of the provisions of the Treaty and the Protocol of 6 February 1989, as specified in the Joint Contractual Plan. The effect of Hungary's conduct was to render impossible the accomplishment of the system of works that the Treaty expressly described as "single and indivisible".

The Court moreover observes that, when it invoked the State of necessity in an effort to justify that conduct, Hungary chose to place itself from the outset within the ambit of the law of State responsibility, thereby implying that, in the absence of such a circumstance, its conduct would have been unlawful. The State of necessity claimed by Hungary—supposing it to have been established—thus could not permit of the conclusion that, in 1989, it had acted in accordance with its obligations under the 1977 Treaty or that those obligations had ceased to be binding upon it. It would only permit the affirmation that, under the circumstances, Hungary would not incur international responsibility by acting as it did. Lastly, the Court points out that Hungary expressly acknowledged that, in any event, such a State of necessity would not exempt it from its duty to compensate its partner.

50. In the present case, the Parties are in agreement in considering that the existence of a State of necessity must be evaluated in the light of the criteria laid down by the International Law Commission in Article 33 of the Draft Articles on the International Responsibility of States that it adopted on First reading. That provision is worded as follows: (text omitted here, see

Art. 25 of AESIWA afore).

51. The Court considers, first of all, that the State of necessity is a ground recognized by customary international law for precluding the wrongfulness of an act not in conformity with an international obligation. It observes moreover that such ground for precluding wrongfulness can only be accepted on an exceptional basis. The International Law Commission was of the same opinion…Thus, according to the Commission, the State of necessity can only be invoked under certain strictly defined conditions which must be cumulatively satisfied; and the State concerned is not the sole judge of whether those conditions have been met.

52. In the present case, the following basic conditions set forth in Draft Article 33 are relevant: it must have been occasioned by an "essential interest" of the State which is the author of the act conflicting with one of its international obligations; that interest must have been threatened by a "grave and imminent peril"; the act being challenged must have been the "only means" of safeguarding that interest; that act must not have "seriously impair (ed) an essential interest" of the State towards which the obligation existed; and the State which is the author of that act must not have "contributed to the occurrence of the State of necessity". Those conditions reflect customary international law. The Court will now endeavour to ascertain whether those conditions had been met at the time of the suspension and abandonment…

53. The Court has no difficulty in acknowledging that the concerns expressed by Hungary for its natural environment in the region affected by the Gabcikovo-Nagymaros Project related to an "essential interest" of that State…The Court recalls that it has recently had occasion to stress, in the following terms, the great significance that it attaches to respect for the environment, not only for States but also for the whole of mankind: "The environment is not an abstraction but represents the living space, the quality of life and the very health of human beings, including generations unborn. The existence of the general obligation of States to ensure that activities

within their jurisdiction and control respect the environment of other States or of areas beyond national control is now part of the corpus of international law relating to the environment."

57. The Court Concludes from the foregoing that, with respect to both Nagyniaros and Gabcikovo, the perils invoked by Hungary, without prejudging their possible gravity, were not sufficiently established in 1989, nor were they "imminent"; and that Hungary had available to it at that time means of responding to these perceived perils other than the suspension and abandonment of works with which it had been entrusted. What is more, negotiations were under way which might have led to a review of the Project and the extension of some of its time-limits, without there being need to abandon it…

Moreover, the Court notes that Hungary when it decided to conclude the 1977 Treaty…Hungary was, then, presumably aware of the situation as then known…the need to ensure the protection of the environment had not escaped the parties…

What is more, the Court cannot fail to note the positions taken by Hungary after the entry into force of the 1977 Treaty. …

The Court infers from all these elements that, in the present case, even if it had been established that there was, in 1989, a State of necessity linked to the performance of the 1977 Treaty, Hungary would not have been permitted to rely upon that State of necessity in order to justify its failure to comply with its treaty obligations, as it had helped, by act or omission to bring it about.

59. In the light of the conclusions reached above, the Court…finds that Hungary was not entitled to suspend and subsequently abandon, in 1989, the works on the Nagyrnaros Project and on the part of the Gabčíkovo Project for which the 1977 Treaty and related instruments attributed responsibility to it.

……

5. References and Recommended Reading Materials

(1) James Crawford, *State Responsibility: The General Part*, Cambridge University Press, 2013.

(2) Geoffrey Wawro, *From Nuremberg To The Hague: The Future Of International Criminal Justice*, Cambridge University Press, 2003.

(3)〔新西兰〕尼尔·博伊斯特、〔英〕罗伯特·克赖尔:《东京国际军事法庭法律新论》,梅小侃、龚志伟译,上海交通大学出版社2021年版。

(4)梅小璈、梅小侃编:《梅汝璈东京审判文稿》,上海交通大学出版社2013年版。

Chapter XIV Peaceful Settlement of Disputes

1. Introduction

International disputes are mainly caused by the differences and contradictions between countries in interest claims, rights claims and even understanding of objective facts. Due to the different causes and nature of international disputes, they are generally divided into four categories: legal disputes, political disputes, mixed disputes and factual disputes. The means of settling international disputes can be divided into peaceful means and force means. The means of peaceful settlement of international disputes can be divided into political means and legal means. The political methods include negotiation, consultation, investigation, mediation and reconciliation. Legal methods mainly include arbitration and judicial methods. Forced settlement is generally considered to include such dispute settlement methods as counter-report retaliation and blockade interference. The current international law advocates the peaceful settlement of international disputes.

The United Nations plays a vital role in the peaceful settlement of international disputes. Among the major organs of the United Nations, besides the ICJ, the Security Council, the General Assembly and the Secretariat are mainly responsible for the peaceful settlement of disputes. In addition to the United Nations, regional bodies or arrangements also play an important role in the peaceful settlement of international disputes. E. g., the

Chapter XIV Peaceful Settlement of Disputes   441

UNCLOS has its own unique mechanism for the peaceful settlement of international disputes, including the exchange of views between the disputing parties, reconciliation and binding adjudication. Judgments that are binding include the awards of the International Tribunal for the Law of the Sea, the International Court of Justice, arbitral tribunals and special arbitral tribunals.

2. Preliminary Reading and Assignment

2.1 Convention for the Pacific Settlement of International Disputes (1907)①

Article 1

With a view to obviating as far as possible recourse to force in the relations between States, the Contracting Powers agree to use their best efforts to ensure the pacific settlement of international differences.

Article 2

In case of serious disagreement or dispute, before an appeal to arms, the Contracting Powers agree to have recourse, as far as circumstances allow, to the good offices or mediation of one or more friendly Powers.

Article 6

Good offices and mediation undertaken either at the request of the parties in dispute or on the initiative of Powers strangers to the dispute have exclusively the character of advice, and never have binding force.

Article 8

The Contracting Powers are agreed in recommending the application, when circumstances allow, of special mediation in the following form:

In case of a serious difference endangering peace, the States at variance

---

① See Convention for the Pacific Settlement of International Disputes, https://docs.pca-cpa.org/2016/01/1907-Convention-for-the-Pacific-Settlement-of-International-Disputes.pdf, last visited on Jan. 8, 2022. The text of the Convention reproduced here is a translation of the French text adopted at the 1907 Peace Conference. The French-language version is authoritative.

choose respectively a Power, to which they entrust the mission of entering into direct communication with the Power chosen on the other side, with the object of preventing the rupture of pacific relations.

For the period of this mandate, the term of which, unless otherwise stipulated, cannot exceed thirty days, the States in dispute cease from all direct communication on the subject of the dispute, which is regarded as referred exclusively to the mediating Powers, which must use their best efforts to settle it.

In case of a definite rupture of pacific relations, these Powers are charged with the joint task of taking advantage of any opportunity to restore peace.

Article 9

In disputes of an international nature involving neither honour nor vital interests, and arising from a difference of opinion on points of facts, the Contracting Powers deem it expedient and desirable that the parties who have not been able to come to an agreement by means of diplomacy, should, as far as circumstances allow, institute an International Commission of Inquiry, to facilitate a solution of these disputes by elucidating the facts by means of an impartial and conscientious investigation.

Article 10

International Commissions of Inquiry are constituted by special agreement between the parties in dispute.

The Inquiry Convention defines the facts to be examined; it determines the mode and time in which the Commission is to be formed and the extent of the powers of the Commissioners.

It also determines, if there is need, where the Commission is to sit, and whether it may remove to another place, the language the Commission shall use and the languages the use of which shall be authorized before it, as well as the date on which each party must deposit its statement of facts, and, generally speaking, all the conditions upon which the parties have agreed.

If the parties consider it necessary to appoint Assessors, the Convention of Inquiry shall determine the mode of their selection and the extent of their powers.

Article 20

The Commission is entitled, with the assent of the Powers, to move temporarily to any place where it considers it may be useful to have recourse to this means of inquiry or to send one or more of its members. Permission must be obtained from the State on whose territory it is proposed to hold the inquiry.

Article 37

International arbitration has for its object the settlement of disputes between States by Judges of their own choice and on the basis of respect for law.

Recourse to arbitration implies an engagement to submit in good faith to the Award.

Article 38

In questions of a legal nature, and especially in the interpretation or application of International Conventions, arbitration is recognized by the Contracting Powers as the most effective, and, at the same time, the most equitable means of settling disputes which diplomacy has failed to settle.

Consequently, it would be desirable that, in disputes about the above-mentioned questions, the Contracting Powers should, if the case arose, have recourse to arbitration, in so far as circumstances permit.

Article 41

With the object of facilitating an immediate recourse to arbitration for international differences, which it has not been possible to settle by diplomacy, the Contracting Powers undertake to maintain *the Permanent Court of Arbitration*, as established by the First Peace Conference, accessible at all times, and operating, unless otherwise stipulated by the parties, in accordance with the rules of procedure inserted in the present Convention.

Article 43

The Permanent Court sits at The Hague.

An International Bureau serves as registry for the Court. It is the channel for communications relative to the meetings of the Court; it has charge of the archives and conducts all the administrative business.

The Contracting Powers undertake to communicate to the Bureau, as soon as possible, a certified copy of any conditions of arbitration arrived at between them and of any Award concerning them delivered by a special Tribunal.

They likewise undertake to communicate to the Bureau the laws, regulations, and documents eventually showing the execution of the Awards given by the Court.

Article 45

When the Contracting Powers wish to have recourse to the Permanent Court for the settlement of a difference which has arisen between them, the Arbitrators called upon to form the Tribunal with jurisdiction to decide this difference must be chosen from the general list of Members of the Court.

Failing the direct agreement of the parties on the composition of the Arbitration Tribunal, the following course shall be pursued:

Each party appoints two Arbitrators, of whom one only can be its national or chosen from among the persons selected by it as Members of the Permanent Court. These Arbitrators together choose an Umpire.

If the votes are equally divided, the choice of the Umpire is entrusted to a third Power, selected by the parties by common accord.

If an agreement is not arrived at on this subject each party selects a different Power, and the choice of the Umpire is made in concert by the Powers thus selected.

If, within two months' time, these two Powers cannot come to an agreement, each of them presents two candidates taken from the list of

Members of the Permanent Court, exclusive of the members selected by the parties and not being nationals of either of them. Drawing lots determines which of the candidates thus presented shall be Umpire.

Article 48

The Contracting Powers consider it their duty, if a serious dispute threatens to break out between two or more of them, to remind these latter that the Permanent Court is open to them.

Consequently, they declare that the fact of reminding the parties at variance of the provisions of the present Convention, and the advice given to them, in the highest interests of peace, to have recourse to the Permanent Court, can only be regarded as friendly actions.

In case of dispute between two Powers, one of them can always address to the International Bureau a note containing a declaration that it would be ready to submit the dispute to arbitration.

The Bureau must at once inform the other Power of the declaration.

Article 62

The parties are entitled to appoint special agents to attend the Tribunal to act as intermediaries between themselves and the Tribunal.

They are further authorized to retain for the defence of their rights and interests before the Tribunal counsel or advocates appointed by themselves for this purpose.

The Members of the Permanent Court may not act as agents, counsel, or advocates except on behalf of the Power which appointed them Members of the Court.

Article 63

As a general rule, arbitration procedure comprises two distinct phases: pleadings and oral discussions.

The pleadings consist in the communication by the respective agents to the members of the Tribunal and the opposite party of cases, counter-cases, and, if necessary, of replies; the parties annex thereto all papers and documents called for in the case. This communication shall be made either directly or through the intermediary of the International Bureau, in the order and within the time fixed by the "Compromis".

The time fixed by the "Compromis" may be extended by mutual agreement by the parties, or by the Tribunal when the latter considers it necessary for the purpose of reaching a just decision.

The discussions consists in the oral development before the Tribunal of the arguments of the parties.

Article 81

The Award, duly pronounced and notified to the agents of the parties, settles the dispute definitively and without appeal.

Article 82

Any dispute arising between the parties as to the interpretation and execution of the Award shall, in the absence of an Agreement to the contrary, be submitted to the Tribunal which pronounced it.

Article 84

The Award is not binding except on the parties in dispute.

When it concerns the interpretation of a Convention to which Powers other than those in dispute are parties, they shall inform all the Signatory Powers in good time. Each of these Powers is entitled to intervene in the case. If one or more avail themselves of this right, the interpretation contained in the Award is equally binding on them.

Article 91

The present Convention, duly ratified, shall replace, as between the Contracting Powers, the Convention for the Pacific Settlement of International Disputes of the 29th July, 1899.

2.2 General Act of Arbitration①

Article 17

All disputes with regard to which the parties are in conflict as to their respective rights shall, subject to any reservations which may be made under Article 39, be submitted for decision to the Permanent Court of International Justice, unless the parties agree, in the manner hereinafter provided, to have resort to an arbitral tribunal.

It is understood that the disputes referred to above include in particular those mentioned in Article 36 of the Statute of the Permanent Court of International Justice.

Article 18

If the parties agree to submit the disputes mentioned in the preceding article to an arbitral tribunal, they shall draw up a special agreement in which they shall specify the subject of the dispute, the arbitrators selected, and the procedure to be followed. In the absence of sufficient particulars in the special agreement, the provisions of The Hague Convention of October 18th, 1907, for the Pacific Settlement of International Disputes shall apply so far as is necessary. If nothing is laid down in the special agreement as to the rules regarding the substance of the dispute to be followed by the arbitrators, the tribunal shall apply the substantive rules enumerated in Article 38 of the Statute of the Permanent Court of International Justice.

Article 19

If the parties fail to agree concerning the special agreement referred to in the preceding article, or fail to appoint arbitrators, either party shall be at

---

① See 1928 General Act (Pacific Settlement of International Disputes), https://cil.nus.edu.sg/wp-content/uploads/2017/08/1928-General-Act-of-Arbitration.pdf, last visited on Jan. 8, 2022. Adopted in Geneva, Switzerland on 26 September 1928. Official texts in French and English. This General Act was registered with the Secretariat, in accordance with its Article 44, on August 16, 1929, the date of its entry into force.

liberty, after giving three months' notice, to bring the dispute by an application direct before the Permanent Court of International Justice.

2.3 Covenant of the League of Nations[①]

Article 2

The action of the League under this Covenant shall be effected throught he instrumentality of an Assembly and of a Council, with a permanent Secretariat.

Article 12

The Members of the League agree that, if there should arise between them any dispute likely to lead to a rupture, they will submit the matter either to arbitration or to inquiry by the Council, and they are in no case to resort to war until three months after the award by the arbitrators, or the report by the Council. In any case under this Article the award of the arbitrators shall be made within a reasonable time, and the report of the Council shall be made within six months after the submission of the dispute.

Article 13

The Members of the League agree that whenever any dispute shall arise between them which they recognize to be suitable for submission to arbitration and which cannot be satisfactorily settled by diplomacy, they will submit the whole subject-matter to arbitration.

Disputes as to the interpretation of a treaty, as to any question of international law, as to the existence of any fact which if established would constitute a breach of any international obligation, or as to the extent and nature of the reparation to be made for any such breach, are declared to be

---

① See Covenant of the League of Nations, https://www.ungeneva.org/en/covenant-lon, last visited on Jan. 8, 2022. The Treaty of Versailles was ratified in the Palace of Versailles Hall of Mirrors on 28 June 1919. The Covenant of the League of Nations is Part I of the Treaty. The Covenant had three main objectives in 26 articles for the League of Nations: to ensure collective security, to assure functional cooperation, and to execute the mandates of peace treaties.

among those which are generally suitable for submission to arbitration or judicial settlement.

For the consideration of any such dispute, the court to which the case is referred shall be the Permanent Court of International Justice, established in accordance with Article 14, or any tribunal agreed on by the parties to the dispute or stipulated in any convention existing between them.

The Members of the League agree that they will carry out in full good faith any award or decision that may be rendered, and that they will not resort to war against a Member of the League which complies therewith. In the event of any failure to carry out such an award or decision, the Council shall propose what steps should be taken to give effect thereto.

Article 14

The Council shall formulate and submit to the Members of the League for adoption plans for the establishment of a Permanent Court of International Justice. The Court shall be competent to hear and determine any dispute of an international character which the parties thereto submit to it. The Court may also give an advisory opinion upon any dispute or question referred to it by the Council or by the Assembly.

Article 15

If there should arise between Members of the League any dispute likely to lead to a rupture, which is not submitted to arbitration or judicial settlement in accordance with Article 13, the Members of the League agree that they will submit the matter to the Council. Any party to the dispute may effect such submission by giving notice of the existence of the dispute to the Secretary General, who will make all necessary arrangements for a full investigation and consideration thereof.

For this purpose the parties to the dispute will communicate to the Secretary General, as promptly as possible, Statements of their case with all the relevant facts and papers, and the Council may forthwith direct the publication thereof.

The Council shall endeavour to effect a settlement of the dispute, and if such efforts are successful, a statement shall be made public giving such facts and explanations regarding the dispute and the terms of settlement thereof as the Council may deem appropriate.

If the dispute is not thus settled, the Council either unanimously or by a majority vote shall make and publish a report containing a statement of the facts of the dispute and the recommendations which are deemed just and proper in regard thereto.

Any Member of the League represented on the Council may make public a statement of the facts of the dispute and of its conclusions regarding the same.

If a report by the Council is unanimously agreed to by the members thereof other than the Representatives of one or more of the parties to the dispute, the Members of the League agree that they will not go to war with any party to the dispute which complies with the recommendations of the report.

If the Council fails to reach a report which is unanimously agreed to by the members thereof, other than the Representatives of one or more of the parties to the dispute, the Members of the League reserve to themselves the right to take such action as they shall consider necessary for the maintenance of right and justice.

If the dispute between the parties is claimed by one of them, and is found by the Council, to arise out of a matter which by international law is solely within the domestic jurisdiction of that party, the Council shall so report, and shall make no recommendation as to its settlement.

The Council may in any case under this Article refer the dispute to the Assembly. The dispute shall be so referred at the request of either party to the dispute, provided that such request be made within fourteen days after the submission of the dispute to the Council.

In any case referred to the Assembly, all the provisions of this Article and of Article 12 relating to the action and powers of the Council shall apply to the action and powers of the Assembly, provided that a report made by the Assembly, if concurred in by the Representatives of those Members of the League represented on the Council and of a majority of the other Members of the League, exclusive in each case of the Representatives of the parties to the dispute, shall have the same force as a report by the Council concurred in by all the members thereof other than the Representatives of one or more of the parties to the dispute.

Article 16

Should any Member of the League resort to war in disregard of its covenants under Articles 12, 13 or 15, it shall *ipso facto* be deemed to have committed an act of war against all other Members of the League, which hereby undertake immediately to subject it to the severance of all trade or financial relations, the prohibition of all intercourse between their nationals and the nationals of the covenant-breaking State, and the prevention of all financial, commercial or personal intercourse between the nationals of the covenant breaking State and the nationals of any other State, whether a Member of the League or not.

It shall be the duty of the Council in such case to recommend to the several Governments concerned what effective military, naval or air force the Members of the League shall severally contribute to the armed forces to be used to protect the covenants of the League. …

2.4 Peaceful Settlement in UN Regime

Article 33[1]

1. The parties to any dispute, the continuance of which is likely to endanger the maintenance of international peace and security, shall, first of

---

[1] See United Nations Charter, Chapter Ⅵ: Pacific Settlement of Disputes (Articles 33-38), https://www.un.org/en/about-us/un-charter/chapter-6, last visited on Jan. 8, 2022.

all, seek a solution by negotiation, enquiry, mediation, conciliation, arbitration, judicial settlement, resort to regional agencies or arrangements, or other peaceful means of their own choice.

2. The Security Council shall, when it deems necessary, call upon the parties to settle their dispute by such means.

Article 92[①]

The International Court of Justice shall be the principal judicial organ of the United Nations. It shall function in accordance with the annexed Statute, which is based upon the Statute of the Permanent Court of International Justice and forms an integral part of the present Charter.

Article 93

1. All Members of the United Nations are *ipso facto* parties to the Statute of the International Court of Justice.

2. A State which is not a Member of the United Nations may become a party to the Statute of the International Court of Justice on conditions to be determined in each case by the General Assembly upon the recommendation of the Security Council.

Article 94

1. Each Member of the United Nations undertakes to comply with the decision of the International Court of Justice in any case to which it is a party.

2. If any party to a case fails to perform the obligations incumbent upon it under a judgment rendered by the Court, the other party may have recourse to the Security Council, which may, if it deems necessary, make recommendations or decide upon measures to be taken to give effect to the judgment.

Article 96

1. The General Assembly or the Security Council may request the

---

① United Nations Charter, Chapter XIV: The International Court of Justice (Articles 92-96), https://www.un.org/en/about-us/un-charter/chapter-14, last visited on Jan. 8, 2022.

Chapter Ⅳ　Peaceful Settlement of Disputes　　　　453

International Court of Justice to give an advisory opinion on any legal question.

2. Other organs of the United Nations and specialized agencies, which may at any time be so authorized by the General Assembly, may also request advisory opinions of the Court on legal questions arising within the scope of their activities.

2.5　Questions and Assignments

(1) How many ways of settlement are referred in these conventions above?

(2) What are the resemblances and differences between the dispute settlement regime in League of Nations and United Nations? Which one is more effective? Why? Find out how many wars or regional armed conflicts have happened after the establishment of UN. Do these wars or conflicts indicate that the regime provided by the UN has failed?

(3) Learn about the history of the League of Nations' investigation on Japan's seizure of Northeast China, especially the Lytton Report,[①] and, give

---

[①] Lytton Report are the findings of the Lytton Commission, entrusted in 1931 by the League of Nations in an attempt to evaluate the Mukden Incident, which led to the Empire of Japan's seizure of Northeast China. The Lytton Report contained an account of the situation in Northeast China before September 1931, when the Mukden Incident took place as the Japanese army (without authorization from the Japanese government) seized the large Chinese province of Northeast China. The Report described the unsatisfactory features of the Chinese administration and giving weight to the various claims and complaints of Japan. It then proceeded with a narrative of the events in Northeast China subsequent to September 18, 1931, based on the evidence of many participants and on that of eyewitnesses. It devoted particular attention to the origins and development of the State of Manchukuo, which had already been proclaimed by the time the Commission reached Northeast China. It also covered the question of the economic interests of Japan both in Northeast China and China as a whole, and the nature and effects of the Chinese anti-Japanese boycott. Soviet Union interests in the region were also mentioned. Finally, the Commission submitted a study of the conditions to which, in its judgment, any satisfactory solution should conform, and made various proposals and suggestions as to how an agreement embodying these principles might be brought about. In spite of care to preserve impartiality between the conflicting views of China and Japan, the effect of the Report was regarded as a substantial vindication of the Chinese case on most fundamental issues. In particular, the Commission stated that the operations of the Imperial Japanese Army following on the Mukden incident could not be regarded as legitimate self-defense.

an 8-10 minutes speech in English based upon your findings and your own comments about the peaceful settlement provided by the League of Nations. Find out how many wars and regional armed conflicts have happened after the establishment of the UN.

(4) Based on the cases excerpted in this chapter and chapters before, e. g., the *Tehran Hostage Case* in Chapter XII, make a brief presentation about the whole process of ICJ's proceeding to hear a contentious case and give an explanation in an 8-10 minutes speech in English.

3. Terminologies and Explanations

3.1 Diplomatic Methods of Dispute Settlement

(1) *The negotiation*

It is the simplest and most utilized way in international disputes. It consists basically of discussions between the interested parties with a view to reconciling divergent opinions or at least understanding the different positions maintained. For example, the United States and China negotiated after the friction of trade to enter the first phase of the agreement. Negotiation does not involve any third party, at least at that stage, and so differs from the other forms of dispute management. In addition to being an extremely active method of the settlement itself, negotiation is normally the precursor to other settlement procedures as the parties decide amongst themselves how best to resolve their differences. It is by mutual discussions that the essence of the differences will be revealed and the opposing contentions elucidated. Negotiating does not always succeed since they do depend on a certain degree of mutual goodwill, flexibility and sensitivity. Failure to enter an agreement by negotiation may be a requirement to initiate an adjudication process, like in the WTO.

(2) *Good offices and mediation*

The employment of the procedures of good offices and mediation involves the use of a third party, whether an individual or individuals, a State or group of States or an international organization, to encourage the contending parties to come to a settlement. Unlike the techniques of arbitration and adjudication, the process aims at persuading the parties to a dispute to reach satisfactory terms for its termination by themselves. Technically, good offices are involved where a third party attempts to influence the opposing sides to enter into negotiations, whereas mediation implies active participation in the negotiating process of the third party itself. The dividing line between the two approaches is often difficult to maintain as they tend to merge into one another, depending upon the circumstances. One example of the good-office method is the role played by the US President in 1906 in concluding the Russian-Japanese War, or the function performed by the USSR in assisting in the peaceful settlement of the India-Pakistan dispute in 1965. The UN Secretary-General can sometimes play an important role by the exercise of his good offices. An example of this was provided in the situation relating to Afghanistan in 1988.

(3) *Inquiry*

The inquiry is a logical solution to adopt while differences of opinion on factual matters underlie a dispute between parties. Reputable observers always conduct it to ascertain precisely the facts in contention. Provisions for such inquiries were first elaborated in the 1899 Hague Conference as a possible alternative to arbitration. However, the technique is limited in that, it can only have relevance in the case of international disputes, involving neither the honor nor the vital interests of the parties, where the conflict centers around a genuine disagreement as to particular facts which can be resolved by recourse to an impartial and conscientious investigation. Therefore, the use of commissions of inquiry in accordance with the Hague Convention of 1907 proved in practice to be extremely rare. The value of inquiry within specified institutional frameworks, nevertheless, has been evident. Its use has increased within the United Nations generally and in specialized agencies, such as in human rights and public health protection.

(4) *Conciliation*

The conciliation involves a third-party investigation of the basis of the dispute and the submission of a report embodying suggestions for a settlement. It involves elements of both inquiry and mediation, and in fact, the process of conciliation emerged from treaties providing for permanent inquiry commissions. Conciliation reports are only proposals and do not constitute binding decisions. So, they are different from arbitration awards. Conciliation is extremely flexible and, by clarifying the facts and discussing proposals, may stimulate negotiations between the parties. The rules dealing with conciliation were elaborated in the 1928 General Act on the Pacific Settlement of International Disputes (revised in 1949). The conciliation procedure was used in the Iceland-Norway dispute over the continental shelf delimitation between Iceland and Jan Mayen island. The solution proposed by the Commission was for a joint development zone, an idea that would have been unlikely to come from a judicial body reaching a decision solely based on the legal rights of the parties.

3.2 Legal Method

(1) *Arbitration*

According to the American Bar Association, an arbitration is a process where disputing parties agree that one or several individuals can make a decision about the dispute after receiving evidence and hearing arguments. It is different from mediation because the neutral arbitrator has the authority to make decision on the dispute. The arbitration process is similar to trial in that the parties make opening Statements and present evidence to the arbitrator. Compared to traditional trials, arbitration can usually be completed more quickly and is less formal. Before conciliation was established, interstate arbitration had long been a part of the scene, having the same political provenance. The salience of arbitration increased considerably after the successful Alabama Claims arbitration of 1872 between the US and Great Britain. ① At this stage, arbitral tribunals were often invited by the parties to resort to "principles of justice and equity" and to propose extra-legal compromises. However, by the end of the 19th century, arbitration was primarily, if not exclusively, associated with a process of decision according to law, supported by appropriate procedural standards. The contrasts with judicial settlement (as it developed post-1922) are principally these: the agency of decision in arbitration would be designated "arbitral tribunal" or "umpire"; the tribunal consists of an odd number, usually with national representatives; the tribunal is usually created to deal with a particular dispute or class of disputes; and there is more flexibility than in a system of compulsory jurisdiction with a standing court. Due to this distinction, States see arbitration as a suitable mechanism for settling a certain class of dispute and indeed, of the cases referred to interstate arbitration, the majority have concerned territorial or quasi-territorial disputes. ②Brierly provides another explanation as to those basic issues that distinguish all sorts of arbitration from judicial settlement. First, the parties choose the arbitrators or how they are to be appointed; Second, the parties choose the applicable law; Third, enforcement may depend on resort to a regular national legal order and forms of judicial settlement.

(2) *The adjudicated or judicial settlement*

There is no sharp line between arbitration and judicial settlement: the latter category is applicable to any international tribunal settling disputes involving States following international law. Moreover, the permanent institutions developed historically from arbitral experience. As a result, it is

---

① Andrew Clapham (ed.), *Brierly's Law of Nations: An Introduction to the Role of International Law in International Relations*, 7th Ed., Oxford University Press, 2012,, pp. 410-416.

② See James Crawford (ed.), *Brownlie's Principles of Public International Law*, 8th Ed., Oxford University Press, 2012, , pp. 719-720.

now common to see the development of integrated systems of dispute resolution which include international "courts" of relatively formal jurisdiction and process, whilst reserving certain sui generis questions for arbitral tribunals convened under the procedures of the same system, for example, in the procedures of the WTO (the panel procedure).

The "World Court" is the label commonly applied to the PCIJ and the ICJ, the latter a new creation in 1945 but substantially a continuation of the earlier body. The Permanent Court began to function in 1922, benefiting from previous experience. *Brownlie's* points out clearly that the arbitration practice contributed to the development in two ways. Its positive influence shows in certain similarities between the Court and arbitral practice: the institution of national judges, the use of special jurisdictional agreements, the power to decide *ex aequo et bono*, and the application of some basic principles. E. g. , absent contrary agreement, an international tribunal may determine its jurisdiction. The negative influence was more decisive, since criticism of the Permanent Court of Arbitration, that it was not a standing court and could not develop jurisprudence.

A crucial issue for the creation of a standing international tribunal in which States may have confidence is judicial appointment. The Statute emphasizes the independence of judges once appointed. No judge may exercise any political or administrative function, engage in any other professional occupation, act as agent or counsel in any case, or participate in the decision of a case with which they have previously been connected in another capacity.

Besides the Court's contentious jurisdiction over disputes referred to it by States, the Court may be requested by the UN General Assembly or the Security Council "to give an advisory opinion on any legal question. " The ICJ has consistently treated this advisory jurisdiction as a judicial function, and it has assimilated the proceedings in most respects to those used in the contentious jurisdiction. Indeed in certain cases, the advisory opinion may actually resolve a dispute by decisively applying the law. Nevertheless, the

ICJ's advisory jurisdiction could invoke complicated consequences while the legal question submitted concerns concrete disputes between States; for example, the *Chagos Archipelago Case*.

4. Cases and Materials

Read the following cases and think about the questions:

(1) What is the difference between contentious cases and advisory cases?

(2) What are those conditions that the ICJ could establish advisory jurisdiction? How does the advisory case promote the development of international law?

(3) What are the shared idea and differences between those Statements submitted by China and US?

(4) Why do we support Argentinian for its claim over the disputed U.K.-controlled Malvinas Islands? Give some reasons based on the *Chagos Case* below.

4.1 *The Chagos Archipelago Case* [1]

(1) *Request from the UN General Assembly (para.1)*

The questions on which the advisory opinion of the Court has been

---

[1] See *Legal Consequences of the Separation of the Chagos Archipelago from Mauritius in 1965*, Advisory Opinion, ICJ Reports 2019, p. 95. In its Chagos Advisory Opinion, ICJ addressed two questions posed in a request from the UN General Assembly. First, had Mauritius' decolonization been completed when it gained independence in 1968, after the excision of the Chagos Archipelago? Second, what were the legal consequences flowing from the United Kingdom's continued administration of the Archipelago? It was thought that the Court might shy away from giving an Opinion in this case as, arguably, it concerned a bilateral sovereignty dispute that the United Kingdom had not agreed to have resolved by judicial decision. However, as it turned out, the Court delivered surprisingly robust responses to the questions posed. The Opinion—and the numerous Separate Opinions that accompanied it—offer a thorough re-evaluation of the customary international law concerning the right to self-determination in cases of decolonization. During the procedure, Thirty-one Member States of the United Nations and the African Union filed written Statements, and ten States and the African Union filed written comments on the written Statements. Ten States and the African Union subsequently presented written comments on these written Statements. Twenty one States and the African Union participated in the oral proceedings, which took place from 3 to 6 September 2018.

requested are set forth in resolution 71/292 adopted by the General Assembly of the United Nations (hereinafter the "General Assembly") on 22 June 2017. By a letter dated 23 June 2017 and received in the Registry on 28 June 2017, the Secretary-General of the United Nations officially communicated to the Court the decision taken by the General Assembly to submit these questions for an advisory opinion. Certified true copies of the English and French texts of the resolution were enclosed with the letter. The resolution reads as follows:

The General Assembly, ··· *Decides*, in accordance with Article 96 of the Charter of the United Nations, to request the International Court of Justice, pursuant to Article 65 of the Statute of the Court, to render an advisory opinion on the following questions:

(a) Was the process of decolonization of Mauritius lawfully completed when Mauritius was granted independence in 1968, following the separation of the Chagos Archipelago from Mauritius and having regard to international law, including obligations reflected in General Assembly resolutions 1514 (XV) of 14 December 1960, 2066 (XX) of 16 December 1965, 2232 (XXI) of 20 December 1966 and 2357 (XXII) of 19 December 1967?

(b) What are the consequences under international law, including obligations reflected in the above-mentioned resolutions, arising from the continued administration by the United Kingdom of Great Britain and Northern Ireland of the Chagos Archipelago, including with respect to the inability of Mauritius to implement a programme for the resettlement on the Chagos Archipelago of its nationals, in particular those of Chagossian origin?

(2) *Events Leading to the Adoption of The Request* (paras. 26-53)

The Chagos Archipelago consists of a number of islands and atolls. The largest island is Diego Garcia, located in the south-east of the archipelago. Between 1814 and 1965, the Chagos Archipelago was administered by the United Kingdom as a dependency of the colony of Mauritius. On 14 December 1960, the General Assembly adopted resolution 1514 (XV) entitled

"Declaration on the Granting of Independence to Colonial Countries and Peoples". On 27 November 1961, the General Assembly, by resolution 1654 (XVI), established the Committee of Twenty-Four, a special committee on decolonization, to monitor the implementation of resolution 1514 (XV).

In February 1964, discussions commenced between the United States of America and the United Kingdom regarding the use by the United States of certain British-owned islands in the Indian Ocean. The United States expressed an interest in establishing military facilities on the island of Diego Garcia. On 29 June 1964, the United Kingdom also commenced talks with the Premier of the colony of Mauritius regarding the detachment of the Chagos Archipelago from Mauritius. On 8 November 1965, by the British Indian Ocean Territory Order 1965, the United Kingdom established a new colony known as the British Indian Ocean Territory (hereinafter the "BIOT") consisting of the Chagos Archipelago, detached from Mauritius, and the Aldabra, Farquhar and Desroches islands, detached from Seychelles. On 16 December of the same year, the General Assembly adopted resolution 2066 (XX) on the "Question of Mauritius", in which it expressed deep concern about the detachment of certain islands from the territory of Mauritius for the purpose of establishing a military base and invited the "administering Power to take no action which would dismember the Territory of Mauritius and violate its territorial integrity".

On 20 December 1966, the General Assembly adopted resolution 2232 (XXI) on a number of territories including Mauritius. The resolution reiterated that "any attempt aimed at the partial or total disruption of the national unity and the territorial integrity of colonial Territories and the establishment of military bases and installations in these Territories is incompatible with the purposes and principles of the Charter of the United Nations and of General Assembly resolution 1514 (XV)".

The talks between the United Kingdom and the United States resulted in the conclusion on 30 December 1966 of the "Agreement concerning the

Availability for Defence Purposes of the British Indian Ocean Territory" and the conclusion of an Agreed Minute of the same date. Based on the Agreement, both States agreed that the Government of the United Kingdom would take any "administrative measures" necessary to ensure that their defence needs were met. The Agreed Minute provided that, among the administrative measures to be taken, was "resettling any inhabitants" of the islands.

On 15, 17 and 19 June 1967, the Committee of Twenty-Four examined the Report of Sub-Committee Ⅰ and adopted a resolution on Mauritius. In this resolution, the Committee "deplores the dismemberment of Mauritius and Seychelles by the administering Power which violates their territorial integrity, in contravention of General Assembly resolutions 2066 (ⅩⅩ) and 2232 (ⅩⅪ) and calls upon the administering Power to return to these Territories the islands detached therefrom".

Between 1967 and 1973, the entire population of the Chagos Archipelago was either prevented from returning or forcibly removed and prevented from returning by the United Kingdom. The main forcible removal of Diego Garcia's population took place in July and September 1971.

On 12 March 1968, Mauritius became an independent State and on 26 April 1968 was admitted to membership in the United Nations. Sir Seewoosagur Ramgoolam became the first Prime Minister of the Republic of Mauritius. Section 111, paragraph 1, of the 1968 Constitution of Mauritius, promulgated by the United Kingdom Government before independence on 4 March 1968, defined Mauritius as "the territories which immediately before 12th March 1968 constituted the colony of Mauritius". This definition did not include the Chagos Archipelago in the territory of Mauritius.

In July 1980, the Organisation of African Unity (hereinafter the "OAU") adopted resolution 99 (ⅩⅦ) (1980) in which it "demands" that Diego Garcia be "unconditionally returned to Mauritius". On 9 October 1980, the Mauritian Prime Minister, at the thirty-fifth session of the United Nations

General Assembly, stated that the BIOT should be disbanded and the territory restored to Mauritius as part of its natural heritage.

In July 2000, the OAU adopted a decision expressing its concern that the Chagos Archipelago was "excised by the colonial Power from Mauritius prior to its independence in violation of United Nations resolution 1514".

On 30 December 2016, the 50-year period covered by the 1966 Agreement came to an end; however, it was extended for a further period of twenty years, in accordance with its terms.

On 30 January 2017, the Assembly of the African Union adopted resolution AU/Res. 1 (XXVIII) on the Chagos Archipelago which resolved, among other things, to support Mauritius with a view to ensuring "the completion of the decolonization of the Republic of Mauritius".

(3) *Jurisdiction and Discretion (Paras. 54-91)*

When the Court is seised of a request for an advisory opinion, it must first consider whether it has jurisdiction to give the opinion requested and if so, whether there is any reason why the Court should, in the exercise of its discretion, decline to answer the request. The Court's jurisdiction to give an advisory opinion is based on Article 65, paragraph 1, of its Statute…

The Court then turns to the requirement in Article 96 of the Charter and Article 65 of its Statute that the advisory opinion must be on a "legal question". In the present proceedings, the first question put to the Court is whether the process of decolonization of Mauritius was lawfully completed having regard to international law when it was granted independence following the separation of the Chagos Archipelago. The second question relates to the consequences arising under international law from the continued administration by the United Kingdom of the Chagos Archipelago. The Court considers that a request from the General Assembly for an advisory opinion to examine a situation by reference to international law concerns a legal question. The Court therefore concludes that the request has been made in accordance with the Charter and that the two questions submitted to it are legal in character.

The Court accordingly has jurisdiction to give the advisory opinion requested by resolution 71/292 of the General Assembly.

Some participants in the present proceedings have argued that there are "compelling reasons" for the Court to exercise its discretion to decline to give the advisory opinion requested. Among the reasons raised by these participants are that, first, advisory proceedings are not suitable for determination of complex and disputed factual issues; secondly, the Court's response would not assist the General Assembly in the performance of its functions; thirdly, it would be inappropriate for the Court to re-examine a question already settled by the Arbitral Tribunal constituted under Annex Ⅶ of UNCLOS in the Arbitration regarding the Chagos Marine Protected Area; and fourthly, the questions asked in the present proceedings relate to a pending bilateral dispute between two States which have not consented to the settlement of that dispute by the Court.

Whether advisory proceedings are suitable for determination of complex and disputed factual issues? The Court observes that an abundance of material has been presented before it including a voluminous dossier from the United Nations. Moreover, many participants have submitted written Statements and written comments and made oral Statements which contain information relevant to answering the questions. Thirty-one States and the African Union filed written Statements, ten of those States and the African Union submitted written comments thereon, and twenty-two States and the African Union made oral Statements. The Court notes that information provided by participants includes the various official records from the 1960s, such as those from the United Kingdom concerning the detachment of the Chagos Archipelago and the accession of Mauritius to independence. The Court is therefore satisfied that there is in the present proceedings sufficient information on the facts before it for the Court to give the requested opinion. Accordingly, the Court cannot decline to answer the questions put to it.

Chapter Ⅳ Peaceful Settlement of Disputes 465

Whether the Court's response would assist the General Assembly in the performance of its functions? The Court considers that it is not for the Court itself to determine the usefulness of its response to the requesting organ. Rather, it should be left to the requesting organ, the General Assembly, to determine "whether it needs the opinion for the proper performance of its functions".

It follows that in the present proceedings the Court cannot decline to answer the questions posed to it by the General Assembly in resolution 71/292 on the ground that its opinion would not assist the General Assembly in the performance of its functions.

Whether it would be appropriate for the Court to re-examine a question allegedly settled by the Arbitral Tribunal constituted under UNCLOS Annex Ⅶ in the Arbitration regarding the Chagos Marine Protected Area? The Court recalls that its opinion "is given not to States, but to the organ which is entitled to request it". The Court observes that the principle of *res judicata* does not preclude it from rendering an advisory opinion. … In any event, the Court further notes that the issues that were determined by the Arbitral Tribunal in the Arbitration regarding the Chagos Marine Protected Area are not the same as those that are before the Court in these proceedings. It follows from the foregoing that the Court cannot decline to answer the questions on this ground.

Whether the questions asked relate to a pending dispute between two States, which have not consented to its settlement by the Court? The Court notes that the questions put to it by the General Assembly relate to the decolonization of Mauritius. The General Assembly has not sought the Court's opinion to resolve a territorial dispute between two States. Rather, the purpose of the request is for the General Assembly to receive the Court's assistance so that it may be guided in the discharge of its functions relating to the decolonization of Mauritius.

Moreover, the Court observes that there may be differences of views on legal questions in advisory proceedings. However, the fact that the Court may have to pronounce on legal issues on which divergent views have been expressed by Mauritius and the United Kingdom does not mean that, by replying to the request, the Court is dealing with a bilateral dispute. In these circumstances, the Court does not consider that to give the opinion requested would have the effect of circumventing the principle of consent by a State to the judicial settlement of its dispute with another State. The Court therefore cannot, in the exercise of its discretion, decline to give the opinion on that ground. In light of the foregoing, the Court concludes that there are no compelling reasons for it to decline to give the opinion requested by the General Assembly.

4.2 Declaration by Vice-President Xue

While in full agreement with the Advisory Opinion of the Court, Vice-President Xue (hereinafter "she") highlights some aspects with regard to the application of the non-circumvention principle in this case. She notes that the dispute between Mauritius and the United Kingdom concerning the issue of the Chagos Archipelago has been going on for decades, but the two States hold divergent views on the nature of the subject-matter of the issue. Whether this bilateral dispute constitutes a compelling reason for the Court to exercise its discretional power to decline to give a reply to the questions put to it by the General Assembly is one of the core issues that was intensely debated in the proceedings.

She recalls the Court's jurisprudence on the fundamental importance of the principle of consent, it considers that there is a compelling reason to decline to give an advisory opinion, if "to give a reply would have the effect of circumventing the principle that a State is not obligated to allow its disputes to be submitted to judicial settlement without its consent". This non-circumvention principle equally applies to the present proceedings.

However, the fact of a pending bilateral dispute, by itself, is not considered a compelling reason for the Court to decline to give an advisory opinion. What is decisive is the object and nature of the request. In light of its consistent jurisprudence, the Court has to examine whether the object of the request is for the General Assembly to "obtain enlightenment as to the course of action it should take", or to assist the peaceful settlement of the dispute, and whether the legal controversy arose during the proceedings of the General Assembly and in relation to matters with which it was dealing, or arose independently in bilateral relations.

The object of the Request is not to resolve a territorial dispute between Mauritius and the United Kingdom, but to assist the General Assembly in the discharge of its functions relating to the decolonization of Mauritius. It therefore does not consider that to give the requested opinion would not have the effect of circumventing the principle of consent.

First of all, the scope of Question (a) put to the Court by the General Assembly is specifically defined. The Court is requested to determine, at the particular time when Mauritius was granted independence, whether the decolonization process of Mauritius was lawfully completed. The issue of the Chagos Archipelago has to be examined on the basis of the facts and the law as existed at that time and against the historical background of the decolonization of Mauritius.

The evidence submitted to the Court demonstrates that the detachment of the Chagos Archipelago by the United Kingdom was not simply the result of a normal administrative restructuring of a colony by the administering Power, but part of a defensive strategy particularly designed in view of the prospective independence of the colonial Territories in the western Indian Ocean. In other words, the very root cause of the separation of the Chagos Archipelago lies in the decolonization of Mauritius.

Whether the "consent" of Mauritius' Council of Ministers, which was still under the authority of the administering Power, can be regarded as representing the free and genuine will of the people of Mauritius is a crucial issue that the Court has to determine in accordance with the principle of self-determination under international law, as it has a direct bearing on Question (a).

She observes that both the United Kingdom itself and the United Nations treated the detachment of the Chagos Archipelago as a matter of decolonization rather than a territorial issue. The archives of the Foreign Office of the United Kingdom reveal that at the time when the detachment plan was being contemplated, the United Kingdom officials were aware, and even acknowledged, that by detaching the Chagos Archipelago and other islands to set up the British Indian Ocean Territory, the United Kingdom was actually creating a new colony.

From its inception, the plan to dismember the colonial territories in the western Indian Ocean gave rise to serious concern to the United Nations Special Committee on Decolonization. Resolution 2066 (XX) adopted by the General Assembly on 16 December 1965 was a direct response to the action taken by the United Kingdom. Despite the repeated calling from the General Assembly, the construction of the military base on Diego Garcia unfortunately went ahead as planned. Although Mauritius was eventually taken off the list of non-self-governing territories after its independence, the deep concern expressed by the General Assembly was left unaddressed. It is in this frame of reference that the Court is requested to consider the questions put to it by the General Assembly.

In characterizing the issue between Mauritius and itself as a bilateral dispute concerning the sovereignty over the Chagos Archipelago, the United Kingdom claims that the dispute between the two States did not arise until 1980. This claim apparently takes the issue of the Chagos Archipelago out of its historical context.

In her view, the fact that Mauritius raised the issue in the United Nations in 1980 does not necessarily mean that a bilateral dispute concerning the sovereignty over the Chagos Archipelago arose from that time. On 9

October 1980, the Mauritian Prime Minister' at the thirty-fifth session of the General Assembly' caled on the United Kingdom to disband the BIOT and return the Archipelago to Mauritius as "its natural heritage". This intervention indicates that the genuine issue between the two States is not about territorial sovereignty, but essentially bears on the applicability of the terms of the detachment of the Chagos Archipelago and its consequential effect on the decolonization process of Mauritius.

Lastly, She considers it necessary to give some further consideration to the claim that the issue of the Chagos Archipelago had not been put on the agenda of the General Assembly for nearly five decades and, meanwhile, Mauritius had resorted to bilateral channels and third-party mechanisms for settlement with the United Kingdom.

She takes the view that as an independent sovereign State, Mauritius has the right to raise the issue with the United Kingdom through the means it sees fit. This freedom of choice of means is inherently embraced in the principle of sovereignty and the right to self-determination. Equally important, so long as decolonization remains incomplete, the General Assembly's mandate under the Charter of the United Nations on matters concerning decolonization has no temporal limitation.

She emphasizes that the right to self-determination is one of the fundamental principles of international law that was well established during the decolonization movement after the Second World War. The paramount importance of the principle of self-determination is reflected in its *erga omnes* character in the sense that it not only confers a right on the peoples of all non-self-governing territories to self-determination, but also imposes an obligation on all States to see to it that this right is fully respected. She States that as an exercise of its substantive right, Mauritius' endeavours to resolve the issue of the Chagos Archipelago with the United Kingdomthrough bilateral and third-party procedures do not by themselves change the nature of the issue as a matter of decolonization, nor do they deprive the General Assembly of its mandate on decolonization under the Charter of the United Nations. ···

4.3　Written Statement of the People's Republic of China①

3. When the General Assembly voted on the draft resolution that has now become resolution 71/292, China abstained in the voting and made an explanatory statement, reiterating "China's firm support for the decolonization process and its understanding of the position of Mauritius on the question of decolonization". ···

4. China would like to further elaborate its positions on the international law issues involved in this case···

5. Decolonization has been an important function of the United Nations. Article 1 of the Charter of the United Nations at the outset declares that one of the purposes of the United Nations is "to develop friendly relations among nations based on respect for the principle of equal rights and self-determination of peoples···".

The relevant provisions and institutional arrangements stipulated in Chapter Ⅸ, Chapter Ⅺ, Chapter Ⅻ, Chapter ⅩⅢ ··· have ensured progress in promoting the self-determination of peoples and the process of decolonization after World War Ⅱ. As the Chinese delegation pointed out on 6 October 2003 at the Special Political and Decolonization Committee of the 58th Session of the General Assembly, "it has remained a cardinal goal in the endeavour made by the United Nations to help the colonial countries and peoples to exercise their right to self-determination and strive for independence".

6. The principle of self-determination of peoples has gradually crystallized as a principle of international law in the course of the decolonization movement. A large number of countries in Asia, Africa and

---

① See ICJ, Legal Consequences of the Separation of the Chagos Archipelago from Mauritius in 1965 (Request for Advisory Opinion), Written Statement of the People's Republic of China, 1 March 2018, https://www.icj-cij.org/public/files/case-related/169/169-20180301-WRI-03-00-EN.pdf, last visited on Jan. 8, 2022.

Latin America, which were under colonial rule or foreign occupation at the end of World War Ⅱ, have since exercised their right to self-determination and declared independence. This right has been accepted by States as an inalienable right conferred by international law upon peoples under colonial domination or foreign occupation. ⋯

7. To supplement resolution 1514 (XV), the General Assembly on 15 December 1960 adopted resolution 1541 (XV), "Principles Which Should Guide Members in Determining Whether or Not an Obligation Exists to Transmit the Information Called for Under Article 73 e of the Charter", clarifying the international obligation of the Administering Members to transmit information in respect of territories whose peoples have not yet attained a full measure of self-government. It provides the modes, and sets forth objective and operable criteria, for the peoples of the non-self-governing territories to exercise the right to self-determination.

10. In the Western Sahara advisory opinion, the Court reiterated that the principle of self-determination is applicable to non-self-governing territories and observed that the principle of self-determination was "defined as the need to pay regard to the freely expressed will of peoples", and that "the right of self-determination leaves the General Assembly a measure of discretion with respect to the forms and procedures by which that right is to be realized".

11. Furthermore, in its judgment in *East Timor* (*Portugal v. Australia*) the Court held that the assertion that the right of peoples to self-determination "has an *erga omnes* character" is "irreproachable", and "the principle of self-determination of peoples has been recognized by the United Nations Charter and in the jurisprudence of the Court; it is one of the essential principles of contemporary international law". ⋯

12. Once a victim of aggression and oppression under imperialism and colonialism, China sympathizes with the peoples under colonial rule and knows full well their sufferings. ⋯ On the international stage, China firmly supports the efforts made by the United Nations to help colonial countries and

peoples exercise their right to self-determination and achieve independence, takes an active part in the United Nations' work of decolonization, and gives strong support, both politically and economically, to colonial countries and peoples, including African countries.

13. Based on the above-mentioned position, China has fully understood and supported Mauritius' legitimate quest for decolonization. ⋯

15. Under international law, every State is free to choose the means of dispute settlement. The jurisdiction of any international dispute settlement mechanism over a dispute between States depends on the prior consent of the parties to the dispute. This is known as the principle of consent, born of the fundamental principle of sovereign equality under international law, enshrined in the Charter of the United Nations and the Statute of the Court, and confirmed in numerous international instruments, including the aforementioned Declaration on Principles of International Law concerning Friendly Relations and Co-operation among States in accordance with the Charter of the United Nations, and the Manila Declaration on the Peaceful Settlement of International Disputes as contained in General Assembly resolution 37/10 of 15 November 1982.

17. In a series of advisory opinions touching upon bilateral disputes, the Court always took a cautious attitude and elaborated why giving an advisory opinion would not entail a breach of the principle of consent. These reasons include among others: that the issue was addressed as a "situation" rather than a "dispute" in the dealings of the United Nations organ that made a request; that the request did not touch the merits of these disputes, giving an opinion would not compromise the legal position of the parties to these disputes, or the opinion was solely concerned with the applicability of certain rules of international law, rather than the application of these rules; and that the questions put to the Court "arose during the proceedings of the General Assembly", "did not arise independently in bilateral relations" and were "located in a broader frame of reference than the settlement of a particular

dispute".

18. China hopes that the Court will pay due regard to the special circumstances in this case and strictly observe the relevant provisions of the Charter of the United Nations and the Statute of the Court in handling the case. While providing legal guidance to assist the General Assembly in fulfilling its function of decolonization, the Court should continue to uphold and respect the principle of consent when a purely bilateral dispute is involved, thus to ensure that its opinion should not have the effect of circumventing or prejudicing this principle.

4.4 Written Statement of the United States[①]

1.2 The United States voted against the General Assembly's referral resolution because it concerns a bilateral territorial dispute between Mauritius and the United Kingdom concerning sovereignty over the Chagos Archipelago. The United States believes that this case raises serious questions about the propriety of utilizing the Court's advisory jurisdiction in light of the fundamental principle that a State is not obliged to allow its disputes to be submitted for judicial settlement without its consent. It is clear that the United Kingdom, one of the parties to this bilateral dispute, has not given that consent.

2.2 ···the present request for an advisory opinion concerns the longstanding territorial dispute between the two States, and in fact represents an attempt to enlist the Court to adjudicate the same sovereignty claim Mauritius has been pressing in other fora.

2.4 The United States explained in the General Assembly debate: "By pursuing the draft resolution, Mauritius seeks to invoke the Court's advisory

---

① See ICJ, Request by the United Nations General Assembly for an Advisory Opinion on the "Legal consequences of the separation of the Chagos Archipelago from Mauritius in 1965", March 1 2018, https://www.icj-cij.org/public/files/case-related/169/169-20180301-WRI-01-00-EN.pdf, last visited on Jan. 8, 2022.

opinion jurisdiction not for its intended purpose but rather to circumvent the Court's lack of contentious jurisdiction over this purely bilateral matter ···. While Mauritius is attempting to frame this as an issue of decolonization relevant to the international community, at its heart it is a bilateral territorial dispute, and the United Kingdom has not consented to the jurisdiction of the International Court of Justice ···. The advisory function of the International Court of Justice was not intended to settle disputes between States."

2.7 In 1966, the United States entered into a bilateral agreement with the United Kingdom regarding the establishment of a joint U.S.-U.K. military facility in BIOT. The 1966 Agreement remains in force today, as amended. Over the years, the United States and United Kingdom have also concluded supplemental agreements. The 1966 Agreement and supplemental agreements have been registered with the United Nations Treaty Office pursuant to Article 102 of the U.N. Charter, and published in the U.N. Treaty Series.

2.8 In 1968, Mauritius gained its independence; its territorial boundaries did not include the Chagos Archipelago. Over a decade later, Mauritius began asserting a claim to sovereignty over the Chagos Archipelago, including in its annual Statements at the opening of the General Assembly.

2.9 Given the joint military facility, Mauritius has raised its territorial claim with the United States on a number of occasions. The United States has been clear in these discussions that the United Kingdom is sovereign over the BIOT. That said, the United States greatly values its warm relations with both Mauritius and the United Kingdom, and has encouraged the two parties to the dispute to resolve the matter on a bilateral basis.

2.10 Prior to this request for an advisory opinion, Mauritius has also pursued its sovereignty claim against the United Kingdom through legal avenues, including by seeking to have the claim adjudicated as a contentious matter with the United Kingdom. Of particular note, Mauritius has sought to bring a contentious dispute against the United Kingdom before this Court. The United Kingdom declined to consent to that procedure for resolving its dispute, preferring instead to engage in direct, bilateral negotiations.

2.17 As such, it is clear that the questions are designed to go directly to issues that are central to the bilateral territorial dispute concerning sovereignty.

5. References and Recommended Reading Materials

(1) J. Michael Greig and Paul F. Diehl, *International Mediation*, Cambridge University Press, 2012.

(2) John Collier and Vaughan Lowe, *The Settlement of Disputes in International Law: Institutions and Procedures*, Oxford University Press, 1999.

(3) Duncan French, Matthew Saul and Nigel White (eds.), *International Law and Dispute Settlement: New Problems and Techniques*, Oxford University Press, 2010.

(4) J. G. Merrills, *International Dispute Settlement*, 5th Ed., Cambridge University Press, 2011.

Chapter XV International Human Rights and Humanitarian Law

1. Introduction

The beginnings of human rights law and humanitarian law are somewhat disjointed. Human rights law had a start in humanitarian law strongly associated with international law governing the justification of wars (*jus ad bellum*) and the conduct of war (*jus in bello*). In the 19th century, the integration of international human rights law and international humanitarian law emerged. For example, States began to adopt the practice of outlawing the trafficking of slaves—a human rights concern. In 1868, the Saint Petersburg Declaration condemned the use of "*dum-dum*" bullets in war, introducing the modern international humanitarian law on which modern international human rights law would be built. Thanks to the international law governing the treatment of aliens and national minorities, the international human rights law began to show its uniqueness. During the same time, some important humanitarian treaties were adopted, such as the 1929 Geneva Convention governing the conduct of war, including the protection of civilians and prisoners of war.

There is a degree of overlap between these two bodies of rules. In the *Cyprus v. Turkey Case*, the European Court of Human Rights (ECHR) declared that in belligerent operations a State was bound to respect not only the humanitarian law laid down in the Geneva Conventions but also fundamental human rights. ① A question that has been raised is whether international humanitarian law is *lex specialis* to the general law or *lex generalis* of international human rights law, thus displacing the latter within its own sphere. The relationship between the principles of international humanitarian law and those of human rights law is further illustrated in the cases of detention of civilians by the forces of one State. ICJ in the case of *Croatia v. Serbia* concluded that, while it would not rule in general and abstract terms on the relationship between the Genocide Convention and international humanitarian law, the rules of international humanitarian law might be relevant to decide whether the acts alleged by the parties constituted genocide within the meaning of Article Ⅱ of the Genocide Convention. ②

This Chapter is to make a brief introduction of the two dynamic areas. Part 2, preliminarily, introduces some important sources of law shared by international human rights law and humanitarian law, such as The Hague Conventions and key provisions constituting the bones of the modern international human rights law and humanitarian law. Part 3 is about the conceptual discussion on some important terminologies underpinning the theories of international human rights law and humanitarian law and some important organizations responsible for the protection of human rights during peace and armed conflicts. And Part 4 will provide some cases on how the mechanisms formulated by the conventions and organizations operate in practice.

---

① See European Court of Human Rights, *Cyprus v. Turkey*, Applieation No. 25781/94, 10 May 2001.

② See *Application of the Convention on the Prevention and Punishment of the Crime of Genocide (Croatia v. Serbia)*, Judgment, ICJ Reports 2015, p. 3, para. 151.

2. Preliminary Reading and Assignment

2.1 Conventions on International Humanitarian Law

(1) 1868 Saint Petersburg Declaration[①]

……

That the progress of civilization should have the effect of alleviating as much as possible the calamities of war; That the only legitimate object which States should endeavour to accomplish during war is to weaken the military forces of the enemy; That for this purpose it is sufficient to disable the greatest possible number of men; That this object would be exceeded by the employment of arms which uselessly aggravate the sufferings of disabled men, or render their death inevitable; That the employment of such arms would, therefore, be contrary to the laws of humanity;

The Contracting Parties engage mutually to renounce, in case of war among themselves, the employment by their military or naval troops of any projectile of a weight below 400 grammes, which is either explosive or charged with fulminating or inflammable substances.

……

(2) Hague Conventions[②]

Convention with Respect to the Laws and Customs of War on Land (Hague, II) (1899)

……

In view of the High Contracting Parties, these provisions, the wording of

---

[①] Declaration Renouncing the Use, in Time of War, of certain Explosive Projectiles Saint Petersburg, 29 November/11 December 1868, http://www.weaponslaw.org/assets/downloads/1868_St_Petersburg_Declaration.pdf, last visited on Jan. 8, 2022.

[②] Hague Conventions of 1899 consisted of three main treaties and three additional declarations entered during the First Hague Conference. The Second Hague Conference, in 1907, signed the 1907 Hague Conventions consisted of thirteen treaties—of which twelve were ratified and entered into force—and one declaration. Among these documents, the most relevant is probably the Convention with respect to the Laws and Customs of War on Land.

Chapter XV International Human Rights and Humanitarian Law   479

which has been inspired by the desire to diminish the evils of war so far as military necessities permit, are destined to serve as general rules of conduct for belligerents in their relations with each other and with populations. ⋯

It could not be intended by the High Contracting Parties that the cases not provided for should, for want of a written provision, be left to the arbitrary judgment of the military commanders.

Until a more complete code of the laws of war is issued, the High Contracting Parties think it right to declare that in cases not included in the Regulations adopted by them, populations and belligerents remain under the protection and empire of the principles of international law, as they result from the usages established between civilized nations, from the laws of humanity, and the requirements of the public conscience. Who, after communication of their full powers, found in good and due form, have agreed on the following:

……

Annex to the Convention: Regulations Respecting the Laws and Customs of War on Land

Article 22

The right of belligerents to adopt means of injuring the enemy is not unlimited.

Article 23

Besides the prohibitions provided by special Conventions, it is especially prohibited: (a) To employ poison or poisoned arms; (b) To kill or wound treacherously individuals belonging to the hostile nation or army; (c) To kill or wound an enemy who, having laid down arms, or having no longer means of defence, has surrendered at discretion; (d) To declare that no quarter will be given; (e) To employ arms, projectiles, or material of a nature to cause superfluous injury; (f) To make improper use of a flag of truce, the national flag or military ensigns and uniform of the enemy, as well as the distinctive badges of *the Geneva Convention*; (g) To destroy or seize the enemy's property, unless such destruction or seizure be imperatively demanded by the necessities of war.

Article 60

The Geneva Convention applies to sick and wounded interned in neutral territory.

(3) *Geneva Conventions*

The First Geneva Convention for the Amelioration of the Condition of the Wounded in Armies in the Field, held on 22 August 1864, is the first of four treaties of the Geneva Conventions. It defines "the basis on which rest the rules of international law for the protection of the victims of armed conflicts". After the first treaty was adopted in 1864, it was significantly revised and replaced in 1906, 1929, and finally 1949.

Convention for the Amelioration of the Condition of the Wounded in Armies in the Field (The 1864 Geneva Convention)

Article 1

Ambulances and military hospitals shall be recognized as neutral, and as such, protected and respected by the belligerents as long as they accommodate wounded and sick.

Neutrality shall end if the said ambulances or hospitals should be held by a military force.

Article 6

Wounded or sick combatants, to whatever nation they may belong, shall be collected and cared for.

Commanders-in-Chief may hand over immediately to the enemy outposts enemy combatants wounded during an engagement, when circumstances allow and subject to the agreement of both parties.

Those who, after their recovery, are recognized as being unfit for further service, shall be repatriated.

The others may likewise be sent back, on condition that they shall not again, for the duration of hostilities, take up arms.

Evacuation parties, and the personnel conducting them, shall be considered as being absolutely neutral.

Convention Relative to the Treatment of Prisoners of War (The 1929 Geneva Convention)

(List of Contracting Parties)

Recognizing that, in the extreme event of a war, it will be the duty of every Power, to mitigate as far as possible, the inevitable rigours thereof and to alleviate the condition of prisoners of war; Being desirous of developing the principles which have inspired the international conventions of The Hague, in particular the Convention concerning the Laws and Customs of War and the Regulations thereunto annexed. ···have agreed as follows.

······

Article 2

Prisoners of war are in the power of the hostile Government, but not of the individuals or formation which captured them.

They shall at all times be humanely treated and protected, particularly against acts of violence, from insults and from public curiosity.

Measures of reprisal against them are forbidden.

Article 3

Prisoners of war are entitled to respect for their persons and honour. Women shall be treated with all consideration due to their sex.

Prisoners retain their full civil capacity.

Article 4

The detaining Power is required to provide for the maintenance of prisoners of war in its charge.

Differences of treatment between prisoners are permissible only if such differences are based on the military rank, the State of physical or mental health, the professional abilities, or the sex of those who benefit from them.

Article 16

Prisoners of war shall be permitted complete freedom in the performance of their religious duties, including attendance at the services of their faith, on the sole condition that they comply with the routine and police regulations prescribed by the military authorities.

Ministers of religion, who are prisoners of war, whatever may be their denomination, shall be allowed freely to minister to their co-religionists.

Article 45

Prisoners of war shall be subject to the laws, regulations and orders in force in the armed forces of the detaining Power.

Any act of insubordination shall render them liable to the measures prescribed by such laws, regulations, and orders, except as otherwise provided in this Chapter.

Article 61

No prisoner of war shall be sentenced without being given the opportunity to defend himself.

No prisoner shall be compelled to admit that he is guilty of the offence of which he is accused.

......

(4) The 1949 Geneva Conventions and Additional Protocols[①]
Convention (Ⅰ) for the Amelioration of the Condition of the Wounded and Sick in Armed Forces in the Field

......

Article 3

In the case of armed conflict not of an international character occurring in

---

[①] The 1949 Geneva Conventions comprise four treaties, and three additional protocols, that establish the standards of international law for humanitarian treatment in war. They were negotiated in the aftermath of the Second World War (1939-1945), which updated the terms of the 1929 treaties, and added two new conventions. As ICRC explains, "The Geneva Conventions and their Additional Protocols are at the core of international humanitarian law, the body of international law that regulates the conduct of armed conflict and seeks to limit its effects. They specifically protect people who are not taking part in the hostilities (civilians, health workers and aid workers) and those who are no longer participating in the hostilities, such as wounded, sick and shipwrecked soldiers and prisoners of war. The Conventions and their Protocols call for measures to be taken to prevent or put an end to all breaches."

the territory of one of the High Contracting Parties, each Party to the conflict shall be bound to apply, as a minimum, the following provisions:

(1) Persons taking no active part in the hostilities, including members of armed forces who have laid down their arms and those placed *hors de combat* by sickness, wounds, detention, or any other cause, shall in all circumstances be treated humanely, without any adverse distinction founded on race, colour, religion or faith, sex, birth or wealth, or any other similar criteria.

To this end, the following acts are and shall remain prohibited at any time and in any place whatsoever with respect to the above-mentioned persons: (a) violence to life and person, in particular murder of all kinds, mutilation, cruel treatment and torture; (b) taking of hostages; (c) outrages upon personal dignity, in particular humiliating and degrading treatment; (d) the passing of sentences and the carrying out of executions without previous judgment pronounced by a regularly constituted court, affording all the judicial guarantees which are recognized as indispensable by civilized peoples.

(2) The wounded and sick shall be collected and cared for.

An impartial humanitarian body, such as the International Committee of the Red Cross, may offer its services to the Parties to the conflict.

The Parties to the conflict should further endeavour to bring into force, by means of special agreements, all or part of the other provisions of the present Convention.

The application of the preceding provisions shall not affect the legal status of the Parties to the conflict.

Article 9

The provisions of the present Convention constitute no obstacle to the humanitarian activities which the International Committee of the Red Cross or any other impartial humanitarian organization may, subject to the consent of the Parties to the conflict concerned, undertake for the protection of wounded and sick, medical personnel and chaplains, and for their relief.

Article 13

The Present Convention shall apply to the wounded and sick belonging to the following categories:

(1) Members of the armed forces of a Party to the conflict as well as members of militias or volunteer corps forming part of such armed forces.

(2) Members of other militias and members of other volunteer corps, including those of organized resistance movements, belonging to a Party to the conflict and operating in or outside their own territory, even if this territory is occupied, provided that such militias or volunteer corps, including such organized resistance movements, fulfil the following conditions;…

(3) Members of regular armed forces who profess allegiance to a Government or an authority not recognized by the Detaining Power.

(4) Persons who accompany the armed forces without actually being members thereof, such as civilian members of military aircraft crews, war correspondents, supply contractors, members of labour units or of services responsible for the welfare of the armed forces, provided that they have received authorization from the armed forces which they accompany.

(5) Members of crews including masters, pilots and apprentices of the merchant marine and the crews of civil aircraft of the Parties to the conflict, who do not benefit by more favourable treatment under any other provisions in international law.

(6) Inhabitants of a non-occupied territory who, on the approach of the enemy, spontaneously take up arms to resist the invading forces, without having had time to form themselves into regular armed units, provided they carry arms openly and respect the laws and customs of war.

……

Convention (II) for the Amelioration of the Condition of Wounded, Sick and Shipwrecked Members of Armed Forces at Sea

......

Convention (III) relative to the Treatment of Prisoners of War[①]

......

Convention (IV) relative to the Protection of Civilian Persons in Time of War[②]

......

Article 3

In the case of armed conflict not of an international character occurring in the territory of one of the High Contracting Parties, each Party to the conflict shall be bound to apply, as a minimum, the following provisions:

(1) Persons taking no active part in the hostilities, including members of armed forces who have laid down their arms and those placed *hors de combat* by sickness, wounds, detention, or any other cause, shall in all circumstances be treated humanely, without any adverse distinction founded on race, colour, religion or faith, sex, birth or wealth, or any other similar criteria. ...

(2) The wounded and sick shall be collected and cared for.

[①] The present Convention replaced the Prisoners of War Convention of 1929. It contains 143 Articles whereas the 1929 Convention had only 97. It became necessary to revise the 1929 Convention on a number of points owing to the changes that had occurred in the conduct of warfare and the consequences thereof, as well as in the living condition of peoples. Experience had shown that the daily life of prisoners depended specifically on the interpretation given to the general regulations. Consequently, certain regulations were given a more explicit form which was lacking in the preceding provisions.

[②] As the ICRC explains: "The Geneva Conventions which were adopted before 1949 were concerned with combatants only, not with civilians." The Convention adopted in 1949 takes account of the experiences of World War II. It contains a rather short part concerning the general protection of populations against certain consequences of war, leaving aside the problem of the limitation of the use of weapons. The great bulk of the Convention (Part III—Articles 27-141) puts forth the regulations governing the status and treatment of protected persons; these provisions distinguish between the situation of foreigners on the territory of one of the parties to the conflict and that of civilians in occupied territory. The Convention does not invalidate the provisions of the Hague Regulations of 1907 on the same subjects but is supplementary to them.

An impartial humanitarian body, such as the International Committee of the Red Cross, may offer its services to the Parties to the conflict.

The Parties to the conflict should further endeavour to bring into force, by means of special agreements, all or part of the other provisions of the present Convention.

The application of the preceding provisions shall not affect the legal status of the Parties to the conflict.

······

Protocol Additional to the Geneva Conventions of 12 August 1949, and relating to the Protection of Victims of International Armed Conflicts (Protocol Ⅰ)

······

Article 1　General principles and scope of application

The High Contracting Parties undertake to respect and to ensure respect for this Protocol in all circumstances.

In cases not covered by this Protocol or by other international agreements, civilians and combatants remain under the protection and authority of the principles of international law derived from established custom, from the principles of humanity and from the dictates of public conscience.

This Protocol, which supplements the Geneva Conventions of 12 August 1949 for the protection of war victims, shall apply in the situations referred to in Article 2 common to those Conventions.

The situations referred to in the preceding paragraph include armed conflicts in which peoples are fighting against colonial domination and alien occupation and against racist regimes in the exercise of their right of self-determination, as enshrined in the Charter of the United Nations and the Declaration on Principles of International Law concerning Friendly Relations and Co-operation among States in accordance with the Charter of the United Nations.

······

Protocol Additional to the Geneva Conventions of 12 August 1949, and relating to the Protection of Victims of Non-International Armed Conflicts (Protocol II)

......

Article 1 Material field of application

This Protocol, which develops and supplements Article 3 common to the Geneva Conventions of 12 August 1949 without modifying its existing conditions of applications, shall apply to all armed conflicts which are not covered by Article 1 of the Protocol Additional to the Geneva Conventions of 12 August 1949, and relating to the Protection of Victims of International Armed Conflicts (Protocol I) and which take place in the territory of a High Contracting Party between its armed forces and dissident armed forces or other organized armed groups which, under responsible command, exercise such control over a part of its territory as to enable them to carry out sustained and concerted military operations and to implement this Protocol.

This Protocol shall not apply to situations of internal disturbances and tensions, such as riots, isolated and sporadic acts of violence and other acts of a similar nature, as not being armed conflicts.

Article 2 Personal field of application

This Protocol shall be applied without any adverse distinction founded on race, colour, sex, language, religion or belief, political or other opinion, national or social origin, wealth, birth or other status, or on any other similar criteria (hereinafter referred to as "adverse distinction") to all persons affected by an armed conflict as defined in Article 1.

At the end of the armed conflict, all the persons who have been deprived of their liberty or whose liberty has been restricted for reasons related to such conflict, as well as those deprived of their liberty or whose liberty is restricted after the conflict for the same reasons, shall enjoy the protection of Articles 5 and 6 until the end of such deprivation or restriction of liberty.

Article 3 Non-intervention

Nothing in this Protocol shall be invoked for the purpose of affecting the sovereignty of a State or the responsibility of the government, by all legitimate means, to maintain or re-establish law and order in the State or to defend the national unity and territorial integrity of the State.

Nothing in this Protocol shall be invoked as a justification for intervening, directly or indirectly, for any reason whatever, in the armed conflict or in the internal or external affairs of the High Contracting Party in the territory of which that conflict occurs.

......

2.2 Conventions on International Right Law

(1) *United Nations Universal Declaration of Human Rights 1948*

Preamble

Whereas recognition of the inherent dignity and of the equal and inalienable rights of all members of the human family is the foundation of freedom, justice and peace in the world,…

Now, therefore, The General Assembly, Proclaims this Universal Declaration of Human Rights as a common standard of achievement for all peoples and all nations, to the end that every individual and every organ of society, keeping this Declaration constantly in mind, shall strive by teaching and education to promote respect for these rights and freedoms and by progressive measures, national and international, to secure their universal and effective recognition and observance, both among the peoples of Member States themselves and among the peoples of territories under their jurisdiction.

......

(2) *Covenants building on the Universal Declaration of Human Rights*

There are 9 core international human rights instruments (see the table below). Each of these instruments has established a committee of experts to monitor implementation of the treaty provisions by its States parties. Some of the treaties are supplemented by optional protocols dealing with specific concerns whereas.

Table 1 The Core International Human Rights Instruments

Conventions	Date	Monitoring Body
International Convention on the Elimination of All Forms of Racial Discrimination (ICERD)	21 Dec. 1965	The Committee on the Elimination of Racial Discrimination (CERD)
International Covenant on Civil and Political Rights (ICCPR)	16 Dec. 1966	The Human Rights Committee (HRC)
International Covenant on Economic, Social and Cultural Rights (ICESCR)	16 Dec. 1966	The Committee on Economic, Social and Cultural Rights (CESCR)
Convention on the Elimination of All Forms of Discrimination Against Women (CEDAW)	18 Dec. 1979	The Committee on the Elimination of Discrimination Against Women (CEDAW)
Convention Against Torture and Other Cruel, Inhuman or Degrading Treatment or Punishment (CAT)	10 Dec. 1984	The Committee Against Torture (CAT)
Convention on the Rights of the Child (CRC)	20 Nov. 1989	The Committee on the Rights of the Child (CRC)
International Convention on the Protection of the Rights of All Migrant Workers and Members of Their Families (ICRMW)	18 Dec. 1990	The Committee on Migrant Workers (CMW)
International Convention for the Protection of All Persons from Enforced Disappearance (CPED)	20 Dec. 2006	The Committee on Enforced Disappearances (CED)
Convention on the Rights of Persons with Disabilities (CRPD)	13 Dec. 2006	The Committee on the Rights of Persons with Disabilities (CRPD)

Selected Articles from ICCPR

Article 1

All peoples have the right of self-determination. By virtue of that right they freely determine their political status and freely pursue their economic, social and cultural development.

All peoples may, for their own ends, freely dispose of their natural wealth and resources without prejudice to any obligations arising out of international economic co-operation, based upon the principle of mutual benefit, and international law. In no case may a people be deprived of its own means of subsistence.

The States Parties to the present Covenant, including those having responsibility for the administration of Non-Self-Governing and Trust Territories, shall promote the realization of the right of self-determination, and shall respect that right, in conformity with the provisions of the Charter of the United Nations.

Article 2

Each State Party to the present Covenant undertakes to respect and to ensure to all individuals within its territory and subject to its jurisdiction the rights recognized in the present Covenant, without distinction of any kind, such as race, colour, sex, language, religion, political or other opinion, national or social origin, property, birth or other status.

Where not already provided for by existing legislative or other measures, each State Party to the present Covenant undertakes to take the necessary steps, in accordance with its constitutional processes and with the provisions of the present Covenant, to adopt such laws or other measures as may be necessary to give effect to the rights recognized in the present Covenant.

Each State Party to the present Covenant undertakes:

(a) To ensure that any person whose rights or freedoms as herein recognized are violated shall have an effective remedy, notwithstanding that the violation has been committed by persons acting in an official capacity;

(b) To ensure that any person claiming such a remedy shall have his right thereto determined by competent judicial, administrative or legislative authorities, or by any other competent authority provided for by the legal system of the State, and to develop the possibilities of judicial remedy;

(c) To ensure that the competent authorities shall enforce such remedies when granted.

......

2.3 Discussions and Assignments

(1) Retreat the conventions on international humanitarian law listed above and find out: what is the connection between human rights law and humanitarian law? What is the key difference between them?

(2) Check the website of ICRC and find the key operations undertaken by it, and make a 5-10 minutes speech about its function in English.

3. Terminologies and Discussions

3.1 International Human Rights and Humanitarian Law

It is clear, of course, that both international humanitarian law and human rights law are based on the same ideals of preserving the dignity of the human being. They both have a " humanitarian character " to use an expression familiar in international jurisprudence. And it is equally clear that, in situations of armed conflict, both these branches of international law can apply simultaneously. Indeed, because of this partial overlap, these two branches of international law may have to be made consistent with one another in ways that sometimes may be seen as compromising the integrity of human rights law.

In the *Legality of the Threat or Use of Nuclear Weapons*, the ICJ took the view that Article 6 of the International Covenant on Civil and Political

Rights (ICCPR), which guarantees the right to life, should be read in accordance with "the applicable *lex specialis*, namely, the law applicable in armed conflict which is designed to regulate the conduct of hostilities". Therefore, "whether a particular loss of life, through the use of a certain weapon in warfare, is to be considered an arbitrary deprivation of life contrary to Article 6 of the Covenant, can only be decided by reference to the law applicable in armed conflict and not deduced from the terms of the Covenant itself". ①

This position has been criticized for creating the impression that, where international humanitarian law is applicable, the applicability of international human rights law would somehow be suspended since it should be treated as *lex generalis*, giving way to the *lex specialis*. That critique seems excessive. The treatment by the court of the relationship of the two branches of law would only seem to apply to the right to life of combatants, and it would be wrong to generalize, from that specific example, to how international humanitarian law and international human rights law should interact in general. Nevertheless, the temptation to treat both as mutually exclusive remains present, and this should come as no surprise. International humanitarian law and international human rights law emerged as answers to different sets of issues, and they were initially intended to apply to different situations. They influence each other in various ways. But these two branches of international law confront us nevertheless with different paradigms, which justifies that we treat them separately for the purposes of study. Generally, the human rights law is characterized by the universal account of the human rights and established regime, especially the UN treaty bodies. And the humanitarian law features at circumstances it applied and those fundamental principles underpinning the provisions, such as the principles of humanity, military necessity, distinction and proportionality.

---

① See *Legality of the Threat or Use of Nuclear Weapons*, ICJ Reports 1996, p. 18.

3.2 Regime of International Human Rights Law

Human rights are a broad area of concern. Thus, it is difficult to make a clear definition of International Human Rights Law. Human rights' potential subject matter ranges from questions of torture and fair trial to social, cultural, and economic rights, for example, the right to housing and water. While human rights is a convenient category of reference, it is also a potential source of confusion. Human rights problems arise in specific factual and legal contexts. They must be decided by reference to the applicable law, whether it is the law of a particular State, the provisions of a convention, or principles of general international law.

(1) *Protection under the UN System*

The multi-lateralization of human rights protection law could date back to the League Covenant of 1919 and associated minorities treaties and mandates. The minorities treaties, in particular, constituted an important stage in recognition of human rights standards. The idea of universal human rights had established until the 1948 Universal Declaration of Human Rights. The Declaration is not a treaty, but many of its provisions reflect general principles of law or elementary considerations of humanity, and the Declaration identified the catalog of rights whose protection would come to be the aim of later instruments. Besides the committees responsible for the execution of these instruments, the UN system also provides some general organs or institutions responsible for the protection and enforcement of human rights, including the treaty bodies listed above.

The General Assembly lacks enforcement powers under the Charter. But it has frequently expressed concerns about human rights violations occurring in different parts of the world. Before the end of the Cold War, the Security Council was unable to act effectively because of the veto, but did use its powers of investigation under Chapter VI from time to time in relation to the situation arising in South Africa (1960). In the period after 1990, the

Security Council began to use its powers in respect of peacekeeping and, based on Chapter Ⅶ, to ensure the provision of humanitarian assistance, as in the case of Somalia in 1992. Extensive operations were undertaken in Bosnia in 1993 with the stated purpose of delivering humanitarian aid. In 1994 the Council authorized certain member States, on a short-term basis, to establish a safe haven in Rwanda for the protection of displaced persons, refugees, and civilians at risk, but the failure to act earlier to prevent the humanitarian catastrophe in Rwanda, has been strongly criticized. It has also authorized forcible intervention in the Libyan Arab Jamahiriya to protect civilians without the territorial State's consent, invoking controversy over the legitimacy of humanitarian intervention after Kofi Annan's constant advocate for human rights.

Besides, the Commission on Human Rights, set up by the Economic and Social Council in 1946, also provided some fact-finding machinery relating to human rights issues. Its principal function has been the preparation of various declarations and other texts. Since 1967 the Commission has established investigatory procedures (the 1235 Procedure) in respect of country-specific complaints of gross violations. In 2006, the Commission was replaced by the Human Rights Council. The Council is an inter-governmental body within the United Nations system made up of 47 States responsible for the promotion and protection of all human rights around the globe. It can discuss all thematic human rights issues and situations that require its attention throughout the year.

The High Commissioner for Human Rights is another important organ under the UN system relating to human rights protection. Both the High Commissioner and the Office have a unique role to promote and protect all human rights.

(2) *Protection under Regional Regime*

Besides, the regional human rights regime also plays an important role today. Three principal regional human rights instruments can be identified,

Chapter XV International Human Rights and Humanitarian Law   495

the African Charter on Human and Peoples' Rights, the American Convention on Human Rights and the European Convention on Human Rights.

The African Charter on Human and Peoples' Rights includes the preamble, 3 parts, 4 chapters, and 68 articles. The Charter recognizes most of what is regarded as universally accepted civil and political rights. They include the right to freedom from discrimination, equality, life and personal integrity, dignity, freedom from slavery, freedom from cruel, inhuman or degrading treatment or punishment, rights to due process concerning arrest and detention the right to a fair trial, freedom of religion, freedom of information and expression, freedom of association, freedom to assembly, freedom of movement, freedom to political participation, and the right to property.

The American Convention on Human Rights was adopted by many countries in the Western Hemisphere in San José, Costa Rica, on 22 November 1969. The bodies responsible for overseeing compliance with the Convention are the Inter-American Commission on Human Rights and the Inter-American Court of Human Rights, both of which are organs of the Organization of American States (OAS).

The European Convention on Human Rights (ECHR; formally the Convention for the Protection of Human Rights and Fundamental Freedoms) is an international convention to protect human rights and political freedoms in Europe. Drafted in 1950 by the then newly formed Council of Europe, the convention entered into force on 3 September 1953. It established the European Court of Human Rights (generally referred to by the initials ECtHR). Any person who feels their rights have been violated under the Convention by a State party can take a case to ECtHR. Judgments finding violations are binding on the States concerned and they are obliged to execute them. The Committee of Ministers of the Council of Europe monitors the execution of judgments, particularly to ensure payment of the amounts awarded by the Court to the applicants in compensation for the damage they have sustained. International law scholars consider the ECtHR to be the most effective international human rights court in the world.

3.3 Fundamental Principles of International Humanitarians Law

If we could use one sentence to describe the international humanitarian law, the following one shall be the most concise and accurate. International humanitarian law (IHL) is the body of rules that applies to armed conflicts. An armed conflict is triggered when there is recourse to armed force. When the opposing parties are States, the armed conflict is international (IAC) whereas when the opposing parties are States and organized armed groups or only armed groups, the armed conflict is non-international (NIAC). The classification of armed conflicts as either IACs or NIACs is critical for legal, political and operational purposes. The existence of an IAC or a NIAC is a question of fact.

International humanitarian law is based on two foundational principles: the principle of humanity and the principle of military necessity. The principle of humanity attempts to "humanize" the conduct of the war by imposing limits on the means and methods of warfare, by according protection to certain categories of persons, by requiring humane treatment of captured persons and, in general, by limiting or mitigating unnecessary suffering. The principle of military necessity allows a belligerent to use lawful means and methods of war to overpower an enemy. Two other principles that derive from the two foundational principles are the principle of distinction and the principle of proportionality. According to the principle of distinction, parties to the conflict should at all times distinguish civilians and civilian objects from combatants and military objectives and afford protection to the former. According to the principle of proportionality, any harm caused by military action to civilians and civilian objects should not exceed the anticipated military advantage expected from the operation.

(1) The Principle of Military Necessity

Military necessity, as understood by modern civilized nations, consists in the necessity of those measures which are indispensable for securing the ends of the war and which are lawful according to the modern law and usages of war. During the Nuremberg Trial, the Tribunal found: "Military necessity permits a belligerent, subject to the laws of war, to apply any amount and kind of force to compel the complete submission of the enemy with the least possible expenditure of time, life, and money. ··· It permits the destruction of the life of armed enemies and other persons whose destruction is incidentally unavoidable by the armed conflicts of the war; it allows the capturing of armed enemies and others of peculiar danger, but it does not permit the killing of innocent inhabitants for purposes of revenge or the satisfaction of a lust to kill. The destruction of property to be lawful must be imperatively demanded by the necessities of war. Destruction as an end in itself is a violation of international law. There must be some reasonable connection between the destruction of property and the overcoming of the enemy forces. It is lawful to destroy railways, lines of communication, or any other property that might be utilized by the enemy. Private homes and churches even may be destroyed if necessary for military operations. It does not admit the wanton devastation of a district or the willful infliction of suffering upon its inhabitants for the sake of suffering alone."[①]

(2) The Principle of Distinction

The principle of distinction is one of the basic rules of international humanitarian law. Subject to this principle, the parties in conflict must differentiate between combatants and non-combatants since the latter may never be the targets of acts of war. There is an elementary reason for this: although war seeks to weaken the enemy's military capacity, it may not target

---

[①] US Military Tribunal, *United States v. Wilhelm List, et al.*, Case No. 47 (Nuremberg, 19 February 1948) Law Reports of Trials of War Criminals, Vol. Ⅷ (1949), p. 66.

those who do not actively participate in the hostilities—either because they have never taken up arms (civilian population), or because they have ceased to be combatants (disarmed enemy troops)—since they are not military personnel. In a case decided by ICTY, the Appeal Chamber ruled that "there is an absolute prohibition on the targeting of civilians in customary international law" and that "the prohibition against attacking civilians and civilian objects may not be derogated from because of military necessity". ①

(3) *The Principle of Proportionality*

In a report presented by ICTY, it explained that: "The main problem with the principle of proportionality is not whether or not it exists but what it means and how it is to be applied. It is relatively simple to State that there must be an acceptable relation between the legitimate destructive effect and undesirable collateral effects. … One cannot easily assess the value of innocent human lives as opposed to capturing a particular military objective." ②

4. Further Reading Materials

Read the following materials and think about the questions below:

(1) How do the human rights protection regimes under the UN work to implement those instruments?

(2) How to consider the humanitarian interventions taken by the United States and other western countries in Libya, Iraq, Afghanistan and Syria?

(3) Why does the world still witness so many armed conflicts and

---

① See ICRC, Practice Relating to Rule 1. The Principle of Distinction between Civilians and Combatants, https://ihl-databases.icrc.org/customary-ihl/eng/docs/v2_rul_rule1, last visited on Jan. 8, 2022.

② ICTY, Final Report to the Prosecutor by the Committee Established to Review the NATO Bombing Campaign Against the Federal Republic of Yugoslavia, https://www.icty.org/en/press/final-report-prosecutor-committee-established-review-nato-bombing-campaign-against-federal, last visited on Jan. 8, 2022.

humanitarian crises while international society has developed a sophisticated human rights protection regime and humanitarian principles and rules? Give a 5-10 minutes speech in English about your own understanding.

4.1 Resolutions and Decisions on Syria War[①]

......

Reaffirming also its strong commitment to full respect for the sovereignty, independence, unity and territorial integrity of the Syrian Arab Republic,

Deploring the fact that March 2021 marks 10 years since the peaceful uprising and its brutal repression that led to the conflict in the Syrian Arab Republic, which has had a devastating impact on civilians, including through grave violations and abuses of international human rights law and violations of international humanitarian law…

Condemning the grave situation of human rights across the Syrian Arab Republic, and demanding that the Syrian authorities meet their responsibility to protect the Syrian population and to respect, protect and fulfil the human rights of all persons within its jurisdiction,

Noting that, under applicable international law, and in line with Security Council resolution 2474 (2019) of 11 June 2019, parties to armed conflict bear the primary responsibility to take all feasible measures to account for persons reported missing as a result of hostilities and to put into place appropriate channels enabling response and communication with families on the search process, and noting also that, in the same resolution, the Council called upon parties to armed conflict to take steps to prevent people from going missing as a result of armed conflict,

---

① HRC, Resolution adopted by the Human Rights Council on 24 March 2021, 46/22, Situation of human rights in the Syrian Arab Republic (A/HRC/RES/46/22), https://digitallibrary.un.org/record/3926644? ln=ru, last visited on Jan. 8, 2022.

Recalling the Statements made by the Secretary-General and the United Nations High Commissioner for Human Rights that crimes against humanity and war crimes are likely to have been committed in the Syrian Arab Republic,

······

Strongly condemns all violations and abuses and the ongoing human rights situation, demands that all parties immediately comply with their respective obligations under international humanitarian law and international human rights law, and emphasizes the need to ensure that all those responsible for such violations and abuses are held to account;

······

Reiterates the call of the Secretary-General for a global ceasefire, the call of the Special Envoy of the Secretary-General for Syria for a complete, immediate and nationwide ceasefire throughout the Syrian Arab Republic and the recent recommendation made by the Commission of Inquiry to immediately institute a permanent ceasefire, in order to provide the space for Syrian-led negotiations and for the restoration of human rights, urges all parties to the conflict to direct their efforts to enact such a ceasefire, and in this regard takes note of the Additional Protocol to the Memorandum on the Stabilization of the Situation in the Idlib De-escalation Area, signed by the Russian Federation and Turkey on 5 March 2020;

······

Welcomes the work and the important role played by the Commission of Inquiry, established by the Human Rights Council in its resolution S-17/1 of 23 August 2011, in supporting essential accountability efforts by investigating all alleged violations and abuses of international human rights law since March 2011 in the Syrian Arab Republic, in order to establish the facts and circumstances and to support efforts to ensure that all perpetrators of abuses and violations, including those who may be responsible for crimes against humanity, are identified and held accountable, demands that the Syrian authorities cooperate fully with the Council and the Commission of Inquiry by

Chapter XV International Human Rights and Humanitarian Law   501

granting the Commission immediate, full and unfettered access throughout the Syrian Arab Republic, and urges all States to cooperate with the Commission in the discharge of its mandate;

......

Strongly condemns the continued use of arbitrary detention, torture and illtreatment, including through sexual and gender-based violence, involuntary or enforced disappearance and summary executions, which the Commission of Inquiry recently noted had been carried out with consistency, in particular by the Syrian authorities, but also by other parties to the conflict;

......

Deeply regrets that the fate of tens of thousands of the victims who were subjected to arbitrary and incommunicado detention and enforced disappearance by the regime, and in lower numbers by the so-called Islamic State in Iraq and the Levant (Daesh) and Hay'at Tahrir al-Sham, remain unknown at the end of nearly a decade of conflict and that, despite the evidence showing that the regime is aware of the fate of most of those it detained, it continues to withhold information, intentionally prolonging the suffering of hundreds of thousands of family members of the forcibly disappeared, and highlights the recommendations of the Commission of Inquiry regarding accountability and supporting victims and survivors and their families, including with psychosocial support and in identifying those missing and disappeared;

Deplores the ongoing humanitarian crisis in the Syrian Arab Republic, which the risks created by the coronavirus disease (COVID-19) pandemic has further exacerbated, and the withholding or hindering of life-saving humanitarian aid by the Syrian authorities, especially in recaptured areas, which has been a recurring feature of the Syrian conflict, demands that all parties comply with their applicable responsibilities and obligations under international human rights law and international humanitarian law and that the Syrian authorities and their State and non-State allies facilitate, and all other parties to the conflict do not hinder, full, timely, immediate, unrestricted and safe humanitarian access, noting that the severity of the humanitarian situation requires the use of all aid modalities, calls for the continuation of cross-border humanitarian support beyond July 2021, including the expansion in number and geographical scope of approved crossing points for such assistance, re-emphasizes the need for immediate, rapid, unimpeded and sustained cross-line access in order to prevent further suffering and loss of life, and calls for respect for humanitarian principles across the Syrian Arab Republic;

……

Expresses deep concern that more than 6.2 million people have been internally displaced within the Syrian Arab Republic, and that the findings of the Commission of Inquiry indicate that many were victims of the crime against humanity of forcible transfer, the war crime of ordering the displacement of civilian populations, or both, and that the commission of multiple war crimes and violations of international humanitarian law prompted many millions to flee internally or seek asylum abroad, also expresses deep concern that repeated displacement has been a feature of the conflict and that Syrians in various parts of the Syrian Arab Republic are routinely denied return to their homes, notably due to restrictions placed on access by the Syrian authorities and the fear of arrest in retaken and formerly besieged areas, and urges all parties to the conflict to take note of the recommendations on this matter made by the Commission;

……

4.2 Joint Statement by the Foreign Ministers of the small group on Syria[①]

1. We, the Foreign Ministers of Egypt, France, Germany, Jordan, the

---

[①] Joint Statement by the Foreign Ministers of the small group on Syria, 26 September 2019, https://2017-2021.state.gov/joint-statement-by-the-foreign-ministers-of-the-small-group-on-syria/, last visited on Jan. 8, 2022.

Kingdom of Saudi Arabia, the United Kingdom, and the United States of America made the following statement on the urgent need for a lasting political solution for Syria, on the basis of United Nations Security Council 2254.

2. The Syrian conflict is in its ninth year, hundreds of thousands of people have died and millions been forcibly displaced. The United Nations assess that in recent months in Idlib, more than 1,000 civilians have been killed and more than 600,000 fled their homes, the humanitarian situation worsened by the targeting of schools, hospitals and other civilian buildings. We deeply regret that the Security Council has failed once again to unite in calling for the protection of civilians, adherence to international humanitarian law, and humanitarian access. We remain fully committed to support such vital measures, and call for an immediate and genuine ceasefire in Idlib. The use of any chemical weapons in Syria shall not be tolerated. We also demand that all parties ensure that all measures taken to counter terrorism, including in Idlib Governorate, comply with their obligations under international law.

3. There can be no military solution to the Syria crisis, only a political settlement. Without that, Syria will remain weak, impoverished and destabilising. We therefore strongly support the UN Secretary General's Special Envoy for Syria in his efforts towards a political settlement in line with Security Council Resolution 2254. We welcome the UN's announcement that all parties have now agreed to the establishment of a Constitutional Committee tasked with beginning this process. This is a long-awaited positive step, but one that still requires serious engagement and commitment to delivery in order to succeed. We encourage the UN to convene the Constitutional Committee, and to start discussion of the substantial issues of its mandate, as soon as possible. It also remains essential to advance all other dimensions of the political process, as outlined in UNSCR 2254.

4. We strongly support Geir Pedersen's broader efforts to implement all of Resolution 2254, including the meaningful involvement of all Syrians,

especially women, in the political process. We fully support efforts towards the mass release of political prisoners and steps to create the safe and neutral environment that would enable Syrians to hold free, fair and credible elections, under UN supervision, in which internally displaced persons, refugees and the diaspora must be able to participate.

5. We stress the importance of accountability in any efforts to bring about a sustainable, inclusive and peaceful solution to the conflict and therefore continue to support efforts to ensure that all perpetrators of abuses and violations of international humanitarian and human rights law, including those who may be responsible for crimes against humanity, are identified and held accountable.

6. As the humanitarian situation across Syria continues to deteriorate, we stress the importance of ensuring safe and unhindered humanitarian access for all those Syrians currently in need of it.

7. We acknowledge the efforts of Syria's neighbours who shoulder the burden of hosting the vast majority of Syrian refugees. We encourage the international community to provide humanitarian assistance as well as financial support to those countries to share the costs of Syria's refugee crisis, until Syrians can voluntarily return home in safety, dignity and security. Any attempts at deliberate demographic change cannot be acceptable. We call on the Regime to cease actions that deter and prevent refugees from returning, and instead to take the necessary positive steps to achieve voluntary, safe and dignified returns.

8. Finally, we express our satisfaction at the liberation earlier this year of all territory once held by Daesh, who have brought such horror to Syria and Iraq, as well as to the rest of the world. However, the threat from Daesh remnants, as well as from other UN designated terrorist groups, remains, and we are resolved to ensure their lasting defeat. A political settlement in Syria remains essential to this outcome.

4.3 Joint Statement by the Representatives of Iran, Russia and Turkey[①]

The representatives of the Islamic Republic of Iran, the Russian Federation and the Republic of Turkey as guarantors of the Astana format:

1. Reaffirmed their strong commitment to the sovereignty, independence, unity and territorial integrity of the Syrian Arab Republic as well as to the purposes and principles of the UN Charter and highlighted that these principles should be universally respected and complied with;

2. Reiterated their determination to combat terrorism in all forms and manifestations and stand against separatist agendas aimed at undermining the sovereignty and territorial integrity of Syria as well as threatening the national security of neighboring countries. Condemned the increasing terrorist activities in various parts of Syria which result in loss of innocent lives. Agreed to continue cooperation in order to ultimately eliminate DAESH/ISIL, Al-Nusra Front and all other individuals, groups, undertakings and entities associated with Al-Qaeda or DAESH/ISIL, and other terrorist groups, as designated by the UN Security Council, while ensuring the protection of civilians and civilian infrastructure in accordance with international humanitarian law. Expressed serious concern with the increased presence and terrorist activity of "Hayat Tahrir al Sham" and other affiliated terrorist groups as designated by the UN Security Council that pose threat to civilians inside and outside the Idlib de-escalation area;

3. Reviewed in detail the situation in the Idlib de-escalation area and highlighted the necessity to maintain calm on the ground by fully implementing all agreements on Idlib;

4. Discussed the situation in the north east of Syria and agreed that long-

---

① Joint Statement by the Representatives of Iran, Russia and Turkey on the International Meeting on Syria in the Astana format, Sochi, 16-17 February 2021, https://www.rusemb.org.uk/fnapr/6986, last visited on Jan. 8, 2022.

term security and stability in this region can only be achieved on the basis of preservation of the sovereignty and territorial integrity of the country. Rejected all attempts to create new realities on the ground, including illegitimate self-rule initiatives, under the pretext of combating terrorism, and expressed their determination to stand against separatist agendas in the east of Euphrates aimed at undermining the unity of Syria as well as threatening the national security of neighboring countries. Expressed concern, in this regard, with the increasing hostilities against civilians. Reaffirmed their opposition to the illegal seizure and transfer of oil revenues that should belong to the Syrian Arab Republic;

5. Condemned continuing Israeli military attacks in Syria in violation of the international law and international humanitarian law and undermining the sovereignty of Syria and neighboring countries as well as endangering the stability and security in the region and called for cessation of them;

6. Expressed their conviction that there could be no military solution to the Syrian conflict and reaffirmed their commitment to advance viable and lasting Syrian-led and Syrian-owned, UN-facilitated political process in line with the UN Security Council Resolution 2254;

7. Emphasized the important role of the Constitutional Committee in Geneva, created as a result of the decisive contribution of the Astana guarantors and in furtherance of the decisions of the Syrian National Dialogue Congress in Sochi;

8. Discussed in detail the fifth round of the Constitutional Committee's Drafting Commission held on 25-29 January, 2021 in Geneva and reaffirmed their determination to support the Committee's work through continuous interaction with the Syrian parties, Constitutional Committee delegates and the UN Secretary-General's Special Envoy for Syria Geir O. Pedersen, as facilitator, in order to ensure its sustainable and effective functioning;

9. Emphasized the importance of ensuring respect to the Terms of Reference and Core Rules of Procedure to enable the Committee to implement

Chapter XV International Human Rights and Humanitarian Law   507

its mandate of preparing and drafting for popular approval a constitutional reform as well as achieving progress in its work;

10. Expressed the conviction that the Committee in its work should be governed by a sense of compromise and constructive engagement without foreign interference and externally imposed timelines aimed at reaching general agreement of its members;

11. Reiterated grave concern at the humanitarian situation in Syria and the impact of the COVID-19 pandemic, recognizing that it presents a profound challenge to all Syria's health system, socio-economic and humanitarian situations. Rejected all unilateral sanctions which are in contravention of international law, international humanitarian law and the UN Charter, particularly in the face of the pandemic. Took note of the Statements made by the UN Secretary-General and the UN High Commissioner for Human Rights in this regard. Called upon the wider UN system, in particular WHO, including through COVAX initiative, to prioritize the vaccination inside Syria;

12. Emphasized the need to increase humanitarian assistance to all Syrians throughout the country without discrimination, politicization and preconditions. In order to support the improvement of the humanitarian situation in Syria and the progress in the process of the political settlement, called upon the international community, the United Nations and its humanitarian agencies, to enhance the assistance to Syria, *inter alia* by developing early recovery projects, including the restoration of basic infrastructure assets—water and power supply facilities, schools and hospitals as well as the humanitarian mine action in accordance with the international humanitarian law;

13. Highlighted the need to facilitate safe and voluntary return of refugees and internally displaced persons (IDPs) to their original places of residence in Syria, ensuring their right to return and right to be supported. In this regard they called upon the international community to provide

appropriate contributions and reaffirmed their readiness to continue interaction with all relevant parties, including the Office of the United Nations High Commissioner for Refugees (UNHCR) and other specialized international agencies;

······

4.4 China's Position on Syria Issue[①]

Continued conflict in Syria has brought sufferings to the Syrian people and impacted peace and stability in the Middle East. China is deeply worried about the situation. China maintains that political settlement is the only realistic way out of the Syrian crisis. All relevant parties in Syria should take credible steps to implement the spirit of the communiqué of the foreign ministers' meeting of the Action Group on Syria, cease fire and stop violence immediately, positively respond to the initiative of holding the second Geneva conference on the Syrian issue, and start and implement a Syrian-led, inclusive political transition as soon as possible. Relevant parties in the international community should provide positive and constructive help for the political settlement of the Syrian issue and avoid taking any action that could further militarize the crisis.

China follows the latest developments in Syria closely. We firmly oppose the use of chemical weapons by anyone. China supports the UN investigation team in conducting independent, objective, impartial and professional investigations. The next step should be determined by the Security Council based on the findings of the UN investigation team. Unilateral military actions that bypass the Security Council will have serious impact on the situation in Syria and the Middle East region and they are also a violation of international law and the basic norms governing international relations.

---

① China's Position on Syria Issue, https://www.mfa.gov.cn/ce/cebw//eng/xwdt/t1076201.htm, last visited on Jan. 8, 2022.

China has maintained an objective and just position and a responsible attitude on the Syrian issue. We are committed to protecting the fundamental interests of the Syrian people, maintaining peace and stability in the Middle East region and upholding the purposes and principles of the Charter of the United Nations and basic norms governing international relations. China has made consistent efforts to promote peace and encourage dialogue, firmly supported and actively promoted the political settlement of the Syrian issue, and supported Mr. Brahimi, UN-Arab League Joint Special Representative for Syria, in making impartial mediation. China will respect and support any settlement plan on the Syrian issue as long as it is widely accepted by all relevant parties in Syria. China has watched closely the humanitarian situation in Syria. We have provided humanitarian assistance to the Syrian people, including Syrian refugees in other countries, as our ability permits, and will continue to do so.

5. References and Recommended Reading Materials

(1) James Griffin, *On Human Rights*, Oxford University Press, 2008.

(2) Nicholas Tsagourias and Alasdair Morrison, *International Humanitarian Law: Cases, Materials and Commentary*, Cambridge University Press, 2018.